D1451854

Young

Adolescence
Transition from childhood to maturity
Second edition

B. Geraldine Lambert
University of Southwestern Louisiana

Barbara F. Rothschild
Louisiana State University, Alexandria

Richard Altland
Veterans Administration Hospital, Houston

Laurence B. Green
University of North Florida

Brooks/Cole Publishing Company
Monterey, California
A Division of Wadsworth Publishing Company, Inc.

To George

Printed in the United States of America

10 9 8 7 6 5 4 3 2

Library of Congress Cataloging in Publication Data

Adolescence.

    Includes bibliographies and index.
    1. Adolescence.   2. United States—Social conditions
—1960–   I. Lambert, Bertha Geraldine, 1922–
HQ796.A333   1978   301.43′15′0973   77-15476
ISBN 0-8185-0251-7

Cover photo by IPA/Jeroboam, Inc.

Photos: page 1 by Russell Abraham/Jeroboam, Inc.; page 31 by Jim Pinckney; page 69 by Elizabeth Crews/Jeroboam, Inc.; page 105 by IPA/Jeroboam, Inc.; page 127 by Robert Burroughs/Jeroboam, Inc.; page 149 by Ken Graves/Jeroboam, Inc.; page 175 by Robert Eckert/Jeroboam, Inc.; page 191 by James Motlow/Jeroboam, Inc.; page 237 by Mitchell Payne/Jeroboam, Inc.; pages 273 and 339 by Peeter Vilms/Jeroboam, Inc.; and page 313 by Emilio A. Mercado/Jeroboam, Inc.

Acquisition Editor: Todd Lueders
Production Editor: Marilu Uland
Interior Design: Sharon Marie Bird
Cover Design: Jamie S. Brooks
Typesetting: David R. Sullivan Company, Dallas, Texas

Preface

It is our belief that adolescent behavior is not restricted to teenagers—that at any age one's behavior can be adolescent. Thus, in this text we do not limit our discussion of adolescence to chronological, physiological, or legal boundaries. We focus instead on adolescence as a behavioral transition from childhood to maturity.

This second edition deals with such current problems as drug and alcohol abuse, school violence and vandalism, adolescent suicide, runaways, and the difficulties in communication between the generations, as well as with the more traditional topics of physical, emotional, and social development. A new chapter on the development of morals and other values has been added and includes a discussion of such innovative techniques as peer counseling. We have tried to avoid duplicating the subject matter usually covered in introductory and educational psychology courses, one of which generally serves as a prerequisite for adolescent psychology. Hence, we have limited our discussion of such topics as cognitive development and intelligence testing, except as they pertain to the adolescent period.

More than 300 new references have been added in this edition, including sources not only in psychology but also in education, history, sociology, medicine, and philosophy. Also cited are some newspaper and magazine articles, as well as interviews with experts in certain fields, because we believe that students should be encouraged to seek information in a wide variety of places before reaching their own conclusions about a subject.

At the end of each chapter are "Thought Provokers"—questions designed to encourage the student to draw upon his or her own opinions, experiences, and attitudes in exploring the problems of adolescence. The comprehensive Glossary of important terms will facilitate understanding of the ideas presented in the text.

As was the first edition, this new book is directed to undergraduates in psychology, education, home economics, and sociology. It can also be useful to parents, teachers, counselors, and other adults who work with adolescents.

Behind the scenes of every book there is usually a sizable group of people who have helped to make it possible. In our case these include the following individuals who kindly consented to serve as reviewers: Eastwood Atwater of Montgomery County Community College, Jerome Kristal of San Jose City College, Larry Weber of Virginia Polytechnic Institute, Janis Bohan of Metropolitan State College, and Cora Patterson of the University of Southwestern Louisiana.

In addition, there were several others without whose assistance we would surely have faltered. Among these were Raymond Cleveland, James DeLee, and Ed Michael of Louisiana State University at Alexandria, who made possible a sabbatical leave for one of the authors for the completion of this book; Joan M. Vater, who did the research on delinquency and educational problems; Carol McGee, who assisted in compiling our extensive bibliography; Roberta Wade, who proofread the entire manuscript and contributed numerous helpful suggestions from the student's point of view; and George H. Rothschild, Sr., who served as lay reader and critic during the entire writing process. One of the authors, Barbara Rothschild, assumed full responsibility for the revision of this, the second edition.

B. Geraldine Lambert
Barbara F. Rothschild
Richard Altland
Laurence B. Green

Contents

11 Career selection   313

12 The adult/adolescent communication gap   339

What is adolescence? 1

It was the best of times, it was the worst of times. It was the age of wisdom, it was the age of foolishness. It was the season of light, it was the season of darkness. It was the spring of hope, it was the winter of despair . . . .

Charles Dickens
"A Tale of Two Cities"

Dickens' description of the adolescence of France following the French Revolution can easily be stretched to include the adolescent in today's swiftly changing world of turmoil, conflict, and upheaval. As appropriate as his description is, however, we must go a few steps further and attempt to provide a workable definition for our discussion of adolescence. How can we define the term in a way that will enhance our understanding of this transitional period?

A definition of adolescence

We believe that *adolescence* can best be shown to be a behavioral/cultural concept if we first point out the inadequacies in the traditional attempts to define the term chronologically, physi-

1

cally, or legally. In the past, the usual definition of adolescence has tied it to an age span, with the starting age varying from 10 to 13 and the concluding age varying from 19 to 21, depending on whose definition we read. It has been quite natural, then, for studies of adolescence to be limited to population groups in the second decade of life, and the research and theory cited in this book inevitably reflect the limitations imposed by this traditional definition.

It is our belief that a more realistic and meaningful definition of adolescence may be in order—a definition that relies more on behavioral terms than on chronological age to explain the concept. As readers progress through this book, they are invited to keep in mind our behavioral definition and to decide for themselves whether they find it more workable and meaningful than the traditional age-span definition.

Surrounding us today are many 35- or 40-year-old people, who manifest behavior that we consider to be typical of the "adolescent" period of life. And there also seems to be justification in noting that this behavior appears to predominate in the life-styles of many individuals. Thus, we are no longer able to accept the idea that adolescence is a period in life between the age of "childhood" and the age of "adulthood."

The major thesis of this book is that adolescence is a behavioral phenomenon that occurs between childlike behavior and "mature" behavior. Accordingly, our goal is to establish adolescence in terms of (1) an identifiable starting point, at which time childlike behavior should be fading and (2) a general pattern of behavior signaling the end of adolescence and the attainment of "maturity."

When does adolescence begin?

A particular "starting point" that marks the beginning of the adolescent period can be identified with the onset of those physical changes that result in *puberty*. This *physiological* milestone is a useful guide, for it is the forerunner of some rather dramatic and sudden behavior changes.

Although we can approach the beginning of the adolescent period by focusing on physical changes, it is not adequate to consider the period as a whole simply from the physiological point of view. Although at puberty there is a sudden and dramatic increase in the release of sex hormones resulting in the development of certain sexual characteristics, of greater importance is the fact that significant sexual thought and behavior accompany this event. And, it is the emotional, social, and intellectual overtones of sex that are more deterministic of "maturity" or "immaturity" than the physiological event alone. The research of Bierich (1975), Ehrhardt and Meyer-Bahlburg (1975), Eichorn (1975), Prader (1975), Wettenhall (1976) and others has demonstrated the dynamic effects of early or late puberty on the behavior of both boys and girls in the spheres of social, emotional, and intellectual development. Furthermore, we cannot readily accept the capability for reproduction as a criterion of adult "maturity"; parental abuse and neglect of children, as well as other forms of parental irresponsibility so prevalent today, testify to a lack of mature behavior among people who have achieved parenthood.

    If physiological occurrences alone cannot be used to define adolescence, can we perhaps resolve the issue by stating that adolescence encompasses those years between the onset of puberty and the magic age of 18? From a legal point of view, this might be true, but there is absolutely no evidence available that at the age of 18 an individual automatically ceases to behave as an adolescent. It no longer seems sufficient to consider adolescence as a phenomenon that can be defined in legalistic or chronological terms. Although laws regarding the age of adulthood in each state of the United States and in Canada do not vary as much as they once did, any attempt to declare adolescence to be at an end when "adulthood" is reached is doomed to failure, for maturity cannot be equated with such adult prerogatives as voting, drinking, marrying, and driving a car.

When does adolescence end?

    Having reached these dead ends, what can we state about adolescence that will help us understand this transitional period? Our approach is to seek a definition with an end point that will, as clearly as possible, establish those behavioral traits that characterize the nonadolescent. If individuals possess these traits by the age of 18, or at 21, or 30, or even older, it can be said that they are no longer adolescent. Our focus, then, is on examining the concept "maturity" to determine the behavioral traits that characterize the mature person.

    What is maturity?   Although most of us seem to recognize when people are behaving maturely and when they are not, the concept "maturity" is so great in scope that it defies precise definition. We are faced with a task similar to that confronted by a physicist asked to define "electricity." Although we can be told whether electricity is present and what it can and cannot do, once the definition goes beyond "a flow of electrons," it's in trouble. Nevertheless, if our thesis of behavioral adolescence is to have any substance, an attempt at definition must be made.

As a first step, let us see what insight we can gain from a quick look at some views of "maturity" as proposed by some of the outstanding personality theorists. Alfred Adler (1935, 1939) believed that we reach maturity as we learn to overcome our feelings of inferiority. We conquer these feelings by developing our potential for social functioning and our ability to create meaning in our lives from our heredity and our experience. Harry Stack Sullivan (1953) describes maturity as the process of transforming one's "self-system" from that of an anxiety-ridden organism to that of a stabilized, secure human being. The essence of this process is developing satisfying interpersonal relationships. Henry Murray and Clyde Kluckhohn (1953) emphasized that maturity grows out of our need to belong to and be accepted by a functioning group, which we achieve by compromising between our own impulses and the demands, interests, and impulses of other people.

Abraham Maslow (1954) defined maturity as being dependent on "self-actualization," a term he coined to describe the process of fulfilling one's genetic potential as opposed to depending on external forces to shape one's personality. If we look at Gordon Allport's personality theory (1955), we see that maturity results when individuals shift their loyalties from self to possessions and loved objects and, ultimately, to abstract moral and/or religious ideas. For Erich Fromm (1955), however, people move toward maturity because of their desire to create, which he described as their "productive orientation." This orientation helps individuals relate to themselves, to others, and to nature, eventually in a mature way. Carl Rogers (1961) believes that to be considered mature one must be able to accept oneself ". . . as a decidedly imperfect person, who by no means functions at all times in the way he would like to function" (p. 17). The person who reaches this conclusion can then work toward changing the self in order to become more personally effective with other people and thus more mature in his or her functioning.

According to Erik Erikson (1968), maturity is achieved when one has resolved the identity crisis and knows who one is, where one is going, and who one is to become. Expanding on Erikson's theory, Marcia (1968) suggests that, in the resolution of this crisis, the mature individual makes personal commitments to a vocation, to a religious belief, and to a personal system of values, as well as resolving his or her attitude toward sexuality.

This brief look at concepts of maturity as proposed by various personality theorists should make the reader aware of the general level of thought and behavior that must be present before a person can be described as "mature." There are, however, other traits of maturity that could be mentioned at this point. These include the ability to forego immediate pleasures for long-range goals, the ability to persevere or to stay with a task or situation until it has been completed or ends, the capacity to confront frustration and defeat without collapse, the ability to be dependable and to live up to one's responsibilities, and the fortitude to make a decision and to stand by it. One additional thought should also be noted before we attempt to define maturity. The usual definition of this concept delineates it as a state of adulthood; however, because such a definition can imply that behavior development or change ceases at the onset of maturity, it is not accurate for our purposes. Rather, we would like to point out that, during middle age and old age (which traditionally and perhaps erroneously have also been considered chronological periods of life), any previously acquired behavioral pattern can change to a more effective pattern.

As can be seen by the numerous approaches used to define or describe the concept of maturity, it is almost impossible to arrive at a comprehensive definition. We believe, however, that it is possible to arrive at a general description of this concept.

> Maturity is the state of life which occurs when one's biological and psychological potential develop through favorable growth and experience and interact with the social and physical world to the extent that self-controlled, productive, and stable behavior clearly dominates[1] the personal and societal spheres of life; although inappropriate and ineffective behavior does not disappear, it is uncommon; and there are always possibilities for later change in the behavior structure.

And it is with the attainment of this general level of behavior that adolescence ends. It should be evident that maturity is not likely to occur automatically at the age of 18 or 21, for maturity connotes a healthy personality capable of consistent effective functioning in the intellectual, emotional, and social spheres of existence. English and English (1964) have provided short descriptions of what characterizes mature functioning in each of these areas: intellectual maturity reflects the acquisition of "practical wisdom"; emotional maturity is marked by "steady and socially acceptable emotional behavior"; and social maturity is described as "mastery of effective social techniques." From these criteria and from our review of personality theo-

---

[1]Quantification of the phrase "clearly dominates" is difficult; 51% of the time would not be appropriate, whereas 99% of the time would be overly optimistic. It would tend to imply, however, that effective mature behavior would be evident in most situations.

ries, it is probable that the behavioral state described as "maturity" cannot be approached before 25 or 30 years of living.

It should also become evident that it is not merely living through the adolescent period that is of the greatest importance; it is the nature of the adolescent experience—physical, intellectual, social, and emotional—that will provide a weak or strong foundation for a mature adulthood. It would appear that the experiences of adolescence are as important to the final character of the adult as are the experiences of childhood. Although an individual comes to adolescence from childhood with a fundamental structure of personality, it is during adolescence that many rapid and dynamic changes in behavior take place.

What, then, is adolescence and what should characterize an individual during this stage of life?

> Adolescence is a dynamic, developmental process—roughly spanning the years from the onset of the pubertal process to "maturity"—during which youths come to terms with themselves and with their unique place in the environment; they transit from childhood to maturity (as we have defined it).

The phrase "come to terms with themselves" is not meant to imply that young people should adopt a passive acceptance of the status quo or believe that they are pawns in the hands of fate. Rather, the phrase describes the dynamic, unique growth potential of each individual and the ability to exercise some control over one's development. This growth concept, as noted by Allport (1955), Rogers (1961), and Nixon (1962), involves a constant striving toward the final goal of becoming one's self. Whether one ever reaches this goal is debatable; it is the striving toward it that really matters—the continual striving that will sustain behavior in the inevitable moments of defeat.

To endeavor to come to terms with one's self includes the physical self, the intellectual self, the social self, and the emotional self. Actually, no one comes to terms with all aspects of the self at any given period. Generally, the individual will tackle one aspect at a time as the occasion arises.

> Susan, 15, is a vivacious girl with a pretty face. However, she constantly complains about her appearance. She feels that, because of her 5'9" height, she is much too tall for the boys to ask her for dates. As a consequence, she slouches in an attempt to disguise her height, which only makes her appear to be taller and more gawky than she actually is. Susan has not yet accepted her physical self.

John, 19, is a college sophomore from a working-class family. His father has a limited education and is employed as a custodian in a hospital. His older sister, the first in the family ever to attend college, is in law school. John thinks he also wants to be an attorney. However, he has rather low reading comprehension and actually dislikes reading; he is therefore not well suited to enter the field of law. On the other hand, he has a strong interest in, and an aptitude for, mathematics. John has not yet demonstrated that he has come to terms with his intellectual self.

Sixteen-year-old Frank, outwardly somewhat arrogant and cocky, has difficulty in gaining the acceptance of his peers. He wants to assert his leadership skills, but he hasn't learned to recognize that his plans and ideas cannot always be carried out; he is not willing to listen to those of others in the group and refuses to do things their way rather than his. He has not come to terms with his social self.

Nancy, an only child of 18, wishes to attend college out of town, but her parents do not want her to leave home. Although she really would like to go away to school, and her family is well able to afford the additional expense, she timidly accedes to their demands. In counseling sessions she has expressed considerable hostility toward her parents because of their refusal to permit her to leave home. In addition, she has shown guilt resulting from her suppressed anger at them, although she attempts to deny that such feelings exist. For a considerable time, the combination of hostility and guilt has adversely affected her performance at the local college. Nancy has not yet learned to come to terms with her emotional self.

When we speak of coming to terms with one's "unique place in the environment," we are referring to both the physical and the interpersonal aspects of living in a real world of things and of people. Individuals must not only find their places in a physical world, they must also find their places in an *interpersonal* world, and they must do so as individuals uniquely separate from, yet within, society. For example, poverty is a physical condition, and generally it is dealt with in a physical manner by providing welfare money, food, and clothing. However, in such treatment, the emotional and social effects of poverty tend to be overlooked. Although social services have come to terms with the physical world of people on welfare, they have failed to recognize the unique interpersonal and *intrapersonal* world of poverty.

The words "transition from childhood to maturity" connote a phase in life through which one must pass. It is not a question of passing through successfully or unsuccessfully; rather, it is a question of passing through or not passing through. Additionally, in the dynamic striving toward maturity, an individual may reach a certain point and then experience a *traumatic* episode, such as the death of a parent, and *fixate* or begin a drastic *regression* in behavior. Although it might not appear normal for a person to regress drastically, it is indeed an aspect of the growth process, and it requires recognition and consideration. One should note that a normal passage through adolescence is not characterized by a smooth progression that correlates with the passing of the chronological years. The period is erratic in nature, typified by peaks of success and valleys of defeat, but the total process reflects a progression toward maturity.

Theories of adolescence

Rereading Dickens' quotation can give us a clue to the nature of the adolescent period. "Best"–"worst," "wisdom"–"foolishness," "light"–"darkness," and "hope"–"despair" reflect the typical polarities that are said to make up adolescence. Indeed, an examination of the literature and theories of adolescence brings to light two basic positions, which themselves create a kind of polarity.

One position characterizes adolescence as a period of inevitable and useful "storm and stress." The other position maintains that if too many emotional or traumatizing events occur, the personality will become distorted for life. Consequently, a somewhat smooth, relatively nontraumatic, transitional period is advocated. In addition, explanations or theories of adolescence tend to be categorized in terms of stage theory (which suggests that life develops in separate, distinct stages) or of continuity theory (which views adolescence not as a distinct period of life but as part of the continuity of human development from infancy to adulthood).

An examination of the literature of the past 70 or 80 years reveals that an interesting sequence of thought has taken place. Shortly after the turn of the century, G. Stanley Hall (1904) wrote a two-volume treatise on adolescence, *Adolescence: Its Psychology and Its Relation to Physiology, Anthropology, Sociology, Sex, Crime, Religion, and Education*, in which he introduced the notion that the adolescent period is one of *storm and stress* (or, as was so fashionable in those days, in German, *Sturm und Drang*). Hall reflected his thoughts about adolescence in such statements as "The 'teens' are emotionally unstable" (Vol. 2, p. 74) and "We here see the instability and fluctuation now so characteristic" (Vol. 2, p. 75). These quotations suggest that Hall considered turmoil to be an unavoidable fact of life for the adolescent; he left no room for environmental influence.

In evaluating Hall's *Sturm und Drang* theory, we must admit that the "instability and fluctuation" are readily apparent in adolescent behavior. Young people can be seen exhibiting dynamic energy one hour, extreme lethargy the next. They can demonstrate a great degree of *euphoria* one day and almost complete *depression* the next. They can show vain conceit one moment and ultramodesty the next. Furthermore, their *egocentric* selfishness of wanting to do their own "thing" can be later replaced with great *altruism* toward those less fortunate than themselves. (These topics are treated in detail in Chapter 6.)

Hall's attempts to place adolescence in a historical context ("now so characteristic") tend to reflect his acceptance of Ernst Heinrich Haeckel's classic concept that *ontogeny is a brief but rapid recapitulation of phylogeny*, a theory that stated that the development of the individual parallels the historical evolutionary development of the human species. Hall attempted to relate Haeckel's concept to the human life span by comparing the life of children ages 8 through 12 with the savage era of human history; ages 12 through 22 or 25, with the stage of human development called barbarism; and age 25 into adulthood, with that part of history called civilization. One might describe Hall's theory as being a *biogenetic* one in that he appears to be saying that adolescence is built into us—that it's hereditary, and therefore not very vulnerable to modification.

About a quarter of a century later, anthropologist Margaret Mead reported on her studies of primitive cultures in Samoa (1928a) and New Guinea (1928b) that she had observed that adolescence didn't seem to be a stormy, stressful experience for these youngsters. They were initiated into the adult world when they were ready. As young girls became capable of reproduction, they married, had children, and took care of their households. When young boys were physically able to hunt and became sexually mature, they married and took their places in society as hunters and as workers. Mead concluded that the stormy nature of adolescence was a "cultural invention" and not the inevitable aspect of development that Hall had suggested. In fact, her cross-cultural research of that period, as well as that of later years (1939), indicates that there are two possible means of avoiding the storm and stress of adolescence: (1) through a continuity of one's role in life, evolving with the gradual granting by society of status, privilege, and responsibility to its young people and (2) through specific rites, usually at the time of puberty, by which the new status of the young person is recognized.

Another hypothesis, the Developmental Task Theory of Robert Havighurst (1972), proposes that, at each stage of life, we are confronted with certain tasks that must be accomplished at least somewhat successfully if we are to be adequately prepared to go on to the next stage. The successive mastery of these tasks contributes to the individual's adjustment to life and lays the foundation necessary for tackling the next stage. These *developmental tasks* have been defined as the skills, knowledge, functions, and attitudes that must be acquired at certain points in life and are mastered through physical maturation, social learning, and personal strivings. At the adolescent stage these developmental tasks include the following:

1. Achieving new and more mature relations with age-mates of both sexes.
2. Learning and accepting a socially approved masculine or feminine social role.
3. Accepting one's physique and using one's body effectively.
4. Achieving emotional independence from parents and other adults.
5. Preparing for marriage and family life.
6. Preparing for a satisfying occupational role.
7. Acquiring a set of values and a system of ethics.
8. Desiring and achieving socially responsible behavior.

If one has not sufficiently mastered a physical, intellectual, social, or emotional task at any given level or age, then the task at the next level will be less easy to accomplish, and the probability of completing later tasks will be reduced.

As can be seen by the list of adolescent developmental tasks, learning and accepting a socially approved adult masculine or feminine role is one area that needs to be mastered during this period. The following example illustrates what may occur when a person fails to accomplish this important developmental task.

Charles was a 16-year-old youth from a lower-class socioeconomic background. An illegitimate child of a mother who had never married, he was reared in a home with two sisters and no father. Nor were there any close male relatives with whom Charles could identify. He was taught solely by women teachers, and although at one point he joined a Boy Scout troop, it dissolved shortly after he became a member. He later sought the friendship of a gang of neighborhood youths with whom he started to identify. Gradually he began to adopt many of their pseudomasculine traits. On one occasion he joined the gang in robbing a railroad refrigerator car, apparently in the belief that such behavior reflected courage and daring. Placed on probation as the result of this delinquent act, he soon got into further difficulties at school and was finally sent to the state reformatory. After a 6-month term, he was released and returned to the custody of his mother and thus to the same matriarchal environment. Once again he resumed his relationship with those he mistakenly regarded as truly masculine. A few months later he was involved in a fight with one of the gang members and was fatally wounded. Of course, one can only speculate that if Charles had had a positive masculine figure with whom to identify, he might have been able to master the task of learning and accepting a satisfying masculine role and avoided the companionship of the gang possessing such pseudomasculine traits. Nonetheless, the evidence is sufficient to indicate that he had never resolved the task of learning and accepting a socially approved masculine role.

Thus, it can be inferred from the Havighurst theory that if there are developmental tasks that must be accomplished at certain stages in life, then adults have the responsibility for seeing that adolescents are confronted with these tasks at the appropriate age. Like Mead, Havighurst seems to indicate that, by learning the appropriate tasks at certain chronological ages, young people can avoid the "hard knocks" of adolescence and be better off for it.

Still another stage theory, that of Erik Erikson (1963, 1968), proposes that the life span is divided into eight stages, each of which is characterized by a psychosocial conflict that must be resolved if a person is to reach maturity. Adolescence, the fifth stage, is concerned primarily with the conflict arising between the acquisition of a satisfying identity versus the failure to do so, which results in *role* diffusion. The resolution of this *identity crisis* involves confrontation with seven subtasks, which are discussed at some length in Chapter 6. Erikson further suggests that an individual cannot find a lasting identity if there is no personal conflict during adolescence. Although young people will inevitably make mistakes along the way and will experience repeated failure, he maintains that they must still be permitted to experience such conflict in their decision making, which is so vital to mature development.

Social-learning theorists Albert Bandura (1964) and Rolf E. Muuss (1976), who believe that most learning of behavior takes place through observation and imitation, question such stage-theory assumptions as those of Havighurst and Erikson. They perceive the problems of adolescence as being culturally determined and the result of social expectations, rather than as an inevitable occurrence in development. Muuss feels that external social experiences exert greater impact on changes in behavior than do any internal physical maturational processes, as suggested by the stage theorists. He believes that environmental factors, such as *socioeconomic status*, culture, home environment, and exposure to different models of behavior and different patterns of discipline, explain the differences in adolescent development and the fact that, in our own society although many find the period to be exceedingly rough and stormy, others experience relatively smooth sailing. He also points out that changes in behavior reflect changes in an environmental situation and that the behavior in even one adolescent may vary from rebellious, insensitive, and disobedient to sensitive, conforming, and considerate, depending on the situation involved.

Friedenberg (1959) has taken still a different position. He states that many problems of youth occur because adults have taken over the tasks that adolescents should be permitted to undertake themselves. He proposes that adults have not allowed young people to experience the conflicts that can prepare them for adulthood and maturity.

> A few years ago, in a small southern city, a group of high school students took the initiative in organizing a teenage center to provide recreation and a meeting place for adolescents during their free time. They enlisted the aid of several interested adults, who, in turn, secured from the city an old building, which they proceeded to remodel and paint without asking the youths to assist in the alterations. Although the young people at first shared in formulating rules and regulations, they soon found themselves being pushed into the background as adults took over most of the policy making. The center quickly came to reflect adult standards and values rather than those of the adolescents. According to one of the adults who worked in the program, the students' loss of interest seemed to be directly related to increased adult domination. Within a few years the center closed its doors.

In examining Friedenberg's theory, it seems appropriate to describe it as a dialectic[2] pathway to maturity; by experiencing conflicts and confrontations, and resolving them as much on their own as possible, young people grow in psychological stature and progress toward maturity.

Although Hall (1904) maintained that conflict is a natural biogenetic phenomenon, and Friedenberg (1959) maintained that conflict derives from a social dialectic process involving interper-

---

[2]A *dialectic* is a process by which one idea, a thesis, is confronted with the opposite idea, an antithesis; the amalgamation of these opposing forces, a synthesis, results in a higher truth.

sonal and intrapersonal confrontations, it seems that both men would agree that "from the crucible of conflict comes the steel of character." Implicit in their thinking (with which we agree) is the idea that all human beings, when they reach the point of adolescence, must be permitted by adults to experience conflicts and battles, from which they will emerge more mature individuals. Friedenberg (1959) summarized the importance of adolescent conflict in the following statement: "Adolescent conflict is the instrument by which an individual learns the complex, subtle, and precious differences between himself and his environment. In a society in which there is no difference or in which no difference is permitted, the word 'adolescence' has no meaning" (p. 13).

We hypothesize that, whereas the violent, militant young people on college campuses in the late sixties and early seventies were searching for identity, they actually forced themselves into a conflict that had been denied them earlier in life. The affluent, permissive adult society of their parents wanted an easier life for its children than it had experienced during the depression of the 1930s. The irony of this is that, during the years from ages 14 through 17, confrontation and conflict with the world of adults is much safer than confrontation with the law and society at ages 18 to 25.

Although we have discussed several theories and divergent points of view regarding the nature of adolescence, it is apparent that there are many arenas in which young people must do battle and emerge with some degree of success if they are to attain maturity. Of course, the critical issue facing any adults who deal with adolescents is the extent and nature of the conflicts and the limits to which they can permit youngsters to proceed. How deeply should an adult let a youth suffer defeat and failure? There is no single answer. Individual adolescents will have their own tolerance limits, beyond which it may be dangerous to allow them to go. And the questions "How far is safe and productive?" and "When does the conflict become destructive?" are the basis of the dilemma that makes rearing children so difficult and so demanding of adult knowledge, patience, and wisdom.

Goals of the adolescent period

Toward what goals should the adolescent be moving during this transitional period? We hope that, during the unfolding of this book, all the goals of maturity will come into focus at various times. At this point, however, let us take a brief look at what are probably the major tasks of the adolescent period. Many of these were cited in

Havighurst's Developmental Task Concept (1972), but there are others that we believe should be included.

Accepting one's physical self

First, all individuals must come to terms with their bodies or their physical selves, for the body can be described as a symbol of the self or body image. On the one hand, moderate care of the physical body, including proper diet, exercise, and good body hygiene, can enhance the attributes with which each person is endowed and can therefore enhance self-confidence. On the other hand, we can readily destroy our self-image, as well as our physical selves, by abuse, disuse, and neglect. Coming to terms with one's body does not demand surrender to one's imperfections, nor does it demand an unrealistic attempt to conform to the ideal physical image of a Miss America or an All-American football hero. On the contrary, physical acceptance involves making the most of one's imperfections and learning to accept the physical changes of growing up and aging.

For instance, consider our example of 5'9'' Susan. Once she can accept her height as an asset rather than as a liability, she will improve her posture and will appear less ungainly and awkward. Her new poise and self-confidence will be a sign that she has come to terms with her height.

Attaining emotional control

One sign of emotional maturity is the ability to avoid extremes; adherence to either extreme would prove to be damaging to the individual's adjustment. Thus, one must attain a balance between a childish free expression of emotions without inhibition and a complete suppression of all emotion. Somewhere between the utterly uninhibited expression of emotion by the typical child and the Victorian suppression of all emotions, adolescents must come to accept their feelings as real and valid, and they must recognize their responsibility for channeling those feelings into constructive outlets. In addition, adolescents face the task of learning to expect and accept the inevitable frustration of failure without degrading themselves or disintegrating into uncontrolled rage or immobilized fear of future failures.

Resolving the identity crisis and developing a positive self-concept

Erikson (1968) has hypothesized that the resolution of the identity crisis is the most critical task in the life span of the human being, that failure to confront and solve this task reflects the individual's failure to reach maturity. Part of the task of resolving this conflict is the development of a positive *self-concept* or *self-image*. As Goldenson (1970) has noted;

> A consistent, well organized conception (knowledge of) his ideals, abilities, and possibilities gives him a sense of personal identity and a point of departure (or a frame of reference) for developing a lifestyle of his own (that is not totally incompatible with the society in which he lives). On the other hand, the individual who entertains deep doubt about who he is tends to feel lost, confused, and alienated from himself and from other people [p. 1180].

Included in this understanding or self-knowledge is the concept not only of who and of what one is, but also of who and of what one is not. However, a knowledge of the self alone, although necessary, is not in itself sufficient. For example, one may know that one is a very poor student—and this is important in developing a realistic self-concept—but of even greater importance is how the individual feels about this "deficiency." Do such people feel less valuable as human beings? How do those in their sociocultural environment make them feel? In other words, how does knowledge of the self (self-concept) affect one's feelings about one's worth (self-esteem)?

To gain greater insight into how the attitudes about oneself can affect behavior, compare the following self-descriptive monologues proposed by Coopersmith (1967, p. 47). For a positive self-attitude:

> I consider myself a valuable and important person, and am at least as good as other persons of my age and training. I am regarded as someone worthy of respect and consideration by people who are important to me. I'm able to exert an influence upon other people and events, partly because my views are sought and respected, and partly because I'm able and willing to present and defend these views. I have a pretty definite idea of what I think is right and my judgments are usually borne out by subsequent events. I can control my actions toward the outside world, and have a fairly good understanding of the kind of person I am. I enjoy new and challenging tasks and don't get upset when things don't go well right off the bat. The work I do is generally of high quality and I expect to do worthwhile and possibly great work in the future.[3]

For a negative self-attitude:

> I don't think I'm a very important or likeable person, and I don't see

[3]From *The Antecedents of Self-Esteem*, by S. Coopersmith. Copyright © 1967 by W. H. Freeman and Company. This and all other quotations from this source are reprinted by permission.

much reason for anyone else to like me. I can't do many of the things I'd like to do or do them the way I think they should be done. I'm not sure of my ideas and abilities, and there's a good likelihood that other people's ideas and work are better than my own. Other people don't pay much attention to me and given what I know and feel about myself I can't say that I blame them. I don't like new or unusual occurrences and prefer sticking to known and safe ground. I don't expect much from myself, either now or in the future. Even when I try very hard, the results are often poor, and I've just about given up hope that I'll do anything important or worthwhile. I don't have much control over what happens to me and I expect that things will get worse rather than better.

Whereas self-knowledge is certainly important for the development of maturity, what is also needed is self-acceptance. The recognition and acceptance of one's self does not imply passive, abject surrender to the status quo; rather, it suggests that a person must possess the determination and motivation to change those aspects of the self which he or she may not like.

At maturity the self-concept should be characterized by a high level of self-esteem, self-acceptance, and self-direction, all of which are prerequisites to self-actualization and the fulfillment of one's potential. To attain these levels, there are two questions for every adolescent and concerned adult to ponder. How does a person determine who and what he or she is (self-concept) and how does a person develop a healthy feeling about self (self-esteem)? These questions are dealth with in more detail in subsequent chapters of the book.

Achieving social maturity

Social maturity centers around the ability to establish good interpersonal relationships. Adolescents begin to recognize that their very existence has no meaning other than that meaning given to it by themselves and by others. Without friends and family to reflect our wishes, attitudes, and feelings, we remain strangers to ourselves. In turn, social maturity demands that we become sensitive to the needs and feelings of others—that we acquire a degree of empathy and understanding in our interpersonal relationships.

Allport (1955) and Toynbee (1956) have theorized that human beings have two innate conflicting forces: (1) a striving for individuality and (2) a striving to belong to a society. And, of course, we cannot acquire either without doing a disservice to the other; a synthesis is demanded. People who are completely self-centered, striving only for their own welfare, are eventually cast out of society. And individuals who place "belonging" above all else sacrifice their individuality and thereby lose their identity. When one recalls Friedenberg's (1959) and Erikson's (1963, 1968) position that the primary task of adolescence is to develop an identity, it becomes evident that complete subservience to society prevents the acquisition of maturity. The adolescent's goal is to acquire a unique identity and still function *within* the limits set by society, for one characteristic of maturity is relative success in resolving this conflict.

Developing satisfying heterosexual relationships

The goal of developing satisfying *heterosexual* relationships is fraught with many pitfalls, especially in our rapidly changing society with its "new morality." Many of these problems are discussed in Chapter 5. At this point, however, we will mention that, because of the swiftly changing times, behavior deemed abnormal a quarter of a century ago might be considered quite normal in today's world. Take for example the fact that in the past it was always assumed that the male would assume the lead in heterosexual social and sexual relationships. This assumption no longer holds true. Under most circumstances it is now quite acceptable for women to make the advances. As a consequence of such changing behavior patterns, the aim of striving toward satisfying heterosexual relationships may be more complex than it was.

It should also be noted that this goal needs to include the achievement of heterosexual compatibility—that is, emotional, intellectual, and social compatibility free of distorting sexual overtones. Observation of contemporary adolescent and pseudo-adult behavior suggests that many heterosexual relationships are marred by the discomfort that comes from viewing members of the opposite sex as sex symbols, rather than as complementary individuals who can enhance the meaning and significance of each other's existence. Because of this orientation, many young people equate rejection by the opposite sex with failure as a human being. The result is often the trying out of certain artificial, unnatural roles because of a fear of risking rejection by acting naturally or being "real." For heterosexual relationships to be handled maturely, men and women must be able to relate to each other for reasons other than self-aggrandizement, sensual pleasure, or reproduction alone.

Acquiring a stable system of values

Another aim of adolescence is the acquisition of a relatively stable value system on which to base one's behavior. Without a value system to guide their thoughts and actions, individuals will find themselves at a loss to know how to behave from one situation to the next. This problem is intensified because our society presents the adolescent with so many different values. Choosing from among these values involves frustration, pressure, conflict, and time—time to try and to sift; time to try again and to sift again, and again, and again. This goal is discussed at length in Chapter 7.

Developing intellectual sophistication and sensitivity

Individuals of intellectual sophistication and sensitivity relentlessly question what they hear or read, and they have an urgent need for their questions to be answered (Nixon, 1962). Intellectual sophistication demands a balance between gullibility (a belief in everything) at one extreme and agnosticism (skepticism toward everything) at the other extreme. Neither position alone can ensure effective intellectual functioning.

In acquiring intellectual sensitivity, one must develop an ability to face reality. One of the most basic realities is failure. In a demonstration of intellectual sensitivity, one is able to come to grips with failure by intellectually picking up the pieces and putting them back together, gaining knowledge from the experience and going on from there.

Let us look again at the case of John, who thought he wanted to become an attorney. When he began to recognize his weaknesses in English and his lack of aptitude in reading, he sought vocational counseling. Test results and an understanding counselor revealed to John his strong mathematical ability and increased his interest in math. Consequently, he decided to change his major field from prelaw to accounting, from which he ultimately graduated with success. John was learning to face failure realistically and constructively—he was gaining intellectual sensitivity.

Young people must also discover that it is necessary to come to terms with the idea that freedom is no guarantee of success. They need to learn that if success is guaranteed, they will not be able to decide for themselves what success is or how to attain it; the definition of success and the means of reaching it are determined by the guarantor. Thus, intellectual sensitivity involves understanding that "freedom" means freedom to fail as well as freedom to succeed. For adults, this understanding implies that allowing adolescents to make decisions should not have built-in guarantees of success. In being given freedom to arrive at their own decisions, young people should gradually become more proficient at making them.

Attaining a satisfying occupational status and economic independence

Another goal toward which adolescents must strive is the wise selection of, and preparation for, a satisfying vocation, one which will also provide the basis for achieving economic independence. Such selection in our society is especially difficult because of the lack of opportunity for early job experiences, the wide gap between the world of school and the world of work, the frequent existence of an over-abundance of choices in selecting a career, and a common lack of youthful knowledge about the opportunities, skills, and demands of various occupational fields. These topics are discussed in more detail in Chapter 11.

Achieving the wise use of leisure time

One more aim of adolescence should be the acquisition of the wisdom and skills needed to enjoy one's leisure time. The transitional period of adolescence spans those years in which youths can establish patterns in their use of leisure time that will persist throughout their lives.

The combination of increased longevity, a constantly lower age of retirement, and shorter working hours demands adequate planning and the development of the wise use of leisure time. Failure to come to grips with this problem during the formative years of life may result in premature physical and mental deterioration through illness, boredom, and psychological atrophy. Berg (1965), in his presidential address to the Southwestern Psychological Association, pointed out that behavioral scientists had better involve themselves in this problem, that, unless people begin to learn how to re-create their psychological, physical, and spiritual selves through leisure-time activities, the need for the treatment of emotional disorders will increase tremendously.

Adolescents, in particular, are confronted with this task of planning for their present as well as their future leisure time. Failure to resolve this problem may cause them to seek excitement and adventure through such antisocial behaviors as delinquency and drug abuse. In many instances they may be aware of some of the activities in which they would like to participate but may lack the funds necessary to pursue such pastimes. Consequently, it is necessary for them to learn to spend their leisure time in activities that are not beyond their financial resources but that provide educational, social, and possibly even spiritual benefits. During these years young people are also preparing for their future retirement because they are forming leisure-time habits that they will probably carry throughout their lifetime. They must come to realize that their ability to socialize, to be accepted, to be employed, to be alone, and to be satisfied or happy is in part determined by their use of leisure time. This topic is discussed at greater length in Chapter 3.

Thus, from the numerous goals that have been cited as necessary for the adolescent to attain, the reader may understand the reasoning of many behavioral scientists, including the authors, who suggest that it requires approximately 25 years of living before one really begins to achieve maturity. It may well be that many, if not most, people never achieve complete "maturity" in all aspects of their lives. Nevertheless, no matter how many years it takes, the problems of adolescence must be confronted and reckoned with if "maturity" is ever to be attained. Adolescence should be marked by a continual striving to achieve those behaviors that mark the mature human being.

Adolescence in historical perspective

The concept of adolescence is a relatively recent one in the history of civilization. In fact, until the 18th century adolescence was confused with childhood, which was also of very short duration. During the middle ages children of the lower classes were apprenticed to adults and mixed with them as soon as they were capable of managing without their mothers or nannies, usually by the age of 7. At that time they entered the community of adults, sharing the work and the play of companions, old and young alike. Formal education was almost unknown, except among the few aristocratic elite (Aries, 1962).

Actually, the ancient Greeks had been aware of the differences and transition between childhood and adulthood, believing that this transition could be accomplished through an education, an idea that medieval civilization later failed to note.

With the beginning of modern times, in the 17th century, there was a revival of education and a recognition that the child was not ready for adult life and required special treatment, a sort of isolation, before being permitted to join adult society. It was this trend that ultimately led to society's becoming aware of a transitional period between childhood and adulthood. But even at the beginning of this era, ambiguity existed between childhood and adolescence on the one hand and the category of youth on the other (Aries, 1962).

The concept of adolescence was initially introduced in America around 1880 (Demos & Demos, 1969). It appears to have reflected the social changes that were occurring on this continent toward the latter part of the 19th century and the beginning of the 20th. It was promoted by three major social movements: (1) compulsory and usually public education, (2) child labor laws, and (3) special legal procedures pertaining to juveniles (Bakan, 1971).

Around 1900 adolescence also became a subject of concern for moralists and politicians; gradually people began to wonder what young people were thinking, and writers began to inquire about their ideas. With World War I youthful troops at the front became solidly opposed to the older generation behind the lines. Following combat, an awareness of the unique needs and problems of youth arose, based on a common feeling experienced by ex-servicemen throughout the nations that had participated in the war. From that point the concept of adolescence expanded. "Henceforth marriage, which had ceased to be a settling down, would not put an end to it: the married adolescent was to become one of the most prominent types of our time, dictating its values, its appetites, and its customs. Thus our society has passed from a period which was ignorant of adolescence to a period in which adolescence is the favorite age. We now want to come to it early and linger in it as long as possible" (Aries, 1962, p. 30).

It was once said that "The more things change, the more they remain the same." This statement made by Alphonse Karr in 1849 seems to be true of the adolescent experience as far back as ancient Greece. In fact, it is nearly impossible to find a period in history during which the younger and older generations have not been at odds with each other over values, standards, morals, and the exercise of judgment and restraint (Fredenburgh, 1968). In order to give today's reader a sense of this continuity, we will present a brief description of what it has meant to be an adolescent in each of the decades of the 20th century. Each decade is marked by ambivalent strivings. On the one hand is a need to hold on to the security of childlike dependence; on the other is the need to establish independence and autonomy.

The good old days

Often referred to as "The Good Old Days," the period from 1900 to 1920 was characterized by nostalgia and sentimentality reflected in the music of the times, which toward the end of that era picked up its tempo through the introduction of ragtime and the dancing that accompanied it. This was also the period of big-time football and other college athletics, which, although frequently quite brutal, offered one possibility for democratic opportunity. Star football players were often first- or second-generation Americans (Lee, 1970).

Higher education for women had emerged only a few decades prior to 1900, and women who attended college were still being regarded with some suspicion. They were often called "Flappers," a term coined by H. L. Mencken. However, it was from the opening of numerous women's colleges that the movement for women's suffrage gained momentum (Lee, 1970).

In many ways this period was one of transition from the Victorian era to the "Roaring Twenties." The need for more education was becoming apparent. Nevertheless, of 21.5 million persons between the ages of 5 and 18 in the United States between 1900 and 1920, only 15 million were enrolled in public schools and only 10.5 million (approximately 50 percent) were in average daily attendance (*Statistical Abstracts of the United States*, 1931). Because of economic necessity, many adolescents had to leave school in order to help support their families. Of the 1910 population, 16% of the boys and 8% of the girls between the ages of 10 and 13 were gainfully employed, whereas 41% of the males and 20% of the females 14 and 15 years old and 79% of the males and 40% of the females between the ages of 16 and 20 were gainfully employed. Thus, young people in the first two decades of this century assumed the role of economically contributing adults in society; consequently, they held the status of adults.

The period was characterized by a spirit of progressivism and reform led by Theodore Roosevelt, who at the age of 43 had become the youngest president in the history of the United States and was highly admired by youth for his energy and vitality (Lee, 1970). At the same time, interest in pioneering in flight was sparked by the Wright Brothers in 1903, so that by the beginning of World War I many young men, who were preparing to volunteer, often dreamed of flying airplanes themselves. Carrie Nation was demonstrating for prohibition, which ultimately led to a movement advocating temperance and abstinence from alcoholic beverages (Dulles, 1965; Lee, 1970).

The roaring twenties

By the "Roaring Twenties," World War I, "the war to end all wars," had become only a memory for most adolescents and their parents. Yet, its influence could be seen in the job market as returning veterans competed with the rest of the population for jobs. Recently passed child-labor laws began to have an effect on school attendance, since young adolescents could no longer find employment in the sweat shops that had exploited young workers during earlier decades. Among those 14 and 15 years of age, only 23% of the males and 12% of the females were reported to be employed—a decline of almost 50%. And, for the first time in the nation's history, more than one-half of those between the ages of 5 and 18 (55%) were in daily attendance in the public schools.

The twenties was the decade of the young, as would be true of the sixties. Youths served as models for their middle-aged parents. "If the daughter started the flapper style, it was her mother who kept it going" (Lee, 1970, p. 23). The novels of F. Scott Fitzgerald set the tone for this decade, an era characterized by much hedonism and living for the moment. The slogan of this period was "back to normalcy," a philosophy that reflected the desire to return to a stable era of peace.

In the political arena of the twenties, young women participated in suffrage demonstrations, which ultimately brought about the passage of the Nineteenth Amendment. At the same time, it was the era of "The Big Red Scare" with resultant intolerance and censorship on the college campuses, where there was little room for student radicalism (Lee, 1970). Politically, it was a time marred by the Teapot Dome Scandal and other questionable activities among public officials, particularly President Warren G. Harding. Some evidence of political revolt among students did begin to develop with a trend toward pacifism as reflected in the formation of the National Student Committee for the Limitation of Armaments in 1922.

In the social sphere there was a revolt in manners and morals among students. Prohibition was in effect, but young people engaged in considerable illegal drinking. Control over sexual behaviors declined, and freer attitudes toward the opposite sex developed. There were petting parties (it was rumored that many girls and women carried contraceptives in their vanity cases), and the fashionable short skirts sparked a national campaign by the YWCA against this scandalous dress of the "flappers." Charles Lindbergh became the dashing hero of the decade for many young people when he made his solo transatlantic flight in 1927.

The great depression

The stock market crash in 1929 brought the "Roaring Twenties" to a close, and a much less exuberant decade followed. By 1932, 13 million Americans were unemployed, and wages were 60% lower than they had been in 1929 (Lee, 1970). As a consequence, school attendance again rose; by 1930, more than 66% of the children between the ages of 5 and 18 were attending school. Students became much more serious minded and concerned about economic and political problems. This was evident in the large number of young people who were participating in radical political activities, such as demonstrating, picketing, organizing the unemployed, signing the Oxford Pledge against bearing arms for their country, and holding Army Day antiwar rallies and strikes. According to Lipset (1966), more than 100,000 students were members of the American Student Union, an amalgamation of the most radical groups of that time. Other estimates have placed participation in antiwar parades as high as 200,000.

Since economic hardship made it difficult for young people to marry, there was an extended increase in premarital sex (Allen, 1939). One survey of a group of young business-class males revealed that 70% reported that they had experienced sexual intercourse prior to marriage (Lynd & Lynd, 1937). And sales of contraceptives to single as well as to married people totaled in the millions of dollars. At the same time, marriage and family life became more revered than it had been in the twenties. However, those who did marry found it extremely difficult to establish economic independence and often lived with their parents.

The repeal of Prohibition in 1933 seemed to cut down on adolescent consumption of alcohol, possibly because the thrill of defying the law was absent.

World War II

By 1940, the hardship of the depression years was subsiding, but a second world war appeared to be imminent. Although most young men were accepting their draft calls, it was apparent that some were skeptical about their country's entering another war. To Morale Officers in the Army, it appeared that the chief aim of the servicemen in the 1940s was to return home as quickly as possible (Allen, 1952). Young women, as well as young men, shouldered much responsibility during World War II. Many joined armed forces auxiliaries such as the WACs or WAVES. Others volunteered to work in the United Services Organizations or for the Red Cross. And still others went to work in factories or civil service jobs, which had been vacated by men drafted into the service of their country.

Thus, the war gave many young people new ways of asserting their independence and new experiences through travel and news of other countries. These new factors showed up most strikingly in the number of GIs who went back to school (with the important help of the GI Bill of Rights) when they returned from the war. It was 1946 that became the year of change, and college life would never be the same again, as the GI Bill provided many with their first opportunity for a higher education. Most of the students were very mature and very serious about their studies. Many of them were married, and their lives were often difficult financially and in many other ways (despite the new availability of married students' housing). However, they demonstrated a type of camaraderie and spirit that has not since been duplicated, with a degree of cooperation, common purpose, and friendship far stronger than that found among fraternity or sorority members today. As Lee pointed out, "The students of the Forties became the parents of the college students of the late Sixties. Should it be surprising to find a generation gap?" (1970, p. 87).

The silent generation

The focus on war and peace in the forties shifted to a focus on rapid scientific and technological advances in the fifties. The most influential of these advances was television, which made it possible for young people to see world events as they happened and opened their eyes to available material goods through advertising.

The affluence brought on by technological advances also made have-nots more visible. The 1954 Supreme Court decision to abolish segregation in the public schools had a major influence on young people. Civil rights demonstrations, sit-ins, and rallies set the stage for the turmoil of the sixties. Ghettos and "Blackboard Jungles" (violence-ridden inner-city schools) also became more visible. Changing neighborhoods began to result in rising juvenile delinquency rates and interracial gang wars and rumbles.

But in many ways the fifties was the decade of the silent generation, which evolved primarily from youths' lack of commitment or forcefulness in the political arena. People didn't want to "rock the boat." The question has arisen about why this silence ensued after World War II. Perhaps it reflected America's mood at that time: tired of war, fearful of inflation, and frightened by Communism (Lee, 1970).

The sixties

Many parallels can be drawn between adolescents of the sixties and their counterparts in preceding decades. In the sixties, the trend toward increasing school attendance continued as employment opportunities for youth declined. It was a decade of tremendous technological and scientific progress dramatized by the space programs. Young people found their heroes among the astronauts. The distaste for war evidenced in the thirties and forties reasserted itself even more intensely in the sixties, as young people saw the grime of war on their television screens and failed to find meaningful reasons for American involvement in Vietnam. Racial hostilities broke into riots, and protest spread to the college campuses. It became the era of the "in"–the sit-in, the sleep-in, and the stand-in. Radical organizations like the Students for a Democratic Society and the Black Panthers attracted numerous disillusioned adolescents into their membership. As Lee has summarized this period so succinctly, it became a time of "confrontation, escalation, and protest" (1970, pp. 136-137).

The emancipation of women, which had begun with passage of the Nineteenth Amendment in 1920 and continued through female participation in the war effort during the 1940s, also grew and gained strength in the form of the Feminist movement.

While many were protesting, others were expressing private interests in improving society. Nationally, internationally, and locally, youth volunteered their services in social causes. Idealism also asserted itself, as some found answers in new religious movements, while others helped to promote an amendment to the United States Constitution that would give those between the ages of 18 and 21 the right to vote.

Drug use began to replace drinking as a form of adolescent rebellion, and sexual permissiveness became the rule rather than the exception. More and more young people were entering college and going on to acquire advanced degrees, extending their financial dependence on their families longer than their predecessors had. (It has been hypothesized that this sacrifice of economic independence may have been a partial explanation of the need for the young people in the sixties to assert themselves through political activity.) In any case, "a prophetic minority" offered a different perspective and radical remedies to serious problems of society and used radically new political techniques in doing so (Lee, 1970).

The seventies

Although the seventies began with much adolescent rebellion and activism, this mood abruptly and pervasively turned to a state of silence and apathy rather reminiscent of the era of the 1950s. Bell (1976) has suggested that on the college campuses this sudden change reflected: (1) public hostility that arose toward the colleges and universities during the years of activism and rebellion and (2) private disillusionment among youth over their inability to change the system. At the same time, there was a gradual decline in college enrollments, in part because economic inflation made it difficult to meet the costs of a higher education and in part because college graduates were discovering that a college degree was no longer an inevitable passport to a high-level occupation.

The apathy also appeared to have reflected youthful disenchantment with a government that had witnessed political scandals reaching all the way to the presidency of the United States. Youths who had fought for the right to vote for citizens between the ages of 18 and 21 now failed to exercise their own right to vote. Students who had once marched into Mississippi to help Blacks gain their right to vote and obtain access to public facilities were now shrugging their shoulders over the Watergate scandal, saying that it had always been that way. To many adults, such indifference was more disturbing than the activism of the sixties. They began to feel that, should such attitudes continue to prevail as today's youths enter adulthood, control of the government could readily pass into the hands of a very few power-hungry leaders at the expense of democracy's erosion.

Alcohol had once again assumed first place over other mind-altering substances, and there was a concurrent increase in alcoholism. The question arose whether this was another attempt by adolescents to combat the helplessness they were feeling over their inability to bring about change and the hopelessness they were experiencing over their government's moral decline.

Thus, it can be seen that, from the era of the Wright Brothers to the era of moon and planet exploration, adolescents have tended to react against adult authority, power, and ineptitude. They have protested—sometimes actively, sometimes passively—against schools, government, wars, social injustices; in short, they have considered the older generation to have failed and have tended to look toward their assertion of independence as the beginning of new solutions.

Chapter summary

We have introduced the hypothesis that the period of adolescence is not determined solely by chronological age or by physiological factors; rather, we have suggested that it is a transitional process involving a dynamic interaction of interpersonal and intrapersonal behavior in a real and physical world. This definition raises questions about what the nature of this transitional period should be. We have hypothesized that a certain amount of conflict is beneficial in that it develops the individual's decision-making ability, which is a prerequisite for mature functioning.

We have pointed out what is meant by mature behavior according to leading personality theorists. A number of goals have been discussed as being necessary for the adolescent to achieve maturity.

What's the matter with kids today...?

NEW YORK, N.Y. (AP) — A cry "strike against war" resounded on many campuses today, summoning students to drop their books at 11 a.m. and demonstrate for peace. Even before the movement got officially underway it resulted in bruises for about 20 persons.

In a riot-launched peace drive on Brooklyn last night, about 500 students of an evening high school joined 2,000 other persons in trying to persuade 1,500 remaining students to join their ranks.

There was a melee in which police swung night sticks and demonstrators swung fists and feet. After the wild turmoil was over, two policemen were treated for sprains and bruises and a citizen for scalp wounds. Many others limped away before the ambulance surgeon could get to them. Eight persons were arrested.

Detectives said known reds led some of the groups of rioters.

CAMBRIDGE, Mass. (AP) — Flying grapefruit and onions today turned an anti-war meeting of Harvard students into a burlesque battle.

There seemed to be a division of thought on the subject of war versus peace.

More than 2,000 students gathered in the Harvard Yard for an anti-war conclave called by the National Student League and the Student League for Industrial Democracy.

BALTIMORE (AP) — An anti-war demonstration by liberal students from the Johns Hopkins University today turned out to be anything but peaceful.

Five minutes after the demonstration opened in a Hopkins assembly hall, the air was filled with oratory cat calls, overripe tomatoes and eggs of undetermined age.

(The Cambridge story noted that the National Student League distributed circulars demanding that ROTC be abolished and criticizing the Civilian Conservation Corps (CCC) as too military.)

Sound familiar?

These reports went out over the Associated Press wire more than 35 years ago and were carried by The Washington (D. C.) Evening Star on April 13, 1934.

These included the following: accepting one's physical self, attaining emotional control, resolving the identity crisis and developing a positive self-concept, achieving social maturity, developing satisfying heterosexual relationships, acquiring a stable system of values, developing intellectual sophistication and sensitivity, attaining a satisfying occupational status and economic independence, and achieving the wise use of leisure time. However, we have noted that, in striving toward these goals, adolescents encounter numerous problems and pitfalls that may prevent them from attaining maturity in all aspects of their lives.

We have also noted that these problems of adolescence do not seem to have changed much over the decades. In our survey of the past century, we have attempted to point out certain common denominators of adolescence, such as resistance to adult authority through political activism, misuse of liquor or drugs, and social protests. We have discussed the increase in school attendance throughout the 20th century and the concurrent decrease in job opportunities for young people. Common to adolescents of all eras have been the ambivalent strivings toward both childlike dependence and adult independence.

Thought provokers

1. How do you think the Dickens quotation applies to adolescence?
2. What have been some of the various definitions of the term adolescence? What is your interpretation of this term?
3. How would you define the term maturity?
4. What should be the primary goals of the adolescent period? Do you think anyone can achieve all of these objectives by the time he or she has reached the mid-20s?
5. Are there problems not mentioned in the text that you find to be of major concern to you? If so, what are some of these problems?
6. What is meant by the statement that the concept of adolescence is a relatively recent one?
7. What are the similarities and differences between today's adolescents and those of the past?

References

Adler, A. The fundamental views of individual psychology. *International Journal of Individual Psychology*, 1935, 1, 5–8.

Adler, A. *Social interest*. New York: Putnam, 1939.

Allen, F. L. *Since yesterday*. New York: Harper & Row, 1939.

Allen, F. L. *The big change*. New York: Harper & Row, 1952.

Allport, G. W. *Becoming*. New Haven: Yale University Press, 1955.

Aries, P. *Centuries of childhood: A social history of family life* (R. Baldick, trans.). New York: Knopf, 1962.

Bakan, D. Adolescence in America: From idea to social fact. *Daedalus*, 1971, 979–995.

Bandura, A. The story decade: Fact or fiction? *Psychology in the Schools*, 1964, 1, 224–231.

Bell, J. N. Silence on campus. *Harpers*, 1976, 252(1510), 18–24.

Berg, I. A. Cultural trends and the task of psychology. *American Psychologist*, 1965, 20, 203–207.

Bierich, J. R. Sexual precocity. *Clinics in Endocrinology and Metabolism*, 1975, 4(1), 107–142.

Coopersmith, S. *The antecedents of self-esteem*. San Francisco: W. H. Freeman, 1967.

Demos, J., & Demos, V. Adolescence in historical perspective. *Journal of Marriage and the Family*, 1969, 31, 632–638.

Dulles, F. R. *A history of reaction—Americans learn to play* (2nd ed.). New York: Appleton-Century-Crofts, 1965.

Ehrhardt, A. A., & Meyer-Bahlburg, H. F. L. Psychological correlates of abnormal pubertal development. *Clinics in Endocrinology and Metabolism*, 1975, 4(1), 207–222.

Eichorn, D. H. Asynchronizations in adolescent development. In S. E. Dragastin & G. H. Elder (Eds.), *Adolescence in the life cycle: Psychological change and social context*. Washington, D. C.: Hemisphere, 1975.

English, H. B., & English, A. V. *A comprehensive dictionary of psychological and psychoanalytical terms*. New York: McKay, 1964.

Erikson, E. H. *Childhood and society* (2nd ed.). New York: Norton, 1963.

Erikson, E. H. *Identity: Youth and crisis*. New York: Norton, 1968.

Fredenburgh, F. A. An apologia for the hippie generation. *Mental Hygiene*, 1968, 52(3), 341–348.

Friedenberg, E. Z. *The vanishing adolescent*. Boston: Beacon, 1959.

Fromm, E. *The sane society*. New York: Holt, Rinehart & Winston, 1955.

Goldenson, R. M. (Ed.). *The encyclopedia of human behavior: Psychology, psychiatry, and mental health* (Vol. 2). New York: Doubleday, 1970.

Hall, G. S. *Adolescence: Its psychology and its relation to physiology, anthropology, sociology, sex, crime, religion, and education*. New York: Appleton-Century-Crofts, 1904.

Havighurst, R. J. *Developmental tasks and education* (3rd ed.). New York: McKay, 1972.

Lee, C. B. T. *The campus scene: 1900—1970*. New York: McKay, 1970.

Lipset, S. M. Student opposition in the United States. *Government and Opposition*, 1966, 1, 351–374.

Lynd, R. S., & Lynd, H. M. *Middletown in transition*. New York: Harcourt Brace Jovanovich, 1937.

Marcia, J. E. The case history of a construct: Ego identity status. In E. Vinacke (Ed.), *Readings in general psychology*. New York: American Book, 1968.

Maslow, A. H. *Motivation and personality*. New York: Harper & Row, 1954.

Mead, M. *Coming of age in Samoa*. New York: Morrow, 1928. (a)

Mead, M. *Growing up in New Guinea*. New York: Morrow, 1928. (b)

Mead, M. *From the South Seas: Studies of adolescence and sex in primitive societies*. New York: Morrow, 1939.

Murray, H. A., & Kluckhohn, C. Outline of a conception of personality. In C. Kluckhohn, H. A. Murray, & D. Schneider (Eds.), *Personality in nature, society, and culture* (2nd ed.). New York: Knopf, 1953.

Muuss, R. E. The implications of social learning theory for an understanding of adolescent development. *Adolescence*, 1976, 11(41), 61–85.

Nixon, R. E. *The art of growing*. New York: Random House, 1962.

Prader, A. Delayed adolescence. *Clinics in Endocrinology and Metabolism*, 1975, 4(1), 143–156.

Rogers, C. *On becoming a person*. Cambridge, Mass.: Riverside, 1961.

Statistical abstracts of the United States, U. S. Department of Commerce, Bureau of Foreign and Domestic Commerce. Washington, D. C.: U. S. Government Printing Office, 1931.

Sullivan, H. S. *The interpersonal theory of psychiatry*. New York: Norton, 1953.

Toynbee, A. *An historian's approach to religion*. New York: Oxford, 1956.

Wettenhall, H. N. B. Growth problems. In J. R. Gallagher, F. P. Heald, & D. C. Garell (Eds.), *Medical care of the adolescent*. New York: Appleton-Century-Crofts, 1976.

The family's influence on adolescent development 2

As are families, so is society. If well ordered, well instructed, and well governed, they are the springs from which go forth the streams of national greatness and prosperity—of civil order and public happiness.

William Makepeace Thayer
(1820–1898)

As they reach adolescence, many young people begin to feel that they have become young adults and therefore no longer require any parental guidance. They assume that their families will now have little influence over them and their behavior. Although this is indeed a period marked by increasing independence and assertiveness, family attitudes and practices do continue to play important roles in the adolescent's development, as do family environment, the *subculture*, and socioeconomic factors.

With the beginning of the adolescent period, the family continues to be a primary socializing agent, although its authority must yield at times to competing socializing forces such as the peer group, as well as to the adolescent's growing need for independence. Family members are also called upon to cope with the problems and perils of their teen-agers' increasing sexual interest and the troublesome, often disturbing, ambivalence about their changing role in the family. Thus, the central problem facing the parents of adolescents is how to help their children gradually acquire *autonomy*, or the freedom to choose to be self-governing individuals, and yet continue to provide certain restraints and limitations. As Douvan and Adelson (1966) have so succinctly stated, "The problem the parent faces is in adjusting his loosening of control to the child's capacity to regulate himself, letting the reins slacken at the right time and in the right way, neither holding them so tightly that the child resists nor releasing them so suddenly as to endanger him" (p. 163). Achieving a satisfactory balance between these two factors depends to a considerable extent on parental practices and attitudes during childhood as well as in adolescence. Even the types and the degree of conflict between the two generations will be affected by the parental practices and attitudes pursued throughout the child's life.

It is true that in recent years questions have arisen concerning the dissolution of the family and the possible decline in its importance in the *socialization* process—that is, its role in the teaching of the younger generation to behave in ways prescribed by society. It is true, too, that the family has been in trouble for at least two centuries as the schools, the mass media, and the rapid changes in society have influenced the role of the family and diminished its strength as a social institution. Nevertheless, the family continues to be the single most powerful institution in the shaping of human life (Frankel, 1976). We believe, therefore, that it is desirable to begin the study of adolescence with a look at various facets of the family and their impact on adolescent development.

Variations in family structure

Parental power structure

To a considerable extent, parental behavior will be determined by the type of power structure that characterizes the family. Elder (1962) has classified child-rearing practices into seven categories: (1) autocratic, in which children are not allowed to express their views or participate in any decisions affecting them; (2) *authoritarian*, in which adolescents may contribute to the solution of a problem but must always yield to their parents' final decision and judgment; (3)

democratic, in which youth is encouraged to participate actively in family decision making, although final approval rests with the parents; (4) equalitarian, in which there are minimal role differences between parents and offspring, with both generations having equal say in family matters; (5) permissive, in which young people are given greater responsibility than their parents for making decisions affecting them; (6) *laissez faire*, in which adolescents have the choice of following or disregarding parental wishes in their decision making; and, finally, (7) ignoring, in which the parents divorce themselves from their adolescents' behavior and allow them to go their own way without question.

According to one study conducted by Elder (1962), about one-third of all adolescents in the United States reported that their families possessed a democratic structure. However, they often perceived their fathers as being more autocratic or authoritarian than their mothers, whom they more frequently described as permissive or equalitarian.

Despite Elder's conclusions regarding the widespread existence of the democratic or equalitarian family pattern, a later study (Kandel & Lesser, 1969) comparing the parental power structures of adolescents in the United States with those in Denmark noted that authoritarian patterns are still the most prevalent in the United States yet very infrequent in Denmark, where the typical family structure is democratic. It was also observed that U. S. parents establish more rules and provide fewer explanations for adolescents than do Danish parents. Kandel and Lesser concluded that the prevalence of authoritarian attitudes among many parents in the United States reflects a tendency in our culture to treat adolescents as children longer than is usual in Denmark. They believe this situation is an outgrowth of the fact that, in the United States, youths remain in school longer than do Danish children and are therefore not expected to make adult decisions as early. It is possible that this delay in the acquisition of autonomy by adolescents in the United States may reflect either a lack of parental discipline or, perhaps, inconsistent parental control when their children were very young. The more firm but democratic discipline of younger children in Denmark may very well contribute to the development of self-discipline in adolescence, which in turn encourages Danish parents to allow their adolescent children greater freedom.

Regardless of one's conclusions about the prevalence of one power structure or another, it is evident that there are numerous factors affecting what type of family structure emerges. For example, the age of the individual appears to have some impact on family attitudes, for both parents are more likely to treat older adolescents more permissively than those still in their early teens. The sex of the child also influences parental practices, for although there is some evidence of change, boys still tend to be given more freedom and independence earlier than girls (Douvan & Adelson, 1966). Family size is another variable affecting the family structure. Parents of large families have been noted to be more authoritarian and less equalitarian than those of small families. Other factors that influence family structure include the socioeconomic class, ethnic background, and level of education reached by the parents. Those from the lower social classes often have had less formal education and a more limited knowledge of the developmental needs of adolescents than do those from other social levels. As a consequence, they are more likely to adopt autocratic or authoritarian attitudes and practices (Elder, 1962). On the other hand, middle-class parents tend to be more permissive and more relaxed in the discipline of their children as well as more open in their expression of affection (Bronfenbrenner, 1961).

Within the framework of the family power structure there are other elements that have an impact on the adolescent. For instance, the consistency or inconsistency of parental discipline can have a marked effect on the child's behavior (Bath & Lewis, 1962). There may also be discrepancies in parental power. The father may be more dominant than the mother, creating a *patriarchal* family structure; the mother may be more dominant than the father, contributing to a *matriarchal* pattern; or conceivably the parents' individual influence may be equal, and they may follow equalitarian child-rearing practices (Bowerman & Elder, 1964). It should be noted, however, that dominance is not synonymous with autocratic or authoritarian control. It should also be pointed out that adolescents report that their parent of the same sex tends to be more powerful and less permissive with them than their parent of the opposite sex (Rothbart & Maccoby, 1966).

The type of parental power structure determines, to a considerable extent, the kind of discipline generally used by the parents, although no parent is likely to rely solely on one kind of reinforcement, sanction, or punishment. Douvan and Adelson (1966) divide sanctions into three categories: physical punishment, a deprivation of privileges, or psychological punishment. Parents who resort to physical punishment can usually be described as authoritarian or autocratic in their approach to child rearing. The form of punishment they choose may be partly motivated by their need to vent their own turmoil or anger and their focus on immediate results rather than on the long-range goal of encouraging the development of self-discipline in their children. Those who resort to a deprivation of privileges tend to stress the need for youths to pay for their misdeeds. On the other hand, parents who rely on psychological punishment, such as statements that they are disappointed by certain behaviors, are usually attempting to encourage the child's development of his or her own inner controls and conscience. Parents who employ this means of discipline would generally be termed equalitarian or democratic. It should be pointed out, however, that not all parents who resort to physical punishment are being autocratic or excessively punitive. Some children actually respond more positively and prefer fairly administered physical methods, which may serve to release tension and diminish anxiety and produce a feeling in the misdoers that they have paid for their errant ways. Conversely, some types of psychological punishment may actually be more vindictive and cruel than certain physical methods. For example, parents who tell their children they don't love them because of certain behaviors can cause the youngsters to feel, if only temporarily, that they are not individuals of worth and value.

The effects of parental practices and attitudes

Adolescent behavior is strongly influenced by the kinds of practices and attitudes that grow out of the family power structure. For instance, in another study conducted by Elder (1963), more than 70% of the adolescents with parents classified as democratic and permissive reported that their parents frequently provided explanations for their rules and actions, whereas less than 40% of the adolescents with autocratic parents made the same statement. Furthermore, it has been observed that young people with democratic parents are more likely to model their behavior on that of their parents and to associate with peers approved by their parents than are those from autocratic homes. In addition, it was noted that democratic parents are also more likely to be consistent in their attitudes and practices and to encourage the acquisition of independence and autonomy in their youngsters than are autocratic parents (Elder, 1963).

Where inconsistencies in parental practices do prevail, or where coercive methods of discipline are employed, greater conflict between the two generations is likely to occur (Edwards & Brauburger, 1973). In fact, when parents demand compliance from their teenagers, the cost is considerable, usually resulting in the decline of effective parent/adolescent relationships and the breakdown of communication between the two generations. And as one might expect, adolescents subject to coercive parental rules are much less likely to adhere to these rules when their parents are absent than are young people subject to democratic practices (Raven & French, 1958). On the other hand, those with democratic parents who explain the reasoning behind their restraints and restrictions tend to maintain conformity with those rules. Apparently, frequent explanations indicate the presence of considerable parental warmth (Elder, 1963). In any case, when young people participate, at least to some extent, in decision making that affects them, two results become apparent: (1) participation tends to facilitate communication between the two generations and (2) youths feel that they have had a role and consequently some responsibility in establishing rules pertaining to them. Such guidance is more likely to be perceived as just by a child than the handing down of rules by parents in an arbitrary manner. Arbitrary parental behavior is apt to result in delayed self-reliance for the adolescent, strained affectional relationships, and a widening of the communication gap between the two generations (Elder, 1962; Douvan & Adelson, 1966).

It has been noted that parents are able to govern their families in a democratic manner if they feel comfortable in their own roles and feel fairly confident about their abilities as parents. Such feelings are subtly conveyed to their offspring, who in turn develop their own inner controls and self-direction, as well as gradual confidence in their ability to make their own decisions (Douvan & Adelson, 1966).

Parental power structure, practices, and attitudes also appear to have an impact on adolescent motivation and achievement, although the reports on this topic have been rather controversial. For example, Bronfenbrenner, (1961), in a study of fathers and sons found that both responsibility and leadership in young people are encouraged by relatively greater power and prominence of the same-sex parent. Males demonstrate a greater sense of responsibility when the father is the chief figure of authority. In fact, he noted that the most dependent and least reliable boys tended to be those who described their family power structure as equalitarian. In a study of 19,200 White high school boys from unbroken homes in Ohio and North Carolina, Bowerman and Elder (1964) also observed that academic motivation appeared to be highest among those who perceived their fathers as the head of the family and as democratic in their relationships with their sons. On the other hand, another investigator reported that a male adolescent in a mother-dominated family may be more achievement oriented because the parent (mother) demanding excellence in the son's performance is usually also the nurturant parent and the one holding the greater emotional power over the children. There has also been some evidence to indicate that achievement-oriented people tend to recall their childhood and their relationships with their parents as characterized by emotional rejection (Straus, 1962). In any case, it is quite possible that an autocratic family structure contributes to a greater dependency on others in decision making—a result that can carry over to low educational goals and to low levels of aspiration. A study by Elder (1963) of White public school adolescents from unbroken homes disclosed that approximately 50% of the boys and girls in grades seven through nine with autocratic parents felt doubtful about completing high school, a trend of considerable significance to those involved with the dropout problem. Such parental dominance was noted especially among parents of the lower socioeconomic class, Roman Catholic parents, and parents who headed large families (Elder, 1962). (This topic is discussed in more detail in Chapter 10.) Apparently, youths' autonomy in making decisions and their level of motivation are strongly dependent on the nature of the parent/child relationship.

Sex-role identification

As you may recall, Havighurst (1972) described the acquisition and acceptance of a masculine or feminine role as one of the most important developmental tasks of adolescence. Among the major factors contributing to the accomplishment of this task have been the interpretations of the sex roles by the parents, the extent to which the parents have served as models to their youngsters and parental response to their offspring, especially to those of the other sex. In recent years, however, these factors have become more complex as a result of the decreasing polarization of the two sex roles and the changing concepts as to what traits are appropriate or satisfying to the individuals. And although traditional sex stereotypes have tended to persist, new experiences with different models of men and women have begun to exert an impact on sex-role learning (Deaux, 1976).

Acquiring a satisfying sex role involves the process of *sex-role identification*. According to Lynn (1966), "Sex-role identification . . . refers to the *internalization* of the role typical of a given sex in a particular culture and to the unconscious reactions characteristic of that role" (p. 466). Parents play a major role in this process, although there is considerable controversy over how they influence the development of the sex role in their children. Some studies indicate that females acquire a strong feminine identity through close identification with their mothers and that males develop a sturdy masculine identity through strong identification with their fathers (Mosby, 1966; Lynn, 1966). Others suggest that identification depends on which parent is perceived as having the greatest control of desirable privileges, such as the use of the family car or telephone. Such a parent tends to be perceived as holding more parental control and consequently higher status, and youngsters are more likely to identify with that parent's interests, attitudes, and behaviors than with those of the parent viewed as having less command in the family power structure (Grinder & Spector, 1965). Still other investigators maintain that the father, through his responses to his daughter, may influence her acquisition of "femininity" more strongly than her mother (Johnson, 1963; Heilbrun, 1965).

According to one theory of sex-role development, that of the *reciprocal-role* hypothesis (Johnson, 1963), a father's behavior and the nature of his relationships with his sons and his daughters has traditionally tended to be quite different. That is, he has tended to assume an *instrumental role* toward his sons—a role characterized by an emphasis on disciplined responsibility and the encouragement of goal acquisition. In other words, the father has typically served, according to this explanation, as an interpreter and a teacher of the world beyond the family. The son's instrumental orientation has been said to be facilitated by his fear of overt punishment and his desire for paternal respect. Toward his daughter the father has usually maintained a more nurturant, *expressive role* with the goal of encouraging her development of femininity. He has been a giver of love and a source of pleasurable affective responses, thereby filling the role of male admirer and serving as a prototype of her future husband (Smart & Smart, 1972).

According to the reciprocal-role theory, the mother's role in the family traditionally has been perceived as being an expressive one. She has been regarded as being loving, affectionate, and supportive and as making no distinctions in her attitudes toward children of both sexes. It has been hypothesized that her children learn most of their expressive behavior from her—a process that begins with their earliest attachment to her.

Included in this analysis of the reciprocal roles of mothers and fathers have been the concepts of identification and modeling. Children tend to identify with certain sex-typed behaviors in their parents. For example, a son's development of strong, assertive, "masculine" traits would reflect his close identification with a dominant father, whereas a daughter would be likely to model the more nurturant traits in her mother.

There are psychologists who would argue with this explanation of sex-role identification. They would say that fathers and mothers need not necessarily fill set instrumental and expressive roles, respectively, in order for their sons and daughters to acquire certain traits. That is, they would be more inclined to attribute a father's different treatment of his sons and daughters to his own socialization and learned attitudes that boys should be active and assertive and girls should be passive and home oriented. Several studies have shown that boys and girls are treated differently according to preconceived notions of what is masculine or feminine and that these children eventually conform to the expectations implicit in the differential treatment (Johnson, 1963; Lynn, 1966; Maccoby & Jacklin, 1974). It has been suggested, therefore, that there is reason to examine the traditional patterns of child rearing as social developments, rather than as built-in, "natural" roles.

Until recently, studies of the father and his influence on child rearing and sex-role development had generally been negligible. In the 1960s, however, it became apparent that the impact of paternal practices in these areas was considerable (Walters & Stinnett, 1971). For example, Lynn (1966) noted that boys tend to experience more difficulty in establishing same-sex identification than girls. He suggested that this tendency may reflect the fact that girls have traditionally had more daily contact with their mothers than boys have had with their fathers. At the same time, it has been observed by some investigators that boys are more susceptible to the influence of their parents than girls are (Bronfenbrenner, 1961). This susceptibility may offer an explanation for the fact that boys tend to be more likely than girls to develop learning problems and emotional disorders when the parent/child relationship is an inadequate one (Walters & Stinnett, 1971). In instances in which one parent is observed to have less influence in the family than the other, the identification of the adolescent tends to be lower with both parents. When the father is the less powerful of the two, identification with him appears to be more impeded than when the mother is the weaker of the pair (Bowerman & Bahr, 1973). These observations further raise the question of how sex-role development is affected when the father plays a very passive role in the family power structure or is frequently or permanently absent from the home. In a study conducted by Rohrer and Edmonson (1960) it was found that women who were reared in a matriarchal home (one characterized by a strong, dominant mother and a submissive father or an absent father) are likely both to establish the matriarchal pattern in their own homes and to live with or near their mothers. In the case of boys, Barclay and Cusumano (1967) state that "The absence of an adequate male model within the family forces the male child to identify with available male models in the external environment" (p. 249). Boys from such homes, who come under the influence of older boys who are members of gangs, often demonstrate the presence of considerable sex-role conflict, which is reflected in their compulsive rejection of anything they consider to be feminine and in their tendency to adopt many pseudomasculine traits (Rohrer & Edmonson, 1960). (Such overcompensatory behavior might not be so common if our society were to deemphasize the need for strong sex-role adherence.) It has also been noted that young people whose fathers are absent from the home often show low academic achievement. In fact, one study indicated that a positive correlation exists between underachievement in males and a lack of sex-role identification (Granlund & Knowles, 1969).

Martin, the youngest of five children, lost his father when he was 2 years old. The other siblings, who were all girls, tended to baby and spoil their younger brother. Martin developed into a poor student, and it was noted by his teachers that he consistently underachieved in his academic performance both in public school and later on at college. During his adolescence he acquired many pseudomasculine traits, including considerable boasting, cockiness, and deceit, as well as a general lack of perseverance. As an adult he began to drift from one job to another and from one business to another, constantly depending upon his older sisters to "bail him out" of his difficulties. He married, and his wife eventually had to take over the major support of the family, while Martin continued to rationalize his failures and shortcomings, blaming everything in his environment but himself. Many psychologists would say that Martin would have turned out differently if his father had lived to provide him with a more responsible masculine image.

At the present time, one of the major problems of sex-role development confronting our society is that of sex-role stereotyping. To combat this phenomenon, which has been so prevalent, Rossi (1964) suggested a redefining of sex roles by society so that people of both sexes might develop such positive human traits as the nurturance typically associated with women and the initiative and assertiveness usually characterized as masculine. This trend seems to be developing gradually, perhaps accelerated by the decline in discrimination by higher educational institutions and by a decrease in job discrimination.

The influences of siblings, family size, and birth order

In addition to parental practices and attitudes, the adolescent's behavior is also affected by other familial factors, including *siblings* and their sex, size of family, and *ordinal position* (birth order) within the family constellation.

The roles of siblings

It has been said that the relationships between and among brothers and sisters in most homes are second only to the parent/child relationships (Irish, 1964). Such sibling associations may have a lasting influence upon an individual's ultimate adult roles (Sutton-Smith, Roberts, & Rosenberg, 1964).

Much emphasis has been placed on the effects of sibling rivalry in human development, but there has been little empirical research into the effects of other kinds of interactions between brothers and sisters. Irish (1964) has suggested eight functions of sibling relationships: (1) They provide a means of socialization, in that young people can try out different behaviors with their brothers and sisters before they attempt them with the world beyond the family. (2) Siblings, especially the older ones, can act as *surrogate* (substitute) parents to the younger members of the family. (3) Siblings can serve as teachers. For example, in the acquisition of such skills as learning to ride a bicycle, older siblings might prove more able teachers than their parents. (4) Since they are closer in age and experience, siblings may understand certain problems of their brothers and sisters better than adult members of the family. (5) Brothers and sisters can often contribute to sibling emotional security by serving as safer targets than their parents for the release of emotional tension. In conjunction with this function they may also render services as counselors and confidants. (6) Siblings may act as role models for one another. For instance, the role established by her older sister may serve as a model for a young girl to follow. (7) Siblings can be sources of motivation through challenge and stimulation. Younger siblings may often accept challenges from older brothers and sisters that they might not accept from parents. (8) Siblings contribute to a feeling of belongingness, which provides a sense of security within the family structure. We would add that siblings may serve yet another function. Often a brother or sister will serve as a liaison between parents and a given child or adolescent, acting to arbitrate disputes between the two generations.

Of course, certain negative aspects are possible in sibling associations. Parental and sibling relationships may create so much security within the family constellation that its young members become reluctant to leave even for short visits, feeling insecure or "homesick" when they are away from home. In a family with many children there may be added difficulties engendered by the presence of so many children with varying needs. In the clamor for the satisfaction of these needs, the less assertive, less outgoing members of the family may often be overlooked, or the talents of some may be sacrificed to satisfy the needs of others. Rivalry and jealousy, sometimes accompanied by the teasing and bullying of younger family members by older brothers and sisters, can also disrupt satisfying, cordial interpersonal relationships and impede the attainment of personal and social adjustment, both inside and outside the family (Irish, 1964).

It should be noted, however, that only children are often in an even more unfavorable position, for at home they have only their parents to whom they can turn and from whom they can learn (Toman, 1961). They may also be denied the opportunity to develop the early socialization patterns—such as sharing—that commonly exist in larger families and that are so necessary for later development of satisfying relationships with their peers.

Age and sex differences of siblings

The age differences between siblings usually will affect the relationships between them. For example, if siblings are 6 or more years apart, they will tend to grow up like only children. If there is less than the 6-year age difference, however, they are often a threat to each other's power and command over their parents. Generally, the closer in age they are, the more severe the conflicts between them, but the greater their tendency to hold on to one another later in life (Toman, 1961).

The sex of siblings also appears to have considerable influence, particularly on the sex-role behavior of each youngster in the family. Sutton-Smith and his colleagues (1964) noted that in a family of two boys, the male twosome usually develops traditionally "masculine" qualities, such as dominance and independence, and a strong motivation toward economic and financial activities. In the case of a female twosome, it was observed that the girls appeared to exhibit traditionally "feminine" traits, such as submissiveness and dependency, and interest in the more "feminine" vocations, such as nursing or teaching. If two siblings are of different sexes, they tend to show more expressive creativity than do either of the other two-sibling patterns. McCormick and Baer (1975) also reported in a study of two-child intact families that first-born males and second-born females appeared to be more extroverted than others. They suggested that the older male's identification with the father might contribute to the son's more outgoing personality, perhaps because of his having greater opportunity than a younger sibling to interact with the adult male world. It was also disclosed by this study that those with opposite-sex siblings tend to show more neurotic tendencies than those with same-sex siblings. It was hypothesized that opposite-sex siblings may regard each other as rivals competing for parental attention to a much greater extent than do same-sex siblings. It is also possible that in a strongly sex-typed society, adolescents (and adults) feel very threatened by any identification with, or modeling of, other-sex characteristics.

On the other hand, a study by Brittain (1966) disclosed that girls with brothers near their own age exhibit more conformity toward parental expectations, whereas girls with sisters seem to be more conforming toward their peers. He suggested that these trends may reflect the greater sibling rivalry that exists in families with two daughters, a conclusion that contradicts the findings of McCormick and Baer cited earlier. Brittain hypothesized further that the competitiveness between same-sex siblings may contribute to hostility toward the parents and hence conformity away from them or that, possibly, a peer-group orientation may reflect the modeling of female-sibling behavior and early awareness of the need for peer conformity.

Other research (Douvan & Adelson, 1966) has noted that first-born girls with younger brothers may be likely to experience problems in the development of a meaningful, satisfying, self-actualizing sex role. Such difficulties are reflected in hostile, competitive feelings of first-born girls toward their younger brothers. These investigators also found, however, that a second-born daughter in a two-girl family may experience even greater difficulties with her sex role, as her parents may consciously or unconsciously convey to her their disappointment in not having a son. Thus, the second-born girl, like many first-born girls with younger brothers, may sometimes wish she were a boy, and this concern may cause her to reject the idea of marriage. Witness the case of Laura.

> Laura, the second-born and youngest child in a college-educated family of two daughters, became the focal point of her father's regret that he did not have a son. Although a mediocre student, she was a likeable individual and a leader in school. Through her father's urging, she became president of her junior college student body, and at his insistence she went on to the large state university that he had attended, although she had expressed a desire to attend a smaller school. After graduation, at his prompting, she entered law school. She had difficulty in meeting the stringent demands placed upon her by the curriculum and almost failed. Ultimately, she obtained a law degree, but at considerable cost. Laura became an extremely tense, anxiety-ridden young woman, who found it necessary to take tranquilizing drugs to maintain the pace established for her by her father because of his disappointment that he had no son.

Family size

The number of siblings within a family constellation also appears to have an impact on the development of the children. According to Douvan and Adelson (1966), adolescents from small families seem to possess greater poise and self-confidence in their relationships with adults than do those from larger families. They are likely to be more social-minded, and they tend to date earlier, engage in more leisure-time activities, and belong to more organized social groups than do adolescents raised in large families. They are oriented toward long-range goals, are more concerned with future educational plans, and are more interested in bettering themselves and in achieving a higher status than that of their parents. In other words, they are more active, energetic, motivated, and future oriented than their counterparts from larger families. Adolescents from small families also appear to be closer to their parents and in some ways identify more intimately with them, sharing more recreational activities, relying more often on their advice, and confiding in them and in other adults more frequently than do youths from larger families.

In keeping with the findings of Douvan and Adelson, Holtzman and Moore (1965) found that adolescents from larger families report that there is a greater distance between their interests and those of their parents. Such young people from large families tend to be more peer oriented and rely more on the advice of their contemporaries than on that of their parents. They are more likely to choose a model from among young adults, older brothers or sisters, and other young acquaintances. Those from large families also tend to be less independent of their parents and other adult authority, yet at the same time, they manifest ambivalence and resentment about this dependency, as well as a lack of well-developed autonomy and internal controls.

These variations in adolescents from large and small families seem to be independent of the factor of social class, for they exist among both middle-class and lower-class youths (Douvan & Adelson, 1966). However, distinctions in the patterns of family power and authority between large and small family units do seem to play a role. For example, parents of large families seem to be more traditional, strict, and punitive in expressing their authority than parents of small families. They are more likely to be autocratic or authoritarian —relying on physical punishment, permitting their children little opportunity to participate in decision making, and generally expecting unquestioning obedience and respect. On the other hand, parents of small families (usually two children) more often appear to be democratic or equalitarian, encouraging personal responsibility, high achievement, and early independence in their offspring. A further difference in socialization stems from the fact that individuals from sizable families are frequently expected to assume responsibility for their younger siblings, a practice that allows them less time for membership in social groups and for participation in leisure-time activities.

Exciting new research has also disclosed the existence of a positive relationship between the size of the family and the intelligence of its children. Zajonc has reported that the fewer the number of progeny in a family constellation, the brighter its children will be (cited by Trotter, 1976). He hypothesizes that, with each additional member, the family's intellectual environment declines and suggests that not only size but also spacing is important; in a family with two children it would be desirable to space them far apart. The longer the older child would be able to remain in an environment "undiluted" by another childish mind, the brighter that first-born would be likely to be. Furthermore, the second-born child, if separated by several years from the older sibling, would be arriving in an intellectually more mature environment.

Birth order

Although the influence of birth order is affected by other factors such as family size, chronological age differences, and the sex of other siblings, research indicates that the role of any individual in the family group is at least partly determined by his or her ordinal rank within the family structure—that is, whether the child was the first-born, second-born, or last-born will affect his or her development.

Initial interest in the effects of birth order on the individual's development was manifested in the past century. Sir Francis Galton first reported such data in 1874, when he published the book English Men of Science. Through his examination of the biographical data of these outstanding men of science, he discovered that only sons and first-born sons were more prevalent among this group of renowned men than might have been possible by chance alone. He concluded that because of the law of primogeniture, under which the eldest sons inherited the bulk of the family estate, they were able to become financially independent and follow their own inclinations. Galton also suggested that parents tended to treat an only son and a first-born son as a companion and to give him greater responsibility than later-born sons.

Among the best-known modern research on the effects of ordinal position is that of Bossard and Boll (1955). In a six-year study of 100 families of at least six children, with a total of 879 living children (458 males and 421 females), they observed that each child selected and filled a specific role in the family structure, with the role selected being determined in large part by the child's ordinal position, by the roles already preempted by the older children, and by the parental and sibling attitudes and behavior toward them. Eight distinct role patterns emerged from this investigation:

1. Every family identified at least one child as filling a role in which he or she assumed the direction or supervision of other siblings or provided them with some type of service. Usually, but not always, this was the oldest child in the family. A male, often the oldest son, would assist his parents and serve as a father surrogate in the absence of the father. Among daughters, it was most frequently the eldest who served as a second mother.
2. A second child was most likely to be described as a popular, sociable, likable youngster, who, realizing that the responsible role was filled, sought to gain recognition and self-esteem through the use of personal charm, rather than through the use of personal power.
3. Another child was apt to be a socially ambitious individual with the term "social butterfly" serving as the most suitable description of the youngster's behavior. Usually this was a girl ranking third, fourth, or fifth in birth order, and it was noted that she tended to turn from the family to the community for recognition.
4. Fourth in the order of frequency was the role described as a studious one, wherein the child apparently searched for and found recognition through academic achievement. This role seemed to be equally divided between male and female offspring, who were described as being quiet, hard working, and preoccupied with their studies.
5. A fifth role was distinguished as being that of the self-centered isolate, who demonstrated a reluctance to participate in family activities and a general withdrawal from the family and family life. Three situations seemed to contribute to the development of the isolate: (a) sometimes it was observed that the child was the odd number in a family in which the other siblings tended to pair off; (b) in other instances, it was noted that this child was likely to possess a

unique interest or hobby not shared by other family members; (c) in other cases, it was reported that in families characterized by early parent/child conflict, youthful rebellion against the parents spread to a more widespread behavioral pattern of rebellion marked by self-imposed isolation.

6. A sixth role was described as that of the irresponsible child, who commonly withdrew from responsibilities. He or she was the one most likely to lose possessions, "forget" to do homework, or neglect household chores.

7. Another role was assumed by a child in poor health or one generally described as being unwell. This child might have a physical defect that created special problems or suffer from a chronic illness or perhaps feign illness as a means of gaining recognition or justifying failures.

8. And in almost every family, there seemed to be a spoiled sibling, usually the last-born child or one who had held that position for several years. It has been suggested that the discipline for the last-born member of the family may be less severe and less rigid; such a child may also be given fewer responsibilities, while at the same time enjoying more opportunities and privileges.

According to Bossard and Boll (1955), ". . . in a large family each child's drive for recognition is expressed in a specialized role related to the roles already pre-empted" (p. 77). In addition, each family member is confronted with different patterns of expectations. The eldest child faces only the expectations of his or her parents, whereas the second-born is confronted with the expectations of both the parents and the older sibling, and so on. It has been suggested by these investigators that, with the passage of time, sibling expectations based on their own roles and experiences may accumulate and ultimately outweigh the expectations of parents.

Other investigators (Parsons & Bales, 1955) have noted that balance in the family structure demands that *all* roles within the *nuclear family* (the family unit consisting of parents and their children living at home) must be filled, meaning that one child may assume several roles. For example, in smaller families of two or three children it seems plausible that one child may possess the traits of several roles. The elder of two children might be not only the responsible child but also the studious one and the *social isolate*, whereas the younger child might be not only spoiled but also sociable and irresponsible. This theory has been extended to explain certain behavior shifts that tend to occur when cultural expectations based on sex are incongruent with family expectations based on birth order (Hancock, 1967). The case of Laura, cited earlier in this chapter, illustrates this point. Ordinarily the second child in the family would not be likely to be as achievement oriented as Laura, but the expectations of her father caused her behavior to shift to some extent from the usual role of the second-born child.

Other studies have indicated that first-born children tend to be the most adult oriented (McArthur, 1956; Altus, 1966, Brody, 1968). They are most likely to be the target of parental pressures, ambitions, and anxieties, whereas later-born children probably will escape these pressures. With the first-born child, parents usually set high standards. In addition, Zajonc has noted that the oldest child tends to be intellectually brighter than his or her siblings (cited by Trotter, 1976). Therefore, it is not surprising that the first-born child is the one in the family most likely to receive a higher education, possess the greatest motivation, and achieve eminence. These children also communicate more frequently with their parents than do younger children (Peterson & Sharpe, 1972). Because these youngsters are so closely identified with their parents, they usually develop strong inner controls or a powerful conscience—sometimes to an inhibiting extent. Often they are more sensitive, withdrawn, high-strung, less sociable, and less accepted by their peers than later-born children.

According to Douvan and Adelson (1966), middle children tend to demonstrate two unique traits. First, they show a lack of motivation (described as "downward mobility"), apparently reflecting their demoralization at having to compete with their older siblings. Second, they seem to show a low internalization of controls. In other words, conscience is apt to be less strongly developed in middle children than in their siblings.

Last-born children generally possess the strongest peer-group ties of any of the children in the family, relying less upon the family for the satisfaction of their social needs and as primary sources for their self-esteem than do older siblings (McArthur, 1956). They also appear to be less bright than the others in the family (Trotter, 1976) and tend to communicate less with their parents (Peterson & Sharpe, 1972). Generally, they are particularly loyal to their friends and often feel that they can be as close to them as to any members of their family. They seem to be the least adult oriented of any of their siblings. The fact that they are less subject to the environmental stimulation of adults might offer one explanation of why they tend to be intellectually inferior to their brothers and sisters.

Only children also occupy a unique position. Bossard and Boll

(1960) suggest that certain common hazards or handicaps tend to characterize only children. They observe that these youngsters have no other children with whom to engage in play and competition within the intimacy of the family. In addition, they fail to receive important lessons in living with others that brothers and sisters would provide, for siblings offer a chance to obtain intimate knowledge about those of a similar age, ability, and type. They can reflect each other's thoughts and behavior and provide assistance in self-correction and self-discipline. The parents of only children also tend to be oversolicitous, possibly because their attention is focused on the one child. Perhaps fear of losing an only child is also greater.

On the positive side, Schachter (1963) observed that the percentage of only children among graduate students at the University of Minnesota was considerably higher than their percentage in the general population. He thought it possible that the only child is more able and thus demonstrates greater persistence in remaining in school than children from larger families. However, such a tendency may also reflect the more favorable economic position possessed by only children.

More recent research (Falbo, 1976) has also indicated that only children tend to be more independent and more trustworthy and to possess higher verbal IQs than children with siblings, which may reflect the fact that only children are likely to spend more time with their parents during the formative years and thereby acquire more adult-like behavior. This same study disclosed that, contrary to popular belief, such children are no more neurotic, selfish, or lonely than children from larger families.

Other studies of the effects of birth order (Miller & Zimbardo, 1966; Radloff & Helmreich, 1968) have also revealed interesting data of possible significance in the selection of job applicants for positions of responsibility. They note that the eldest child and the only child appear to possess a stronger need to affiliate or to lean on others in times of stress than those in other ordinal positions. The need to affiliate may reflect the greater feelings of insecurity that are typical of first-born and only children. Often parents feel very insecure with their first child, and their insecurity is reflected in the subsequent behavior of this eldest or only child.

Toman (1970) suggested that ordinal position may also affect how one selects a spouse, a friend, or a business partner. He noted that the pattern of a new relationship tends to duplicate the pattern of an old one and that the greater the similarity between the two, the more likely it is that the new relationship will be a lasting one, as well as a happy one. He pointed out that brothers and sisters constitute a child's first peers and are usually present during the crucial formative years. Therefore, the eldest child who tended to dominate younger siblings would probably be happiest as the dominant partner in marriage; conversely, younger brothers and sisters, accustomed to being followers and being dominated, will be likely to select friends and occupations that will allow them to remain followers and dependent on others to lead them.

A common statement echoed by parents of more than one child is the fact that the personality of each of their children is so different from that of the others. Although there appears to be a central core of temperament that may be inherited, it is very likely that one's ordinal position in the family is superimposed upon this pattern of innate predisposition and offers one explanation of the wide diversity in individual traits that ultimately develop within the family constellation.

Environmental factors and the family

Not only is adolescent development influenced by parental practices and attitudes, the family power structure, the size of the family, the sex of the children, and the ordinal position of the individual, but adolescent behavior is also affected by such environmental factors as the family's socioeconomic status, the subculture, family mobility, the absence of a parent from the home, and the employment of the mother.

Socioeconomic status

In contrast to Western European countries, where until recently heredity was the chief determinant of social class, social status in the United States and Canada has been based mainly upon economic level. Several measurements of American social class have been devised; perhaps one of the most frequently used has been the *Index of Social Position* (Hollingshead, 1975). According to this index, socioeconomic class can be determined primarily by three factors: (1) the family's residential address, (2) the occupation of the household head, and (3) the years of formal education completed by the head of the household. Through an assessment of these three factors, five social classes have been delineated. In brief, Class I members may be described as belonging to the upper class. Few have achieved this status solely through their own efforts but tend to have inherited wealth and lineage. These are usually the community's professional and business leaders; they are college educated, and they possess high incomes. Although the lines between Classes I and II have recently become blurred, those in Class II would be defined as upper-middle class. Their achievements have resulted mainly from their own efforts. They have had some formal education beyond high school graduation; their household heads occupy managerial positions and engage in the lesser-ranking professions; and they usually are described as "well-to-do." Unlike Class I members, however, they have rarely inherited their wealth. Members of Class III are typically referred to as middle class. They are high school graduates, often with some college background, and the heads of their families are usually employed in salaried and clerical pursuits, own small businesses, are semiprofessionals or technicians, or serve as plant supervisors. Class IV, described as the lower-middle or working class, is frequently composed of second- or third-generation members of an ethnic group. They have less formal education than those of Class III, and many household heads are not high school graduates. Most Class IV males are engaged in skilled or semiskilled manual labor in mines and mills. Class V or the lower class, if employed, is mainly composed of semi-skilled and unskilled factory hands and laborers. Generally, most adults in this group have failed to complete elementary school. They typically live in urban slums, their households are characterized by brittle family ties and many broken homes, and they tend to be resigned to a life of frustration and defeat. Although this classification was the outgrowth of the Elmstown study undertaken in the late 1940s (Hollingshead, 1949), when he revisited this community in the early 1970s, Hollingshead concluded that "The class structure is changing, but it has not disappeared, nor is it likely to disappear in the foreseeable future. Class status is related in one way or another to the functioning of every institution in the community. The central axis around which it revolves is the occupational role that the adult member of a nuclear family occupies in the structure of the community's institutions" (1975, p. 353).

Another approach that has been used in describing class structure has been that of Packard (1959), who also delineates five categories but has taken a perspective somewhat different from that of Hollingshead. He suggests that there are two major divisions in our present class system: (1) the college-diploma elite, consisting of the real upper class and the semi-upper class, who are at the helm of society; and (2) the supporting classes, composed of the limited-success class, the working class, and the real lower class. Thus, Packard considers the main class divisions to have changed since the 1940s when the primary division appeared to fall between the white-collar class and the blue-collar class. He points out that this change may reflect the greater demand for a college diploma as a prerequisite for many upper-class and semi-upper-class occupations. At the same time, clerical jobs, which once were considered white-collar, have frequently been downgraded, whereas factory work has become cleaner and has offered greater remuneration than many white-collar occupations.

Why is it necessary in a study of parental practices and attitudes to delineate socioeconomic classes in a democratic society such as those that exist in the United States and Canada today? The answer lies in the fact that each socioeconomic class is characterized by a unique pattern of norms, values, and concerns that generate different types of parental responses to problems created by adolescent development—problems that occur uniformly within all social classes (Kobrin, 1962). For example, the middle class tends to encourage impulse control, planning for future goals, and raising one's status in society—aims that demand the acceptance by youth of adult authority. Achievement orientation—that is, motivation toward attaining worthwhile goals—is significantly higher among Class I, II, and III boys than among those from Class IV and V, although other factors, such as family size and ordinal position, may also play a role in the acquisition of motivation (Rosen, 1961). No such information is currently available on girls. The lower classes, because they are not governed by a positive program in child training, tend to foster impulsiveness, aggressive behavior, and independence from adult authority, while placing less emphasis on achievement. Among such groups there is often a general lack of opportunity to gain knowledge about child care and effective parenting, particularly in respect to the psychological aspects of development. In addition, parents from the lower socioeconomic levels tend to be limited in the time and energy they have available to devote to rearing their children.

Socioeconomic factors can also affect how young people respond to the demands of the adult world, especially during the period of late adolescence. Middle-class norms, which emphasize supervised training and socializing institutions, prepare young people to accept a certain amount of authority. By contrast, adolescents of the lower socioeconomic classes are often given unlimited freedom and are thus unlikely to accept adult authority as valid. Although they may not overtly manifest more rebellious behavior than do middle-class youths, those from the lower class frequently find it difficult to assimilate certain elements of adult authority, and sometimes tend to come into scrapes with the law (Kobrin, 1962).

Lower-class adolescents are also much more likely to perceive themselves in a negative way than are higher socioeconomic-class youths. Kimmel and Stein (1973) observed that because of their many negative experiences, youths from poor families often feel that they must submit passively to the demands of others; remain self-deprecative; seek pleasure as an end in itself without striving for any sense of achievement; and avoid blame, rejection, or loss of affection—all of which are perceived by such youngsters as inevitable facts of life. Conversely, young people from the higher socioeconomic levels usually tend to see themselves as needing to accomplish difficult tasks that are culturally desirable and to cooperate with others, as well as to seek and enjoy an awareness of their own inner sensory experiences.

Another area of difference between middle- and lower-class adolescents is how they resolve the conflict between their dependency needs and their need to become independent and acquire autonomy. Middle-class parents, who are likely to be protective and controlling with their children, more readily accept the dependency needs of their adolescents and sometimes prolong them by encouragement. Lower-class parents, however, being less protective and controlling, may facilitate the acquisition of early independence among their youth, especially among their sons (Kobrin, 1962; Straus, 1967).

Lack of parental interest and involvement in their youngsters' problems is also noted to be more common among lower-class parents, although sometimes this pattern exists among middle-class parents as well (Douvan & Adelson, 1966). Such a lack of parental concern, however, may merely reflect the family's struggle and preoccupation in supplying its children with the basic needs of food, shelter, and clothing rather than its indifference toward the other needs of their young people. The reader should keep in mind the fact that all kinds of child-rearing patterns appear in every socioeconomic class. The trends we have been discussing are common ones that can be attributed generally to socioeconomic factors.

Sociocultural factors

Closely associated with the socioeconomic elements that affect parental practices and attitudes are those of the subculture in which the family may live. The subculture is characterized by distinctive patterns of values, behaviors, and ideologies that provide a style of life uniquely different from that of the predominant culture and those of other subcultures. Sometimes we refer to the term minority in describing such a group—a minority being defined as a group whose members share racial or ethnic traits, or possibly both, that differ from the traits of the dominant culture and who tend to be regarded and treated as being "different."

It is an unfortunate fact that in the United States a preponderance of the members of these minorities live at the lowest financial and social class levels. They include the migrant workers, Blacks, Puerto Ricans, Native Americans (American Indians), Mexican-Americans, and the so-called poor-Whites of Appalachia. Thornburg (1975) presents a rather clear picture of the plight of these minorities who ". . . tend to have little feeling of personal identity, . . . and to perceive themselves as always subject to the will of other men or of God" (p. 227). In other words, they generally perceive themselves as being "pawns in the hands of fate" rather than as able to exert any control over their environment. Many such families are now third-generation welfare recipients, and as such their fatalistic attitudes have become deeply ingrained in their offspring.

Because we usually perceive ourselves as we think others see us, the self-concept of these people tends to be quite low. For example, Beglis and Sheikh (1974) investigated the factor of race by comparing the self-concepts of Black and White children. They noted that, at the sixth-grade level, the self-concepts of the Black children were more basic, elementary, and immature than those of the White children. The Black youngsters seemed to be less aware of what they could accomplish or what they could become. On the other hand, Samuels (1973) determined that social class was even more potent than race in the determination of the self-concept. Her study showed that middle-class children, whether Black or White, possessed higher self-concepts than lower-class children of either race. Apparently it was the social status of the child's family rather than the minority status that determined how the youngster felt about himself or herself.

One of the problems that is most pervasive among minority groups is that of effective communication with people of the predominant culture. For example, Black dialect and phraseology frequently make it hard for the prevailing culture to understand the Black minority and, conversely, for the Black minority to understand the White community. This is particularly apparent in the classroom, where students and teachers often fail to understand one another. In order to facilitate better communication, some educators have suggested that Standard English be taught as a second language to children from minority groups in the first grade.

Almost one-half of all Black families live in poverty (Thornburg, 1975), many of these being father-absent families. As a consequence, the family pattern is frequently characterized by the mother serving as the head of the house because of the father's absence by reason of death, divorce, separation, or desertion (Thornburg, 1975). Prolonged paternal absence may have marked negative effects on the development of young males, often resulting in antisocial behavior (Biller, 1970). With the lack of a male model, many youths experience difficulty in finding a satisfying, socially acceptable sex role. They may confuse rash, daring, acting-out behavior with masculine behavior and thereby develop early tendencies toward juvenile delinquency.

Another sizable minority likely to be confronted with a communication problem is the Mexican-American community, which tends to be concentrated along the Rio Grande Valley dividing Texas from Mexico and in certain areas of the southwestern United States. Because many of these youths speak only Spanish in their homes, English must be introduced to them as a second language. However, since Spanish, like the Black dialect, tends to remain the prevailing language at home, these youngsters are at a disadvantage as they continue their education.

In contrast to the typical Black family, however, the Mexican-American family pattern tends to be patriarchal, with the father clearly in command and usually resorting to authoritarian child-rearing practices (Thornburg, 1975). The family is generally large and, as such, its importance is sometimes over-stressed to the detriment of such values as the need for education and the desirability of delaying immediate gratification for long-range goals.

Another Spanish-speaking minority, the Puerto Rican, is a more literate group than its Mexican-American counterpart. Many Puerto Ricans acquire a knowledge of English before entering the United States, and they tend to be more self-supporting than many of the other minorities (Thornburg, 1975). As a consequence, if their adolescents can avoid the temptations offered by the numerous delinquent gangs who frequent the urban slums where many Puerto Rican families reside, then they tend to show higher achievement motivation than adolescents of other minority groups. Nevertheless, they often meet with resistance when they try to establish an identity outside their own culture.

Malloy (1976) has reported that persons of Spanish background are beginning to push for separatism because of their failure to gain an identity outside of their own minority. To deny identification with the predominant culture to an estimated population of 11.2 million people of Spanish origin is detrimental to society at large.

The poor-Whites in Appalachia demonstrate much lower tendencies toward achievement. Typically, families are geographically isolated and suspicious of outsiders. They often regard education as an expendable commodity. Many of them live in mining towns owned by mining companies with paternalistic attitudes toward their employees. Since jobs tend to be passed down from one generation to another, this subculture can see little need for education—an attitude that appears to be readily imparted to their offspring.

Another geographically isolated group is the Native Americans, two-thirds of whom still live on reservations mainly in the southwestern region of the United States (Thornburg, 1975). Because their parents encourage them to adhere to their cultural heritage, Indian youths often resist entering the mainstream culture. Thus, they also tend to become school dropouts, whether they attend schools on the reservation or in nearby towns.

It is of interest to note, however, that recently some groups of Native Americans, for example in the state of Maine, have begun to demand reparations for land that they believe was unjustly taken from them by early American settlers. With the expression of such assertiveness and with the opportunities afforded by newly acquired monetary resources and education, achievement among this group will undoubtedly improve.

One of the major problems confronting America today is the question of whether minorities should be encouraged to enter the mainstream culture. According to Thornburg, we should "give those living in a marginal existence freedom of choice to participate—or not to participate—in the dominant culture (1975, p. 226)." Others would disagree, believing that we should provide different minorities with the means to assimilate, that otherwise we will be fostering a social structure so divisive that violence might be the only alternative. Certainly, we have witnessed the success of the assimilation of numerous ethnic groups who immigrated to the United States in the late 19th century. Most of these entered mainstream America but still managed to hold on to traits unique to their own subcultures.

Family mobility

At the turn of the century, a vast majority of Americans were born and reared in a community and stayed to marry, raise their children, and die in that same community, often in the same home as well. In recent years, however, it has been estimated that one out of five families moves every year, many from one city or town to another (Birren, 1970). This increased mobility, which has considerable impact on family life, reflects the tendency of business, industry, and the armed forces to transfer their personnel with relative frequency, as well as the need of many Americans to seek better employment opportunities or their desire to search for "greener pastures." Such mobility can be difficult for all members of the family but no more so than for adolescent members, who develop extremely close ties with their peers at this stage (see Chapter 3). In such instances, youthful family members may feel as if they are leaving part of their families behind when they move. And if the moves are too frequent, they will begin to refrain from establishing any new close interpersonal relationships as they move into one strange community after another. In addition, gaps in their learning often occur as they transfer from one school to another. They may begin to feel more and more inadequate and insecure as they find themselves constantly uprooted from their comfortably familiar surroundings.

In one community visited by one of the authors, the members of the local mental-health treatment center reported a common behavior pattern, which they termed "Air Base Syndrome." Among the typical symptoms was excessive anxiety, usually noted in the mother but sometimes observed in the children as well. In addition, many parents engaged in sexual promiscuity, the use and abuse of hard drugs, and excessive drinking, while their youngsters tended to display unruly behavior, were difficult to discipline, and were beset by numerous academic problems. Transferred frequently from one military post to another, with the fathers absent from the homes for extended periods of time, the mothers often were forced to make many parental decisions alone. At the same time, their youngsters were confronted with the problems of adjusting to new schools and to new communities. The impact of such moves, especially during the high school years, was noted to be quite traumatic for many young people, sometimes resulting in youths' dropping out of school. At the same time, it should be pointed out that some adolescents of military families have reported that such mobility has caused their families to become especially close knit, for the family proves to be a major source of stability and security in an otherwise swiftly changing environment.

In certain respects, people who move from one military installation to another, may have an advantage over civilians who move from one city or town to another. There are usually similarities between military posts, for example in the social structure, that do not necessarily prevail from one community to another in the world at large. Therefore, children and adolescents whose parents are employed in business or industry may experience greater emotional trauma if their families are subject to frequent transfer than the offspring of military personnel.

The broken home and the one-parent family

The broken home may be defined "... as the 'core unit' in which one parent is no longer present, owing to death, divorce, no marriage, or illness" (Kaseman, 1974, pp. 113-114). In addition, there are families in which the parents are "living together" but in reality are psychologically separated.

In 1973 more than 8 million children were being reared in single-parent families—one out of every seven youngsters (Kaseman, 1974). An additional 12 million children under the age of 18 were living in homes that were not characterized by an intact first marriage—that is, one in which one of the natural parents was no longer present but in which a stepparent had entered the family constellation. Only one-half of all Black children under the age of 18 were living with both their parents (Norton & Glick, 1976). And it has been hypothesized that during the next few decades as many as 40% of all children will be affected by marital disruption (Bane, 1976). In view of these disturbing statistics, it is important to take a realistic look at the effects of the broken home and the one-parent family, for whether the family has been broken by death, divorce, or psychological estrangement, it appears to influence the adolescent's development and behavior. The time of the parental loss also appears to have an impact. Hetherington (1972) noted that the first five years in the lives of both boys and girls seem to be the most critical period for father absence to occur.

Hetherington (1972) further observed that the effects of paternal absence are different for sons than for daughters. She noted that, for boys, the absence of the father tends to result in a disruption of sex-role typing during the preschool years and that in adolescence these boys are likely to demonstrate overcompensatory masculinity. On the other hand, for girls, the effects of paternal absence only become perceptible as they reach the adolescent period, when they appear to experience difficulty in relating to males but show little deviation in the usual sex-typed behaviors or in their interpersonal relationships with females. Whether father absence is due to death or to divorce also appears to affect female behavior. Daughters who were very young at the time of parental divorce tend to exhibit greater aggressiveness toward males as they grow older, whereas daughters who were at a very early age at the time of paternal death seem to become very reticent in their relationships with males as they enter adolescence. It was suggested that paternal absence for girls may result in a lack of opportunity during the formative years to interact with a loving, attentive male and thereby increase their apprehension and decrease their skill in relating to the other sex. Differences in the expression of this insecurity, suggests Hetherington, may lie in the negative maternal attitudes of the divorced mother toward the other sex and toward marriage, as contrasted with the more positive attitudes of the widowed mother toward her deceased husband and toward married life.

Individuals from broken homes also seem to have fewer friends; apparently the formation of friendships is impeded by the need for these young people to work after school or to care for younger siblings in the home while their mothers work (Douvan & Adelson, 1966). Boys tend to be "loners," rarely belonging to organized groups. Girls also seldom belong to clubs or engage in leisure-time activities, which may further reflect increased home responsibilities for daughters rather than any psychological difficulties in accepting divorce.

However, the possibilities of emotional disturbance are greater for adolescents who have experienced early parental loss. For example, in one study of 85 adolescents referred for psychiatric evaluation, 36.4% had suffered such a loss compared with only 11.6% of an unscreened school sample (Seligman, Gleser, Rauh, & Harris, 1974).

Throughout the United States and Canada it has been customary for divorced mothers to obtain custody of their children unless fathers have been able to substantiate that such placement would result in an environment injurious to the health or morals of the child. However, this practice is changing. Blaine (1966) has suggested that children over 12 years of age should live with the parent of the same sex whenever possible. In view of the impact of the father on the sex-role identification of both sons and daughters, the courts' traditional awarding of custody of the children of both sexes to the mother in a major proportion of divorce cases needs to be scrutinized and questioned very carefully.

It has further been suggested that schools make special efforts to place children from broken homes in classes taught by male teachers and that boys be provided with male "tutors" (older high school or college students) when they demonstrate a need for extra academic help or masculine emotional support.

The working mother

Since World War II, more and more mothers with children under the age of 18 have gone into the labor force. By 1974 more than one-half of all the women between the ages of 18 and 64 were gainfully employed (U.S. Women's Bureau, 1974). This trend has raised numerous questions about the effects of mothers working outside the home on the behavior and development of their children. Although the results of research often have proved to be inconclusive, the consequences of maternal employment on adolescents tend to point to four possible factors: (1) the sex of the adolescent, (2) whether the mother is employed part time or full time, (3) the socioeconomic status of the family, and (4) the stability of the family constellation (McCord, McCord, & Thurber, 1963; Douvan & Adelson, 1966; Wallston, 1973).

At one time, the employment of the mother either on a part-time or full-time basis was thought to have a greater effect on adolescent girls than on adolescent boys (Douvan & Adelson, 1966). Traditionally it was believed that daughters of working mothers carried heavier household responsibilities than did daughters in homes in which the mother was not employed. However, a later study of both boys and girls (Propper, 1972) disclosed that differences in the amount of housework reported by adolescents of working mothers versus those of nonworking mothers is slight. In addition, it was noted that there was little substantiation for the hypothesis that household tasks are so time and energy consuming that adolescent children of working mothers have less time for leisure, extracurricular activities, and part-time work than children of nonworking mothers.

Douvan and Adelson, in their study of adolescent girls (1966), did suggest that full-time maternal employment may cause a premature separation of adolescent daughters from their parents, as reflected in their tendency to date and go steady early and in the minimal amount of time they spend with their families. They note that such behavior may be indicative of the possibility that the emotional needs of these young women are not being met at home and must therefore be satisfied elsewhere.

A difference in motivation may distinguish part-time working mothers from those employed full time. Some women who work on a part-time basis appear to be less motivated by economic necessity and more inspired by a need for self-fulfillment than do many women employed full time (Douvan & Adelson, 1966). The results of this motivational pattern among mothers employed part time can be observed in the behavior of their daughters. In addition to a high level of energy, which is also quite apparent in the behavior of their mothers, daughters of part-time working mothers tend to show early development of autonomy, independent thinking, and early self-reliance, all behavior traits which their parents seem to encourage. Apparently these daughters rather closely model the behavior of their mothers. In contrast to daughters of mothers employed full time, these girls also seem to have a closer and a happier relationship with their parents. But it is of interest to note that they are not as oriented toward the typically feminine interests as girls of mothers working full time, for they tend to choose more "masculine" vocational goals and more often aspire to upward social mobility.

A third factor in maternal employment, which appears to have some effect on female adolescent behavior, is that of socioeconomic class. Among the middle class, the development of daughters of mothers employed full time seems to be quite similar to that of daughters with mothers employed part time. Girls from both groups exhibit a higher degree of participation in leisure activities and in organized groups and an earlier acquisition of autonomy and self-reliance than do girls of working lower-class mothers or even nonworking middle-class mothers (Douvan & Adelson, 1966). In the lower class, however, daughters of mothers working full time are unlike girls of middle-class, full-time working women, for they are more emotionally dependent upon their mothers and less encouraged by their parents to become self-reliant. These daughters may feel neglected and tend to experience deprivation in their family life, probably not as a result of intentional behavior on the part of their mothers but because of the fact that these mothers are often harassed and overextended in their commitments.

Among lower-class families in which maternal employment may be an economic necessity, sons of working women are less likely to report their fathers to be the males they most admire than do sons of nonworking women. Apparently, at such lower-class levels when the mother works, her employment seems to make the father appear to be less effectual as a provider and hence a less convincing ideal for his son (Propper, 1972). It has also been observed that sons from lower-class, working-mother backgrounds are more apt to exhibit greater rebellious behavior against adult authority and are likely to show evidence of poorer conscience development than do boys from other environments. They also seem to possess a short-term perspective and a low level of energy, hold part-time jobs less frequently than boys from other groups, belong to fewer organized activities, and engage in fewer leisure pastimes (Douvan & Adelson, 1966).

On the other hand, McCord and his colleagues (1963), in a *longitudinal study* of 140 boys from lower-class families, have suggested that it is not so much the lower-class background and the working mother that determine the effects of maternal employment on the sons as it is the stability of the home. Working mothers from unstable homes tend to increase the dependency of their male offspring and increase their sons' chances of engaging in delinquent behavior. Although all of the youngsters in this study were from a lower socioeconomic-class neighborhood, few of the boys reared in stable homes, regardless of their mothers' working, had become criminals. Certainly the quality of the relationship between mother and child, rather than the quantity of time spent together, would partly determine the impact of the mother's working. Perhaps it would be logical to conclude that if a family is unstable, and if the mother is cold and distant, then maternal employment may increase the possibilities that youths will become delinquents and criminals.

Ways and means of helping parents and youths cope with adolescent problems

It has often been said that the peer group serves adolescents as a *reference set* and as a support for common youthful dilemmas or predicaments. On the other hand, parents have generally had no group toward whom they could turn for guidance and reassurance at this period in their children's lives. Often suffering from what might be described as an "adjustment reaction of parenthood" when earlier applied principles of child rearing no longer seem applicable, these parents commonly begin to experience grave doubts about their adolescent children and about themselves (Helfat, 1967).

Even though child-guidance material and the mass media may temporarily reassure them that they share numerous problems in common with other parents of adolescents, these aids still fail to provide many parents with support sufficient to withstand the emotional trauma of this period in the lives of their children. To combat this dilemma, one program entitled "The Parents Exchange on Problems of Youth" was established in Silver Spring, Maryland (Cooper, 1967). Meeting once a week with a professional worker and volunteer mental-health aides (all having adolescents of their own), this group started with the goals of identifying areas of particular concern to parents of youths, eliciting information, providing support and reassurance, offering suggestions, and exchanging ideas on adolescent and parent mental-health issues. In other words, the function of this group was primarily that of group education, rather than group therapy, for its emphasis was focused on the healthy factors in the personality rather than the deviant, and the parents met to share common problems and experiences.

Another approach has been that of Parent Effectiveness Training, based on the principles introduced by Thomas Gordon (1970). In the community of one of the authors, such a program developed as an outgrowth of attempts to combat the problems of drug abuse. Parents met one night a week for six weeks at a local high school, where they learned from trained professionals and paraprofessionals more effective means of coping with their teenagers and their problems. The program proved to be so popular that it was offered again during the semester to a second group of parents (Randolph, 1976).

For youths, programs of peer counseling have been developed. Selected, mature high school students receive a semester of training in self-awareness, values clarification, communication, and problem solving. They then serve as counselors to younger adolescents, as well as to their contemporaries (Randolph, 1976). This topic will be discussed in more detail in Chapter 7.

Chapter summary

Despite the denial of many adolescents, parental practices and attitudes continue to assume significant roles throughout the period of adolescence. Numerous factors influence the various patterns of child rearing pursued by parents. These include the family power structure, the number and sex of the children, and the ordinal position or birth order of each. Environmental elements, such as socioeconomic class, subculture, residential mobility, the broken home and/or the one-parent family, maternal employment, and family stability, also have an impact on parent/adolescent interaction. Siblings, too, contribute to the behavior and development of each individual within the family constellation.

Just as adolescents need the support and reassurance of their peer group during this often trying period, it is becoming more evident that parents, too, need the support of others in order to share some of the problems pertaining to their young people and to maintain their confidence in themselves as parents. It has been suggested that discussion groups and training in parental effectiveness be made readily available to parents of adolescents. In addition, young people, through peer counseling, can provide opportunities for adolescents to discuss problems they may be experiencing with their parents, as well as in other areas of their lives.

Thought provokers

1. Try to think about families you know that exemplify what Elder has delineated as the seven different parental power structures: (1) autocratic, (2) authoritarian, (3) democratic, (4) equalitarian, (5) permissive, (6) laissez faire, and (7) ignoring. What effects have these various power structures had, especially on the adolescent children in the family?
2. What are some of the various discipline patterns and what are

their effects on the attitudes and behavior of the adolescents in the family? What are the effects of inconsistent parental discipline? What sociological and psychological factors may play a role in the type of discipline administered?

3. How do you think sex-role identification develops? Do you disagree with the authors? What effects may changing sex roles have on the development of children and adolescents?

4. Can you think of any functions not covered by the text that siblings may perform? What are some of the disadvantages of having siblings?

5. What is your ordinal rank in the family? Do you think you fill the role as described by the authors? How about your siblings?

6. Compare the social-class structure of Hollingshead with that of Packard. Which do you believe to be more pertinent today? What effects might social class have on the behavior of students in the classroom?

7. Has your family been a mobile family? If so, discuss the effects, both good and bad, that you believe this mobility has had on you.

8. Do you come from a broken home? If so, what favorable and unfavorable effects do you believe this factor has had on your development?

9. How do you feel about working mothers? What positive and negative effects do you think their working may have on the development of their children and adolescents?

10. What are some of the ways of helping parents and youths resolve adolescent problems?

References

Altus, W. D. Birth order and its sequelae. *Science*, 1966, *151*, 44–48.

Bane, M. J. Marital disruption and the lives of children. *Journal of Social Issues*, 1976, *32*(1), 103–117.

Barclay, A., & Cusumano, D. R. Father absence, cross-sex identity, and field-dependent behavior in male adolescents. *Child Development*, 1967, *38*(1), 243–250.

Bath, J. A., & Lewis, E. C. Attitudes of young female adults toward some areas of parent–adolescent conflict. *The Journal of Genetic Psychology*, 1962, *100*(2), 241–253.

Beglis, J. F., & Sheikh, E. C. Development of the self-concept in Black and White children. *Journal of Negro Education*, 1974, *43*(1), 104–110.

Biller, H. B. Father absence and the personality development of the male child. *Developmental Psychology*, 1970, *2*, 181–201.

Birren, J. E. The abuse of the urban aged. *Psychology Today*, 1970, *3*(10), 37–38;76.

Blaine, G. B., Jr. *Youth and the hazards of affluence.* New York: Harper & Row, 1966.

Bossard, J. H. S., & Boll, E. S. Personality roles in the large family. *Child Development*, 1955, *26*(1), 71–78.

Bossard, J. H. S., & Boll, E. S. *The sociology of child development*. New York: Harper & Row, 1960.

Bowerman, C. E., & Bahr, S. J. Conjugal power and adolescent identification with parents. *Sociometry*, 1973, *35*, 366–377.

Bowerman, C. E., & Elder, G. H., Jr. Variations in adolescent perception of family power structure. *American Sociological Review*, 1964, *29*(4), 551–567.

Brittain, C. V. Age and sex of siblings and conformity toward parents versus peers in adolescence. *Child Development*, 1966, *37*(3), 709–714.

Brody, J. E. It can be tough to be first-born. *The New York Times*, Sunday, February 18, 1968.

Bronfenbrenner, U. The changing American child—A speculative analysis. *Journal of Social Issues*, 1961, *17*(1), 6–17.

Cooper, M. The parents exchange on problems of youth. *Community Mental Health*, 1967, *3*(4), 355–357.

Deaux, K. *The behavior of women and men*. Monterey, Calif.: Brooks/Cole, 1976.

Douvan, E., & Adelson, J. *The adolescent experience*. New York: Wiley, 1966.

Edwards, J. N., & Brauburger, M. P. Exchange and parent–youth conflict. *Journal of Marriage and the Family*, 1973, *35*(1), 101–107.

Elder, G. H., Jr. Structural variations in the child rearing relationship. *Sociometry*, 1962, *25*(3), 241–262.

Elder, G. H., Jr. Parental power legitimation and its effect on the adolescent. *Sociometry*, 1963, *26*(1), 50–65.

Falbo, T. Does the only child grow up miserable? *Psychology Today*, 1976, *9*(12), 60–65.

Frankel, C. The impact of changing values on the family. *Social Casework*, 1976, *57*(6), 355–365.

Gordon, T. *Parent Effectiveness Training*. New York: Peter H. Wyden, 1970.

Granlund, E., & Knowles, L. Child–parent identification and academic under-achievement. *Journal of Consulting and Clinical Psychology*, 1969, *33*(4), 495–496.

Grinder, R. E., & Spector, J. C. Sex differences in adolescents' perception of parental resource control. *The Journal of Genetic Psychology*, 1965, *106*(2), 337–344.

Hancock, F. T. An empirical investigation of the relationship of ordinal position, sex, and sex of sibling to socialization, personality, and choice of behavior among adolescents in one- and two-child families. *Dissertation Abstracts*, 1967, *28*(2-A), 781–782.

Havighurst, R. J. *Developmental tasks and education* (3rd rev. ed.). New York: McKay, 1972.

Heilbrun, A. B., Jr. An empirical test of the modeling theory of sex-role learning. *Child Development*, 1965, *36*, 789–799.

Helfat, L. Parents of adolescents need help too. *New York State Journal of Medicine*, 1967, *67*(20), 2764–2768.

Hetherington, E. M. Effects of father absence on personality development in adolescent daughters. *Developmental Psychology*, 1972, *7*, 313–326.

Hollingshead, A. B. *Elmstown youth*. New York: Wiley, 1949.

Hollingshead, A. B. *Elmstown youth and Elmstown revisited*. New York: Wiley, 1975.

Holtzman, W. H., & Moore, B. M. Family structures and youth attitudes. In M. Sherif & C. W. Sherif (Eds.), *Problems of youth: Transition to adulthood in a changing world*. Chicago: Aldine, 1965.

Irish, D. P. Sibling interaction: A neglected aspect in family life research. *Social Forces*, 1964, *42*(3), 279–288.

Johnson, M. M. Sex-role learning in the nuclear family. *Child Development*, 1963, *34*, 319–333.

Kandel, D., & Lesser, G. S. Parent–adolescent relationships and adolescent independence in the United States and Denmark. *Journal of Marriage and the Family*, 1969, *31*(2), 348–358.

Kaseman, C. M. The single-parent family. *Perspectives in Psychiatric Care*, 1974, *11*(3), 113–118.

Kimmel, D., & Stein, M. I. Variations in self-rated personality needs as a function of sex, age, and socioeconomic status from adolescence to middle age. *Proceedings of the 81st Annual Convention of the American Psychological Association,* 1973, *8*, 777–778 (Summary).

Kobrin, S. The impact of cultural factors on selected problems of adolescent development in the middle and lower class. *American Journal of Orthopsychiatry*, 1962, *32*, 387–390.

Lynn, D. B. The process of learning parental and sex-role identification. *Journal of Marriage and the Family*, 1966, *28*(4), 466–470.

Maccoby, E. E., & Jacklin, C. N. *The psychology of sex differences*. Stanford, Calif.: Stanford University Press, 1974.

Malloy, M. T. We want no melting pot. *The National Observer*, August 7, 1976, 1; 12.

McArthur, C. Personalities of first and second children. *Psychiatry*, 1956, *19*, 47–54.

McCord, J., McCord, W., & Thurber, E. Effects of maternal employment on lower-class boys. *Journal of Abnormal and Social Psychology*, 1963, *76*(2), 177–182.

McCormick, K., & Baer, D. J. Birth order, sex of subject, and sex of siblings as factors in extroversion and neuroticism in two-child families. *Psychological Reports*, 1975, *37*(1), 259–261.

Miller, N., & Zimbardo, P. G. Motives for fear-induced affiliation: Emotional comparison of interpersonal similarity? *Journal of Personality*, 1966, *34*(4), 481–503.

Mosby, D. V. P. Maternal "identification" and perceived similarity to parents in adolescents as a function of grade placement. *Dissertation Abstracts*, 1966, *26*(11), 6841.

Norton, A. J., & Glick, P. C. Changes in American family life. *Children Today*, 1976, *5*(3), 2–4; 44.

Packard, V. *The status seekers*. New York: McKay, 1959.

Parsons, T., & Bales, R. F. *Family, socialization and interaction process*. Glencoe, Ill.: Free Press, 1955.

Peterson, R. A., & Sharpe, L. K. Effects of ordinal position: Tripartite analysis. *Psychological Reports*, 1972, *30*(3), 890.

Propper, A. M. The relationship of maternal employment to adolescent roles, activities, and parental relationships. *Journal of Marriage and the Family*, 1972, *34*(3), 417–421.

Radloff, R., & Helmreich, R. *Groups under stress: Psychological research in SEALAB II*. New York: Appleton-Century-Crofts, 1968.

Randolph, S. Faculty member, Rapides Parish Schools, Alexandria, Louisiana. Interview, November, 1976.

Raven, B. H., & French, J. R. P., Jr. Legitimate power, coercive power, and observability in social influence. *Sociometry*, 1958, *21*, 83–97.

Rohrer, J. H., & Edmonson, M. S. *The eighth generation*. New York: Harper & Row, 1960.

Rosen, B. C. Family structure and achievement orientation. *American Sociological Review*, 1961, *26*, 574–585.

Rossi, A. S. Equality between the sexes. In R. J. Lifton (Ed.), *The woman in America*. Boston: Houghton Mifflin, 1964.

Rothbart, M. K., & Maccoby, E. E. Parental differential reactions to sons and daughters. *Journal of Personality and Social Psychology*, 1966, 4, 237–243.

Samuels, S. C. An investigation into the self-concepts of lower- and middle-class Black and White kindergarten children. *Journal of Negro Education*, 1973, 42(4), 467–472.

Schachter, S. Birth order, eminence and higher education. *American Sociological Review*, 1963, 28, 757–768.

Seligman, R., Gleser, G., Rauh, J., & Harris, L. The effect of earlier parental loss in adolescence. *Archives of General Psychiatry*, 1974, 31(4), 475–479.

Smart, M. S., & Smart, R. C. *Children: Development and relationships.* New York: Macmillan, 1972.

Straus, M. A. Conjugal power structure and adolescent personality. *Marriage and Family Living*, 1962, 24, 17–25.

Straus, M. A. The influence of sex of child and social class on instrumental and expressive family roles in a laboratory setting. *Sociology and Social Research*, 1967, 52(1), 7–21.

Sutton-Smith, B., Roberts, J. M., & Rosenberg, B. G. Sibling association and role involvement. *Merrill-Palmer Quarterly of Behavior and Development*, 1964, 10, 25–38.

Thornburg, H. D. *Development in adolescence.* Monterey, Calif., Brooks/Cole, 1975.

Toman, W. *Family constellation.* New York: Springer, 1961.

Toman, W. Birth order rules all. *Psychology Today*, 1970, 4(7), 45–49.

Trotter, S. Zajonc defuses I.Q. debate: Birth order work wins prize. *APA Monitor*, 1976, 7(5), 1,10.

U. S. Women's Bureau. *The myth and the reality.* Washington, D. C.: U. S. Government Printing Office, 1974.

Wallston, B. The effects of maternal employment on children. *Journal of Child Psychology and Psychiatry*, 1973, 14, 81–95.

Walters, J., & Stinnett, N. Parent–child relationships: A decade review of research. *Journal of Marriage and the Family*, 1971, 33(1), 70–111.

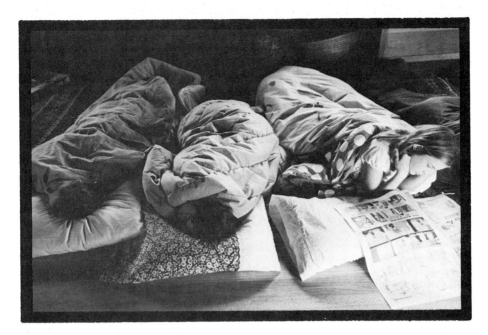

Adolescent
social development   3

> The most powerful and the most lasting friendships are usually those of the early season of our lives, when we are most susceptible of warm and affectionate impressions.
>
> William Melmoth
> (1710–1799)

The socialization process during adolescence assumes an importance second only to that which occurs during infancy. During adolescence, the final stage of intensive socialization, the striving toward maturity, takes place. Once maturity is reached, personality traits become somewhat fixed, and modifications in social behavior become relatively difficult (McGovern, 1967). With the onset of adolescence, social development demands that young people start to free themselves from what one psychologist has called the "social incubator" of the family (Nixon, 1962). But like butterflies emerging from their cocoons, adolescents are at first unsure of themselves and lack sufficient experience and perspective to make the leap from the security of the family to the outside world. Thus, in their need to

69

establish independence from the family, to resolve the conflict of who they are and what their roles in life will be, and to establish autonomy, they turn to their peer group.

In brief, the peer group has been defined as ". . . a peripheral subculture of [the adolescent's] own making, which cherishes values and establishes criteria of status distinct from those of the adult community" (Ausubel, 1954, p. 343). Some behavioral scientists also describe peer groups as reference groups that enable young people to assess their own problems, drives, and goals (Sherif & Sherif, 1965).

Major functions of peer groups

The peer group serves many functions, but probably none is more important than its provision of the kind of environment for growth and acquisition of knowledge about the self that the family is generally unable to offer and that few individuals are capable of finding alone. The peer group also presents opportunities for its members to learn and try out new roles, to observe others experimenting with their roles, and ultimately to revise old ones that no longer prove to be effective. Such modification of former styles of behavior enables youths to discover more adequate means of functioning in society. When they become capable in a given role, they may frequently transfer their newly discovered knowledge from one group to another (Horrocks & Benimoff, 1966; McGovern, 1967). For example, youths who become leaders in their own crowd may acquire skills that will enable them to become leaders in other groups, such as their high school student council.

Through membership in a peer group, young people also acquire a certain status. All peer groups become distinctive in their dress, their language, their loyalty and dependability, and their participation in extracurricular activities at school, as well as in other pursuits. In turn, individuals are generally classified according to the group of which they are members (Hollingshead, 1975). It is through the adoption of such symbols of peer-group status that adolescents begin to acquire their own identity separate from that of "child" in the family.

The peer group further facilitates adolescent emancipation from the family by helping youths to balance their ambivalent needs for independence and dependence. In a group of their contemporaries, where they are more likely to be treated as equals, they can begin to move out of the subordinate position they hold in their relationships with adults (McGovern, 1967). Thus, the peer group can provide young people with an instrument for bargaining with adults.

Through the support of their friends they can often gain privileges already held by other members of the group. For instance, when an adolescent daughter tells her mother that all of the other girls in her crowd can stay out with their dates until midnight, it puts considerable pressure on her parents to reconsider her 11 o'clock curfew. However, Blos (1967) points out that if peer-group relationships merely replace childhood dependencies and fail to provide for growth and development, then they are not fulfilling their proper functions.

The development of a social, personal, and sexual identity, known as the process of *individuation*, is facilitated by membership in a peer group (Blos, 1967). Friends can help young people acquire a clear, stable identity in a number of ways: (1) they assist adolescents in resolving their conflicts within themselves and with others; (2) they teach them respect for competence (presumably social competence), which is necessary for the acquisition of maturity and autonomy; (3) they instruct them in how to act in social situations, especially those involving heterosexual relationships; and (4) they are a source of feedback to youths about their personality and behavior, thereby enabling them to assess their own development and modify their actions when necessary (McGovern, 1967).

The peer group can also offer its members an opportunity for an intimate relationship, a need that seems to permeate all youthful behaviors. Such intimacy has been defined as ". . . the need for deep involvement with another person" (Mitchell, 1976, p. 275). Apparently, young people find it difficult to cope with the daily stresses of their lives without someone in whom they can confide and communicate their problems, although it should be pointed out that such a need is not unique to this stage of life.

One of the primary sources of sex education is the peer group, for one's contemporaries can often provide information on topics that are likely to be avoided by adults (McGovern, 1967). Peers can help adolescents prepare to make decisions about premarital sexual activity and about marriage; the peer group provides a setting in which young people can try out various *psychosexual* and sociosexual roles. In addition, the peer group develops its own norms of sexual behavior, which generally serve as guidelines for individual behavior.

Participation in many group recreational activities is facilitated by membership in a peer group. Such activities are usually informal, often relatively inexpensive, and generally unsupervised by adults (Horrocks & Benimoff, 1966). Adolescent leisure-time pursuits can range from endless "rap" sessions and just "fooling around" to active participation in sports, such as tennis and drag racing, to attendance at spectator functions, such as football games, movies, and rock concerts. Because leisure activities are a part of the socialization process in the adolescent (Noe, 1969), this topic will be discussed in more detail later in this chapter. At this point, it might be noted that such activities are important to the adolescent's social development, because they offer opportunities for young people to develop leadership and autonomy, to test themselves socially, and to establish their own values.

Peer-group communication

Without a doubt, one of the most common and most time-consuming activities of adolescence is just plain talk, often called a "rap session" or "bull session." Such sessions first take place in the context of *unisexual* peer groups—those made up of all girls or all boys.

Sometimes a peer relationship may serve no other purpose than that of a sounding board, wherein one member functions primarily as a listener (Douvan & Adelson, 1966). At other times, it provides a two-way street for the exchange of ideas, thoughts, and feelings. In reality, the seemingly never-ending conversations of young people are actually practice sessions in the skills needed for successful social interaction. The results of failure to engage in frequent conversations can often be seen in orphanages and corrective institutions and among low socioeconomic groups (Staton, 1963). One of the authors had the opportunity to observe several classes of students in a high school located in a slum area. Quite evident among a majority of the students was a lack of verbal facility, possibly reflecting limited conversation in the home and a fear of ridicule and rejection for verbal ineptitude. Such a lack of practice in conversational skills often results in retarded intellectual and social development.

The peer group seems to have a language all its own, a language that tends to change to some extent with each succeeding generation. Such verbalization not only enables members of the group to communicate with one another but also provides a barrier that excludes outsiders. Thus, the common language creates a feeling of group identity, a sense of belonging, and a degree of status (McGovern, 1967).

Perhaps the adolescent idioms of today are more descriptive and more earthy than those of past generations. Some of the current terms used openly in the presence of adults would have caused more than raised eyebrows two or three decades ago. Undoubtedly, much of this idiomatic language reflects the impact of our mass media and our technological advances. In addition, the earlier tendency to "protect" women from the so-called common or unpleasant realities of life has lost much of its force, and many frank terms that were once confined to all-male gatherings are expressed just as readily by females as by males in our present society. But in any case, adolescent language is a natural outgrowth of the world in which young people live today and is possibly a vital factor in expanding and helping to keep the English language alive today. The White House Conference in 1950 concluded that lengthy adolescent conversations developed not only social skills but also greater insight into how others think and feel, thereby enabling young people to develop a more complete sense of self-identity (Midcentury White House Conference on Children and Youth, 1951).

Since the invention of the telephone, adolescents have been known to tie up the lines for several hours at a time. Although few parents are enthusiastic about the practice, it is likely that telephone conversations serve many of the same purposes as face-to-face talk sessions. Such dialogue provides opportunities for youths to learn to express their ideas, determine their effect on others, gauge the meaning of what their peers are saying, and evaluate the significance of ideas left unsaid or incomplete.

The peer-group structure

The adolescent peer-group social system appears to vary from school to school, from one geographical region to another, and from rural areas to urban ones. In fact, it may even vary from one year to the next within the same school (Newman, 1976). Nevertheless, there are two major categories of peer groups that tend to prevail in all types of schools—cliques and crowds—with the main determining factor being the size of the group.

Cliques

Cliques are generally smaller than crowds, ranging anywhere from two to nine members with the mode of such groups being five. Hollingshead (1949) offers the following definition: "A clique comes into existence when two or more persons are related one to another in an intimate fellowship that involves 'going places and doing things' together, a mutual exchange of ideas, and the acceptance of each personality by the others" (p. 205).

Cliques tend to be of a "closed" nature—that is, they have an "elite" membership and generally forbid entrance by "outsiders." Usually, cliques can be defined as one of three types: (1) school cliques, (2) recreational cliques, or (3) institutional cliques, such as church youth groups (Hollingshead, 1949). During early adolescence cliques are always unisexual in nature, but, according to Dunphy (1963), a transformation in structure may take place during the middle-adolescent period, at which time some cliques may become heterosexual.

An interesting study of school cliques conducted in Sydney, Australia, between 1958 and 1960 uncovered 44 cliques among a total of 303 predominantly middle-class boys and girls, who were about equally divided in the number of each sex and ranged in age from 13 to 21. The small size of these cliques—they had an average of 6.2 members—reflected the intimate relationships of the group, which was also characterized by a strong cohesiveness (Dunphy, 1963). Perhaps it is no coincidence that the size of the clique tends to be comparable to that of the average family, a fact that may help to explain the ready transfer of adolescent allegiance from family to peer group.

Cliques are generally composed of members of the same socioeconomic class or of adjacent classes and tend to be limited to those in the same grade level at school. Membership is voluntary but dependent upon the acceptance of other group members and is terminated by the mutual consent of these same group participants. Members usually have a common set of values, interests, tastes, and moral standards, which allows for considerable intolerance and contempt for those who are different. However, a moderate amount of difference can add to the dynamics of the group, as Douvan and Adelson (1966) suggest: "Qualities of personality must vary between friends enough to give the relation the zest, tension, and enrichment that comes out of differences" (p. 184). Should such conflict become too severe and hence become the group's *raison d'être*, then the clique may evolve into a gang (Hollingshead, 1949).

However, it should be noted that there are several major differences between a clique and a gang: (1) whereas a clique is relatively small, a gang may number into the hundreds through an interlocking membership. (2) A clique is less formal and less organized than a gang, which is usually characterized by a formal leadership, stated functions and goals, and regular times or places for assembling. (3) A clique is likely to be a middle-class group that reflects middle-class values, whereas a gang is apt to reflect the lower-class culture, especially the delinquent subculture (see Chapter 8). (4) A clique prefers social and recreational activities, whereas a gang tends to engage in antisocial or deviant behavior. (5) Both groups demand certain standards of behavior from their members and place certain sanctions on them, but a clique uses manipulation and control, avoidance or rejection, and constructive criticism, whereas the gang tends to resort to physical coercion (McGovern, 1967).

Crowds

The average crowd is considerably larger than the average clique. In his study of the Australian students cited earlier, Dunphy (1963) noted that there were 12 crowds among the 303 students, with the crowd size varying from 15 to 30 members and average membership being 20.2. He concluded that a crowd is basically "an association of cliques" with the average crowd composed of 3.1 cliques but ranging in number from no more than 4 cliques to no fewer than 2. At the same time, he observed that not all cliques are associated with crowds. However, clique membership appeared to be a necessary prerequisite for membership in a crowd; in no case did a person belong to a crowd without concurrently being a member of a clique.

The large size of the crowd prevents the formation of intimate relationships, and members tend to regard each other as "acceptable associates" rather than as "real buddies." The functions of the crowd also tend to differ from those of the clique. Whereas a clique is usually preoccupied with conversation and communication, a crowd is more concerned with organized social activities such as parties and dances, which tend to take place on weekends in contrast to clique functions, which are most likely to occur during the week (Dunphy, 1963).

Membership in a crowd does offer one very important benefit not generally available from membership in a clique. It provides a means of transition from puberty to courtship, permitting progress from unisexual to heterosexual relationships through interclique activities that allow group members to practice new roles in a heterosexual setting (McGovern, 1967).

Adolescent social structure from another perspective

In addition to classifying the peer group according to size, we might also categorize it according to its social type. In a study of the social-group structure of male seniors in one California high school, Poveda (1972) noted that one's social position in the peer group could be delineated not necessarily according to group size or social class but on a continuum he described as "insider-outsider," with several groups between the two extremes. He described "insiders" as those participating in a peer-oriented life and "outsiders" as students referred to by others as "clods," "duds," or "lames," a fairly sizable group composed of about 13% of the males in the senior class. In the center of this continuum was a relatively large group of "average" or "normal" male seniors (about 34%), who participated to a varying extent in the adolescent social system, perhaps engaging in one or two activities of particular interest to them but not becoming actively involved in the school's prestigious events. This group Poveda described as being socially invisible, whereas the "clods" were usually quite visible due to their lack of social skills or because of some other negative trait.

He further suggested that, among those considered to be peer-oriented, there were two distinctive categories and a cluster of additional minor types. The two major peer-oriented groups consisted of the "athlete/upper class," which was oriented toward school social activities, and the "in-crowd," which consisted of those whose peer affiliations tended to take place outside the realm of the school. Many of the latter, who composed 24% of the males in the senior class, were heavily involved in the use of drugs and in other rebellious activity. Because their social activities usually occurred away from the environment of the school, they were described as the "out-of-sight" group.

The "athlete/upper class," which consisted of about 16% of the senior-class boys, regarded itself as the popular elite with an exclusive membership. A satellite of this group was that of the "brain/athlete/upper class," about 13% of the male seniors, a group that strongly identified with the "athlete/upper class" and aspired to be accepted by it. Students in this satellite group appeared to be somewhat more friendly and sociable than their other classmates and prided themselves on being well rounded.

Although Poveda's study was based on the results obtained only from male seniors in one high school, it does provide a frame of reference for additional research on the existing social structure among adolescents. Such continued study is needed, because the academic success or failure of youths is often based partly on their social standing. For example, Poveda noted that many of those who would have been considered members of the "in-crowd"—that is, the rebellious youths who tended to socialize mainly outside school —had already become dropouts.

One interesting question that arises in regard to adolescent social status is that of whether it can be changed or modified. An unusual report by a high school student of her observations on the high school social system (Jones, 1976) suggests that, although students recognize the existence of a status system, they do not understand it. She goes on to note that, although adolescents with low status, for example the "clods," look up to their classmates at the top of the social hierarchy and try to model their behavior after them, the roots of this status system form in the earlier years of the students' education and that, once established, such status does not change, regardless of the adolescents' present traits. Although Jones feels that propinquity is largely to blame and can be modified through shuffling and reshuffling students every two years to keep them moving and to prevent them from coagulating, we believe that this is only a partial solution to a complex problem. Other remedies might include small-group projects within the classroom involving youths from various social strata. Such groupings may offer positive learning experiences, as well as facilitate the development of new friendships, and remove some of the barriers existing within the social structure.

Factors affecting peer-group membership

It is generally agreed that adolescents, regardless of their standing in the social hierarchy, must develop an increasing ability to get along with their peers if their personal and social adjustment is to be adequate (Bowerman & Kinch, 1959). According to McGovern (1967), getting along requires that young people conform to a certain extent to the social values of the group, that they possess a sufficient number of common interests, and that they come from similar socioeconomic backgrounds. Of course, the emphasis on compliance can become so strong that group members almost seem to be prisoners of group norms, depending on them for advice in how to dress, how to talk, what to do, and even what to think and believe (Douvan & Adelson, 1966). Staton (1963) has suggested that this kind of confor-mity reflects the tremendous insecurity of youths who are trying to adjust to a strange and fearsome, yet often delightful, social structure. But such conformity is by no means limited to young people; many adults also exhibit a high degree of conformity, reflecting their own uneasiness and anxiety about the rapid changes with which they must also contend in today's world.

Douvan and Adelson, in their study of adolescent girls (1966), found that girls in middle adolescence who possess such personality traits as sensitivity, warmth, tact, and sympathy are the ones most likely to prove acceptable as friends to other girls. During this period, girls seek like-sexed peers who will provide understanding and emo-tional support during their inevitable trials, discoveries, and despairs. Prior to forming such friendships, however, girls will tend to visually assess each other before deciding to associate, for appearance and dress do seem to have an impact on the formation of teenage friendships and social interactions. If a girl's clothing does not reflect current adolescent fashions, she may be rejected by her peers or labeled as "different" before she can establish her worth as an individual. Sometimes, however, such deviant appearance may reflect youthful attempts to gain peer-group attention and acceptance (Allen & Eicher, 1973). Once friendships are established, however, the investment can become so great that to lose a friend through disloyalty or through mobility is almost like losing a part of the self and can indeed prove to be a painful experience (Douvan & Adelson, 1966).

In his classic study of ten Midwestern high schools in the United States, Coleman (1961) notes that athletic accomplishments appear to be important in the attainment of status and acceptance among adolescent boys, a finding substantiated by the later research of Poveda (1972) cited earlier. Coleman suggests that athletes visibly lead their teams to victory for their schools and for their communities. This visibility is not true of outstanding scholars, who have few means of bringing glory to their schools, since their achievements are basically personal and sometimes attained through competition at the expense of their peers. Those who acquire the greatest status and acceptance appear to be students who are actively engaged in visible activities that they are able to call their own. In addition to athletics, visible functions would include active participation on school newspapers, in drama clubs, and in social affairs. Scholars who are not engaged in any of these activities generally fill rather passive roles.

A study by Horowitz (1967) also supports Coleman's observations but further discloses that a combination of athlete and scholar is the most popular of all, in contrast to Poveda's (1972) results, which disclosed the "brain/athlete" to be second in the social hierarchy. The results of three studies reported by Friesen (1968) dispute all of these findings. Approximately 15,000 students from 19 public high schools in an eastern Canadian city, a large western Canadian city, and a central Canadian urban and rural area participated in his research. The 10,019 subjects who participated in one study reported that the traits that would gain acceptance by the most elite group were friendliness (51.3%), good looks (25.4%), money (13.8%), athletic ability (7.0%), and academic excellence (2.5%). These same 10,019 subjects felt that popularity was determined by the following criteria: membership in the leading crowd (64.3%), athletic stardom (18.7%), possession of a nice car (12.7%), and academic excellence (4.2%). Interestingly, however, in all three studies students most wanted to be known as outstanding scholars, a choice far ahead of their desire for athletic recognition. Apparently, those selecting athletic success as most important recognize that it can provide immediate gratification, especially among the peer group, but that it has little value for the future. This indicates that adolescents recognize the discrepancy between peer-group values and the values necessary to later success in life. From the results of the studies reported by Horowitz, Poveda, and Friesen, it appears that the enduring, respected values among adolescent boys are, in order of importance: (1) academic achievement, (2) athletic prowess (in males), and (3) popularity; among adolescent girls they are: (1) academic achievement, (2) popularity, and (3) athletic prowess (in males).

In summary, Friesen makes three important observations: (1) Young people fail to give adequate support to academic excellence and give most visible recognition to star athletes. (2) Athletic achievement is actually attained only by a relatively small group. (3) Although popularity is desired by most students, only about 25% of the students in Friesen's studies claimed to be in the elite group, only 22.6% had been elected to any type of leadership during their junior or senior years of high school, 28% expressed concern about being accepted and liked, and 28% never socialized with their peers.

The results of these various studies suggest that there is room for greater recognition among adolescents of academic excellence. Some have suggested that "letters" be given for scholastic achievement as well as for athletic performance. Rallies in which outstanding scholars participate in teams against scholars from other schools might be another means of extending recognition to outstanding academic performance and would also enable scholars to bring glory to their schools.

Another factor that appears to affect peer-group membership is that of race. Gottlieb and Tenhouten (1965) noted that, as Blacks enter a previously all-White school, they initially enter only those activities involving a minimum amount of interracial interaction and refrain from seeking membership with their White peers in school-related groups, a situation also noted at the college level by one of the authors of this textbook. As the percentage of Blacks increases, two distinct, separate social systems emerge, and the interaction between the two is usually very limited. If the Black students ultimately become a majority, they then engage in all of the activities offered by the school and act much like the White students who once constituted the majority.

Among individual students there are a number of factors contributing to the selection of friends. Strong similarities in values, attitudes, and other traits appear to be characteristic of many adolescent friendships. In fact, Gray and Gaier (1974) have suggested that such similarities seem to assist youths in establishing a personal identity by providing them with a sense of security and serving as a reflection of themselves, a likeness that tends to provide an image pattern.

In every school there are some students who may be described as popular and toward whom classmates seem to gravitate. At the other end of the continuum are those to whom no one seems to pay much attention, youths who might be called "loners" or social isolates. Most young people tend to fall somewhere between these two extremes. Of course, the factors contributing to social acceptance in one school might not be the same as those at another school. Nevertheless, there are certain traits that tend to contribute to popularity. Physical attractiveness and good grooming, as defined by a given group, appear to be important to social approval (Cavior & Dokecki, 1973), as do friendliness, enthusiasm, a sense of humor, and cheerfulness, at least among youths of middle-class society. Ordinal rank or birth order may also play a role in popularity. Later-born children appear to be more popular than early- or first-born children, a situation that seems to hold true across racial and ethnic lines (Miller & Maruyama, 1976). Apparently, the younger children acquire social skills from their older siblings.

At one time or another, many adolescents experience social rejection by their peer group. Dunphy (1963) found that youths could be rejected if they ignored the authority of the group or if they failed to keep up with their peers in dating. Horrocks and Benimoff (1966) also found that some adolescents are never accepted by their contemporaries. On two occasions one year apart, they administered a *sociometric* questionnaire to the entire student body of a junior high school and a high school in a Midwestern community with a population of about 10,000. The students were asked to list the names of their best friends. On the first occasion, about one-seventh (102 of 749) of the students were chosen by no one. On the second sociometric questionnaire, this figure rose to about one-fourth, or 157 of 549 students. In comparing the responses to both questionnaires, the investigators noted that 24 adolescents were not selected at either rating period.

Ausubel (1954) classified adolescents who experience social rejection into three main groups: (1) those who are socially unacceptable to their peers because they possess personality traits, physical characteristics, or interests that are unacceptable to the group; (2) young people who themselves reject the peer group because they find it emotionally disturbing or unrewarding, possibly because they lack certain necessary social skills or have deviant personality traits; and (3) youths who are neither accepted nor rejected by the group but who demonstrate a strong interest in other activities, which they prefer to pursue even at the risk of peer-group rejection. For example, a young person interested in a career as a pianist might be willing to forego social contacts in order to devote his or her free time to practicing the piano. Conceivably, all three situations could even apply to the same individual. An adolescent might be rejected by the group because of undesirable personality traits (such as excessive bragging about the social status of his or her family), as a result withdraw from engaging in any social interaction with the group because of failure to acquire the necessary social skills, and then turn to the piano in an effort to compensate for the social rejection.

As the study by Horrocks and Benimoff (1966) pointed out, however, youths accepted by their peers at one time might later find themselves rejected, or, conversely, one rejected during an early stage of social development may later be accepted. The group norms may change as the group gets older, and behavior once accepted may no longer be approved. For instance, the girl who becomes popular through her clowning during the early teen years may later find herself rejected for the same behavior. Or the boy who does not start to date when many of his friends do may have little in common with them and consequently face rejection, yet later be reaccepted into the group when he begins dating.

At the same time, it should be noted that there are potential dangers inherent in the peer group. For example, it may encourage risky or antisocial behavior or emphasize values that later prove to be inapplicable to adult life. The peer group's rigid structure may also reinforce the youthful tendency to maintain a facade to such an extent that the adolescent becomes reluctant or unable to discard it in favor of the emotional intimacy so important during these years (Mitchell, 1976). Nevertheless, although there are some adolescents who prefer to go their own way, many young people become quite unhappy when they find they are not accepted by their peers. Social rejection can impair the ability to learn, as well as emotional adjustment. Consequently, there is a strong argument for schools to provide counseling services that can help teenagers come to terms with some of the problems that make it difficult for them to relate to their peers. Such services, which might be provided by professionals or by peer counselors, could enable them to modify such personality traits as a lack of concern for others, tactlessness, or excessive timidity. Encouragement through empathic counseling also could give some adolescents the boost they need to get them to participate in extracurricular activities that could help them become more visible and more accessible to their classmates.

Peer-group leadership

Dunphy (1963), in his field study of adolescent peer groups, noted that, although they usually deny the presence of a group leader, group members implicitly accept one member in a leadership role. Clique leaders usually represent their group to those outside it, cooperate with other cliques, and play a larger role in decision making than do other group members. They generally become better known than their followers to the members of other groups, and the group is often identified by the leader's name as his or her group. Clique leaders tend to occupy a position in which they can impart the wishes and ideas of their followers to those of other cliques (who may be in the same crowd). Such standing affords them a degree of power and status.

Crowd leaders, on the other hand, appear to occupy a coordinating, integrating position. These leaders have traditionally been male (although this situation may be changing) and generally serve also as leaders of the largest, most heterosexually advanced clique in the crowd. Holding a role superior to that of other clique leaders, a leader of the crowd can exercise considerable influence over other clique leaders (Dunphy, 1963).

Certain traits seem to be deemed necessary by group members for skillful leadership. Certainly the leader of a crowd must possess sufficient organizational skill to coordinate the activities of different cliques. Dunphy (1963) also observed that crowd leaders are generally more advanced in their heterosexual social development; they date more frequently, go steady more often, and go steady earlier than other members of the crowd. In addition, they tend to serve as confidants and counselors in matters of heterosexual problems and exert considerable pressure in encouraging their followers to attain more mature development in their heterosexual relationships.

Popularity and leadership, however, are not necessarily synonymous. A young person may be very popular and well liked, but this fact does not inevitably ensure that he or she will be accepted as a leader. At the same time, it is unlikely that a leader could remain unpopular and disliked for any period of time and still retain a position of leadership (Ausubel, 1954).

Leadership among youth is often rather tenuous and easily subject to the whims and desires of group members (Staton, 1963). Sometimes the needs and goals of the group change and demand new leadership. At other times, although leaders may occasionally be less conforming to group norms than their followers, they may do something that seriously displeases their peers and interferes with the attainment of certain group aims and thereby find themselves replaced by another individual as group leader (Wiggins, Dill, & Schwartz, 1965).

Does a peer-group culture really exist?

One of the most controversial issues in the area of adolescent social development has been the question of whether or not there is a genuine peer-group culture. As early as 1942, Parsons (1954) claimed that there was a youth culture unique to the United States. He described its characteristics as irresponsible behavior with heavy emphasis on "having a good time," much heterosexual socializing, and reluctance to comply with adult norms and demands. However, a study in the mid-fifties (Elkin & Westley, 1955) of adolescents and their parents from a suburban, well-to-do, upper-middle-class community in Montreal, Quebec, disclosed that the youth culture was subject to control by parents and that it was marked by acceptance of parental values. It showed that unique interests, language, and customs among adolescents do exist but that the stereotype of a youth culture is erroneous, at least in middle-class society. It further noted that many youths in this community learned to forego immediate gratification of their desires for future goals—a pattern of behavior that was believed to be contradictory to the views of the youth-culture advocates. Consequently, Elkin and Westley concluded that the adolescent peer culture was a myth. However, it should be pointed out that this study, which is over 20 years old, dealt primarily with a select segment of society, and it may no longer be characteristic even of this group.

In the 1960s, Coleman (1961), Smith (1962), and McGovern (1967) observed that a distinct youth culture did exist that was relatively independent of parental control and generally in conflict, rather than in harmony, with adult society. Coleman stated that the

> . . . setting apart of our children in schools—which take on ever more functions, ever more extracurricular activities—for an ever longer period of training has a singular impact on the child of high school age. He is cut off from the rest of society, forced inward toward his own age group, made to carry out his whole social life with others his own age. With his fellows, he comes to constitute a small society, one that has most of its important interactions *within* itself, and main-

tains only a few threads of connection with the outside adult society [1961, p. 3].

And Smith concurred, pointing out that "The autonomy of youth culture has been verified by the setting up of norms, which although they change from institution to institution, in all cases dominate and pattern youth behavior" (1962, p. 218).

During this same decade, a more middle-of-the-road approach was expressed by several social scientists (Bealer, Willits, & Maida, 1964; Epperson, 1964; Snyder, 1966; Brittain, 1967). They suggested that adolescents possess multiple loyalties, which vary according to the situation. The fact that young people withdraw from many family functions, preferring peer-group activities, does not necessarily imply a rejection of parental norms. They also noted that society tends to concentrate on the "idiosyncratic aspects of adolescent behavior" (Bealer et al., 1964) and thereby overlooks the similarity in values that does exist between the generations. Too often, perhaps, investigators have assumed that conflict occurs between parents and their children in all areas because it occurs in some.

Also during the 1960s, various studies by Brittain (1963, 1967) indicated that young individuals are inclined to turn to those who they believe will provide them with the most competent advice and that they perceive their peers and their parents as being competent in different areas. According to Brittain, adolescents appear to adhere to peer-oriented counsel in social values, which are subject to rapid change and in which they can anticipate immediate consequences rather than long-range effects. For example, they would probably rely on their friends in regard to matters of taste in dress, whereas they would be likely to consult their parents on such issues as whether or not to work part-time while attending school or on matters involving important, difficult decisions, such as what college to attend.

However, a more recent study by Larson (1972) suggests that junior high and high school teenagers conform less to either parents or peers than the studies of Brittain had indicated. In a study of 1542 7th, 9th, and 12th graders, he reported that a majority of youths are parent oriented, only a minority favor peer orientation, and a sizable proportion see no reason to differentiate between the two. Larson further reported that adolescents tend to choose to comply with parents in current-oriented situations, whereas, on future-oriented issues, the content of the matter and moral factors appear to be of greater importance than either parent or peer pressures. At the same time, it was noted that those who are parent oriented rarely choose to comply with the wishes of their peers, whereas those giving equal weight to the opinions of both are less likely than their parent-oriented contemporaries to comply with parental wishes. It was further observed that neither parent or peer orientation nor pressures from either had the ability to modify the choices of a majority of youths. In other words, orientation was not necessarily correlated with choice; almost as many parent-oriented as peer-oriented adolescents selected choices that were incongruent with parental expectations or wishes.

On the other hand, other research of the seventies has tended to concur with the earlier viewpoints expressed by Coleman (1961), Smith (1962), and McGovern (1967). Poveda (1972) states that the social position of adolescents in North America has been one of segregation and subordination. He suggests that the withdrawal of young people from the adult world has posed a threat to society, that youthful fads and customs contribute to uncertainty among the older generation about future trends in adolescent development and about the possibility of youths' reaching the point at which they challenge adult institutions rather than become assimilated into them, as they have traditionally done in the past.

Margaret Mead (1970a) has even argued that our accelerated society in a sense makes adults within its midst "immigrants" from the past, trying to assimilate the present, whereas youths are the native-born population of the present, emigrating into the future. She believes that, in order to survive socially and emotionally, as well as physically, young people must learn their values and attitudes from their peers, not from adults who, as immigrants, speak the wrong language and work in the wrong manner to achieve what, ultimately, often prove to be the wrong ends. In fact, she concludes that adults can learn much from the younger generation.

Another point of view is that of Weiner (1972) and Cohen (1976), who both believe that the teenage population has not one but many cultures, with a world of difference between them, and that they think and act as differently from each other as adults do. Weiner goes on to state that there is little evidence to support the idea that most adolescents are rebelling against parental values. He believes that a majority of young people demonstrate a minimal amount of turmoil, that most of them resolve their identity problems without any major disruptions, that they usually respect their parents and wish to be like them, and that they do not generally regard themselves as outcasts of society but, rather, as an integral part of it. Weiner even suggests that youths tend to be more concerned with achievement and study habits than with sports, recreation, popularity, or instant gratification.

As you can see, there are many points of view on the issue of the peer-group culture, and it would be difficult at this time to state absolutely that it does or does not exist. At the same time, however, it should be noted that there are certain factors that certainly increase or decrease the impact of peers on the adolescent.

For example, Bronfenbrenner (1970) observed that, among middle-class American adolescents, those from families in which the parents were absent from home for extended periods of time showed greater susceptibility to peer-group influence and were more likely to go along with the group than those from homes in which the parents were more readily available. He also observed that the shift from parents to peers as a major source of influence was occurring at a younger age than it had a decade or two ago.

It has also been reported that, the lower the quality of adolescent interaction with adults, the higher the peer-group involvement (Iacovetta, 1975). It has been further observed not only that peers have greater influence on teenagers today than they did in the mid-sixties but also that lower-class youths are more influenced by their peers than are those of the middle class (Lasseigne, 1975). Higher-socio-economic-class adolescents seem to be more concerned about the opinions of their parents than about those of their peers, although this preference for parental opinions appears to decline somewhat with age from early junior high school through much of high school and then tends to increase again between grades 11 and 12 (Curtis, 1975). It was suggested by Floyd and South (1972) that the inability of parents to meet many of the needs of their offspring during the junior high and high school years causes many youths to find the opinions of other young people with similar needs and experiences more helpful.

To counteract the strong pull of the peer group at this stage, perhaps parents and teachers should strive to make youths feel that they are a very integral part of society by granting them greater status and more responsibility and by making them feel needed—for example through encouraging their participation in community service.

Dating

Although people tend to regard the terms dating and courtship as synonymous, the terms actually refer to two distinct activities. The practice of courtship has existed for many centuries and is an adult-oriented pattern of behavior with the ultimate goal of marriage, whereas dating, which is a relatively recent, American phenomenon, is geared toward present needs and desires and has no long-range aims. Although it is true that dating tends to accompany courtship, as well as chronologically precede it, the date is basically an end in itself; it provides heterosexual relationships during the period of prolonged adolescence (Smith, 1962; Rogers, 1969).

Dating is an originally American institution that was first introduced in our cities among college students in the 1920s. It reflected the new female emancipation, the increase in the amount of leisure time, the greater freedom available to young people, higher standards of living, greatly expanded commercial recreation, and the widespread development of coeducational institutions. In the late 1930s and early 1940s, dating activities emerged at the high school level (Burchinal, 1969), and today we see junior high school and even grade school youths emulating the dating patterns of their older brothers and sisters.

Adolescent dating patterns

Of all of the adolescent institutions, dating tends to vary the most from adult norms, as Smith (1962) points out: "Romantic love is least relevant during dating, although it simulates romantic love by using its language devoid of 'meaning' " (pp. 147–148). Surprisingly, it is often the parents who unknowingly perpetuate the idealization of romance by their belief in the myth that romance will "change all" (Cervantes, 1965). They tend to regard dating as a romantic pastime, whereas their adolescent offspring, although they may describe their dating in romantic terms, tend to view it primarily as engaging in fun and having a good time. Until the early sixties, sex taboos were rather rigorously enforced during adolescent dating and were relaxed only as youth approached marriage or in cases of exploitive dating.

Three dating patterns seem to have emerged among today's North American youth: group dating, competitive or multiple dating, and noncommitment steady dating. The first pattern, which has developed primarily during the past decade, involves boys' and girls' getting together and going out in a group, a situation that frequently involves the sharing of expenses between the sexes. This phenomenon may occur at any level from grade school to college. The second pattern, competitive or multiple dating, is characterized by a frequent change of dating partners and no serious emotional involvement. It remains a common practice for most North American young people, at least for some period during high school, and tends to be the most highly approved form of intersexual relationship for this age group. In Europe, however, such competitive dating is less frequently practiced and less readily approved, for dating there tends to follow a pattern of going with one person for a period of time, rather than "playing the field," with the thought that the steady relationship might lead to a permanent one. Because, in North America, dating one person for a period of time tends to lead to greater emotional involvement than multiple dating, termination of such a relationship can be quite traumatic (Husbands, 1970). In the United States and Canada the third basic pattern of dating, that of noncommitment steady dating, involves dating only one person at a time. This pattern may vary from the so-called sitting-steady relationship, which commonly occurs among junior high school students who do most of their heterosexual socializing in school and on the telephone, to such an extent that it becomes the first stage in courtship, leading to marriage or to cohabitation. Higher-socioeconomic-class adolescents are less likely to go steady than lower-class youths, a phenomenon that tends to reflect a greater tendency toward future-oriented behavior and career preparation among more affluent young people (Larson, Spreitzer, & Snyder, 1976).

However, it should be noted that, until recent years, the motivation for dating frequently differed according to sex. Girls have traditionally dated with the objective of marriage and have been more likely to become emotionally involved, although these tendencies are changing. Boys, on the other hand, have more commonly been motivated to date by a desire for recreation and have been less apt to become deeply involved in their dating relationships (Skipper & Nass, 1966). Even today it appears that many girls perceive dating as a means to marriage more often than do boys, since, until the past decade or so, their socioeconomic future and their life chances —in fact, their very identity—were primarily determined by their husbands.

In our society, males have traditionally taken the assertive, asking role, whereas girls have tended to take the passive, answering role. These roles, however, are presently changing; girls are becoming just as assertive as boys and many have adopted the asking role in dating relationships (Place, 1975; Vener & Stewart, 1974).

In regard to dating patterns, the question also arises as to what factors initially trigger the desire to date. Some psychologists believe that initial dating is motivated primarily by a desire for companionship rather than by sexual attraction (McKinney, 1960). Other psychologists believe that there is an element of sexual attraction underlying every adolescent heterosexual relationship. But it is apparent in many youthful friendships that young people relate to each other as individuals regardless of the sex of their companions (Staton, 1963).

Primary functions of dating

Although current North American dating patterns possess many negative aspects, which will be discussed shortly, dating does serve a number of positive functions. Certainly, it provides an easier, less abrupt transition from unisexual to heterosexual relationships than courtship alone would be likely to afford (Burchinal, 1969). It also gives adolescents an opportunity to establish and test their psychosexual roles and offers them numerous occasions to learn many of the social graces demanded by adult society. Dating presents favorable circumstances for engaging in various sexual experiences and discovery, and it serves as a means of assessing one's popularity and social success as well. Perhaps most important of all, dating offers a combination of circumstances conducive to developing a love relationship and ultimately finding a mate (Skipper & Nass, 1966).

Problems in dating

Although it serves many useful functions, adolescent dating does present a variety of problems. The question of when to begin dating, the problems of the delayed dater and the nondater, the question of whether to go steady, the difficulty in genuine interaction because of role-playing, and the inadequacies of dating as a preparation for marriage are all problems that may arise in adolescent dating. In addition, many young people experience considerable anxiety and unpleasantness in their dating relationships. Sometimes they encounter parental disapproval and resistance toward their friends. At other times they hear reports of unpleasant dating experiences from their peers or encounter such unfortunate experiences themselves. As a consequence, youths are often exceedingly unhappy in their social relationships, and there is a need to take a serious look at some of the difficulties that are caused or exacerbated by dating norms and expectations.

Early dating.   Since World War II, young people have begun dating at an earlier and earlier age (Morgenstern, 1961; O'Dwyer, McAllister, & Davis, 1967). A study by Kuhlen and Houlihan (1965) compared adolescent heterosexual interests in 1942 with those in 1963. They noted that in 1963 there was a greater display of heterosexual interest during grades 6 to 12, with boys being a bit less reticent than they were in 1942.

Several social scientists have expressed considerable concern over the trend toward earlier dating (Morgenstern, 1961; Douvan & Adelson, 1966; O'Dwyer et al., 1967). They feel that an early dating pattern can have many unfortunate consequences. Early daters, especially girls, seem to become socially precocious, showing early development of pseudosophisticated versions of such social traits as poise and nonchalance, while at the same time lagging in their emotional development. Precocious dating tends to bring a premature end to childhood and to force young people to try to behave as adults, before they are emotionally ready to do so. There are often gaps left in their development, and the formation of deeper character traits, such as the postponement of immediate gratification for long-range goals, is often hindered. Early dating can also lead to premature "steady" relationships, an overemphasis on sex, and frequent, often unfortunate, teenage marriages (see Chapter 9).

A number of explanations have been offered for this trend toward early dating: (1) the emphasis on sex and romance, especially by the mass media, (2) the strong desire for success in our competitive society, since during the adolescent period success tends to be gauged by the attainment of popularity, (3) considerable peer-group pressure for individuals to conform to certain norms of heterosexual activity, (4) excessive permissiveness among many parents, who are reluctant to say "no" and find it difficult to apply sensible limits to the behavior of their children, and (5) the attempts by many parents to experience vicarious pleasure through their children, who they often fear will not achieve popularity, athletic success, or other goals the parents have for their children (Morgenstern, 1961; O'Dwyer et al., 1967).

Solutions to this problem of premature dating lie both with parents and with educators. Parents can demonstrate their love and affection by offering their time, attention, and understanding and by serving as models for desirable behavior. Mothers and fathers can also set definite limits on behavior, accompanied by logical reasons for such limits, and can thus help their adolescent children to accept certain responsibilities along with their acquisition of certain privileges. At the same time, parents can help by listening to the problems related to them by their adolescents and by providing a sympathetic outlet for young people to safely verbalize their fears and anxieties without being ridiculed or criticized (O'Dwyer et al., 1967; Gordon, 1970).

The fact that early dating and teenage marriages are so much more prevalent in North America than in Western Europe poses some interesting questions for educators. Young people in Western European countries begin to date later, possibly because they do not attend coeducational schools and therefore have less opportunity for heterosexual relationships. In fact, Blos (1971) has suggested that we consider educating the two sexes separately during the early adolescent years, the years from 11 to 14. This is the period when boys tend to lag behind girls in their physical and social maturation and girls, in turn, often appear to push boys into heterosexual social activities for which the boys are not yet ready and for which they have little interest. However, it has yet to be proved whether separate schools for boys and girls would delay the onset of dating, delay the practice of "going steady," and postpone many premature marriages, or even whether it would be beneficial to youthful social development.

If coeducation during early adolescence continues to be the norm, however, there are still ways in which our schools might be able to discourage early dating. They could offer social activities that involve group associations of both sexes, such as bowling, and discourage social activities that promote twosome dating. The school curriculum could be set up to encourage maximum interaction between the two sexes through coeducational courses in physical education, sex education, and homemaking (which have already been instituted in some schools), through mixed-group projects, and through class discussions on topics of concern to both boys and girls. Through such intermingling, boys and girls might gain a better understanding of each other, while the aura of glamour and romance could be minimized with such close contact (coeducational dormitory living has achieved this minimization effect on many college campuses today). Educators can also provide parents with pertinent material on topics such as "going steady" and can work together with parents to establish a practical set of codes for adolescent behavior (Morgenstern, 1961).

The late dater and the nondater.   It should be noted that the norm for initial dating may vary according to several factors. It may differ from one geographic area to another, with adolescents from urban communities usually beginning to date earlier than those from rural areas (Burchinal, 1969). It also will vary according to socioeconomic level. Young people from the lower classes generally begin dating sooner than those from the middle and upper classes. Variations in the onset of dating can be seen according to educational level as well; school dropouts are likely to start dating at an earlier age than those who continue their education (Cervantes, 1965).

But regardless of these differences, those who do not begin to date at the time considered appropriate by their peers are likely to suffer from several unfortunate social and emotional consequences. The late dater, the adolescent who does not begin to date by the junior or possibly the senior year of high school, and the nondater are both likely to become anxious and to develop feelings of isolation. Such adolescents may feel that they are missing certain crucial experiences afforded by the dating institution and may even experience difficulty in forming same-sex friendships, especially with those of their own age. Social life will tend to be minimal for these adolescents, thereby retarding their social maturation. Late dating or nondating may also cause young people to remain more dependent on their families (Douvan & Adelson, 1966).

There are several plausible explanations for the failure of adolescents to begin dating at the usual time—that is, during middle adolescence (15–16 years of age). Extensive research among nondating girls by Douvan and Adelson (1966) (no such research is available on boys) disclosed that they were socially immature, had little awareness of a boy's needs or of how to demonstrate sensitivity and an understanding of others. They had no concept of what is involved in a stable, loyal, trusting heterosexual friendship. They were oblivious to the fact that young people tend to seek those who make them feel more secure and adequate and who help enhance their self-concept (Staton, 1963). These girls tended to have distorted ideas about what traits lead to popularity, believing only good looks and social facility to be important. They were usually quite self-conscious, egocentric, low in self-confidence, and lacking in a sense of humor. They engaged in few extracurricular activities, organized social groups, or other forms of leisure-time recreation. Although they were generally just as attractive as those who dated, they tended to display fewer traits of "femininity." Sometimes their delay in dating reflected a disturbed family situation or an overdependence on their families (Douvan & Adelson, 1966).

If late daters and nondaters display deviant behavior patterns or seem very unhappy about their lack of dates, they could probably benefit from counseling by sympathetic adults or possibly from peer counseling, which will be discussed in more detail in Chapter 7. Since parents are too likely to be emotionally involved with their children's failure to date, understanding teachers, young adults who are not too remote from the problems of adolescence, or sensitive, mature peers often prove to be more effective in working with these young people. The trend in recent years toward role changes that allow girls more control over the dating process may prove beneficial to both boys and girls who are late daters or nondaters.

Going steady.   There are probably few adolescent social patterns that create more conflict between the generations than the widespread practice of going steady. According to Cervantes (1965), going steady is the heterosexual interaction pattern that has traditionally been characteristic of the youth culture. Although the pattern may be changing, going steady seems to be the dating "ideal" from grade school through graduate school. This dating pattern usually involves a commitment not to date others and a degree of emotional involvement that is often described as "being in love." It has been estimated that the proportion of 11th- and 12th-grade students who go steady at any given time varies from about 20% to 33%. By the time they have graduated from high school, between 50% and 75% of all students will have pursued this pattern of dating at some time (Reiss, 1961; Broderick, 1967).

Definite arguments, both favoring and opposing this practice, have been presented. Some youths regard going steady as being more prestigious than multiple dating. It is also believed that such a single attachment provides the opportunity for the youthful experience of ambivalence, a conflict that is essential in any close interpersonal relationship. "Without legitimate sources of conflict, dating couples have no chance to test the strength of their mutual attachment, to realize that hostility may be externalized without endangering the basis of their relationship, or to appreciate the increased cohesion when an erotic relationship survives what may at the time be seen as an irreparable breach" (Husbands, 1970, p. 459). Steady dating also provides the opportunity for emotional intimacy, which is perhaps the most difficult need to gratify during the adolescent years. In addition, going steady does make conversation and other social interaction easier and eliminates the need for frequent adjustment to the new, unfamiliar habits and attitudes of many different dating partners. Whether eliminating the need for adjustment to others is entirely advantageous is debatable, however, for it often appears to be stultifying to the young person's social development (Staton, 1963). Steady dating also facilitates the association of sex and affection, a situation that is less likely to develop in casual dating (Rogers, 1969) and one that may lead to precocious sexual behavior that adolescents may be unable to handle emotionally.

At the same time, particularly during early and middle adolescence, there are several arguments against the practice of going steady, which was once described as a "demi-marriage," in words if not in deeds ("The Teen-Agers," 1966). Parents, especially, tend to disapprove of this dating pattern, because they believe that it interferes with opportunities for adolescents to get to know many kinds of people. They also fear that it will lead to excessive sexual intimacy and/or to early cohabitation or marriage. Teachers, too, condemn this dating pattern, for they often believe that scholastic interests are subordinated to the interests of the steady relationship and that discipline problems arise as a result. Frequently, youths who go steady separate themselves from their peers and from group activities (Staton, 1963). Larson et al. (1976) have suggested that going steady may be a type of compensatory behavior that is sought because of personal insecurity and because of low levels of educational or vocational aspirations.

Although many adolescents in the sixth, seventh, and eighth grades may describe themselves as going steady, the term may refer only to the fact that they walk home from school with the same partner day after day and converse with that individual nightly on the telephone. According to Douvan and Adelson (1966), however, girls in their early teens who form a serious, stable, exclusive association with one partner are likely to be quite socially immature and to possess poorly formed concepts of unisexual friendships as well as of heterosexual relationships. The development of adolescent intimacy in a heterosexual relationship requires that both boys and girls first experience such emotional involvement with a same-sex peer (Mitchell, 1976).

For both sexes, going steady with one person tends to remove them from associations with others of the same sex as well as with others of the opposite sex. They are likely to have misconceptions about friendship and popularity with others and often fail to acquire an awareness of the need for traits that are essential to the development of an intimate relationship—for example, trust, confidence, and sharing (Mitchell, 1976). Adolescents who go steady experience a gap in their social development when they forego intimate same-sex relationships which are necessary for the development of a strong identity and the formation of a full capacity for genuine object love. This deficiency may be reflected in the adolescent's inability to establish emotional intimacy with his or her steady, with whom the relationship is likely to be relatively superficial because they have not had the opportunity of learning genuine affection through unisexual friendships. Although girls who go steady may be more poised and self-confident than girls who do not during early adolescence, they tend to possess little interest in personal achievement and in education, while demonstrating a strong interest in traditional adult feminine goals, including those of wife, homemaker, and mother (Douvan & Adelson, 1966).

This preoccupation with traditional feminine goals may help to explain the relationship of early steady dating to teenage marriages. Broderick (1967) described going steady as the "beginning of the end." He believes that this dating pattern leads to a social and emotional commitment, through which youths often slide into marriage. He notes that about 80% of steady couples have given some serious consideration to marriage and about 40% have informally agreed to marry. The longer two people go steady, the more likely they are to announce their intention to marry, with over one-half expecting to marry each other after one year of going steady. If such steady dating begins in early or middle adolescence, it is not surprising that there is such a high incidence of teenage marriages (see Chapter 9).

At the same time, it should be pointed out that a socio-economic-class distinction does exist. Among those in high school who go steady and plan on attending college, few will be likely to marry their high school sweethearts. On the other hand, those who drop out of school or who terminate their education with graduation from high school are much more likely to marry their high school partners (Cervantes, 1965). Apparently those who defer marriage tend to be willing to endure other delayed gratification, to minimize the romantic cult, and to concentrate on educational and vocational preparation while they acquire emotional maturity.

It was also reported in one study (Larson et al., 1976) that those who are only children or have few siblings are more likely to go steady than those with three or four brothers and sisters. This may reflect the tendency of the only child and the first-born child to possess a stronger need to affiliate (Warren, 1966).

Other difficulties in dating.   In addition to the problems just cited, the institution of dating is beset by other difficulties. Many young people, especially as they first begin to date, experience strong feelings of anxiety and insecurity. They often report feeling shy and fearful of doing and saying the wrong thing. Filled with well-meant parental advice, both dating partners tend to play their respective roles with considerable clumsiness (Saxton, 1977). Even college students report considerable insecurity in their dating relationships (Skipper & Nass, 1966). As a result, emotional intimacy, which is rare in an insecure individual, may be missing, and hence dating continues to involve only superficial relationships (Mitchell, 1976).

Dating frequently proves to be frustrating for young people in another way. Among boys, especially, the natural culmination of sexual pairing off is sexual intercourse, a practice that until recently has been frowned upon outside the framework of marriage, especially for girls, and is still discouraged for adolescents by most segments of society.

Dating can also encourage certain attitudes and behavior patterns that will prove very inappropriate in marriage. For example, attitudes such as "good girls don't, bad girls do," which are found particularly among middle-class girls during their years of adolescent dating, may be quite difficult to relinquish in marriage, thereby creating potential difficulties in marital adjustment.

Current North American dating patterns tend to discourage the formation of the intimate relationships necessary for a successful marriage. Even if they do interact with many different partners through multiple dating, young people tend to play the same roles over and over again, hiding their true selves from each other and adopting a facade or assuming a role they feel will meet with approval and acceptance. Consequently, there is little opportunity to make accurate comparative judgments of their dating partners (Husbands, 1970). What is more likely to occur is that dating becomes so ritualized that couples remain on guard to avoid any deep interpersonal relationships (Hettlinger, 1970). Such behavior is not likely to be very conducive to enabling two people to learn to know each other. On the contrary, they will tend to seek in their future mates superficial traits, such as gaiety, charm, and charisma, that are pleasant to possess but "irrelevant to the needs of marriage" (Douvan & Adelson, 1966, p. 208).

In addition, those who are homely or unattractive are often not dated, even though they may possess a fine character and many positive personality traits, because physical attractiveness appears to be an important factor in dating for both males and females, but especially for women (Cunningham, 1976). In fact, one study indicated that the dishonest individual with good looks and social sophistication is likely to be a frequent dater, whereas the honest and dependable but physically unattractive individual is less likely to date. It was further noted that students often said that they would prefer not to date at all rather than date someone who they considered to be homely and/or socially unsophisticated (Herold, 1974).

Alternative living patterns

Since the mid-sixties, a number of new practices and ideas have appeared that may help to counteract the failure of many young people to develop close, meaningful heterosexual relationships, especially among middle-class college-aged students. One of these innovations has been that of the commune, or tribal family. Such relationships have generally consisted of "... persons usually not blood kin (other than children) who have a semipermanent economic, sexual, and dwelling relationship on the basis of common needs and interests" (Downing, 1970, pp. 120–121). These tribal-family units have been described as seeking freedom from middle-class norms, which they have come to regard as frustrating and inhibiting growth and self-actualization, through (1) the selection of their own values, (2) the right of all members to determine their own conduct, including their sexual behavior, and to define their own sexual roles, (3) a deemphasis on work as a panacea for all social problems, (4) a sharing of all property, based on the belief that the rights to property should be subordinate to human rights and needs, and (5) an acute awareness of one's social responsibilities. Such living arrangements, however, have not been an unqualified success. Many participants, after a year or so of communal living, find that they are ready to return to their own individual homes and communities. From the positive point of view, communes have represented a brave social experiment and an attempt to resolve some of society's most perplexing problems. On the negative side, they have proved, in some cases, to be no more than a type of "hippie live-in" with the potential for considerable psychological harm (Biever, 1974).

Another alternative living pattern that is being practiced is that of cohabiting, or living together. Many regard cohabitation as a natural aspect of a strong dating relationship. Others feel that such experiences will help them decide whether or not the relationship should be formalized and become a permanent one. Mead (1976) has fittingly referred to this pattern of living as an "arrangement." Thus far, however, research has not indicated whether cohabitation, when it leads to marriage, results in any happier marriages than more traditional patterns of courtship.

An offshoot of the trend toward cohabitation is the recent emergence of coeducational dorms, which first opened on college campuses around 1970 ("Intimate Revolution in Campus Life," 1970). Results tend to indicate that such living arrangements deemphasize sex and place it in a more practical perspective. Apparently, the familiarity of daily living in such dormitories promotes nonromantic heterosexual friendships. Some have suggested that this intimate coeducational living might be a more practical preparation for marriage than the romantic dating and courtship patterns that have been pursued by most adolescents. It may even provide one explanation for the decline in marriage rates during the past decade, in that it may have eliminated some of the myths surrounding marriage.

Margaret Mead (1970b) suggested that the establishment of two stages of marriage might also help to counteract the difficulty in developing close heterosexual relationships. She proposed that couples first engage in an *individual marriage*. Such a marriage would be legally recognized and licensed, but it would not include parenthood. The second stage would be that of a *parental marriage*, with goals directed toward the formation of a family. A license would also be required for this relationship, but it would be more difficult to obtain and possible to acquire only after the parties involved had demonstrated a successful adjustment in an individual marriage. Whether such an approach to marriage and the formation of a family would ever become an accepted practice is debatable, but it does deserve consideration as a possible solution to the high incidence of divorce and as a possible means of decreasing the number of children growing up in broken homes.

Leisure-time activities among adolescents

Because many leisure-time activities contribute to the socialization process in adolescents and because the wise use of leisure time is becoming more and more of a problem both for youth and for their elders, this topic should not be overlooked in the study of adolescent psychology.

The use of leisure time appears to be particularly critical during early adolescence, when youths are usually regarded as being too young to hold part-time jobs or even to do meaningful volunteer work. For example, in a survey of students in the psychology class of one of the authors, seven out of ten students recalled that during their early adolescence they had not known how to cope with their leisure time, and they particularly requested that this book contain a section dealing with the subject.

One valuable group of recreational activities, of course, lies in the area of sports. The cliché that "sports build not only strong bodies but also strong minds" certainly is true, for sports involve decision making, pressures, and stress, as well as the need to develop good sportsmanship (Noe, 1969).

Another large category of leisure-time pursuits includes various hobbies and handicrafts, which can contribute to the development of an esthetic attitude and to esthetic appreciation in young people and can also encourage the use of creative and inventive talents (Noe, 1969). To cite one example, a 16-year-old boy, who was a very disinterested, underachieving student, spent his leisure time designing a miniature rocket. It was so well constructed that it was able to lift off under its own power from the driveway of his home. Parents can often encourage the development of such interests; according to one study of 1000 subjects, it was reported that 70% of all hobbies had begun in the home, with parents providing the instruction 44% of the time (Nash, 1960).

Associations and organizations, such as clubs and interest or hobby groups, also provide contact for the adolescent with the social world and lead to the development and training of youths in the fundamental values of society. Such groups can often take over certain functions of the family and the school in fostering and transmitting cultural values (Noe, 1969).

Although television viewing is heaviest at the beginning of the adolescent period, with the typical youth of 11–13 spending an average of three hours per day in such activity, the amount of time spent in this recreational pursuit begins to decline after the age of 13. This decrease probably reflects the increasing social development of teenagers as they gradually spend more and more time away from home and begin to develop new interests (Schramm, Lyle, & Parker, 1961). In those cases in which heavy viewing continues beyond early adolescence, Coleman (1961) suggested that this behavior reflects the "status frustration" hypothesis, wherein adolescents whose achievements are ignored or unrewarded make extensive use of the mass media. There also seems to be a difference in the amount of television watching according to socioeconomic class. Schramm et al. (1961) noted that middle-class tenth-graders appear to be more oriented toward activities of the real world, which leaves them less time and desire for television. Working-class tenth-graders, on the other hand, seem to be more oriented toward fantasy, as reflected in their extensive television viewing and in their choice of reading material, which often consists primarily of comic books and pulp magazines.

Some youths, like many of the older generation, are characterized by a "do-something complex" (Rothschild & Altland, 1975). They develop anxiety about having too little time and develop boredom if they have too much time (which can lead to delinquency). In their attempts to solve their problems and forget the time, they frantically seek activity or companionship. Parents can encourage such young people to allow time during the day for fantasy, thought, and meditation. Instead of being concerned and inquisitive when their adolescent children retreat to their own rooms and suggesting that they are up to no good, parents should support this behavior. Through such contemplation, youths may come to recognize that their ceaseless activity may be serving as an escape from problems that they have not tried to solve or that they have come to regard as unsolvable. If youths are using activity as an escape, then parents need to be at hand to listen from a nonjudgmental point of view and to offer advice when it is sought.

Chapter summary

One of the most important aids to adolescent social development is the peer group, which offers a valuable means of transition from the warmth, safety, and intimacy of the family to the insecurities of adult society. The peer group serves many functions: it offers opportunities for youths to learn and to experiment with new social roles, facilitates the development of identity, encourages discovery about self and about others, contributes to a feeling of belonging and status, and provides an environment conducive to learning to communicate with other people.

Factors involving acceptance by one's contemporaries vary from age to age and from one socioeconomic and ethnic group to another, but numerous authorities believe that athletic prowess and popularity have been given too much weight by too many young people. Although being accepted by the peer group demands a certain degree of social skill, many additional social skills are acquired through adolescent participation in the peer group. If initially rejected by it, adolescents may fail to develop adequate poise in their social relationships with others, a factor that may affect other facets of their adjustment.

Normal social development during this period of transition generally moves from primarily unisexual or same-sex friendships, which are concentrated in the clique in early adolescence, to both unisexual and heterosexual relationships in middle adolescence, first involving crowds, then moving to group dating, and later to paired dating. Those who deviate too widely from the normal pattern of socialization because of peer-group rejection, precocious dating, delayed dating, nondating, or prematurity in going steady are likely to show immaturity and gaps in their social development.

One of the most controversial questions about the peer group is whether or not a peer-group culture actually exists. Several points of view have been presented in regard to this issue, and the reader is free to decide how he or she feels about this matter.

Dating and courtship, often regarded as synonymous, actually differ in their goals and in the degree of emotional involvement demanded. Although dating offers many positive values, it also presents such difficulties as widespread feelings of insecurity and anxiety and the encouragement of certain behaviors that tend to be inappropriate to successful marital adjustment.

One other facet of adolescent social development is that of learning to make wise use of leisure time, which is initially encouraged in the home with parents usually serving as instructors. Failure to master the use of leisure time may result in anxiety or boredom, states of mind that may even lead to delinquent behavior.

Thought provokers

1. Do you recall your own peers and peer groups in early adolescence (12–14)? In middle adolescence (15–17 years of age)? Of

whom did they consist? In what ways were they similar to you? What advantages did they offer you? What disadvantages did they present?

2. Do you think peer groups of today differ much in structure and function from those of 10 years ago? Of 25 years ago? If you believe that there are perceptible differences, what are some of them?

3. Do you believe that a peer-group culture really exists? Give arguments supporting your position.

4. Do you know of adolescents rejected by their peers? If so, what might their peers do to help them become more accepted? What could you as teachers do to help them overcome such rejection?

5. How do you think leaders emerge among adolescents? Cite examples from your own personal experiences, if possible. How can teachers help develop leadership in their students?

6. Do you think dating among adolescents is different today than it was a generation ago? If so, in what ways does it differ?

7. At what age do you think young people should start to date? Explain why you feel a certain age to begin dating should be set.

8. What are some of the problems you have encountered in dating?

9. How do you feel about going steady among young adolescents (under age 16)?

10. Why are leisure-time activities important to the adolescent's social development?

References

Allen, D. C., & Eicher, J. B. Adolescent girls' acceptance and rejection based on appearance. *Adolescence*, 1973, 8(29), 125–138.

Ausubel, D. P. *Theory and problems of adolescent development.* New York: Grune & Stratton, 1954.

Bealer, R. C., Willits, F. K., & Maida, P. R. The rebellious youth subculture—A myth. *Children*, 1964, 11(2), 43–48.

Biever, L. A review of: Communes U. S. A. By Richard Fairfield. *The Family Coordinator*, 1974, 23, 91.

Blos, P. The second individuation process of adolescence. *The Psychoanalytic Study of the Child*, 1967, 22, 162–168.

Blos, P. The child analyst looks at the young adolescent. *Daedalus*, 1971, 100(4), 961–978.

Bowerman, C. E., & Kinch, J. W. Changes in family and peer orientation of children between the fourth and tenth grades. *Social Forces*, 1959, 37, 206–211.

Brittain, C. V. Adolescent choices and parent-peer cross pressures. *American Sociological Review*, 1963, 28, 385–391.

Brittain, C. V. An exploration of the bases of peer-compliance and parent-compliance in adolescence. *Adolescence*, 1967, 2(8), 445–458.

Broderick, C. B. Going steady: The beginning of the end. In S. B. Farber & R. H. L. Wilson (Eds.), *Teenage marriage and divorce*. Berkeley, Calif.: Diablo Press, 1967. Pp. 21–24.

Bronfenbrenner, U. *Two worlds of childhood: U. S. and U.S.S.R.* New York: Russell Sage Foundation, 1970.

Burchinal, L. G. Adolescent dating attitudes and behavior. In M. Gold & E. Douvan (Eds.), *Adolescent development: Readings in research and theory*. Boston: Allyn & Bacon, 1969. Pp. 199–202.

Cavior, N., & Dokecki, P. R. Physical attractiveness, perceived attitude, similarity, and academic achievement as contributors to interpersonal attraction among adolescents. *Developmental Psychology*, 1973, 9, 44–54.

Cervantes, L. F. *The dropout: Causes and cures*. Ann Arbor: University of Michigan Press, 1965.

Cohen, J. The impact of the leading crowd on high school change: A reassessment. *Adolescence*, 1976, 11(43), 373–381.

Coleman, J. S. *The adolescent society*. New York: Free Press, 1961.

Cunningham, J. D. Boys meet girls: Patterns of interaction and attribution in heterosexual attraction. *Journal of Personality and Social Psychology*, 1976, 34(3), 334–443.

Curtis, R. L. Adolescent orientations toward parents and peers: Variations by sex, age, and socioeconomic status. *Adolescence*, 1975, 10(40), 483–494.

Douvan, E., & Adelson, J. *The adolescent experience*. New York: Wiley, 1966.

Downing, J. The tribal family and the society of awakening. In H. A. Otto (Ed.), *The family in search of a future*. New York: Meredith, 1970. Pp. 119–135.

Dunphy, D. C. The social structure of urban adolescent peer groups. *Sociometry*, 1963, 26, 230–246.

Elkin, F., & Westley, W. A. The myth of adolescent peer culture. *American Sociological Review*, 1955, 20, 680–684.

Epperson, D. C. A reassessment of indices of parental influence in the adolescent society. *American Sociological Review*, 1964, 29, 93–96.

Floyd, H. H., & South, D. R. Dilemma of youth: The choice of parents or peers as a frame of reference for behavior. *Journal of Marriage and the Family*, 1972, 34(4), 627–634.

Friesen, D. Academic-athletic-popularity syndrome of the Canadian high school society (1967). *Adolescence*, 1968, 3(9), 39–52.

Gordon, T. *Parent Effectiveness Training*. New York: Peter H. Wyden, 1970.

Gottlieb, D., & Tenhouten, W. Racial composition and the social system of three high schools. *Journal of Marriage and the Family*, 1965, 27, 204–212.

Gray, D. F., & Gaier, E. L. The congruency of adolescent self-perceptions with those of parents and best friends. *Adolescence*, 1974, 9(34), 299–303.

Herold, E. S. Stages of date selection: A reconciliation of divergent findings on campus values in dating. *Adolescence*, 1974, 9(33), 113–120.

Hettlinger, R. F. *Sexual maturity*. Belmont, Calif.: Wadsworth, 1970.

Hollingshead, A. B. *Elmstown youth*. New York: Wiley, 1949.

Hollingshead, A. B. *Elmstown youth and Elmstown revisited*. New York: Wiley, 1975.

Horowitz, H. Prediction of adolescent popularity and rejection from achievement and interest tests. *Journal of Educational Psychology*, 1967, 58, 170–174.

Horrocks, J. E., & Benimoff, M. Stability of adolescent's nominee status over a one-year period as a friend by their peers. *Adolescence*, 1966, 1, 224–229.

Husbands, C. T. Some social and psychological consequences of the American dating system. *Adolescence*, 1970, 5(20), 451–462.

Iacovetta, R. G. Adolescent-adult interaction and peer group involvement. *Adolescence*, 1975, *10*(39), 327–336.

Intimate revolution in campus life. *Life*, November 20, 1970, pp. 32–41.

Jones, S. S. High school social status as a historical process. *Adolescence*, 1976, 11(43), 327–333.

Kuhlen, R. G., & Houlihan, N. B. Adolescent heterosexual interest in 1942 and 1963. *Child Development*, 1965, *36*, 1049–1052.

Larson, D. L., Spreitzer, E. A., & Snyder, E. E. Social factors in the frequency of romantic involvement among adolescents. *Adolescence*, 1976, 11(41), 7–12.

Larson, L. L. The influence of parents and peers during adolescence: The situation hypothesis revisited. *Journal of Marriage and the Family*, 1972, *34*, 67–74.

Lasseigne, M. W. A study of peer and adult influence on moral beliefs of adolescents. *Adolescence*, 1975, *10*(38), 227–230.

McGovern, J. D. The adolescent and his peer group. In A. A. Schneiders & contributors (Eds.), *Counseling the adolescent*. San Francisco: Chandler, 1967. Pp. 14–28.

McKinney, F. *Psychology of personal adjustment*. New York: Wiley, 1960.

Mead, M. *Culture and commitment*. Garden City, N. Y. Natural Historical Press, 1970. (a)

Mead, M. Marriage in two steps. In H. A. Otto (Ed.), *The family in search of a future*. New York: Meredith, 1970. Pp. 75–84. (b)

Mead, M. Lecture at Louisiana College, Pineville, Louisiana, March 1976.

Midcentury White House Conference on Children and Youth. *A healthy personality for every child–Fact finding report: A digest*. Raleigh, N.C.: Health Publications Institute, 1951.

Miller, N., & Maruyama, G. Ordinal position and peer popularity. *Journal of Personality and Social Psychology*, 1976, *33*(2), 123–131.

Mitchell, J. J. Adolescent intimacy. *Adolescence*, 1976, 11(42), 275–280.

Morgenstern, J. J. Teenage dating patterns. *NEA Journal*, 1961, *50*, 8–11.

Nash, J. B. *Philosophy of recreation and leisure*. Dubuque, Iowa: William C. Brown, 1960.

Newman, P. R. Social settings and their significance for adolescent development. *Adolescence*, 1976, 11(43), 405–418.

Nixon, R. E. *The art of growing*. New York: Random House, 1962.

Noe, F. An instrumental conception of leisure for the adolescent. *Adolescence*, 1969, 4(15), 385–400.

O'Dwyer, C., McAllister, R. J., & Davis, I. Special aspects of adolescent problems. In A. A. Schneiders & contributors (Eds.), *Counseling the adolescent*. San Francisco: Chandler, 1967. Pp. 49–65.

Parsons, T. *Essays in sociological theory*. New York: Free Press, 1954. Pp. 89–103.

Place, D. M. The dating experience for adolescent girls. *Adolescence*, 1975, *10*(38), 157–174.

Poveda, T. G. A perspective on adolescent social relations. *Psychiatry*, 1972, *35*(1), 32–47.

Reiss, I. L. Sexual codes in teen-age culture. *The Annals of the American Academy of Political and Social Sciences*, 1961, *338*, 53–62.

Rogers, D. Dating. In D. Rogers (Ed.), *Issues in adolescent psychology*. New York: Meredith, 1969. Pp. 376–377.

Rothschild, B. F., & Altland, R. *The therapeutic use of leisure time*. Unpublished manuscript, 1975.

Saxton, L. *The individual, marriage and the family* (3rd ed.). Belmont, Calif.: Wadsworth, 1977.

Schramm, W., Lyle, J., & Parker, E. B. *Television in the lives of children.* Stanford, Calif.: Stanford University Press, 1961.

Sherif, M., & Sherif, C. Problems of youth in transition. In M. Sherif & C. Sherif (Eds.), *Problems of youth: Transition to adulthood in a changing world.* Chicago: Aldine, 1965. Pp. 1–12.

Skipper, J. K., Jr., & Nass, G. Dating behavior: A framework for analysis and an illustration. *Journal of Marriage and the Family,* 1966, *28,* 412–420.

Smith, E. A. *American youth culture.* New York: Free Press, 1962.

Snyder, E. E. Socioeconomic variations, values, and social participation among high school students. *Journal of Marriage and the Family,* 1966, *28,* 174–176.

Staton, T. F. *Dynamics of adolescent adjustment.* New York: Macmillan, 1963.

The teen-agers. *Newsweek,* March 21, 1966, pp. 57–75.

Vener, A. M., & Stewart, C. S. Adolescent sexual behavior in middle America revisited: 1970–1973. *Journal of Marriage and the Family,* 1974, *36*(4), 728–735.

Warren, J. R. Birth order and social behavior. *Psychological Bulletin,* 1966, *65*(1), 38–49.

Weiner, I. B. Perspectives on the modern adolescent. *Psychiatry,* 1972, *35*(1), 20–31.

Wiggins, J. A., Dill, F., & Schwartz, R. D. On "status-liability." *Sociometry,* 1965, *28,* 197–209.

Physical growth and development in the adolescent

4

Your body is where you find yourself. It is where you are and where no one else is. Possession is yours. Where are you and what is happening?

Richard Altland

In order to understand adolescent behavior, one must be aware of the dramatic physical and *biochemical* changes taking place during this period. Adolescence is a developmental period that is unique to the human being,[1] and it encompasses its own specific patterns of physiological, psychological, and social development. This chapter will focus mainly on physiological maturation. (Social maturation was discussed in Chapters 2 and 3, and psychological and emotional development will be discussed in Chapter 6.) One must take into account, however, the fact that these different areas of development

---

[1]The growth of mammals other than humans reveals marked differences in the ages at which various maturational developments occur. In some cases, these changes take place within a span of a few weeks or months. Lower animals have an even earlier attainment of a relatively complete adaptive and sexual capacity. These animals experience neither an adolescent period of growth nor a latency period of quiescence of sexual drives.

are closely interwoven and that each is dependent upon the others to some extent.

Prepuberty, pubescence, and puberty

The process of physical development that results in the end of childhood and the beginning of adolescence involves three overlapping stages: *prepuberty, pubescence,* and *puberty.* Although this sequence is the same for all individuals, the times of onset and the lengths of these periods differ from one person to another (Thornburg, 1975).

Prepuberty begins at the end of childhood with a rapid rise in *hormone* levels, which produces intensified interest in sexuality but very little interest in the other sex. The prepubescent's sexual interest during this stage centers primarily on his or her own body and genitals. It is also a period in which a rapid growth spurt begins and the *secondary sex characteristics,* such as the budding of the breasts in girls and the enlargement of the testes and penis in boys, start to develop. Generally, girls experience these changes two years before boys; the average age of onset of this stage is 10 for females, 12 for males (Tanner, 1975).

Pubescence, the second stage, is characterized by the proliferation of sex cells and near completion of the secondary sex characteristics (Thornburg, 1975). Pubescence begins with the *menarche,* or first *menstruation,* in girls and with the first *ejaculation* in boys. The appearance of these characteristics, however, does not necessarily indicate that the reproductive system is complete. It may be a matter of months or even years before the body is capable of reproduction.

It is only with the third phase, puberty, that girls develop regular *ovulatory menstrual cycles* and the capability for procreation and that boys become capable of producing mature *spermatozoa.* This period generally spans about two years for girls and about three years for boys, ending when all of the secondary sex characteristics have fully appeared and reproductive ability has been reached. Most boys are well into puberty by age 14 (Marshall, 1975), most girls by the age of 15–16.

The term *adolescence,* however, is much broader and more inclusive than *puberty,* for it refers not only to the biological changes but also to psychological maturation, which will be discussed in more detail in Chapter 6. Research has shown that psychological changes during this period do not necessarily parallel the physiological changes; they may begin earlier or later, and they are likely to continue over a longer period of time (Clausen, 1975; Eichorn, 1975;

Eveleth & Tanner, 1975). Adolescence encompasses the years between childhood and maturity and represents a continuation of the
psychological and physical maturational processes initiated during
pubescence. Both physical and psychological development proceed
asymmetrically and at different rates. Sometimes the period of
adolescence is divided into two stages according to physical development; early adolescence (pubescence) and later adolescence
(Clausen, 1975).

Early adolescence continues only through the brief period of
pubescence. Late adolescence begins with the end of puberty but the
body's ability to reproduce does not necessarily indicate sexual and
psychological maturity (Marshall & Tanner, 1968). Psychologically,
late adolescence does not end until the individual resolves the identity crisis, which is discussed in Chapter 6.

Adolescence is characterized by a unique group of developmental problems, which may be physiological, psychological, or social. Several of these problems were discussed earlier. This chapter
will review some of the physiological problems that appear during
adolescence and their impact on behavior. A more complete discussion of adolescent sexual behavior will follow in the next chapter.

The secular trend

There is an increasing tendency, called a *secular trend*, for
physical maturation to occur at a younger age over successive generations. This acceleration is characterized by faster growth, earlier onset
of the adolescent growth spurt, and earlier attainment of adult height
(Muuss, 1970). Although this secular trend has been evident in
human growth and development for several generations, today's
young people are not only reaching puberty, physical maturity, and
sexual maturity at an earlier age than previous generations but also are
becoming taller and heavier as adults. At present, over one-fourth of
the adult male population is over 6 feet in height, and more than
one-sixth of adult women are 5 feet 7 inches tall or more. During the
year 1900, the average height for both sexes was two or three inches
less than it is today. Furthermore, in 1900, individuals reached their
maximal height during their mid-20s; today it is attained at about the
age of 16 or 17 for girls and 18 or 19 for boys. The average age of the
onset of pubescence is now about 12.5 years for girls, down from about
17 years a century ago (Eveleth & Tanner, 1975; Malina, 1974; Tanner,
Whitehouse, Marshall, Healy, & Goldstein, 1975; U. S. Department of
Health, Education and Welfare, 1973).

Another indication of this accelerated biological maturation is the gradual decrease in the average age at which menarche has been occurring among Western European girls and apparently among girls of the United States and Canada as well (Botstein & McArthus, 1976). According to this study, the menarche has been taking place approximately four months earlier in the life of the adolescent girl with each passing decade for the past century. One hundred years ago the average age of menarche was 14–16. Today the typical age at the first menstrual period lies somewhere between 11 and 13 years. This earlier age of menarche further substantiates the presence of a general secular trend, as does the increasing body size (height and weight) and earlier *somatic* or bodily maturity. The fact that research has indicated that this trend is just as evident among girls in temperate climates as among girls in warm climates would also tend to destroy the myth that girls mature earlier in warm climates than in more moderate ones. It also seems probable that this secular trend applies to male as well as female development (Eveleth & Tanner, 1975).

Apparently the rate of adolescent growth and development is influenced by several factors, including genetics, the prenatal environment, and nutrition (Cantwell & Svajian, 1974; Cheek, 1974). Better nutrition seems to explain today's earlier rate of maturation among adolescents. Good nutrition is a primary requisite for normal growth and development; conversely, malnutrition decelerates growth and delays, decreases, or prevents physical maturation, although females seem better able than males to resist the effects of malnutrition. It has been found that chronic malnutrition retards skeletal growth and maturation, delays the menarche, and extends the growth period (Huenemann, 1974). Thus, the fact that nutritional conditions are closely related to standards of living and socioeconomic status may very well explain why children from lower socioeconomic classes tend to physically mature later than those from the middle and upper classes and why parents with a high economic or educational status rear adolescents who biologically mature earlier and become larger adults (Eveleth & Tanner, 1975). The effects of nutrition can also be seen when one compares children from economically advanced nations with children from poorer countries. It is likely that a 6-year-old child from Central America will be smaller than a 4-year-old child in the United States or Canada.

The trend toward earlier physical maturation has important psychological and sociological ramifications. For example, sexual activity and pregnancy may occur at an earlier chronological age. Furthermore, youth who undergo this earlier physical maturity also have a commensurate need for earlier psychological and intellectual development, but this development often lags behind their biological maturation. Parents and other adults may be unrealistic in their expectations of more mature behavior in these adolescents. Such discrepancies in development, along with the prolonged economic dependence of so many young people, have contributed to the lengthening of the adolescent period and its accompanying problems. Recent evidence, however, suggests that the secular trend is beginning to level off (Eichorn, 1975).

Variations in normal physical growth and development

The age at which adolescence begins and the rate and the extent of progress through this period of development vary significantly among the members of a particular race as well as among races throughout the world. The average age at onset of adolescence, however, is 12.5 years for girls and 13.5–14.5 years for boys. There are wide differences in the rates of biological maturation that are considered normal, and such deviations usually fall within two years of the norm or average (Ehrhardt & Meyer-Bahlburg, 1975; Eveleth & Tanner, 1975).

There is a definite distinction between "deviating from the average" and "being abnormal." Growth and development occur in a sequential manner, but there are many normal variations in the time, the rate, and the extent of physical maturing. Since there are different states, rates, and modes of growth, a deviation must show a marked departure from the normal growth pattern before it can be considered to have reached abnormal proportions.

The vast majority of adolescents ultimately attain satisfactory, mature, adult development, but the manner of arriving at that stage of development may vary appreciably from one individual to another. Developmental deviations from the norm often cause emotional stress, because most young people experience some difficulty in accepting any rate of physical growth that is noticeably different from that of their peers. Much of the anxiety and many of the psychosomatic difficulties arising during adolescence are caused by the maladjustment of youths who deviate from the typical, as the following case study illustrates.

Fran, at age 15, is somewhat slow, but not abnormal, in her physical and sexual development, as compared with her peers in the tenth grade. She has not yet begun to menstruate, and her breasts are still undeveloped. As a consequence, she refuses to wear a bathing suit and constantly develops various aches and pains that prevent her from having to dress for gym class. Because of her feelings of physical inadequacy and her fears that she will never develop in a normal manner and catch up with her classmates, she has become a rather shy, withdrawn girl with very few friends.

Developmental age versus chronological age

Because of the complex differential development of the various body organs, the concept of "chronological age" provides an unreliable frame of reference for determining an individual's growth rate. A more valid measure is the adolescent's *developmental age*, which is usually determined by the degree of development of the various secondary sex characteristics or by the extent of bone ossification (*skeletal age*). Skeletal age, or bone age, may vary from what would normally be expected at a given chronological age. For example, an individual can have a skeletal age of 13 and a chronological age of 15, or, conversely, a 13-year-old can have a skeletal age of 15. If healthy adolescents are slow in their skeletal development, they will normally continue growing over a longer period of time. On the other hand, if they are advanced in their skeletal growth, they will usually cease growing at an earlier chronological age (Marshall, 1974; Tanner et al., 1975).

In girls the menarche is so closely related to somatic growth that the age at first menstruation is more closely correlated with their skeletal age than with their calendar age. Lamburg, Kantero, Saarinen, and Widholm (1973) have pointed out that one can usually predict the menarche by the sudden skeletal-growth spurt that generally precedes it by about one year. Skeletal age appears to correlate more reliably with the appearance of other maturational phenomena than does chronological age.

Chronological age is not so important a factor as maturational level, and some early adolescents are exceptionally mature. Girls generally mature physically two years earlier than boys, and girls who have passed menarche normally express more direct interest in heterosexual activities. Physical maturity, rather than age, is the determinant of the time when an adolescent becomes interested in sex and in heterosexual relations.

Thus, the use of the concept of developmental age as an index of growth ensures a more exact prediction of physical maturation than does the use of chronological age alone. Because girls are biologically older than boys from birth to 15 or 16 years of age and because individual differences are so great within each sex, the developmental age has proven to be a more effective measure than chronological age when assessing the physiological and metabolic changes that determine physical maturational development.

Endocrine factors in adolescent development

More than any other stage of development, except for the prenatal period and the first year of life, adolescence is characterized by rapid physical and psychological changes, diversity in behavior and development, and considerable physical growth and psychological maturation. The whole sequence of events constituting adolescence is initiated by the *hypothalamus*. From a low and stable level during childhood, hormone levels in the body increase gradually but considerably, and there is increased sexual development. These changes are triggered by the hypothalamus, which in turn activates the pituitary gland to secrete *gonadotropic* hormones. Increased secretions of the growth and sex hormones follow, bringing about the development of the secondary sex characteristics and ultimately reproductive capability (Blizzard, Thompson, Baghdassarian, Kowarski, Migeon, & Rodriguez, 1974; Grumbach, Roth, Kaplan, & Kelch, 1974). When a girl is 10 or 11 years old, there is a marked rise in the level of the female hormone *estrogen*, and by the time she is 12 or 14, the amount of estrogen being secreted has increased to about 20 times that of her childhood level (Lamburg et al., 1973). In boys the increase in the level of the male hormone *androgen* occurs approximately two years later, and the increase is fourfold. At the same time, in both sexes, a pituitary-produced growth hormone increases height, weight, and muscle tissue. These rapid and extensive growth changes bring greater nutritional demands, particularly for protein, calcium, and iron. Additional dietary demands also occur in the female with the advent of the menarche. The rapid changes in physical growth and development, the greater nutritional requirements that result, and the state of emotional development during this period often cause young people to become apathetic, listless, and fatigued.

The normal maturation of secondary sex characteristics depends on the orderly development and functioning of the complicated hypothalamic/pituitary/gonadal/adrenal mechanism. Puberty is a time of great transition in the functions of the endocrine system. The main activities of the hypothalamic/pituitary mechanism change from governing somatic growth and development to regulating the secretion of the sex hormones. Most of the deviations from the average development encountered during adolescence are due to minor constitutional variations in the endocrine pattern or to temporary imbalances in the secretion of hormones. Abnormal growth and delayed or precocious puberty are usually associated with disorders in hypothalamic hormonal changes (Schonberg, 1975; Sizonenko, 1975).

For several months during prepuberty and before the menarche, there is some acceleration in genital growth in girls, marked by an increase in the secretion of estrogen. Lengthening and widening of the *vaginal* canal occur at this time. Genital development begins quite slowly during the prepubescent period and accelerates during the adolescent growth spurt, which we will discuss shortly. The genital changes that lead to physical sexual maturity are the result of endocrine secretions produced by the ovaries, which are activated by the anterior pituitary gonadotropic hormones (Faiman & Winter, 1974).

The anterior pituitary, thyroid, and adrenal glands all participate to varying degrees in the endocrine system and play various roles in sexual maturation and functioning. Genital growth and development are directly controlled by the pituitary, which stimulates the gonads to increase their production of estrogen and androgen. Genital functioning is also indirectly influenced by the *pituitary*. Although the relationship of the thyroid gland to sexual development is not clearly understood, it is generally agreed that the adrenals act indirectly on genital activity through their production of androgen-like substances (see Figure 4-1).

Pituitary gonadotropic activity initiates the adolescent growth spurt, which takes place under hormonal control (Faiman & Winter, 1974). The sex hormones and growth hormones are responsible for the growth spurt as well as for the onset of menstruation. During a girl's early adolescence, however, menstruation occurs in response to hormonal fluctuations without ovulation taking place. Gradually, the *ovaries* begin to mature and to secrete estrogen, which is responsible not only for *ovulation* but also for vaginal and breast development. On the average, by the time girls are 13.5–14 years old, their breasts have reached a mature shape, although the breasts are likely to continue developing in size for an additional two or three years (Plotnick, Thompson, Beitins, & Blizzard, 1974; Tanner, 1975). Estrogen also initiates the development of deposits of fat in both sexes, while androgen stimulates the development of pubic hair and axillary (armpit) hair and the increased activity of the sebaceous and sweat glands in both boys and girls. In males, increased secretion of androgen accounts for the increase in the size of the *penis,* and in the female these same hormones stimulate the development of the *clitoris.* Thus, one can readily see the close interrelationship of the increased production of sex hormones and the development of both secondary and primary sex characteristics. Although estrogen is primarily a female hormone and androgen is primarily a male hormone, both hormones are present in all individuals, the other-sex hormone simply being present in lesser quantities. These two hormones have a definite impact on

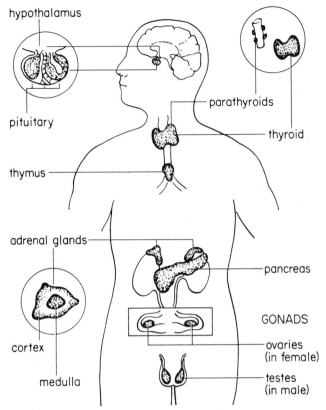

Figure 4-1.   The endocrine glands. (Diagram by Malcolm Le Jeune.)

various aspects of sexual development (Schonberg, 1975; Thomas, 1973).

Anatomical and physiological changes

The adolescent growth spurt

The rate of growth throughout life is not steady. It is most rapid during the prenatal period and infancy, then it declines; it accelerates again between the ages of 6 and 8 and then decreases; and finally it again starts to increase rapidly sometime between the ages of 11 and 16 (Cheek, 1974; Tanner, 1975). Adolescence is ushered in by rapid physical growth, physiological changes, development of the genital organs and secondary sex characteristics, and emotional changes. The adolescent growth spurt, in both males and females, can create a sense of being bigger and stronger and of having greater athletic ability than in childhood. This spurt occurs in all adolescents, but the age at which it appears, its extent, and its duration vary considerably from one individual to another.

In boys the growth spurt commonly begins somewhere between 12 and 16 years of age. Height may increase from 4 to 12 inches, with an average increase of about 4 inches per year (Tanner et al., 1975; "Height and Weight of Youths 12–17 Years, U. S.," 1973). The growth spurt begins earlier in girls, usually starting between the ages of 11 and 14, but it proceeds at a slower rate and results in less extensive growth. Thus, the adolescent girl is frequently taller than boys of the same chronological age. Later, when the boys experience their growth spurt, they catch up with the girls and finally become taller. The average age at which the greatest increase in height takes place is approximately two years earlier in girls (12.6 years) than in boys (14.8 years). From 11 to 13 years of age, girls are usually heavier as well as taller than boys. At physical maturity, men, of course, are generally taller and heavier than women. Also, adolescents who mature early are, on the average, both heavier and taller as adults than those who mature late.

During the growth spurt, all parts of the body are developing but at various rates and at different times. Because of this very uneven growth, boys and girls in early adolescence often appear to be clumsy, awkward, and poorly coordinated. The legs lengthen and complete their spurt first. Next the hips widen, although more noticeably in girls than in boys. This growth is followed by a broadening of the shoulders for both sexes, a change that is more evident in boys than in girls. The fact that males do develop broader shoulders has been suggested as one explanation for their greater physical strength; apparently, broad shoulders help to provide better leverage for the operation of the muscles (Horrocks, 1976). Later, the trunk length and the chest depth increase; in the case of boys, the chest also broadens. In both sexes, excess childhood fat acquired prior to the growth spurt may disappear. After the skeletal growth has subsided, a second rapid increase in weight and muscle, particularly in boys, may take place (Wettenhall, 1976).

As the trunk grows longer in comparison to the arm and leg length, the skeletal framework begins to change. The appearance of long-leggedness gradually disappears. The contours of the body become more rounded as subcutaneous fat deposits increase. The face fills out, and the skin becomes softer and often shows increased pigmentation.

Most of the somatic growth changes have occurred in girls and boys by the ages of 15 and 16.5 years, respectively (Marshall, 1974). Because the rate of skeletal maturation is usually somewhat ahead of the rate of sexual development, many of the bodily changes have already taken place or are occurring by the time of pubescence. Many of the sex differences in biological structure and metabolic function, however, make their appearance later, during the growth spurt. At that time, the secondary sex characteristics begin to develop.

Growth sequence of primary and secondary sex characteristics

Beginning in prepuberty, boys experience a gradual increase in the size of the *testicles,* followed by the appearance of pubic, facial, and then axillary hair and by the enlargement of the larynx and lengthening of the vocal cords. The voice takes on a deeper, adult sound as a result of changes in the larynx. Boys show a more striking change in their voices than girls do. The hallmark of male sexual development finally appears with the formation of spermatozoa (*spermatogenesis*), which is followed by the onset of seminal emission (*oligarche*). The appearance of pubic hair and the enlargement of the testicles normally occur between the ages of 12 and 16 years, whereas the enlargement of the penis and the first ejaculation take place sometime between 13 and 17 years of age. The average age of the first seminal emission—a late development in the pubertal process—is just under 14 years. The penis and testicles of the male nearly double in size between the 9th and 15th years.

The female growth pattern at the time of puberty is largely hidden and less accessible when compared with erection and ejaculation in males. Even the sensitive clitoral area is less accessible than are the male genitals (Botstein & McArthus, 1976; Marshall, 1975).

In girls there initially appears a budding of the breasts, then the appearance of pubic hair, then the menarche, and finally ovulation. Pubescent changes in females accompany estrogen production and are noticeable in increased pelvic width, breast development, and the appearance of pubic hair. The growth of the breasts is most readily apparent because of their more prominent position in the overall body structure. Breast development and pubic hair first become visible at about 10–11 years of age, whereas the menarche occurs, on the average, in the range of 11–13 years, or approximately two years after initial breast development. Menstruation during pubescence is generally irregular, partly due to factors of emotion, tension, and nutrition. Reproductive maturity is usually attained from one to two years after the first menstruation, with maximum fertility developing in the early 20s (Lamburg et al., 1973).

The development of secondary sex characteristics in response to increased secretions of the sex hormones is a highly significant indicator of approaching physical maturity in both sexes. These characteristics develop in a sequential fashion, and their growth is correlated with height, weight, and genital growth. The sequence of development of primary and secondary sex characteristics is outlined in Table 4-1.

Table 4-1. Sequence of development of the primary and secondary sex characteristics

Female	*Male*
Initial increase in breast size	Enlargement of the testes
Growth of straight, pigmented pubic hair	Appearance of straight, pigmented pubic hair
Rapid physical growth	Growth of the penis
Appearance of kinky pubic hair	Voice changes
Menarche	Rapid physical growth
Growth of axillary hair	Development of the beard
Localized fat deposits	Growth of kinky pubic hair and axillary hair
Increased sebaceous-gland activity	First ejaculation
Increasing maturity of reproductive organs	Spermatogenesis
Ovulation	Seminal emission (oligarche)

The menarche and psychological reactions to menstruation

The average age at menarch is 12.5 to 13. However, some normal girls may begin to menstruate as early as 9, while others may not start until the age of 16 (Offer & Offer, 1968). The impact of variations from the average may be quite traumatic for some girls. For example, girls who unexpectedly start to menstruate before the usual age often experience marked surprise, stress, and anxiety. On the other hand, those who are noticeably delayed in the onset of their first menstrual period may regard themselves as abnormal and suffer needless worry and concern (Kaplan, 1975; Lamburg et al., 1973).

Although the adolescent growth spurt is not an essential pre-liminary of the menarche, the peak of accelerated growth usually has passed before the onset of the first menstruation. After the menarche, the growth rate decelerates rapidly and, generally speaking, height will increase only 2 to 3 inches thereafter. There are few increases in height after the age of 16 or 17. Girls who menstruate early (before age 13) are usually taller and heavier throughout adolescence than girls who experience their menarche later (after age 14). After the age of 15, however, the late maturers (at the time of their menarche) will often be taller than early-maturing girls (Wettenhall, 1976).

Genital growth is usually not complete when menstruation begins, and this growth continues slowly for several more years. The menarche is frequently followed by a period of sterility, which lasts until a regular ovulatory menstrual cycle is established. The duration of this period varies considerably; the first *ovulation* (the discharge of the first egg from the ovaries) may occur at menarche, or it may not take place until years later.

Menstruation serves as a profound landmark of psychosexual transformation for girls; boys do not experience this sort of demarca-tion point. The importance of the menarche as a biological marker should not be overlooked in understanding the psychology of female adolescent development.

The menarche initiates a critical period of life-span develop-ment that may elicit a wide variety of psychological reactions. It is a positive experience in that it represents the beginning of adulthood. Girls who are psychologically and intellectually prepared for the menarch can accept this evidence of maturity, and the average girl regards it as a necessary inconvenience in achieving maturity. She accepts menstruation as a normal, although perhaps somewhat dis-turbing, physiological activity. Normally, the major effect of menstru-ation is to enhance her perception of her role as a woman and thereby the importance of her sex role.

However, if a young girl is unprepared for her first menstrual period, she may experience psychological trauma and shock, which may continue with subsequent menses. Girls who are fearful or reluc-tant to accept this sign of female maturation are likely to exhibit various degrees of denial during their adolescent years. However, the female's experience with menstruation need not be problematic if she is adequately prepared for this healthy event (Ehrhardt & Meyer-Bahlburg, 1975).

For several months following the menarche, there is usually a lack of regularity in the extent and timing of the menstrual flow. A high correlation between emotional flare-ups and hormonal changes has been found to be associated with this irregularity in menstruation, particularly during puberty or early adolescence. Apparently, fluctuations in girls' moods and attitudes are rather closely related to various phases of the menstrual cycle. These changes usually occur premenstrually and take the form of anxiety, irritability, depression, disorganization, and a low frustration tolerance.

The psychological effects of early and late physical maturation

Considerable longitudinal research has been undertaken on the psychological effects of early versus late physical maturing, especially among boys (Bierich, 1975; Eichorn, 1975; Wettenhall, 1976). The results have indicated that whether youths physically mature early or late in the adolescent period seems to have a considerable influence on their psychological development.

These studies suggest that the reactions of both adults and peers to the development of the early maturer may have a marked impact on his or her behavior. Because they look older, early maturers may be accorded responsibilities and privileges that ordinarily would be reserved for chronologically older people. Being more developed physically, they are more likely to participate in athletics and thereby attain prestige and prominence, which may then lead to other roles of leadership and responsibility among their peers. Frequently able to meet such challenges and thereby reinforce the impressions of others, early maturers enhance their skills and self-satisfaction and, in turn, tend to have a higher self-concept than late-maturing youths. Early developers may also show an earlier interest in sexual activities.

Conversely, later maturers, because they are delayed in their physical development, may possess attitudes of inferiority and may be excessively dependent on others. Should they feel resentful about the childish status and treatment that have been accorded them, they may react in a rebellious, impulsive manner (Eichorn, 1975). It has also been noted that late maturers more often than early maturers fail to resolve certain conflicts characteristic of adolescence. They are less likely to assume roles of leadership and dominance over others, yet they remain more reluctant to accept gracefully the discipline asserted by those in authority. Not surprisingly, such late maturers, who are more likely to be male, tend to have a low self-concept (McCandless, 1970).

To a considerable extent, the same traits associated with late-maturing boys apply to late-maturing girls as well (Eichorn, 1975). For girls, however, the effects of early versus late physical maturation are somewhat more variable (Rogers, 1969). Some researchers have suggested that girls who physically mature early tend to be more mature in their personality development and to possess more favorable self-concepts (Lamburg et al., 1973) than normal- or late-maturing girls. On the other hand, the girl who matures very early (the one who reaches pubescence in the sixth grade) may feel physically conspicuous. She may develop an interest in the opposite sex that is not reciprocated by boys her own age and be too immature emotionally to cope with older boys at this time (Ehrhardt & Meyer-Bahlburg, 1975; Prader, 1975).

Thus, it appears that early maturation may carry social advantages for boys but social disadvantages for girls. Many adolescents consider tallness to be a physical stigma in girls. At their peak of growth, early-maturing girls are not only taller than their female classmates but also taller than most of their male classmates; they are conspicuously large at a time when physical size is not an asset for girls in our culture. Among boys, increase in size and musculature is an asset because of cultural values. Although early-maturing boys have physical advantages over other boys and are socially in step with girls of their own age, the girl who develops earlier than her classmates may be temporarily isolated.

Many difficulties of modern adolescence are due to the fact that the various physical, mental, and emotional objectives toward which teenagers are expected to strive cannot all be reached at the same time. Delayed pubertal development may take one of two forms: failure of sexual development to begin at the usual age or failure of maturational development to be consistent with chronological age. The wide variation within normal development includes many adolescents who have a heightened sense of differentness. Early- or late-maturing youths are handicapped by their deviation from the average; they feel out of step with their peers both socially and physically. The feeling of differentness in the early or late developer may cause many emotional problems, and early counseling is often helpful in such cases.

The adolescent's sensitivity to physical changes

Following the initial appearance of the secondary sex characteristics, young people develop an intense psychological need for physical sameness with their peers and a considerable concern about any deviations from what they consider to be physically normal. Adolescents are much more sensitive to their growth and development than members of any other age group. Because they feel as they do about their physical development, unwarranted and erroneous beliefs about their bodily changes often arise.

There is an intensification of body awareness during adolescence, based upon the fact that the body is a primary image of oneself. In fact, one's body image is closely related to one's self-concept. Those who have a negative body image also tend to have a low self-concept. Adolescent beauty, or the lack of it, may leave its mark for years. In a survey of more than 62,000 *Psychology Today* readers about their attitudes toward their bodies, unattractive teenagers were the least happy among all survey participants and those now between age 30 and 44 who described themselves as having been beautiful adolescents reported they were most happy (Berscheid, Walster, & Bohrnstedt, 1973).

Rare are the adolescents who even partially understand the basic nature of the changes taking place in themselves and in their peers. The incredible change in the adolescent's appearance results in a great change in the body concept. Perceptions related to an increased awareness of sexual feelings are also integrated into a view of oneself. Thus, a major task for the adolescent is the establishment of self-identity in the face of role confusion. The newly experienced sexuality activates not only questions about maleness or femaleness but also concerns about who one is and how one relates to his or her peers. Many youths band together as a means of testing their identity. The ultimate question for the changing adolescent remains "Who am I?"

Adolescents often present special problems for their parents, teachers, and other adults because of their rapid physical development and the emotional changes that accompany it. They are struggling with an identity conflict, a search for values and standards, and their developing sexuality, all topics to be discussed in more detail in later chapters. Adolescents will vacillate between childish and adult attitudes and behaviors and between the freedom they want and the security they need. The adolescent years are critical in the development of the self-concept generally and of one's body image in particular. For the male adolescent, physical development is especially important; the common belief that one's virility and potency can be equated with the size of the testicles and penis probably contributes to his concern. Similar preoccupations may be found in girls who worry about breast development and menstruation. For example, many young women are worried that their breasts are too small or too large. Other aspects of growth, such as height, weight, and skin problems, also create anxiety in both boys and girls.

Numerous adolescent difficulties can develop from sudden changes in height and weight. Margie began her growth spurt at the age of 11 in the sixth grade. By the time she reached the seventh grade, she was the tallest student in her class, towering above both boys and girls. As the object of many jokes about growing like a weed and looking like a beanpole, she began to feel very inadequate and shy in the presence of her classmates, and she started to withdraw from her old friends.

Like Margie, most young people find it difficult to cope with so much change in such a short period of time (Young, 1968; Glaser, 1969). Consequently, if adolescents discover that they have grown 6 inches in one year, they may fear that there is something wrong with them. Or those who lag behind their friends in physical development may begin to wonder if they will ever mature. For example, a boy who remains shorter than his peers, has smaller genitals, or has less beard and a girl who has smaller breasts, has not yet begun to menstruate, or is very tall or thin may tend to feel not only that they are abnormal but also that they are undesirable and unacceptable to their peers. Perhaps most stressful to these young people are deviations in sexual maturity, height, and weight. Obesity is a particularly sensitive issue for both sexes but especially for girls in our culture. The gangling arms and growing feet typical of adolescence often produce self-consciousness, just as the sudden increases in height often cause posture problems.

Young people's preoccupation with physical appearance often extends to dissatisfaction with some of their own physical traits. Adolescents' unwillingness to accept the changes taking place in their bodies can manifest itself in an obsessive desire to alter their appearance, possibly through plastic surgery, to correct a real or imagined abnormality. Consider the following illustration of this sort of dissatisfaction.

At the age of 15, Mike first mentioned his concern about the appearance of his nose to his parents, who said that they thought his nose looked all right. Shortly afterward, he received his annual school picture and thought that his nose looked quite crooked in the picture. About the same time, he played the central character in a Sunday-school play about a boy with a long nose. He could not remember his lines, although, on other occasions, he had memorized roles without any difficulty. Six months after these two incidents, Mike decided that he wanted to undergo plastic surgery and his parents agreed to permit it. After the operation, Mike, who had been very shy and timid, especially with girls, became much more outgoing and talkative. Socially, he seemed much more sure of himself. He began not only to date regularly but also to volunteer for group activities, which he had never done before. He even showed some improvement in his normally poor academic performance. It is reasonable to speculate that these modifications in his behavior may have been brought about not by any improvement in his appearance but by his own perception of the change in his appearance.

It should be noted that, although such surgery may at times be indicated and may result in a more favorable self-image, adolescents' perceptions of themselves tend to exaggerate physical imperfections. In most instances, time and physical maturity will correct some of this perceptual distortion.

Young people naturally want to be as attractive as possible and so devote considerable time and effort each day to their dress and grooming. Unfortunately, the adolescent period is often accompanied by the trying problem of skin blemishes. The increased activity of the sebaceous glands frequently causes acne to develop, and this proves to be a source of considerable anxiety and embarrassment for many young people. The psychological effects of acne should not be underestimated, because it almost invariably results in emotional distress. Medication, diet, frequent washing, plenty of physical exercise, adequate social activity, and proper rest constitute the normal treatment for acne. Generally speaking, the predisposition to acne is caused by large sebaceous glands with high secretion levels (the secretions are produced by increased androgen levels that normally occur during this time). Since androgen stimulates sebaceous activity and estrogen decreases it, corrective hormone therapy is sometimes medically prescribed for the treatment of acne.

The need for sexual expression

As the adolescent's body grows and secondary and primary sex characteristics mature, new sexual drives develop. We will discuss these sex drives in detail in Chapter 5, but it should be noted at this point that these increasing sexual urges, which are initiated by newly activated genital and hormonal stimuli, can be disturbing to many young people.

Although girls experience an earlier physical growth, boys develop sexual feelings earlier. Early-maturing girls, who are much taller than boys of their age and more mature physically, usually do not want to date boys of their own age, preferring boys a few years older. These older boys, however, tend to possess a sexual drive far in excess of that of early-maturing girls. It is possible that sexual-impulse control is more difficult for adolescent males, because their sexual feelings are intensely aroused at puberty. In addition, they have usually acquired more liberal attitudes than girls toward sex. The fact that the penis and testicles of the male nearly double in size between the 9th and 15th years, the erectile power of the penis, and the occurrence of *nocturnal emissions* may all cause boys to focus attention on their genitals and on genital sensations. On the other hand, girls, whose genitalia are partially concealed, do not tend to experience this focus of attention on their genitals. The female's sexual impulse is ambiguous at puberty and, therefore, more easily repressed and controlled. With the onset of developing sexual feelings, there is social pressure exerted on the female not to establish her sexual identity—to postpone her sexual gratification or achieve it only in fantasy (Marshall, 1975). It is this difference in sexual feelings and attitudes that contributes to many of the difficulties of adolescent dating, which we discussed in Chapter 3.

Chapter summary

The physical and biochemical development of the adolescent is a complex phenomenon that consists of three stages: prepuberty, pubescence, and puberty. These stages involve rapid increases in hormone levels, a rapid growth spurt, the development of secondary and primary sex characteristics, and, finally, the capability for reproduction. Although the sequence of physical maturation is similar for all individuals, its rate varies from one person to another and from one sex to the other, with girls tending to mature about two years earlier than boys.

Any noticeable deviations from the norm or average in physical development, however, are of considerable concern to young people and often have psychological effects. Adolescents are extremely sensitive to physical changes, which are frequently unpredictable and confusing: the fat become thin, the short become tall, and the immature become mature.

Thought provokers

1. Do you recall when you first reached pubescence? Did it take you by surprise? What kinds of feelings did you experience?
2. Did your parents prepare you for the experience of pubescence? If not, how did you feel about their failure to do so?
3. In what ways do you think the secular trend affected your adoles-

cence and that of your peers? What impact did the secular trend in your adolescence have on your parents?

4. Were you physically an early or late maturer? If you were either one of these, what effects did this deviance have on your behavior and on your feelings about yourself?

5. Do you think the D.A. (developmental age) is a more valid measure of physical development than the C.A. (chronological age)? Why?

6. Did your own growth sequence follow the one described in this chapter? If not, how did it differ?

7. During adolescence, did you possess any physical traits that you regarded as deviant? How did you feel about these? What, if anything, did you do about them? Do you feel the same way about these traits today as you did in adolescence?

References

Berscheid, E., Walster, E., & Bohrnstedt, G. The happy American body, a survey report. *Psychology Today,* 1973, 7(6), 119–131.

Bierich, J. R. Sexual precocity. *Clinics in Endocrinology and Metabolism,* 1975, 4(1), 107–142.

Blizzard, R. M., Thompson, R. G., Baghdassarian, A., Kowarski, A., Migeon, C. J., & Rodriquez, A. The inter-relationships of steroids, growth hormone and other hormones on pubertal growth. In M. M. Grumbach, G. D. Grave, & F. E. Mayer (Eds.), *Control of the onset of puberty.* New York: Wiley, 1974.

Botstein, P., & McArthur, J. W. Physiology of the normal female. In J. R. Gallagher, F. P. Heald, & D. C. Garell (Eds.), *Medical care of the adolescent.* New York: Appleton-Century-Crofts, 1976.

Cantwell, Z. M., & Svajian, P. N. *Adolescence: Studies in development.* Itasca, Ill.: F. E. Peacock, 1974.

Cheek, D. B. Body composition, hormones, nutrition and adolescent growth. In M. M. Grumbach, G. D. Grave, & F. E. Mayer (Eds.), *Control of the onset of puberty.* New York: Wiley, 1974.

Clausen, J. A. The social meaning of differential physical and sexual maturation. In S. E. Dragastin & G. H. Elder (Eds.), *Adolescence in the life cycle: Psychological changes and social context.* Washington, D. C.: Hemisphere, 1975.

Ehrhardt, A. A., & Meyer-Bahlburg, H. F. L. Psychological correlates of abnormal pubertal development. *Clinics in Endocrinology and Metabolism,* 1975, 4(1), 207–222.

Eichorn, D. H. Asynchronizations in adolescent development. In S. E. Dragastin & G. H. Elder (Eds.), *Adolescence in the life cycle: Psychological changes and social context.* Washington, D. C.: Hemisphere, 1975.

Eveleth, P. B. & Tanner, J. M. *World-wide variation in human growth.* Cambridge, Mass.: Cambridge University Press, 1975.

Faiman, C., & Winter, J. S. D. Gonadotropins and sex hormone patterns in puberty: Clinical data. In M. M. Grumbach, G. D. Grave, & F. E. Mayer (Eds.), *Control of the onset of puberty.* New York: Wiley, 1974.

Glaser, K. Emotional problems of adolescents. *Maryland Medical Journal,* 1969, 18, 51–54.

Grumbach, M. M., Roth, J. C., Kaplan, S. L., & Kelch, R. P. Hypothalamic-pituitary regulation of puberty in man: Evidence and concepts derived from clinical research. In M. M. Grumbach, G. D. Grave, & F. E. Mayer (Eds.), *Control of the onset of puberty*. New York: Wiley, 1974.

Height and weight of youths 12–17 years, United States 1966–70. U. S. Department of Health, Education and Welfare: National Center for Health Statistics. Washington, D. C.: U. S. Government Printing Office, 1973.

Horrocks, J. E. *The psychology of adolescence* (4th ed.). Boston: Houghton Mifflin, 1976.

Huenemann, R. L., et al. *Teenage nutrition and physique*. Springfield, Ill.: Charles C Thomas, 1974.

Kaplan, J. G. Retarded sexual development in adolescence. *Medical Aspects of Human Sexuality*, 1975, 9(2), 47.

Kugelmass, I. N. *Adolescent medicine: Principles and practices*. Springfield, Ill.: Charles C Thomas, 1975.

Lamburg, B. A., Kantero, R. L., Saarinen, P., & Widholm, O. Endocrine changes before and after the menarche. IV. Serum thyrotrophin in female adolescents. *Acta Endocrinology*, 1973, 74, 695.

Malina, R. M. Adolescent changes in size, build, composition, and performance. *Human Biology*, 1974, 46(1), 117–131.

Marshall, W. A. Interrelationships of skeletal maturation, sexual development and somatic growth in man. *Annuals of Human Biology*, 1974, 1, 29.

Marshall, W. A. Growth and sexual maturation in normal puberty. *Clinics in Endocrinology and Metabolism*, 1975, 4(1), 3–26.

Marshall, W. A., & Tanner, J. M. Growth and physiological development during adolescence. *Annual Review of Medicine*, 1968, 19, 283–300.

McCandless, B. R. *Adolescents' behavior and development*. Hinsdale, Ill.: Dryden Press, 1970.

Money, J., & Clopper, R. R., Jr. Psychosocial and psychosexual aspects of errors of pubertal onset and development. *Human Biology*, 1974, 46(1), 173–181.

Muuss, R. E. Adolescent development and the secular trend. *Adolescence*, 1970, 5(19), 267–284.

Offer, D., & Offer, J. L. Profiles of normal adolescent girls. *Archives of General Psychiatry*, 1968, 19(5), 513–522.

Plotnick, L. P., Thompson, R. G., Beitins, I., & Blizzard, R. M. Integrated concentrations of growth hormone correlated with stage of puberty and estrogen levels in girls. *Journal of Clinical Endocrinology and Metabolism*, 1974, 38, 436.

Prader, A. Delayed adolescence. *Clinics in Endocrinology and Metabolism*, 1975, 4(1), 143–156.

Rogers, D. (Ed.) *Issues in adolescent psychology*. New York: Meredith, 1969.

Schonberg, D. K. Dynamics of hypothalamic-pituitary function during puberty. *Clinics in Endocrinology and Metabolism*, 1975, 4(1), 57–88.

Sizonenko, P. C. Endocrine laboratory findings in pubertal disturbances. *Clinics in Endocrinology and Metabolism*, 1975, 4(1), 173–206.

Tanner, J. M. Growth and endocrinology of the adolescent. In L. I. Gardner (Ed.), *Endocrine and genetic diseases of childhood and adolescence*. Philadelphia: W. B. Saunders, 1975.

Tanner, J. M., Whitehouse, R. H., Marshall, W. A., Healy, M. J. R., & Goldstein, H. *Assessment of skeletal maturity and prediction of adult height. TW2 Method*. New York: Academic Press, 1975.

Thomas, J. K. Adolescent endocrinology for counselors of adolescents. *Adolescence,* 1973, *8*(31), 395–405.

Thornburg, H. D. *Development in adolescence.* Monterey, Calif.: Brooks/Cole, 1975.

Wettenhall, H. N. B. Growth problems. In J. R. Gallagher, F. P. Heald, & D. C. Garell (Eds.), *Medical care of the adolescent.* New York: Appleton-Century-Crofts, 1976.

Young, H. B. Special needs of adolescents. *International Journal of Psychiatry,* 1968, *5*(6), 494–495.

Sexual behavior
in adolescence   5

A mature sexual relationship is part of an honest, nonhurting, interpersonal experience in which both people can be themselves and freely express their sensitivity to each other's needs and desires.

Richard Altland

Sexual behavior probably elicits more interest, discussion, frustration, depression, anxiety, guilt, aggression, displacement, friendliness, and humor than any other single human activity. As in adults, sexual urges in adolescents can be expressed in a great variety of ways. In adolescents, however, the ultimate goal of sexual gratification is to find an appropriate identity for oneself.

Because adolescent physical changes are quite rapid, young people are not always completely prepared to integrate these changes and to adjust to them as swiftly as they occur. Despite the stresses of adolescence, however, the majority of young people ultimately achieve an adequate sexual adjustment, usually by establishing a satisfying heterosexual relationship.

Sexual exploration and experimentation traditionally have

been restricted by arbitrary prohibitions in childhood. Many parents and religions also encourage the limitation of sexual expression in adolescence, and, when these limitations are violated, the young person often experiences considerable anxiety. Adolescents are frequently given inadequate information or assistance in learning about normal sexual expression. As a result, they acquire numerous misconceptions from their peers or from the mass media. Adult discussion on the subject is too often emotional, negative, and concerned more with prohibiting adolescent sexual activities than with helping teenagers understand their awakening sexual urges. Besides failing to offer adequate sexual guidelines and explanations, adults often reveal to adolescents a hypocritical and contradictory set of rules and behavioral examples. For example, our society tends to place a blanket restriction on most adolescent sexual activity, while at the same time it spends millions of dollars each year in advertising geared to arouse and stimulate sexual interest and desires in the teenage market. As a result, many youths begin to question such hypocrisy and to rebel against the limitations that have been placed on their sexual behavior.

In order to understand how sex is perceived and experienced by the adolescent, it will be helpful to examine recent research findings regarding "normal" sexual expression in adolescence and certain behavioral patterns typically associated with adolescent sexual development. Because precise figures are seldom available and the existing statistics often contradict one another, the more informative collective findings of various studies will be used for interpretation. In addition to these general findings, we will look at the incidence of different kinds of sexual response that are typical of adolescent expression at various ages.

There are many forms of sexual expression, and a majority of adolescents have engaged in some form of sexual behavior, such as *masturbation*, homosexuality, petting, or intercourse, by the age of 15 (Castadot, 1975; Gadpaille, 1975; Godenne, 1974; Mitchell, 1975; Schoefield, 1974).

The new morality

When adult morality declares that any adolescent sexual behavior is taboo, the stage is set for conflict. Most adolescents believe that their sexual behavior would be considered immoral by parental standards, but they have come to realize that parental morality is not the only morality. The dilemma of adolescent striving for independence involves, in part, the reexamination of the meaning of morality. Because their moral beliefs often do not parallel those of their parents, some adolescents who engage in behavior thought by adults to be morally wrong may simply deny such behavior if they are questioned about it. Thus, youths may find themselves in situations in which truthful reporting of their behavior results in more conflict than false reporting does. Anxiety then develops from the deception of those who trust them as well as from the sexual activity itself. When adolescents expect disapproval of their behavior, they will manage their lives so as to avoid such negative judgments (Briedis, 1975; Maddock, 1973).

Young people want to decide for themselves what is sexually right and wrong. Most youths believe that it is important that they develop their own personal values—both sexually and otherwise. Within the present adolescent generation, there is a trend away from critical attitudes toward those whose sexual behavior is different. Instead of intolerance, there is an effort to understand and accept varying life-styles. Today many adolescents believe that anything two individuals want to do sexually is moral, as long as they both wish to do it and the activity doesn't hurt them or anyone else. Thus, these young people are unwilling to accept the judgment of adult society that youthful sexual activities are immoral. Adolescents are becoming increasingly tolerant of the sexual behavior of their peers, even though they may decide that such activity is not right for themselves at a given time. Many youths believe that two people do not have to intend to marry each other in order to have sexual relations or have to marry each other in order to live together (Sorensen, 1973).

Many of today's adolescents often impose fewer moral restrictions on their sexual activities than did those of the past. Although they may oppose the use of sex strictly for physical pleasure, an increasing number of adolescents have come to believe that mutual caring, rather than love, is sufficient basis for a sexual relationship (Macklin, 1974). According to Godenne (1974), much of the anxiety, fear, or shame associated with unconventional sexual activities is being alleviated through sexual frankness in movies, books on human sexuality, and courses in sex education. Thus, the new morality is characterized by commitment to personal values rather than to traditional ones. These values are not limited to sexual behavior; they extend to a wide range of other activities, including human rights, social problems, and political questions.

Possible problems and conflicts

Adolescents in our rapidly changing society encounter many problems in the area of sexual behavior. As noted previously, one problem is the conflict engendered by the gap between moral values of parents and those of adolescents. At the same time, youths usually are not taught how to cope with the sexual urges that become very strong during this period. Another problem is that of young people who do decide to engage in various sexual activities and then discover that they feel inadequate or dissatisfied with their experiences, which is usually the result of emotional or social rather than biological or physical factors. For example, teenagers may be sexually inhibited by anxiety, ignorance, disgust, fear of pregnancy, and fear of venereal disease. Sexual inhibition also tends to occur in individuals who have received no sex education or who have been told that sex is bad (Cohen & Friedman, 1975; Woods, 1975).

By rejecting adult and parental sexual values and restraints, adolescents can use their sexual behavior as a form of rebellion. Some youths attempt to escape from parental authority by sexually acting out their problems. Although it enhances the young person's feelings of freedom and independence, this defiant behavior can result in more conflict at home and in a loss of desirable communication with the parents. Most adolescents, however, tell their parents only what they believe their parents will accept, and they resent any questioning about their sexual activity (Salzman, 1974; Toussieng, 1975).

Adolescents may also use their sexual experiences maladaptively. For instance, they may engage in sexual behavior in order to establish their sexual identity, but the prematurity of these sexual experiences often results in a sexual identity that is uncertain and insecure. These early sexual activities may also reflect an unconscious desire for procreation or a wish to bind a dating partner to a more permanent relationship. In addition, these behaviors can represent a desire to achieve an experimental conquest, escape from unpleasant experiences, satisfy peer pressures, or gain status or approval. They may even satisfy a drive for dominance or submissiveness or reflect the presence of self-destructive impulses. Premature sexual experiences, however, may simply be a manifestation of a striving for love or a need to belong to someone (Cohen & Friedman, 1975; Hofmann, 1974; Mitchell, 1975; Woods, 1975).

Unfortunately, many young people are sexually irresponsible; they often act impulsively and give little thought to the possible consequences of their behavior. Although adolescents who realize that they have problems have a more promising prospect of solving them than those who deny the existence of their problems, sexual activity used as a means of solving nonsexual problems can be harmful to the adolescent's well-being. Problems may also result when parental responsibility is shirked, when necessary limits are not set, and when family communication is disturbed. Many adolescent/parent conflicts exist because neither can accept the other's values and attitudes. When neither side is willing to listen to the other's point of view, communication breaks down and the adolescent is forced to deal with his or her sexual problems alone.

Changing attitudes toward sexual behavior

The liberalization of sexual attitudes during the past decade has brought about a shift in values as well. Adolescents are more open and honest with each other than ever before. A new equality between the sexes has resulted in a decline in the old double standard for sexual behavior. Young people feel less anxiety about their sexual behavior and talk about sex openly, without shame or fear (Cohen & Friedman, 1975; Godenne, 1974; Maddock, 1973). The feminist and gay liberation movements, which offer various alternatives to traditional marriages, have also contributed to new outlooks on such topics as masturbation, homosexuality, nonmarital adolescent intercourse, abortion, and venereal disease (Bauman & Wilson, 1976; Berg, 1975). Attitudes toward nonmarital adolescent intercourse, for example, are more liberal today than a decade ago, probably the outgrowth, in part, of the ready availability of contraceptives.

Most adolescents do a lot of thinking about sex. Many of them approve of the new standard of "sex with affection but without commitment." A new attitude has also developed toward previous sexual experience, particularly regarding females; virginity is no longer as highly prized as it once was. Many adolescents are also experiencing *coitus* at an earlier age and are considering alternatives to traditional marriage. An increasing number of older adolescents want to live with a steady dating partner, whether they anticipate marrying that person at a later date or not. More adolescents are planning not to marry or to have children, and, as attitudes toward out-of-wedlock pregnancies are becoming more tolerant, marriages to "legitimize" such pregnancies are becoming less common (Godenne, 1974; Schoefield, 1974).

Masturbation

Although attitudes are changing, society has traditionally decreed that sexual expression, if it is to be socially acceptable, must be delayed several years beyond the time that the sexual impulse reaches its peak in adolescents. Thus, boys and girls in the early period of adolescence find that sexual expression must be suppressed or alternatives to intercourse must be found if their sexual urges are to be satisfied. As a consequence, many youths resort to masturbation, which can be considered a behavior pattern typical of the adolescent (Blaine, 1962).

The genitals, of course, are the leading erogenous zone of the body, and there is ample evidence that erotic feelings appear early in life. Even during the first year, infants discover the pleasurable sensations of genital self-manipulation (Bakwin, 1974). During childhood, the clitoris and the penis remain the most accessible and susceptive erogenous zones. But it is primarily during puberty that there is a heightened readiness for genital stimulation. At this time, the adolescent experiences a reawakening of sexual interests that were relatively dormant throughout the latency or middle-childhood period. Consequently, masturbation becomes a central concern for young adolescents, particularly for boys after the onset of *nocturnal emissions*.

An early-adolescent male, unsure of his developing masculinity, may repeatedly try to reassure himself by masturbating. Rebellious attitudes, feelings of unpopularity, fear of rejection by girls, and a need to explore their new sexuality—all can contribute to this auto-erotic phase of development in boys (Spicer, 1968). Girls tend to use masturbation to release tension and as a substitute for activities in which they feel inadequate. Masturbation for the latter reason would be regarded as reflective of problems in adolescent adjustment (Conger, 1977).

As a youth progresses through adolescence, masturbation begins to take on a deeper psychological significance than that of earlier sexual exploratory behavior. While masturbating, the adolescent fantasizes, perhaps by visualizing the sexual act with a certain desirable partner. This is a normal response to the young person's increasing psychosexual awareness, for it provides a means of learning how to control and integrate one's new genital sensations. Masturbation is not only a very healthy but most likely a necessary practice for optimal sexual development. In fact, it has been suggested that masturbation may well be a step toward the establishment of a sexual identity and the development of a sense of intimacy. It is through such activity that adolescents are first able to face their own sexual excitement; this is then followed by the next step, fusing one's sexual excitement with that of another (Erikson, 1955).

Unfortunately, although many physicians, psychologists, and others have argued that masturbation is a normal, healthy, and even necessary practice, some parents still believe that masturbation is a "dirty" act that can produce physical and mental deterioration or interfere with normal heterosexual development. Such parents often cause their children to carry unnecessary burdens of guilt and anxiety about adolescent masturbation (Spicer, 1968).

During puberty teenage boys have more sexual fantasies, engage in more masturbatory and homosexual experiences, and discuss sexuality more openly than do teenage girls. Although adolescents generally are reluctant to admit that they masturbate, girls have traditionally been more secretive about masturbation than boys (although this seems to be changing). Generally, girls suppress their masturbatory impulses, either partially or entirely, whereas boys masturbate quite frequently throughout adolescence. Whether there is actually more male masturbation or whether this behavior is just more readily admitted by boys than by girls is open to debate. Different developmental patterns of masturbatory behavior, however, do seem to exist between boys and girls.

Up to around 10 years of age, the frequency of masturbation is about the same for both sexes. Boys, however, often have their first adolescent masturbation experience around age 13 and continue to masturbate fairly regularly throughout adolescence. The first ejaculation can be quite anxiety-producing for the male if he has not been educated to expect this occurrence. The female adolescent, on the other hand, usually does not masturbate until late adolescence or early adulthood, and even then masturbation is not so common among females as among males and occurs much more sporadically. Recently, however, adolescent girls have begun to masturbate earlier and more frequently and to talk about it more freely than in the past (Dranoff, 1974; Sorensen, 1973; Woods, 1975).

For males, the onset of regular heterosexual experiences causes a marked decrease in the frequency of masturbation and its complex fantasy associations. Late-adolescent males in the lower socioeconomic classes and those with limited education begin to seek *coitus* as a source of erotic satisfaction, whereas late-adolescent males of higher socioeconomic and educational levels usually engage in petting, rather than coitus. Thus, males from the lower socioeconomic classes tend to experience coitus at an earlier age than other males and to view masturbation as an immature practice (Kerckhoff, 1974).

For females, pubescence is not a time of significant sexuality, especially not in an overt way. For example, there does not appear to be any correlation between the menarche and masturbation. Although there are individual differences, most girls do not seem to experience a marked need or desire for genital activity at this time. It has been suggested that this later development of a strong sexual drive in the female is one underlying explanation of the double standard (or possibly vice versa). In other words, the early strong sexual urge in males makes it more likely that they will actively seek sexual fulfillment during their teens than will females, who at this time apparently experience more moderate sexual drives that don't demand overt expression.

Masturbation is a normal activity among adolescents and is nothing to be ashamed of. The primary reason that people masturbate is for enjoyment; it provides pleasure as well as a release for sexual tension. Most adolescents engage in this behavior without conflict, but some experience anxiety or shame, especially if their parents have indicated that masturbation is abnormal or immoral. Other adolescents find that their desire to masturbate is in conflict with their parents' warning that excessive masturbation is harmful. The absence or inhibition of masturbation in adolescence can lead to sexual dysfunction, because it deprives an individual of the opportunity to explore and satisfy his or her own sexuality. The fantasy thoughts associated with masturbation can help develop sexual identity and establish sexual preferences (Dranoff, 1974; Moore, 1975; Sorensen, 1973; Toolan, 1975). An acceptable program of sex education in the home and in the school can help to minimize the emotional conflicts so often associated with masturbation. Many of today's adolescents need reeducation to free them from the taboos regarding masturbation that they learned in childhood.

Homosexual behavior

No male is completely "masculine" and no female completely "feminine." Consequently, the conflict of bisexuality is normal in adolescent psychosexual development. With their rapidly developing sexual characteristics, most adolescents experience a rather intense identity struggle. The bisexual conflicts and strivings caused by these sexual changes can initiate homosexual tendencies.

Young people normally experience some homosexual interests while progressing toward heterosexual maturity. This transient sexual experimentation, which is common in childhood and adolescence, should not be confused with adult homosexuality, however, because the homosexual behavior of adolescent boys usually does not extend to sexual acts with adult men (Gebhard, Gagnon, Pomeroy, & Christenson, 1967; Gagnon & Simon, 1968). It is important to distinguish between the adolescent attachment for and sexual exploratory behavior with an individual of approximately the same age and that of the adult who prefers to achieve sexual gratification with members of the same sex rather than engage in heterosexual behavior. Adult homosexuality is more than sexuality; it is a life-style, a preference for same-sex companionship and attachment as well as for a same-sex sexual partner.

Some adolescent boys have an occasional, casual homosexual experience before they become adults; others have a more extended homosexual contact. The incidence of adolescent homosexuality for girls appears to be much less common than that for boys, and the experiences are relatively fleeting. Again, one can question whether a female is perhaps less inclined than a male to discuss this type of sexual activity, thus accounting for the reported difference in experience. Although homosexual experiences during the adolescent period are of psychological and social significance, their incidence and frequency are much lower than other forms of sexual behavior.

Many youths engage in transitory homosexual experiences as a normal aspect of their sexual development; these experiences are not incompatible with future adult heterosexual orientation. Even though adult homosexuals in recent years have been able to live more comfortably in our society than they once could, adolescent fondling between members of the same sex frequently engenders fears of latent homosexuality and its social consequences. Actually, homosexual behavior on a continuous basis is usually an adult, rather than an adolescent, phenomenon, with the incidence of nontransitory homosexuality increasing as adolescents grow older. Sometimes, negative attitudes toward heterosexual behavior are passed on from parents to adolescents, who, in turn, become discouraged in pursuing heterosexual relationships and seek out homosexual ones instead (Godenne, 1974; Sorensen, 1973; Woods, 1975).

Petting

A further step in resolving the identity conflicts of bisexuality is the adolescent's gradual progression from homosexual tendencies to overt heterosexual behavior. This behavior involves petting for most and sexual intercourse for many. A majority of young people have a strong awareness of sex and begin their heterosexual experiences with kissing, hugging, and activities variously called "making out," "necking," or "petting."

Petting includes numerous forms of physical contact, excluding penile penetration, designed to effect erotic arousal. Petting can include any part or all of the techniques of foreplay that are usually preludes to intercourse, such as kissing, breast fondling, genital stimulation, and mutual masturbation. Mutual petting to orgasm is a frequent solution to the problem of relieving sexual tensions without intercourse (Maddock, 1973; Sorensen, 1973).

Petting is extremely common among young people. Adolescents of today are petting at an earlier age and with greater frequency than was characteristic of past generations. This increase may reflect the earlier onset of pubescence, the prevalence of early dating and of going steady, and possibly the arousal of erotic urges by the mass media. Young people who pet, especially girls in our culture, may experience considerable conflict. Should one be untouchable, or should one risk acquiring the reputation of being "easy"? One pathway may lead to a dateless adolescence, whereas the other may lead to a quick succession of short-lived, unsatisfying romances (Blaine, 1962). To attain a balance between these two extremes is often a considerable problem for the average adolescent girl (Spicer, 1968).

There appears to be no correlation between the onset of pubescence and the incidence of petting for either sex. Many boys and girls have been pubescent for some time before they begin to pet. Very few males have had any petting experience prior to pubescence, in contrast to females who begin dating at an earlier age. A considerable increase in petting takes place at about the age of 13 for both sexes, an increase that continues throughout adolescence. Although many young people do not require sexual intercourse to obtain sexual satisfaction, there is a tendency to move toward sexual intercourse by middle or late adolescence (Maddock, 1973; Sorensen, 1973).

The first sexual intercourse

The first intercourse is often unpremeditated. It usually occurs with little discussion and without the use of contraceptives. More likely than not, it takes place in the parental home, rather than in an automobile or motel, as was more typical of earlier generations. Although they may enjoy subsequent sexual relations, many adolescent girls do not find their initial experience pleasurable. For both sexes there is usually a considerable amount of anxiety present during the first intercourse, and both parties may have doubts about their adequacy and performance.

The age of the first sexual intercourse is dropping for both sexes, although boys are still starting earlier than girls. According to Goldsmith (1976), by the age of 16 many adolescents have engaged in sexual intercourse. By the time of graduation from college, it has been estimated that two-thirds of the males and one-half of the females will have experienced coitus (Hettlinger, 1974).

Generally, adolescents who have not had sexual intercourse do not believe they are ready for it, have not found the person with whom they desire sexual relations, or refrain from the behavior because of deeply held religious beliefs (Jackson & Potkay, 1973).

Nonmarital adolescent intercourse

It has been suggested that the achievement of a complete sexual identity is difficult to attain without heterosexual experience and experimentation during late adolescence (Simon & Gagnon, 1969). Normal young people reach a point at which they are psychologically ready for intercourse, think about it, desire it, and, in many cases, engage in it. Greater knowledge about and accessibility of contraceptives to all age groups has virtually eliminated the fear of pregnancy as a reason for abstaining from sexual activity. Heterosexual experiences in middle adolescence, however, are often sporadic and experimental. During the late teens, especially when a couple is going steady, intercourse often becomes a fairly regular practice. Thus, patterns of adolescent sexual behavior are frequently well established before some youths ever leave home. (Elias & Elias, 1975).

There are as many reasons for nonmarital adolescent sexual activities as there are adolescents. Teenagers engage in sexual intercourse for pleasure, as a sign of their physical maturity, as a part of their search for new experiences, in response to peer-group pressures and the desire to conform, as an escape from loneliness and from problems, and so on. The practice of adolescent, nonmarital sexual intercourse is affected by a number of factors: socioeconomic status, educational background, geographical location, and religious experience. For example, nonmarital intercourse among adolescents in the United States is more common and begins earlier among the less educated. It is less frequent among rural than among urban youths and among those from the South and the Midwest than among youths from other regions of the country (Braen & Forbush, 1975; Kerckhoff, 1974; Packard, 1968; Pomeroy, 1976; Sorensen, 1973).

There is a great deal of peer pressure, starting at pubescence, to engage in sexual behavior (Toussieng, 1975). The sexually precocious and permissive adolescent tends to push many of his or her peers into heterosexual activity before they are psychologically ready for it (Toolan, 1975). Many of those in early and middle adolescence are not emotionally prepared for sexual involvement, but, ready or not, many of them are engaging in such behavior at earlier and earlier ages.

In their search for love and happiness, young people question the necessity and the practicality of refraining from nonmarital adolescent intercourse. For example, the postponement of sexual activity until marriage, particularly in cases of extended engagements, can lead to unrealistic expectations of future sexual satisfaction. The actual experience after marriage may then prove to be quite disappointing and much less satisfying than the partners had expected it to be. However, whether previous sexual experience contributes to a happy marriage depends on many factors, including the ability to build a mutually satisfying interpersonal relationship, the ability to communicate openly and honestly, the type of instruction each of the partners has received about sexuality, their degree of emotional maturity, and the extent of their mutual concern and affection for each other (Kirkendall, 1974).

Unmarried pregnancy and parenthood

Both the number and the percentage of births to teenage girls are increasing, and statistics indicate no significant change in this trend. Whereas the rate of childbearing among adult women is falling, that for girls under 18 years of age is rising. Although there is a higher incidence of births to married than to unmarried teenagers, a large number of these births represent premarital conceptions. This increase in adolescent pregnancies is related to the fact that most sexually active teenagers do not consistently use any reliable form of contraception; one-half of all out-of-wedlock births are to mothers who already have one child (Juhasz, 1974). More than one-third of all marriages are classified as teenage marriages—that is, marriages in which at least one of the partners is under age 20 (this topic will be discussed in more detail in Chapter 9). Those who do marry in their teens usually begin having children at an early age.

Whether or not to marry in cases of pregnancy is a decision that many girls and boys, as well as their parents, must confront. Although the unmarried mother is not the only one who has a decision to make, she has four basic choices open to her: (1) she can choose to rear the child by herself, (2) she can have an abortion, (3) she can arrange for an adoption, or (4) she can marry the father. The majority of girls appear to favor having the baby and rearing it, with or without marriage. There is no consistently clear-cut evidence to indicate that a forced marriage is any less painful than an out-of-wedlock pregnancy or than rearing the baby alone. Unlike many adults, however, fewer adolescents consider out-of-wedlock pregnancy today to be a social stigma (Boyce & Benoit, 1975; Polsby, 1974; Sorensen, 1973; Zackman & Branstadt, 1974).

Because teenage parents, married or unmarried, often lack the emotional maturity and financial security needed for parenthood, they require a variety of services from the community. For example, one pregnant adolescent may need abortion counseling, another pre-natal care, and another child-care services. One service that has long been overlooked, however, is that of counseling for unwed fathers, whose psychological reactions to parenthood have traditionally been neglected (Juhasz, 1974; Klerman, 1975; Maddock, 1973).

Sex education

As adolescents learn about the anatomy and physiology of human reproduction, they form attitudes that will affect their future sexual behavior. When the acquisition of such knowledge is part of an organized program designed to provide instruction about sexual be-havior or attitudes, the term *sex education* is commonly used.

The goals of sex education should include both the instilling of wholesome attitudes, such as the responsibilities as well as the joys and pleasures of sex, and the imparting of adequate and correct information about sex. Sex-education courses should teach sexual attitudes that will promote good mental health and social adjustment (Staton, 1968). For example, such attitudes of the past as "good girls don't, bad girls do" have often had an adverse effect on sexual adjust-ment in marriage. Thus, through sexual misinformation needless fears and guilt about sex have arisen (Iverson, 1974).

Sexuality is a fact of life from the time of infancy. Even prior to school age, however, many children are exposed, in one way or another, to distorted sexual attitudes from their peers, parents, and other adults. Long before youngsters reach adolescence, for instance, many parents have imparted to their children the idea that their genitals are undesirable and are not to be explored (Hettlinger, 1970). Later, during school and religious training, children and adolescents are often indoctrinated with Victorian or puritanical notions of sexual inhibition and chastity. A sex-education program presented to chil-dren and adolescents previously indoctrinated in such traditions will probably fail in its objective of providing youth with honest informa-tion, healthy attitudes toward one's body and sexuality, and a sense of direction.

Effective sex education, therefore, must operate not through the old mode of externally imposed societal controls but through the new mode of encouraging internal control in adolescents based on what they believe is right as a result of meaningful guidelines and their own personal experience. Society should provide young people with the information they want and need regarding sex; it should then provide them with freedom to experiment for themselves (Nixon, 1962).

Unfortunately, the kind of sex education that has been offered by our schools and colleges has tended to emphasize mainly reproduction, with the psychological aspects of sexual behavior often falling by the wayside. The net result has been that young people usually acquire less knowledge of both physical and psychological factors than they need to make wise, informed decisions. Furthermore, it is often difficult to sexually "reeducate" an adolescent with only a short-term, superficial sex-education program. A frank and honest treatment of sexuality, one that really comes to grips with the intimate practical problems of sexual behavior, is a relatively rare experience for today's youth. With masturbation and petting being commonly practiced and nonmarital adolescent intercourse approaching a similar status, there is an increasing need for a broader program in sex education.

Reliable, objective information concerning what is known about sexual behavior and its effects on human relationships, however, has frequently been difficult to obtain. Young people have too often been exposed to adult society's own confusion and inconsistencies in its handling of controversial sex issues; many hypocrisies, prejudices, myths, and taboos about the role of sex in human behavior still persist. Much that the average youth hears from adults has been prohibitive and guilt-arousing mythology, while he or she has received quite opposite views (sometimes just as inaccurate) from the peer group. Seldom have adolescents had the opportunity to freely discuss sexual matters with a well-informed and willing adult.

Recently, however, adults have begun to reconsider, reevaluate, and reappraise the appropriateness and relevance of their traditional sexual attitudes and standards. Consequently, many contradictory and opposing opinions, practices, and attitudes presently exist about the proper place and importance of sex in our society. Of course, an erroneous assumption, too, has been that sexual problems involve only the younger generations and not the older ones.

Actually, sex education first begins when the preschool child asks such questions as "Where do babies come from?" It is the obligation of parents to answer such questions honestly but simply, without elaboration beyond the immediate answers desired by the child. Unfortunately, many parents are unable to provide such answers for their young children and are even less prepared to cope with their child's need for information when he or she reaches adolescence, often because of their own misconceptions or lack of knowledge (Page, 1967). Thus, young people with an intense curiosity and a need to pursue all possible sources of sex information begin to observe and listen to others in their peer group. The peer group, by default, thus becomes the most important factor in sex education. Sexual interests are experienced and discussed within the peer group and are acted out in accordance with peer expectations and demands. Adolescents are then able to compare and test their own standards of morality with those of adult society; the result is that they often choose to compromise less with adult prohibitions (Bell, 1966).

Young people should be instructed in the psychology as well as the physiology of sexuality. Physiological instruction should include material on the reproductive system and process, the effects of heredity, biochemical functions relating to sex, and differences in the anatomy of the sexes, as well as physiological changes from childhood to adulthood and the impact of these changes on behavior (Staton, 1968). There also should be a discussion of the differences in the intensity of sexual drives between males and females during adolescence and the discrepancy in learned attitudes that underlie these differences. Psychological topics should include the effects of emotional stimuli as they contribute to sexual arousal, the role of love and romance in a girl's sexual desire as opposed to the role of a boy's erotic urges, and the impact of conversation on sexual behavior (Staton, 1968). Many adolescents also need advice on their responsibilities in regard to engaging in sexual activities, as well as information about birth-control methods.

An adequate sex-education program presented by those effectively trained to teach such material would greatly minimize, if not eliminate, adolescent misconceptions, misinformation, and anxiety about sexuality. Such a program, if it is to be successful, must give adolescents honest, factual, and relevant information that will help them to understand that sexual awareness and desires are psychologically normal and that sex is an important part of the individual's overall development.

Rather than the traditional "They are going to learn in the street anyway" form of sex education (Gagnon & Simon, 1969, p. 46), programs should be designed to relate to the current changes in sexual attitudes and behavior. A comprehensive sex-education curriculum should include relevant goals, methods, and content appropriate for different age levels, as well as suggestions on the role that the parents, school, and community can play in sex education (Bracher, 1967; Kinch, 1967). The Sex Information and Education Council of the United States (SIECUS) represents an innovative start in that direction (Hathaway, 1976).

Although some schools are providing adequate programs in

sex education, many adolescents have never had any exposure to such a course (Spanier, 1976). Even though today's youths are better informed about sexuality than previous generations, they still cling to many of the myths and misconceptions of their parents and peer groups. A great number of young people are entering their adult lives with incomplete knowledge and awareness of their own sexuality and of human sexuality in general (Toussieng, 1975).

Society's traditional assumptions that adolescents should not engage in sexual relations and that the less they know about sex, the better have, in the past, deprived teenagers of the information necessary for them to make informed and responsible decisions. The fear that information would lead to experimentation has provided much of the parental resistance to and anxiety about sex education. Many adolescents will engage in sexual behavior regardless of whether they receive sex education and regardless of what society may think.

Interestingly, the majority of teenagers still prefer their parents as sex advisers and as sources of sexual information; however, most of the adolescents' sexual information, much of it based on misconceptions, comes from their friends. Although parents are the earliest models of sexuality, many adolescents believe that their parents do not talk freely about sex and do not provide them with enough information about it, despite the fact that sex is often a source of conflict between them. Young people do not want to be told what they should do; as a matter of fact, they often resist or behave contrary to parental wishes or parental moralizing (Jensen & Robbins, 1975). Parents serve their children best when they guide and counsel, rather than criticize and offer moral lectures (Elias & Elias, 1975).

Sex education should not only be incorporated into the schools and become an integral part of general education but should also be made a continuing experience in the academic curriculum. The schools, however, cannot handle the job without the help of parents and of community services (Gordon, 1974; Reichelt & Werley, 1975).

Improved sex education is a prerequisite for reducing the incidence of teenage pregnancies and the number of unwanted children (Juhasz, 1974), but it is also essential in the effort to stop the massive increase in the incidence of venereal disease (VD) in this country. Most young people are aware of the current epidemic prevalence of VD. Venereal disease, which is transmitted through sexual contact, can be contracted by anyone of any age or socioeconomic level. Older adolescents presently have approximately twice the incidence of venereal disease as younger adolescents. Many youths discover that they have contracted one of the venereal disorders (gonorrhea is most frequent, followed by syphilis), and do not know where to go for diagnosis and treatment. Others are not aware that they have VD. In some states, adolescents cannot legally seek information and treatment of VD without parental consent—and how many youths would be willing to tell their parents that they have a venereal disease? VD-treatment information is now available, however, through a program called Operation Venus, which is providing information to some 3000 callers each month on its toll-free, nationwide hot-line number: 800-523-1885 (Thornburg, 1975).

Teenagers also need a place to talk about their sexuality and discuss what it means to be a sexual human being. Kelly (1976) has devised several innovative approaches to helping young people effectively communicate on this topic; one approach has been that of values clarification, which will be discussed in more detail in Chapter 7. Open communication between the adolescent, the family, and the peer group is especially helpful to adolescents (Rosenberg, Held, & Chilgren, 1975). Published guides are available to provide parents with better ways of talking about sex to young people at various age levels (for example, Gadpaille, 1974; Pomeroy, 1976). Centers where teenagers could talk about sex-related questions, see films, pick up brochures, and obtain resource and referral information in an open, nonjudgmental atmosphere would be particularly useful. Materials available should represent several points of view on controversial matters; young people have a right to an education that enables them to make their own decisions after careful consideration of the facts.

Thus, effective sex education can help today's adolescents establish healthy, responsible sexual behavior. It can teach them to live comfortably with ambiguity, to develop a tolerance of others unlike themselves, and to show respect for different points of view.

Contraceptives and the abortion revolution

Society, traditionally, has been punitive toward pregnancies among unmarried women, particularly teenagers, and has generally provided only the alternatives of a forced marriage, an illegitimate child, or a back-alley abortion. Over the years illegal abortion has been tolerated as a necessary evil but has not been considered a subject for polite conversation. Women who terminated their unwanted pregnancies did so in fear and silence, often risking their lives and suffering much guilt and shame. More recently, many states have sought abortion reform by liberalizing their statutes, by repealing some of their legislation, or by challenging existing abortion laws in the courts. In addition, the sexual revolution, the population explosion, and the demand for equality of the sexes have all contributed to changing attitudes about abortion. One might even say that an abortion revolution in this country is well under way. Today a woman is more likely to die from pregnancy than from a hospital abortion.

Many teenagers fail to use contraceptives and have a poor understanding of sexuality and the consequences of the sexual act. It is not surprising, therefore, that teenage girls receive one-third of all abortions performed in this country. And, as mentioned earlier, unmarried teenage mothers tend to continue to engage in sexual intercourse without adequate protection and often have additional unwanted pregnancies (Goldsmith, 1976; Nadelson, 1976; Nettleton & Cline, 1975).

The hardships of out-of-wedlock pregnancy and the social costs involved are sufficient to justify the development of preventive programs. Attempts to reduce the number of unwanted pregnancies and to lower abortion rates by discouraging nonmarital adolescent intercourse have not been effective. Yet the fact remains that adolescents generally receive insufficient practical information about sexuality and birth control (Castadot, 1975; Johnson, 1974; Schoefield, 1974). In addition, they usually do not start using birth-control methods at the same time that they start to have sexual intercourse. A large number of adolescent sexual activities are episodic and unanticipated, and contraception is, therefore, often unavailable. Because many teenagers do not even understand contraception or are unable to decide which method to use, their utilization of contraceptive protection is often inept, sporadic, and irrational (Cvetkovich, Grote, Bjorseth, & Sarkissian, 1975; Nadelson, 1976).

Thus, adolescents tend to ignore contraceptive precautions and "take their chances." The wide range of excuses offered for not using contraception reflects the many misconceptions prevalent among poorly informed youths. These include the following: (1) pregnancy is unlikely, (2) it only happens to others, (3) it doesn't happen the first time, (4) my sexual encounters are too infrequent, (5) I'm too young, and (6) it's the wrong time of the month. Some adolescents have limited access to contraceptives or do not use them for fear of being discovered by their parents. Others believe that the use of contraceptives interferes with the spontaneity of the sex act, making it seem as though it had been planned (Goldsmith, 1976; Nadelson, 1976).

Young people have both a need and a right to know how to prevent unwanted pregnancy. Effective birth-control counseling in a supportive and nonjudgmental atmosphere is essential to meeting the needs of adolescents. It is important, however, to encourage sensible and responsible use of such measures. Schools and clinics need to make available to teenagers birth-control services that offer educational information, medical examination, and abortion counseling. Since the principle of parental consent is sometimes in opposition to the best health interests of the adolescent, laws allowing minors to seek medical help without parental consent should be enacted. In 1976, the Supreme Court ruled that states cannot require the consent of parents before minors on welfare can be given free contraceptives. Some states, however, still refuse requests for birth-control information and supplies when the teenager refuses to seek parental permission.

In this age of modern contraceptives, many people believe that it is a woman's right to engage in sexual activity without fear of pregnancy and that such activity should not be the direct concern of society. Furthermore, many people advocate the fundamental right of women to choose whether or not to bear children. Birth control, they believe, should be a matter of individual conscience, and legal abortion should be made available on request. There are others, however, who support the "Right to Life" movement and would strongly disagree, at least on the issue of abortion.

Chapter summary

Probably no greater problems confront the typical adolescent in today's rapidly changing world than those in the area of sexual behavior. Because of the wide gap between the attitudes of the older generations and the values and current sexual attitudes and practices of the younger generations, adolescents are often beset with needless guilt and anxiety if they engage in certain sexual behaviors that are more or less commonly practiced today.

A recent report disclosed that adolescents criticize their parents most of all for their failure to provide adequate information on sex and contraceptives (Goldsmith, 1976). There is an emphatic need for a relevant sex-education program encompassing both the psychological and physiological aspects of sexuality. Such a program must focus its attention as much on the formation of healthy attitudes and the development of responsible sexual behavior as on the biological forces if young people are to become emotionally and socially well-adjusted individuals. Until adequate sex education becomes widespread, rising venereal disease rates, increasing numbers of nonmarital pregnancies and out-of-wedlock births, and a growing incidence of unhappy teenage marriages will continue to plague our society.

Thought provokers

1. What is meant by the concept "the new morality"?
2. What are some of the problems and conflicts likely to be experienced by adolescents in regard to sexual behavior?
3. Contrast the erotic feelings of males and females during the early- and middle-adolescent periods. What are some of the effects of this discrepancy?
4. Compare the typical sexual behavior of middle-class boys in mid-adolescence with the typical sexual behavior of lower-socioeconomic-class boys at that same stage of adolescence.
5. What is meant by the phrase "the conflict of bisexuality"?
6. How do you feel about nonmarital adolescent sexual intercourse?
7. What are your feelings about abortion? What other alternatives exist to prevent unwanted pregnancies?
8. Do you feel that sex education should be a function of the school? If not, what individual, group, or agency should be primarily responsible for providing sex education?
9. If you were devising a sex-education program for a school setting, what topics would you include? At what ages would you introduce these various topics? Would you devise a unisexual or a coeducational program? Why?

References

Bakwin, H. Erotic feelings in infants and young children. *Medical Aspects of Human Sexuality,* 1974, 8(10), 200–209.

Bauman, K. E., & Wilson, R. R. Premarital sexual attitudes of unmarried university students: 1968 vs. 1972. *Archives of Sexual Behavior,* 1976, 5(1), 29–38.

Bell, R. R. Parent-child conflict in sexual values. *Journal of Social Issues,* 1966, 22, 34–44.

Berg, D. H. Sexual subcultures and contemporary heterosexual interaction patterns among adolescents. *Adolescence,* 1975, 10(40), 543–548.

Blaine, G. B., Jr. *Patience and fortitude: The parents' guide to adolescence.* Boston: Little, Brown, 1962.

Boyce, J., & Benoit, C. Adolescent pregnancy. *New York State Journal of Medicine,* 1975, 75(6), 872–874.

Bracher, M. The Martinson report: Implications for sex education. *Journal of School Health,* 1967, 37, 491–497.

Braen, B., & Forbush, J. B. School-age parenthood: A national overview. *Journal of School Health,* 1975, 45(5), 256–262.

Briedis, C. Marginal deviants: Teenage girls experience community response to premarital sex and pregnancy. *Social Problems,* 1975, 22(4), 480–493.

Castadot, R. G. Need for, difficulties and experiences with sexual behavior questionnaires among teenagers. *Maryland State Medical Journal,* 1975, 24(4), 40–42.

Cohen, M. W., & Friedman, S. B. Nonsexual motivation of adolescent sexual behavior. *Medical Aspects of Human Sexuality*, 1975, *1*(1), 8–10 ff.

Conger, J. J. *Adolescence and youth* (2nd ed.). New York: Harper & Row, 1977.

Cvetkovich, G., Grote, B., Bjorseth, A., & Sarkissian, J. On the psychology of adolescents' use of contraceptives. *Journal of Sex Research*, 1975, *11*(3), 256–270.

Dranoff, S. M. Masturbation and the male adolescent. *Adolescence*, 1974, *9*(34), 169–176.

Elias, J. E., & Elias, V. D. The sexual world of the adolescent. *Counseling Psychologist*, 1975, *5*(1), 92–97.

Erikson, E. H. The psychosexual development of children. In J. M. Tanner & B. Inhelder (Eds.), *Discussions on child development* (Vol. 3). New York: International Universities Press, 1955. Pp. 168–215.

Finger, F. W. Changes in sex practices and beliefs of male college students: Over 30 years. *Journal of Sex Research*, 1975, *11*(4), 304–317.

Gadpaille, W. J. Counseling parents with sexually active young teenagers. *Medical Aspects of Human Sexuality*, 1974, *8*(7), 127-128.

Gadpaille, W. J. Adolescent sexuality—a challenge to psychiatrists. *Journal of the American Academy of Psychoanalysis*, 1975, *3*(2), 163–177.

Gagnon, J. H., & Simon, W. Sexual deviance in contemporary America. *The Annals of the American Academy of Political and Social Science*, 1968, *376*, 106–122.

Gagnon, J. H., & Simon, W. They're going to learn in the street anyway. *Psychology Today*, 1969, *3*, 46–49.

Gebhard, P. H., Gagnon, J. H., Pomeroy, W. B., & Christenson, C. V. *Sex offenders*. New York: Bantam Books, 1967.

Godenne, G. D. Sex and today's youth. *Adolescence*, 1974, *9*(33), 67–72.

Goldsmith, S. Contraceptive care for minors. *SIECUS Report*, 1976, *4*(3), 1.

Gordon, S. What place does sex education have in the schools? *Journal of School Health*, 1974, *44*(4), 186–188.

Hathaway, B. Innovative experiment in peer sex education in New York City high schools. *SIECUS Report*, 1976, *4*(3), 3.

Hettlinger, R. F. *Sexual maturity*. Belmont, Calif.: Wadsworth, 1970.

Hettlinger, R. F. *Human sexuality: A psychosocial perspective*. Belmont, Calif.: Wadsworth, 1974.

Hofmann, A. D. Brief guide to office counseling: Adolescent promiscuity. *Medical Aspects of Human Sexuality*, 1974, *8*(5), 63–64.

Iverson, S. R. Sex education and adolescent attitudes. (Doctoral dissertation, University of Maryland, 1974). *Dissertation Abstracts International*, 1974, *34*, 13181.

Jackson, E. D., & Potkay, C. A. Precollege influences on sexual experiences of coeds. *Journal of Sex Research*, 1973, *9*(2), 143–149.

Jensen, G. D., & Robbins, M. Ten reasons why "sex talks" with adolescents go wrong. *Medical Aspects of Human Sexuality*, 1975, *9*(2), 6 ff.

Johnson, C. L. Adolescent pregnancy: Intervention into the poverty cycle. *Adolescence*, 1974, *9*(35), 391–406.

Juhasz, A. M. The unmarried adolescent parent. *Adolescence*, 1974, *9*(34), 263–272.

Kelly, G. F. *Learning about sex: A contemporary guide for young adults*. Barron's Educational Services, 1976.

Kerckhoff, A. C. Social class differences in sexual attitudes and behavior. *Medical Aspects of Human Sexuality*, 1974, *8*(11), 10 ff.

Kinch, R. A. Adolescent sex education. *Annals of the New York Academy of Sciences*, 1967, *142*(3), 824–833.

Kirkendall, L. Can premarital intercourse be healthy? In W. B. Frick (Ed.), *Explorations in healthy personality*. Fort Collins, Colo.: Shields, 1974.

Klerman, L. V. Adolescent pregnancy: The need for new policies and new programs. *Journal of School Health*, 1975, 45(5), 263–267.

Macklin, E. D. Cohabitation in college: Going very steady. *Psychology Today*, 1974, 8(6), 53–59.

Maddock, J. W. Sex in adolescence: Its meaning and its future. *Adolescence*, 1973, 8(31), 325–342.

Mitchell, J. J. Moral dilemmas of early adolescence. *Adolescence*, 1975, 10(39), 442–446.

Moore, W. T. Genital masturbation and adolescent development. *Journal of the Philadelphia Association for Psychoanalysis*, 1975, 2(1), 20–37.

Nadelson, C. C. Inadequate contraceptive use among sexually active adolescents. *Medical Aspects of Human Sexuality*, 1976.

Nettleton, C. A., & Cline, D. W. Dating patterns, sexual relationships and use of contraceptives of 700 unwed mothers during a two year period following delivery. *Adolescence*, 1975, 10(37), 45–58.

Nixon, R. E. *The art of growing*. New York: Random House, 1962.

Packard, V. *The sexual wilderness*. New York: Pocket Books, 1968.

Page, E. W. Physically adult, mentally unprepared. In S. M. Farber & R. H. L. Wilson (Eds.) *Sex education and the teenager*. Berkeley, Calif.: Diablo Press, 1967. Pp. 1-7.

Polsby, G. K. Unmarried parenthood: Potential for growth. *Adolescence*, 1974, 9(34), 273–284.

Pomeroy, W. *Your child and sex: A guide for parents*. New York: Dell, 1976.

Reichelt, P. A., & Werley, H. H. A sex information program for sexually active teenagers. *Journal of School Health*, 1975, 45(2), 226–227.

Rosenberg, P. P., Held, J. P., & Chilgren, R. A. Sex education of adolescents and their families. *American Journal of Orthopsychiatry*, 1975, 45(2), 226–227.

Salzman, L. Sexual problems in adolescence. *Contemporary Psychoanalysis*, 1974, 10(2), 189–207.

Schoefield, M. *The sexual behavior of young adults*. Boston: Little, Brown, 1974.

Simon, W., & Gagnon, J. H. Psychosexual development. *Trans-action*, 1969, 6, 9–17.

Sorensen, R. C. *Adolescent sexuality in contemporary America*. New York: World, 1973.

Spanier, G. B. Formal and informal sex education as determinants of premarital sexual behavior. *Archives of Sexual Behavior*, 1976, 5(1), 39–68.

Spicer, F. Sexual problems in adolescence. *Proceedings of the Royal Society of Medicine*, 1968, 61, 510–512.

Staton, T. F. Sex education for adolescents. In J. F. Adams (Ed.), *Understanding adolescence: Current developments in adolescent psychology*. Boston: Allyn & Bacon, 1968. Pp. 248–271.

Thornburg, H. D. *Development in adolescence*. Monterey, Calif.: Brooks/Cole, 1975.

Toolan, J. M. Adolescent concerns about being "normal" sexually. *Medical Aspects of Human Sexuality*, 1975, 9(2), 79–80.

Toussieng, P. W. The inhibited adolescent. *Medical Aspects of Human Sexuality*, 1975, 9(2), 143.

Woods, N. F. *Human sexuality in health and illness*. St. Louis: C. V. Mosby, 1975.

Zackman, J., & Branstadt, W. (Eds.) *The teenage pregnant girl*. Springfield, Ill.: Charles C Thomas, 1974.

Normal development of emotionality in the adolescent 6

Don't laugh at a youth for his affectations; he's only trying on one face after another till he finds his own.

Logan Pearsall Smith (1865–1946)
"Afterthoughts"

Probably no stage of life is characterized by stronger and more rapidly changing manifestations of emotionality than the period of adolescence. According to Stamell (1964), the typical adolescent "becomes easily disturbed by insignificant events and reacts out of all proportion to their insignificance" (p. 1020). Bewildered parents and teachers who are confronted by frequent, intense, and often abrupt mood swings in adolescents begin to wonder if they have failed them or whether these young people have suddenly developed a serious disorder. Even adolescents themselves may sometimes wonder whether their feelings and thoughts are normal and characteristic of their peers as well.

What are some of the reasons behind the frequent display of intense emotionality in these young people? First, as we mentioned in

149

Chapter 4, the many rapid physical and biochemical changes characterizing adolescence are usually accompanied by emotional changes.
Second, the adolescent experiences a conflict between the desire to
grow up and become independent and the wish to hold on to a
childlike passivity and dependency (Daly, 1966). Third, the adolescent is engaged in a search for *identity*, a term that has been used by
Erikson (1963) to describe the feeling of being at home in one's body
and possessing an awareness of where one is going. And fourth,
as Elkind (1967) has suggested, the development of new *cognitive
structures*—new ways of thinking, reasoning, perceiving, and feeling
—makes possible *affective* or emotional experiences not previously
experienced by adolescents.

Emotionality and physical changes

When an adolescent experiences swift changes in body size
and shape, a common reaction to this new image is a lowering of
self-esteem, which puts considerable strain on the already fragile *ego*
(Daly, 1966). Boys and girls in their early teens may compare their size
and shape to that of mature adults and become worried and concerned
when they discover that the comparison is unfavorable to them. They
may feel inferior and ashamed of their bodies and try to withdraw
from social contacts to protect themselves from such feelings. Because
of their uneven physical growth and development, adolescents may
become sullen and depressed. They often retreat to their rooms to
worry for endless hours about these rapid changes and what they
signify and to daydream about a possibly brighter future.

Large increases in hormone secretions also play a major role in
the emotional development of the adolescent. In girls, the beginning
of hormonal changes particularly influences their moods, although
possible adverse learning from mothers, older sisters, and peers can
also contribute to such mood swings. Most female adolescents, however, are at first unable to connect their moodiness with menstruation
and hormonal fluctuations and become upset when their premen-
strual behavior is quite atypical. Boys, too, experience many radical
physical and hormonal changes to which they must become accustomed. Once such changes have taken place, however, they stabilize
and become familiar. Thus, boys are not confronted with the periodic
hormonal changes that girls face every month with their menstrual
cycle (Bardwick, Douvan, Horner, & Gutmann, 1970).

Usually by the end of early adolescence, however, the hormonal and biological processes have become relatively stable, and
this results in some stabilization in the emotions of the adoles-

cent (Group for the Advancement of Psychiatry, 1968). They no longer tend to overreact with the intensity characteristic of early adolescence.

Independence versus dependency needs

One of the major problems among adolescents is the conflict they experience between their desire to become adults independent of their parents and their reluctance to give up their dependency on their parents. This ambivalence can be seen in the fluctuation of the adolescent's level of emotional maturity. One hour he or she appears to be striving toward independence and the achievement of autonomy. The next hour there are childlike demands for limitations on behavior and requests for guidance from parents and other authority figures. During this period of conflict, usually during early adolescence, the parent/adolescent relationship tends to be one of pull and counterpull—toward independence and away from it (Offer & Offer, 1968). Consequently, the adolescent is also ambivalent toward parental advice, wanting it but often acting contrary to it. Sometimes this process of striving toward independence from parents and other adults is referred to as "psychological weaning" (Horrocks, 1976).

Blos (1967) describes this psychological weaning as the second individuation process, the first having been completed at the end of the third year of life. He points out that this process involves "the shedding of family dependencies, the loosening of infantile object ties in order to become a member of society at large, or simply, of the adult world" (p. 163). Failure to achieve this disengagement prevents the young person from seeking out new, extrafamilial objects of affection. Difficulties in resolving this situation may be manifested through acting-out behavior, learning disorders, or patterns of procrastination, moodiness, apathy, and negativism.

The first exhilaration marking the realization of newly acquired independence from one's parents may be accompanied by a depression almost comparable to a state of mourning upon the death of a love object (Blos, 1967). Apparently, the adolescent suddenly begins to realize that he or she is leaving the emotional security of childhood and entering a new, uncertain, insecure stage of life.

When the dependency/autonomy conflict is most intense, the adolescent is likely to engage in deviant behavior, perhaps as a cry for help or as a plea for attention to the stress and strain he or she is undergoing. Frequently it is difficult to determine whether such behavior is transient or permanent, normal or pathological (Blos, 1967). In fact, adolescent turmoil can simulate psychiatric illness to such an extent that it is sometimes difficult to determine whether it is "just a phase" (Masterson, 1967). What initially appears to be the onset of an emotional disorder, however, often proves to be simply a crisis that will eventually resolve itself and may even contribute to the process of identity formation. During the period of early adolescence, deviant behavior resulting from the dependency/autonomy conflict is likely to be characterized by rebellion against and withdrawal from adults and their values. At first, this rebellion is primarily verbal, but it gradually may come to involve more and more acting-out behavior. As adults offer severe criticism, dire predictions, and sweeping negative generalizations about the younger generation, adolescents become more questioning and rebellious against the rules, standards, and values of adult society. It is of interest to note, too, that the adult's own experiences in adolescence usually have little or no value in aiding him or her to understand, communicate with, and relate to those who are now adolescents (Gallatin, 1968; Personality and Growth Series for Adolescents: An Evaluation, 1969).

Although they may speak and act as though they reject any need to be dependent upon their parents or other adults, young people are often relieved when adults place firm but fair limitations on youthful behavior. Such limitations make the adolescent feel more confident and secure and less frightened in exploring areas of behavior within these boundaries (Josselyn, 1967).

> Donna, 16, was told by her mother that she would not be permitted to drive alone in the family car after dark and that, when necessary, her parents would escort her to her destination during the evening. Although vehemently protesting that, among other things, this would interfere with her freedom to attend community little-theater activities and that most of her girlfriends were permitted to drive alone at night, Donna relented. Despite the fact that she was quite vocal in her complaints about this "injustice," her mother overheard her remark to a close friend that she had been somewhat fearful of being alone in the little-theater parking lot following rehearsals or of possibly having car trouble on her way home.

According to Douvan and Adelson (1966), there are three primary goals involved in the process of striving toward independence: behavioral autonomy, emotional autonomy; and moral (or value) autonomy. Behavioral independence or autonomy is generally sought during early adolescence. It involves the assertion of independence in such areas as dating, gainful employment, management of personal finances, and the choice of leisure-time activities and companions. With this striving for behavioral independence generally come a decrease in the amount of time spent with the family and an increase in the time spent with peers. This shift in behavior can often become a point of conflict between the parents and children when parents have difficulty understanding why their adolescent children would, for example, prefer attending a football game with their friends to going out for dinner with their family. The second goal, that of emotional autonomy, has been defined as the extent to which young people are able to shed their childhood emotional ties to the family (Douvan & Adelson, 1966). This goal involves relinquishing much of their childhood dependency, acquiring self-control, self-reliance, and a sense of responsibility, and learning to identify more with parents as close, trusted friends rather than as models to be copied without question. Gold and Douvan (1969) believe that such emotional independence is more difficult to achieve than behavioral independence, especially for girls who are reluctant to cast off earlier emotional ties that had provided them with emotional security. The third goal, moral or value autonomy, which appears to develop in late adolescence or young adulthood, will be discussed at length in Chapter 7.

Parents, teachers, and other adults working with adolescents need to be prepared to handle youthful striving toward autonomy. In the case of parents, it is essential that they agree with each other as to what behavior they will permit, expect, and encourage in their children; otherwise, the adolescent may pit one parent against the other. Together, the parents need to decide how much to slacken the reins of control and when to do so. If they release too much parental responsibility too soon, the adolescent may be presented with more freedom than he or she can cope with. Such premature independence may result in youths' being persuaded to engage in behavior for which they are not ready. On the other hand, if a measure of independence is denied the adolescent or delayed too long, then he or she may remain psychologically unweaned and more or less permanently dependent on parents and other adults. Such dependency can be seen in the spouse who runs home to his or her parents each time there is a quarrel with the marriage partner.

The search for identity

Erik Erikson (1956) has described the stage of late adolescence as the period of the *identity crisis*. During this developmental stage the adolescent engages in a personal redefinition of his or her role in society, a process that can either take the form of intense self-awareness or exist at a less conscious level. A combination of psychological and environmental factors initiates this search for identity and facilitates its development. These factors present the adolescent with a complex, often confusing variety of *self-images* (Bronson, 1959).

According to Erikson (1955), there are seven tasks that must be mastered in order to resolve this identity crisis. These consist of the following:

1. *Time perspective versus time diffusion.* Successful resolution of this task involves the realization that there is a lifetime ahead of the adolescent—that is, that there is enough time for the accomplishment of many goals but not so much time that he or she will not know what to do with it. The fact that this task is difficult for many adolescents can be seen in the typical impatience of youth (for example, in their desire for instant reform in the political realm).

2. *Self-certainty versus identity consciousness.* The development of self-certainty requires that the adolescent first acquire a degree of autonomy and then a particular social status among his or her peers. Social status is usually acquired through close affiliation with a group of like-minded peers. The need for such status helps to explain the young person's tendency to affiliate with cliques, fraternities, and other groups, which often provide a mirror image, or reflection, of the adolescent's self and of who he or she is. Because adolescents are not yet able to develop self-certainty on their own, they seek out peer-group affiliations that will help them develop at least an externally based self-certainty.

3. *Role experimentation versus negative identity.* The task of role experimentation reemphasizes the quotation by Logan Pearsall Smith at the beginning of this chapter: ". . . he's only trying on one face after another till he finds his own." Young people will try affiliating with a number of different groups that have a variety of political and social viewpoints.

4. *Anticipation of achievement versus work paralysis.* Youths overidentify with those who have achieved success in some field of endeavor. Thus, adolescents often idolize rock musicians and frequently emulate their idols' behavior rather than developing their own uniqueness and fulfilling their own potential. Their dreams of achievement are sometimes so impossible to fulfill, however, that these adolescents may eventually give up all hopes of achieving these or any other goals.

5. *Sexual identity versus bisexual diffusion.* This task involves not only the attainment of sexual maturation but also the definition and acceptance of a personally satisfying psychosexual role.

6. *Leadership polarization versus authority diffusion.* The

adolescent must learn to be "a leader of some and a follower of others" (Erikson, 1955, p. 183). No one can be a good leader, however, unless he or she has first learned to be a good follower. Bad leaders, such as leaders of delinquent gangs, may appear to be ideal in the eyes of their youthful followers, but they often have no regard or respect for others.

7. *Ideological polarization versus diffusion of ideals.* This task requires that the adolescent develop a general ideological position. Young people are often impressionistic and may adopt certain ideals without sufficient thought. One of the functions of certain rites, such as fraternity initiations, is to help adolescents establish certain ideals. Unfortunately, such rites often lead to expressions of distinction and thus to the development of snobbishness and intolerance for the ideals of others.

If these seven tasks are not adequately resolved, then "identity confusion," the psychological chaos and conflict arising in many young people, will persist (Erikson, 1968).

In the process of evaluating their past self-images, assessing their present assets and liabilities, reformulating new ideals and goals, and testing new interpersonal relationships, young people often wonder who they really are (Bronson, 1959). With the arrival of adolescence, young people lose the stable *self-concept* they developed in childhood. The loss of this relatively fixed self-image often causes adolescents' appraisals of their social environment to fluctuate and causes them to exhibit wide variations in their interpersonal behavior. Not surprisingly, this identity confusion is likely to be accompanied by considerable inner tension and increased anxiety.

Erikson has suggested that our rapidly advancing technology, which has lengthened the period of adolescence dependence by delaying the acquisition of an occupational identity, has added to the identity crisis. To compensate for the delayed occupational identity, young people may temporarily overidentify with their peers and with their peer leaders to the point that they appear to lose their own individuality. Such behavior may be indicative not only of an attempt to resolve the identity crisis but also of the transference of adolescence dependency needs from adults to the peer group. Even "falling in love" can represent an attempt to solve the problem of who one really is; a young man who becomes a young woman's steady is acquiring status in a certain role. Furthermore, adolescent love can serve as a means of projecting one's diffused self-concept onto another and thus, through its reflection, clarifying one's own identity (Erikson, 1963). Unfortunately, clannish, intolerant behavior and the exclusion from the group of those who are different can serve as a temporary defense against identity diffusion.

A slightly different approach to the resolution of the identity crisis is that of Marcia (1968), who suggests that identity achievement can be defined as the act of becoming committed to an occupation and to an ideology and of experiencing a crisis in achieving these. He delineates four categories to describe the identity status of an individual: (1) Those who have been through the identity crisis but who have developed a personally determined stand regarding their occupation and ideology are described as "identity achieved." (2) Individuals who have accepted with little or no questioning the identity assigned to them by their families are referred to as "identity foreclosed." (3) Those still searching for their own commitments and values are described as being in the "moratorium" stage. (4) Individuals immobilized by self-doubt and alienation from society, family, and peers and those who experience great difficulty in tackling the issues involved in identity resolution are categorized as being in the "identity-diffusion" group.

Using this identity-status scale, Donovan (1975) categorized the identity status of 22 college students (13 males and 9 females) with an average age of 21. He reported that only three subjects could be described as belonging to the identity-diffusion group. These three people had few plans or personal goals and were vague about political, religious, and sexual issues. In addition, they mentioned feelings of inferiority, alienation, and *ambivalence* and felt that they were misfits both at home and among their peers. Six students were described as fitting into the identity-foreclosure group. They appeared to have internalized parental plans for them, generally without question, and they were characterized by inhibited feelings, conventional behavior, and overconcern about the opinion of others. Eleven, or one-half, of the subjects fitted into the identity-moratorium group, but there were several important differences among them. One subgroup seemed to be actively searching for personal goals and commitment even while they appeared to be uncertain about their vocational aims; they were concerned about learning to know themselves and the world about them first. A second subgroup showed a lack of clearly defined goals and values and avoided any commitment even while seeking it. They showed a defensive, diffused attitude about their lack of commitment, however, and Donovan suggested that this subgroup might constitute a fifth identity status—that of "moratorium diffusion." The category of identity achievement contained only two people, both women who were much older than the other students (in their late 30s compared with the average age of 21). It was suggested that both had probably been identity foreclosed at the age of 21 but later had undergone change during young adulthood, resulting in an increased self-awareness. This research by Donovan discloses the possibility that there may well be a developmental sequence in identity formation—foreclosure to moratorium to achievement—and that identity achievement may very likely be a phenomenon of the late 20s or early 30s, when it occurs. Such a hypothesis tends to contradict that of Erikson, who suggests that the identity crisis is settled in the early 20s.

Regardless of one's point of view, it appears that some young people find it necessary to declare a *psychological moratorium* in order to achieve healthy identity development (Blaine, 1965; Erikson, 1968). For instance, a student may temporarily drop out of high school or college in an attempt to reestablish a state of psychological equilibrium and a satisfying identity. Their apathy and listlessness, which are so often disturbing to parents, may very well be masking anxiety resulting from their concern about the void within them—a void that develops when old values are discarded and new ones have not yet been developed to replace them.

> The process of dropping-out often makes the difference because the student is able to get the feeling afterwards that he has made a real change from the established pattern that had been set down for him since early life. When he comes back he feels that he is now going to college for his own reasons. This improves his ability to perform. The other great advantage of dropping-out of college is the feeling of accomplishment which may result from doing a job . . . . This gives him a feeling of confidence which he can carry back into college work [Blaine, 1965, p. 394].

The case of Larry illustrates the possible usefulness of the psychological moratorium.

> Larry was a college dropout. He began his studies at the state university in premedical training, which satisfied the ambitions of his physician father but not Larry's own ambitions. After a year and a half of college, Larry dropped out of school because of low grades and a general disinterest in preparing for the medical profession. He joined the Air Force and began training as a radar technician, a job that he found interesting and gratifying. After his tour of duty, during which he was promoted to staff sergeant, Larry left the service and decided to return to school. With his satisfying experiences in the Air Force behind him, he developed a new enthusiasm for completing his education. This time, however, after seeking out vocational testing, Larry decided to discontinue his premedical training and enter the college of engineering. Pursuing his own selected goals, his grades soared and he ultimately graduated from the university with honors.

Identity formation neither begins nor ends with adolescence; it is a lifetime development (Erikson, 1956). However, by the time a youth has graduated from college, or possibly after an occupational status has been achieved, the typical individual will have fairly well resolved the identity crisis. For those attending trade school or serving apprenticeships for electricians, plumbers, and other skilled trades, the resolution of the identity crisis is likely to occur somewhat sooner. Others, who obtain such jobs as bus drivers, file clerks, and assembly-line workers, resolve the identity crisis at the time that they achieve their occupational status. Nevertheless, the end results are similar for all groups: the development of a sense of who one is and what one's role in life is to be—achievements that require that one incorporate into the self certain identifications with valued people in one's environment. Sometimes this phenomenon occurs rather abruptly, surprising even the young person involved, but, regardless of when it takes place, it is a necessary step on the road to maturity (Blaine, 1965). How does an adolescent know when the problem has been resolved? Often, others are the first to perceive that the identity has been established and to offer such comments as "She knows where she's headed" or "He's comfortable with himself" or "She's found herself" (Knight, 1968).

Cognitive structure and adolescent emotionality

According to Elkind (1968), adolescence is accompanied by the appearance of new cognitive structures and new affective or emotional experiences. He cites the example of prejudice, which he believes is not usually manifested until the adolescent period, when adolescents form small cliques based mainly on socioeconomic class. It has been suggested that the new displays of emotion during adolescence are not necessarily the result of the emerging cognitive structures they parallel but, rather, that the cognitive changes are necessary for the occurrence of the emotional changes.

Elkind bases his hypothesis about the interrelation between cognition and adolescent emotionality on Piaget's theories of cognitive development (Inhelder & Piaget, 1958). According to Piaget, each individual goes through the same sequence of intellectual development, although not necessarily at the same rate of speed or at the same chronological age. The highest stage of cognitive development is that of formal operations, which usually emerges about the beginning of adolescence and provides the basis for certain typical adolescent reactions. This cognitive stage is characterized by the ability to introspect and to think at an abstract level. Adolescents who have reached this stage are able to perceive and consider many different possibilities in their decision making. For instance, they become cognizant of alternatives to their parents' directives and become reluctant to accept these directives without question. They want to learn not only where their parents stand but why, and they are usually prepared to debate parental decisions and to compare them with alternatives being considered by themselves and by peers. Paradoxically, although perhaps troubled by having to arrive at decisions themselves and often finding such decision making to be quite a burden, they still do not want adults to make up their minds for them. As a matter of fact, some adolescents seem to demand that their parents take a stand, if only so that they can rebel against it.

In primitive cultures there is often little of the storm and stress commonly experienced by youths in our Western society (Elkind, 1968). Perhaps this is so because the absence of a more advanced cognitive framework, and thus the possibility of constructing various alternatives in problem solving, eliminates many of the conflicts that adolescents experience in our society. The development of the cognitive tools needed for decision making appears to set the stage for the typical conflicts erupting between parents and their adolescent children. As they become more and more adamant about arriving at their own decisions, young people reject parental values more and more, thereby creating greater dissonance between the two generations.

Other aspects of emotional development in the adolescent

Egocentrism

The whole universe of the preschool child is made up of direct experience (Piaget, 1963). Although there are certain differences between the adolescent's and the preschooler's perceptions of the universe, children in their early teens tend to be just as ego centered as the preschooler. Adolescents typically fail to distinguish between others' thoughts and their own preoccupations, and, consequently, they assume that other people are as obsessed with their behavior and appearance as they themselves are (Elkind, 1967).

Because early adolescents so often believe that the attention of others is focused on them, they frequently behave as though they were performing before an assemblage of people. Elkind (1967) has described this phenomenon as the perception of having an "imaginary audience." It is an audience because the adolescents believe that they are the focus of attention, yet it is imaginary because, in truth, no one is watching them—they are all too busy watching themselves and performing for their own imaginary audiences. This perception of an imaginary audience probably explains much of the self-consciousness characteristic of so many young people. They perceive themselves with a critical eye and believe that their audience will view them just as critically. Their desire for privacy and their reluctance to reveal their inner thoughts to others may also reflect this feeling of being under close scrutiny by a critical assemblage.

At the same time, adolescents are often self-admiring, and again the imaginary audience plays a role in their behavior (Elkind, 1967). Youthful boorishness, loudness, and faddish dress may mirror the discrepancy between what a young person believes others will find attractive and what others actually find attractive. It is not surprising, then, that adolescents often fail to comprehend adults' disapproval of their dress and their manners. A similar manifestation of egocentrism can be seen at heterosexual gatherings in which adolescents seem to be more concerned with being observed than with observing (Elkind, 1967). Thus, those in their early teens become both actors and an audience for others. This dual role is especially noticeable at parties during the early adolescent period. The boys often gather at one end of the room and the girls at the other, each group gawking quite self-consciously at the other; the boys frequently display boisterous behavior, and the girls giggle with embarrassment.

An adolescent's egocentrism is also reflected in a belief in the uniqueness of his or her own emotionality. As Elkind (1967) puts it, "Only he can suffer with such agonized intensity or experience such exquisite rapture" (p. 1031). At a slightly different level, this feeling of uniqueness becomes what Elkind has described as a "personal fable," exemplified by an adolescent boy's belief that he is immortal or an adolescent girl's conviction that an unexpected pregnancy can happen to others but surely will never happen to her.

In addition, egocentrism can be seen in youthful impatience about ideals. Adolescents often believe that merely thinking about something can make it happen "now," without recognizing the practical limitations that prevent or delay implementation of an ideal. This impatience contributes to the rift between adolescents and adults, because most adults come to believe that more can be accomplished through evolution than through revolution.

This egocentrism, which is so typical of early adolescence, begins to diminish by the time adolescents reach the age of 15 or 16 (Elkind, 1967). Apparently the process of *reality testing* takes the place of performance for an imaginary audience, and the teenager begins to develop a genuine concern about the reactions of an authen-

tic audience. This process first occurs at a cognitive level; th
vidual learns to differentiate between his or her own thoughts
thoughts of others. Then, on the affective level, the adolescent gradually learns to integrate the feelings of other people with his or her own
emotions. At the same time, the adolescent discovers that his or her
problems are not unique after all and that it has become socially
undesirable to express such ideas of uniqueness.

Self-consciousness

Closely associated with egocentric behavior in young people is
their experience of considerable self-consciousness and their strong
need for self-confidence (Galdston, 1967). Adolescents are extremely
conscious not only of their bodies but also of their minds. They are
often aware of a sharp discrepancy between the selves they are and
the selves that they wish to become—that is, their *ideal self*. With the
onset of puberty most youths undertake a thorough self-inventory,
comparing not only their body parts but also their motor skills, intellectual abilities, talents, and social skills with those of their peers and
their heroes. It is not surprising that this critical self-appraisal is
accompanied by self-conscious behavior, which makes adolescents
especially vulnerable to embarrassment, slight, and shame, as we can
see in the following illustration.

> Fifteen-year-old Laura is overweight. She is so self-conscious
> about her body image that she is reluctant to walk alone down the
> high school corridors between classes or even to obtain a drink of
> water from the water fountain by herself. Apparently, she feels that, if
> a companion or two accompany her, she will be less conspicuous and
> her body size will be less noticeable.

The quest for self-confidence

When the self-inventory is reasonably complete, the typical
adolescent compiles the results and then directs his or her energies
toward correcting the shortcomings and undesired traits. Galdston
(1967) describes this situation quite vividly: "Adolescence is a time
for discarding unwanted attributes and for building up others in a
'psychological spring housecleaning'" (p. 165).

The deviant behavior displayed by many youths is often an
attempt to deny the existence of a major discrepancy between the
results of the self-assessment and the image of the ideal self (Galdston,
1967). Adolescent rebellion, then, can very well be a manifestation of
the adolescent's dissatisfaction with himself or herself. For example,

a young person who aspires to become an Olympic athlete may discover that he or she doesn't possess the skill, the stamina, or the courage demanded of such an athlete. To silence doubts about himself or herself and feelings of inadequacy, the adolescent may *overcompensate* by turning to patterns of behavior characteristic of a "tough" individual in order to demonstrate the physical strength and courage he or she, in reality, lacks.

Although such behavior can fulfill a need, it can become dangerous to the individual and to the community if it is carried to extremes. In some cases it may even lead to delinquent behavior (Galdston, 1967). The degree of behavioral deviation is generally proportionate to the disparity between the childhood fantasies of the ideal self and the reality of the adolescent self. The young person who falls far short of his or her ideal may eventually discard the ideal altogether. This relieves the painful tension aroused by the disparity but, at the same time, destroys the motivation that might have enabled the adolescent to attain the sought-after goal or to achieve satisfying alternative aims. Discarding the goal of the ideal self leaves a void, which adolescents often misperceive as being solely the result of factors beyond their control rather than the consequence of their own actions. Becoming cynical, such youths may seek relief through sensory stimulation by turning to drugs, which give the illusion of filling the void.

As adolescents develop toward maturity and gradually acquire certain social skills and improved physical coordination, their self-confidence begins to increase. With their new self-assurance, young people usually develop a greater capacity for self-discipline, which enables them, for the first time, to develop an integrated system of personal values (which will be discussed at some length in Chapter 7) and a set of self-determined goals for their future (Karowe & McCandless, 1963). Prior to this stage of growth, adolescent values are frequently an outgrowth of their defiance of adults or an imitation of their peers' values.

Idealism

Adolescence is a period of intense idealism, which has been defined by Webster as "behavior or thought based on a conception of things as they should be or as one would wish them to be" (1960, p. 720). It is true that idealization is also present during childhood, but during that period it focuses on the parents. With the arrival of the teen years, there is a break in this idealization of parents, and the adolescent's idealism becomes centered on peers, teachers, and prominent individuals. Such an object of idealization is admired for his or her skills and values and represents to the young person a desirable model toward which to strive. In the case of peers, the idealization is also an endeavor to find security within the peer group—security that was once provided by one's parents. The fact that peer affiliations change frequently, especially in early adolescence, reflects the tendency of youths to retreat from a relationship when they find that it does not live up to their idealization of it (Russian, 1975).

Certain questions arise in regard to the idealism of youth. First of all, whom does the young person idealize? Is it someone so infinitely superior that the adolescent can never hope to measure up to the ideal? Does such a choice cause the individual to become self-denigrating or to feel optimistic about his or her own potential? Or is the person the adolescent chooses to idealize someone closer to his or her own status in life? There may be the risk of negative as well as positive feedback from such a model. Is the young person able to recognize and tolerate imperfections in the object of his or her idealization? Does the adolescent transfer his or her idealism from one individual or group to another, or is it confined to a single individual or group? (Russian, 1975.)

In any case, the presence of idealism among so many adolescents probably reflects the changes in their cognitive structure that we discussed earlier in this chapter. With the arrival of the stage of formal operations (Piaget, 1963), there is a shift in emphasis in the adolescent's thinking processes from the real to the possible (Inhelder & Piaget, 1958). At this point, youths may no longer base all of their thinking solely on their concrete experiences. They can now think about other possibilities through cognitively experimenting, hypothesizing, and exploring—behavior that can certainly lead to idealistic views of what the world should be like.

In order to cope with their feelings, adolescents often resort to defense mechanisms such as *rationalization*, wherein they attempt to prevent threats to their egos from the objects of their idealism by justifying the idealized one's behavior and making excuses for it. For example, a boy might rationalize that the student-council president, whom he has placed on a pedestal, doesn't notice him because of nearsightedness, when, in truth, this school leader doesn't know he exists. Many adolescents display little practical knowledge about how to make their thoughts or hopes become reality—such as getting the student-council president to notice and take an interest in them—and they show even less interest in working to make it happen (Elkind, 1968).

During this stage of development, the youthful capacity for

idealism often leads adolescents to regard family, religion, and society in general in a derogatory manner because of the wide contrast between the ideal and the real. Adults come under considerable fire for having failed to put their professed ideals into practice. However, few human beings can hope ever to fulfill the idealistic expectations of the adolescent (Elkind, 1968).

Concurrently, young people often fail to demonstrate compassion for human weaknesses within themselves as well as in others. Because of their limited experience, adolescents' perspective is often narrow and their patience with the foibles of humans is extremely short.

Generally, as they approach their mid-20s, youths start to adapt to the realities of life (Elkind, 1968), and they begin to recognize that they will not be able to change the world overnight. This acceptance may reflect the fact that they have given up trying to change society because they have been defeated too many times, or it may be the result of their reassessment of the limitations of previous generations and of their recognition of their own shortcomings. In any case, adolescents gradually appear, at least overtly, to become more acceptant of both the limitations and the shortcomings.

Adolescent defense mechanisms

As young people reach adolescence, they start to show changes in their emotional expression, such as increased intensity in their reactions, more extensive acting-out behavior, and changes in the defenses they use to cope with their problems and conflicts.

During adolescence, the defenses and adaptive behavior patterns that were developed to cope with childhood stresses begin to disintegrate. For example, prior to the teens, children will usually respond to fearsome objects by looking to their parents to protect them. In adolescence, as they undergo new experiences farther and farther away from home and parents, young people have to seek other outlets for the expression of their fears. Hence, the disintegration of childhood behavior patterns is important in that it enables the adolescent to seek new patterns of behavior that will be compatible with the demands of adulthood (Josselyn, 1967).

Young people, then, begin to modify their approach to life through changes and modifications in their *defense mechanisms*. Let's take a look at some typical defensive reactions to the numerous frustrations, conflicts, and pressures with which the adolescent is confronted.

Fantasy

Youthful devotion to idealism is closely related to a reliance on fantasy. In fact, the adolescent period has often been described as a period of dreaming—a time when one can take refuge from the many demands of life by creating, in a childlike manner, an ideal world (Stamell, 1964). A young person engages in fantasies that are frequently unrealistic and antisocial in nature (Piotrowski, 1962). Such daydreams, often lively and strongly emotional, can serve as substitute gratification of many adolescent needs and desires, such as sexual urges, that cannot be satisfied directly.

Unfortunately, parents and others working with adolescents too often assume that such fantasies will inevitably be acted out (Piotrowski, 1962). Antisocial fantasies, however, are indicative of future delinquent behavior only when at least one of two conditions exists: (1) the adolescent regards his or her fantasies as realistic representations of the ways things are or even as actual rehearsals of future behavior, and (2) he or she possesses weak self-control, which allows such fantasies to spill over readily into acting-out behavior. It is essential to distinguish between aggressiveness that serves purely as a defense against emotional stress and aggressiveness that has become deeply entrenched as a character trait. The latter form of aggressiveness is found in the psychopath, an individual who is unable to visualize or to care about the consequences of his or her actions. Actually, fantasy can often prove to be a satisfying and acceptable outlet for the emotions at all stages of life, as well as a valuable source for creative behavior. Provided that an individual is able to distinguish imaginative activity from reality and provided that the individual's self-control is adequate, he or she can indulge in many antisocial fantasies with little danger of their being acted out. Indeed, the crucial aspect of fantasy is not its content but the role it plays in the individual's motives and drives (Piotrowski, 1962).

As a youth develops emotional maturity, he or she normally learns that self-limitations need to be imposed on behavior. However, such controls need not cancel out the freedom to fantasize about and even discuss ideas that would be unacceptable if they were translated into behavior (Karowe & McCandless, 1963).

It can be beneficial to adolescents to learn to discuss their fantasies and feelings in a supportive atmosphere. This may be accomplished, at times, through family councils and parent/child dialogues. We have encouraged this emotional ventilation on numerous occasions in the classroom through class discussion and "bull sessions." Discussing gripes about difficult instructors, problems with parents, and other issues can enable students to express their feelings and can alleviate considerable pent-up hostility. Such discussions can permit adolescents to assume a greater degree of objectivity in their attitudes toward their problems. Unfortunately, far too many adults tend to chastise or belittle young people who do ventilate their feelings. They condemn them for having such thoughts, rather than accepting them and reflecting their ideas back to them.

Fear, anxiety, and guilt and mechanisms for coping with them

Fear, anxiety, and guilt are very much present and are often quite intense during adolescence, although they are less overtly expressed than they were in childhood and are sometimes subtly hidden behind a mask of indifference or apathy. What types of fears are of the greatest concern to today's adolescent, and what kinds of individuals are most likely to possess these fears? Croake and Knox (1971), in a study of 212 randomly chosen ninth-graders in the southeastern United States, disclosed that boys reported fewer fears than girls and that adolescents from the lower socioeconomic class had more fears —especially fears related to their families—than those from the middle class. The most frequent fears of both sexes were of a political nature, perhaps reflecting concern about our present instruments for self-annihilation. This study disclosed an increase in the number of fears reported in an earlier study by Croake (1967), although both investigations revealed that the most frequently cited fears were in the political realm. The later research (1971), however, revealed a decline in the intensity of political fears and an increase in the intensity of fears concerning the supernatural.

One of the authors (B. R.), in 1975, queried college sophomores in an adolescent-psychology class about their fears. The results showed a wide variety of concerns, which included fear of growing up and not knowing what to do with one's life, fear of not succeeding, fear of nuclear war, and fear of an economic depression.

In a much earlier study by Angelino and Shedd (1953), 589 young people, 10 to 18 years of age, from regular public-school classrooms were asked to choose from a list of ten the fears and worries they felt were most commonly held by their peers. The 13- and 14-year-old youngsters of both sexes seemed to be most concerned with school problems. Personal-conduct fears—for example, fear of making mistakes in social behavior—assumed the second-greatest importance for the 13-year-olds, whereas political and economic fears took second place among 14-year-old boys and social relationships second place among 14-year-old girls. By the age of 16, however, political and economic fears appeared to predominate in both sexes. It is very possible that the rapid changes and the uncertainties of our world, accentuated by the mass media, may explain the predominance of political fears among today's adolescents.

A second emotion, that of anxiety, is similar to fear in its affective component, but, unlike fear, its source is frequently vague. Anxiety tends to be more subjective in nature than fear, and it may often prove threatening to the adolescent's self-esteem. Because it is more involved in the personality structure, anxiety is not so easily reduced or alleviated as fear is.

Guilt, another emotion, occurs when an internal conflict develops between an individual's values and behavior. For example, a youth who has been taught by his or her parents that cheating is wrong but copies a friend's homework assignment may experience guilt. Because such conflict between values and behavior tends to be especially characteristic of adolescence, guilt is likely to be quite prevalent at this stage of life. Sometimes such conflict is described as *cognitive dissonance* (Festinger, 1957), a state that can cause a person to experience considerable emotional discomfort. In order to reduce such discomfort, one must either modify one's attitudes, a phenomenon that occurs quite commonly during adolescence, or modify one's behavior.

In coping with fear, anxiety, and guilt, adolescents can utilize several different defense mechanisms. For example, to reduce feelings of guilt about cheating, a youth who is aware that cheating is wrong might rationalize his or her own cheating with the statement that "everyone cheats." Or an adolescent may cope with fears through the process of *intellectualization*—that is, the separation of emotion and intellect—thereby reacting to threatening situations as though he or she is devoid of feeling. Another defense mechanism is the *reaction formation*, in which an individual consciously builds up one attitude in order to contain or overpower a conflicting, repressed emotion. For instance, a student may criticize the extroverted behavior of a popular school leader, when unconsciously he desires to be just like that individual. Through another defense mechanism, *projection*, one attributes to others attitudes and behaviors actually possessed by oneself but that one needs to deny. An example would be that of the young boy who says that none of his peers like him, when actually he doesn't like himself or others. Or, adolescents may resort to the mechanism of *displacement*—that is, the act of making one person the target of feelings actually aroused by another person. For example, a young girl may be angry at herself for flunking a test but take the anger out on the student innocently sitting across the aisle. The girl may even claim that the innocent student interfered with her studying for the test, when in truth that person had nothing to do with her failure. An adolescent is likely to adopt a wide range of such defense mechanisms before arriving at a combination that best protects the self from outside scrutiny (Hornick, 1967).

As it is in most human beings and higher animal species, emotionality in adolescents is often accompanied by physical manifestations: heavy perspiration, muscular tension, increased heartbeat, varying pulse pressure, and overwhelming fatigue. Because the adolescent may be unaware of the precipitating causes of the anxiety, he or she may mistakenly regard these physical signs as conclusive evidence of physical illness. Consequently, preoccupation with one's physical condition can become a defense against real anxieties and fears, as in the following case history.

> Betsy, a high school senior, had gone steady with her boyfriend for about two years. Toward the end of this period they began to engage in heavy petting. Suddenly Betsy became aware of a general aching in her breasts and was immediately convinced that she had developed breast cancer. Reluctant to go to her mother and tell her about the pain or to phone their family physician for an appointment, she became so preoccupied with her physical condition that her grades began to slip. Her homeroom teacher, to whom Betsy was quite attached, noted this sudden drop in grades and requested that she come in one day after school for a visit. At first, Betsy denied that there was anything wrong. Finally she broke down, admitting her fears. With her homeroom teacher's encouragement, Betsy told her mother, who promptly made an appointment with their family physician. A competent, understanding man, he examined her and found no physical basis for her complaint; he suggested that there is often a *psychogenic* explanation for many aches and pains—that is, that emotions can readily affect physical well-being. Betsy reflected on what he had said and finally began to see a possible relationship between the heavy petting in which she had recently engaged and her aching breasts. Raised in a rather strict home, where she had been warned about the potential dangers of such activity, she had developed feelings of anxiety and guilt about engaging in this behavior. In further discussion with her family doctor, Betsy soon gained insight into her problem; her pain disappeared, and her grades subsequently improved.

Boredom and apathy

Adolescent boredom, which seems to have become more prevalent in recent years, can be considered an outgrowth of the egocentrism characteristic of this period (Josselyn, 1967; Schonfeld, 1967).

The following causes for this increasing incidence of boredom have been suggested: (1) an educational system that has frequently failed to meet the needs of many students and that, too often, has lacked relevance to the rapidly changing world in which they live, (2) a culture that has failed to grant status and recognition to its young people, (3) a society that has provided widespread leisure time but has neglected to teach people how to use it wisely, and (4) an affluent civilization that has given the younger generation too much too soon, depriving them of the experience of anticipating and working toward the fulfillment of their own wants and needs.

But regardless of its *etiology*, or causes, boredom has become a major problem for many of today's adolescents, as well as for many adults. Often possessed of too much free time or a feeling that they are not really an integral part of today's society and are not recognized or accepted, both young and old have turned to criminal and delinquent behavior, excessive alcohol consumption, or drug abuse (which we will discuss in more detail in Chapters 8 and 9).

Although often used interchangeably with boredom, *apathy* is slightly different. Whereas boredom is a condition of wandering attention and impaired working efficiency, which simulates a type of fatigue, apathy is an apparent absence of feeling or emotion or an attitude of indifference, which may or may not exist in boredom (Drever, 1952). Boredom and apathy affect those from all socioeconomic classes (Blaine, 1966). They often serve as masks for the anger and resentment experienced by many youths in their striving for status in the community, where they are often shunted aside and regarded as second-class citizens (Brown, 1968).

The development of love and affection

Genuine love, which is significant in the life of any individual, is of very great importance in the emotional development of the adolescent. Unfortunately, many youths, as well as many adults, tend to confuse love and sex and regard them as synonymous. The consequence is often impulsive sexual relationships or a hasty marriage based on biochemical attraction rather than genuine love. Another erroneous assumption is that love is one distinct emotion. Genuine love comprises many emotions that can occur between individuals of the same or opposite sex, of similar or widely different ages, with or without erotic overtones.

Green (1970) has suggested that an individual must go through four rather broad stages in order to achieve the mature affectional relationship called love. During the first stage in infancy, children must learn to love themselves, a situation that is possible only when they receive adequate love from the significant others in their lives —that is, those within the family circle. This stage continues into childhood, when children begin to move from their initial egocentric self-love to a degree of compassion and fondness for others. The second stage, characterized by the development of an affinity for and a love of a peer of the same sex, should occur in early adolescence. During this time two young people can become quite inseparable, confiding their innermost thoughts and feelings to each other and reflecting the beginning of a sense of trust in others. This stage lays the foundation for later heterosexual intimacy. The third stage, which occurs in middle and late adolescence, is marked by the emergence of an affinity and a love for a member of the opposite sex. This is a relationship in which the two people gradually begin to entrust themselves to each other and strive for a comfortable heterosexual relationship. The final stage occurs only with true maturity. According to Erich Fromm (1955), it is the stage in development ". . . in which man relates to man lovingly" (p. 362) or, in other words, develops an affinity for and a love of all mankind.

A major task of adolescence is that of learning to distinguish between normal falling-in-love, which is characterized by mutual feelings, tenderness, idealization, and enhanced physical and psychological functioning, and infatuation, typified by obsession, ambivalence, impaired ego functioning, and acting-out behavior (Christie, 1972). It is true that normal love may occur suddenly and be marked by a tendency to overvalue or idealize the loved one, as well as by some evidence of regression to the parent/child pattern of tenderness and caring. Perhaps of greater significance is the fact that the

> Genital sexual drive can be strong but there is far from being any constant relationship between falling-in-love and genital sexuality. An exciting romance may be accompanied by no great sexual arousal, while intense sexual desire may sometimes be felt for a person who is hardly known or even actually disliked. However, the intensity of romantic love feelings does increase in the presence of an external barrier or internal barrier to gratification of genital sexual drive and clearly decreases in response to genital gratification [Christie, 1972, p. 245].

This statement provides a very plausible explanation for the present decline in the aura of romance surrounding so many heterosexual relationships, which find relatively few barriers to the expression of the genital sexual drive.

It is understandable that adolescents are prone to infatuations or intense crushes. After all, young people are trying to wean themselves from their dependent love for their parents while still living under the family roof. Crushes on teachers, for example, often serve to bridge the gap between dependence on parents and dependence on peers.

Far too many individuals continue to show patterns of short-lived infatuations, however, and they may never achieve a mature love. Adolescents, like their elders, will at times suffer rebuff, ridicule, and even abuse in their interpersonal relationships, and, because of these adverse experiences, they may develop a distrust and cynicism in their relationships with others. Often lacking faith in themselves, they may come to believe that others will not give them total affection without some string attached (Green, 1970). As a consequence, many young people are reluctant to display any genuine, overt affection—a tendency that may continue throughout their lives. Others may well overcome this barrier in due time through the process of trial and error and the acquisition of wisdom gained through a wide variety of interpersonal relationships.

Chapter summary

The intense, frequently uninhibited, rapidly fluctuating emotionality of those in early adolescence is often a source of considerable difficulty and misunderstanding for parents and teachers. Explanations of this erratic, unpredictable behavior include: (1) the swift biological changes occurring during the early adolescent period, (2) the conflict between the desire to become independent and the desire to remain dependent, (3) the search for identity, especially during late adolescence, and (4) the possibility that cognitive changes during late adolescence facilitate certain variations in emotional expression.

Among other aspects of emotional development at this stage of life are a propensity for egocentric behavior, a high degree of self-consciousness, a strong desire to improve oneself in order to enhance the self-image and attain greater self-confidence, and a definite emphasis on a philosophy of idealism. But as in people of all ages —although perhaps differing in underlying causes or etiology—the defense mechanisms of adolescents, including those of fantasy, rationalization, intellectualization, reaction formation, projection, and displacement, serve to protect them from the fears, anxieties, and guilt so prevalent during this period.

Adolescence is also a time of life characterized by the growth and development of genuine love and affection in the individual, a process normally beginning in infancy and continuing through maturity. One of the greatest problems confronting the young person is that of learning to distinguish among the biochemical phenomenon of sex, the experience of infatuation, and the genuine reality of love.

Thought provokers

1. What is your interpretation of the statement "Don't laugh at a youth for his affectations; he's only trying on one face after another till he finds his own"?
2. What are some of the factors contributing to the intensity of adolescent emotionality? Did you have wide mood swings during your early adolescence? How did you feel about these? Did you think you were abnormal?
3. Did you experience much conflict in your need to be independent and your reluctance to give up your dependency on your parents? How did you express this ambivalence?
4. Why does Erikson describe the stage of late adolescence as the period of the identity crisis? Did you experience this problem? Are you perhaps still having some difficulties in resolving this problem?
5. What do you think of the idea of a "psychological moratorium"?
6. What do you think of Elkind's idea of new cognitive structures contributing to the adolescent's experience of new emotional experiences?
7. What factors do you feel substantiate the idea of an adolescent's being egocentric, especially in early adolescence? Or do you disagree with this idea? What arguments support your position?
8. Why do young people tend to be so idealistic? What advantages and disadvantages are there in such idealism?
9. Cite some examples of various defense mechanisms used by adolescents you know.
10. What types of fears are of most concern today to those in middle adolescence? What other kinds of fears are adolescents likely to show?
11. Boredom and apathy among young people have become more prevalent during recent years. What causes might you offer to explain the increase in their incidence?
12. Do you agree with Green that love can exist without erotic urges? Why?

References

Angelino, H., & Shedd, C. Shifts in the content of fears and worries relative to chronological age. *Proceedings from Oklahoma Academy of Science*, 1953, 34, 180–186.

Bardwick, J. M., Douvan, E., Horner, M. S., & Gutmann, D. *Feminine personality and conflict*. Monterey, Calif.: Brooks/Cole, 1970.

Blaine, G. B. Some emotional problems of adolescents. *Medical Clinics of North America*, 1965, *49*, 387–404.

Blaine, G. B. *Youth and the hazards of affluence*. New York: Harper & Row, 1966.

Blos, P. The second individuation process of adolescence. *The Psychoanalytic Study of the Child*, 1967, *22*, 162–186.

Bronson, G. W. Identity diffusion in late adolescents. *Journal of Abnormal and Social Psychology*, 1959, *59*, 414–417.

Brown, W. N. Alienated youth. *Mental Hygiene*, 1968, *52*(3), 330–336.

Christie, G. L. The origins of falling in love and infatuation. *American Journal of Psychotherapy*, 1972, *26*(2), 244–262.

Croake, J. W. Adolescent fears. *Adolescence*, 1967, *2*(8), 459–468.

Croake, J. W., & Knox, F. H. A second look at adolescent fears. *Adolescence*, 1971, *6*(23), 279–284.

Daly, M. J. Physical and psychological development of the adolescent female. *Clinical Obstetrics and Gynecology*, 1966, *9*(3), 711–721.

Donovan, J. M. Identity status: Its relationship to Rorschach performance and to daily life patterns. *Adolescence*, 1975, *10*(37), 29–44.

Douvan, E., & Adelson, J. *The adolescent experience*. New York: Wiley, 1966.

Drever, J. *A dictionary of psychology*. Baltimore: Penguin Books, 1952.

Elkind, D. Egocentrism in adolescence. *Child Development*, 1967, *38*, 1025–1034.

Elkind, D. Cognitive structure and the adolescent experience. *Adolescence*, 1968, *2*(8), 427–434.

Erikson, E. H. The psychosocial development of children. In J. M. Tanner & B. Inhelder (Eds.), *Discussions on child development* (Vol. 3). New York: International Universities Press, 1955. Pp. 168–215.

Erikson, E. H. The problem of ego identity. *Journal of the American Psychoanalytical Association*, 1956, *4*, 56–121.

Erikson, E. H. *Childhood and society* (2nd ed.). New York: W. W. Norton, 1963.

Erikson, E. H. *Identity: Youth and crisis*. New York: W. W. Norton, 1968.

Festinger, L. *Theory of cognitive dissonance*. New York: Harper & Row, 1957.

Fromm, E. *The sane society*. New York: Holt, Rinehart & Winston, 1955.

Galdston, R. Adolescence and the function of self-consciousness. *Mental Hygiene*, 1967, *51*(2), 164–168.

Gallatin, J. E. The development of the concept of rights in adolescence. *Dissertation Abstracts*, 1968, *28*(12-B), 5204.

Gold, M., & Douvan, E. *Adolescent development: Readings in research and theory*. Boston: Allyn & Bacon, 1969.

Green, L. B. *An essay on love: Its character and development*. Unpublished report, University of North Florida, 1970.

Group for the Advancement of Psychiatry. Committee on Adolescence. *Normal Adolescence*. New York: Author. February 1968, *6*(68).

Hornick, E. J. The adolescent crisis today: Emergencies, anxiety, and adolescence. *New York State Journal of Medicine*, 1967, *67*, 1979–1981.

Horrocks, J. E. *The psychology of adolescence* (4th ed.). Boston: Houghton Mifflin, 1976.

Inhelder, B., & Piaget, J. *The growth of logical thinking from childhood through adolescence*. New York: Basic Books, 1958.

Josselyn, I. M. The adolescent today. *Smith College Studies in Social Work*, 1967, *38*(1), 1–15.

Karowe, H. E., & McCandless, F. D. Emotional problems of adolescence. *Postgraduate Medicine*, 1963, *33*, 237–248.

Knight, J. A. Suicide among students. In H. L. P. Resnik (Ed.), *Suicidal behaviors.* Boston: Little, Brown, 1968. Pp. 228–240.

Marcia, J. E. The case history of a construct: Ego identity status. In E. Vinacke (Ed.), *Readings in general psychology.* New York: American Book, 1968. Pp. 325–332.

Masterson, J. F. *The psychiatric dilemma of adolescence.* Boston: Little, Brown, 1967.

Offer, D., & Offer, J. L. Profiles of normal adolescent girls. *Archives of General Psychiatry,* 1968, *19*(5), 513–522.

Personality and growth series for adolescents: An evaluation. *Journal of the National Medical Association,* 1969, *61*(1), 93– 95.

Piaget, J. *The origins of intelligence in children.* New York: W. W. Norton, 1963.

Piotrowski, Z. Treatment of the adolescent: The relative pessimism of psychologists. *American Journal of Orthopsychiatry,* 1962, *32*, 382–387.

Russian, R. B. Idealization during adolescence. *Smith College Studies in Social Work,* 1975, *45*(3), 211–229.

Schonfeld, W. A. The adolescent crisis today: Socioeconomic affluence as a factor. *New York State Journal of Medicine,* 1967, *67*, 1981–1990.

Stamell, B. B. Emotional growth in the adolescent. *Medical Times,* 1964, *92*, 1019–1023.

Webster's New World Dictionary, College Edition. New York: World, 1960.

Adolescent development of morals and other values   7

What is moral is what you feel good after and what is immoral is what you feel bad after.

Ernest Hemingway
"Death in the Afternoon"

Chapter 1 emphasized that one of the major problems of adolescence is the acquisition of a relatively stable set of values by which young people can learn to govern their actions. Today's youths are confronted with so many different values that it is often difficult for them to choose those that will meet their own unique psychological needs and desires and yet enable them to function within the limits set by society. This selection of a suitable set of values, however, is an essential aspect of the adolescent's resolution of the identity crisis (Erikson, 1968), and there is no period of life more critical to values formation than that of adolescence (Konopka, 1973).

In this chapter we will look at some of the various theories of moral development that have evolved over the years. In addition, we will discuss the contributions made by various agencies of society to the acquisition of moral standards and describe those values that seem to be of the greatest concern to today's adolescent.

Theories of moral development

It was John Dewey (1964), the progressive educator, who first introduced the idea that *cognitive development*—that is, the development of the higher mental processes such as reasoning, thinking, and concept formation—lays the foundation for the development of moral values and that moral development occurs in stages that parallel those of cognitive development. He believed the primary purpose of moral education to be the stimulation of active thinking about moral values and of informed decision making. Dewey delineated three levels of moral development: (1) the premoral or preconventional level, wherein moral behavior is motivated primarily by physiological and social impulses, (2) the conventional level of behavior, wherein a person accepts the basic standards of his or her group with little or no critical evaluation, and (3) the autonomous level of moral behavior, wherein the individual's conduct is determined primarily by thinking and judging for himself or herself about whether an act is good or not and wherein the individual accepts the standards of his or her group only after reflective thought.

Jean Piaget, who had long studied cognitive development, began to study it as it related to moral behavior. He endeavored to define stages of moral development through his observations of children playing games governed by rules (Piaget, 1948). His delineation of three stages tended to parallel Dewey's theory. Piaget believed that moral development is an outgrowth of the interaction of cognitive development and social experience and that it progresses through a predetermined sequence. However, his three stages accounted for moral development only up to the age of 12. It failed to account for any further moral development during the adolescent period, except to describe what adolescent behavior should or could be but seldom is.

Lawrence Kohlberg (1958) first hypothesized that, although there are only three basic levels of moral development, each consists of two substages, and that the highest level may be reached only with true moral maturity, which is often never attained. Table 7-1 describes Kohlberg's theory of moral development.

Table 7-1. Definition of moral stages

I. *Preconventional level*

At this level, the child is responsive to cultural rules and labels of good and bad, right and wrong, but interprets these

labels either in terms of the physical or hedonistic consequences of action (punishment, reward, exchange of favors) or
in terms of the physical power of those who enunciate the rules
and labels. The level is divided into the following two stages:

Stage 1: The punishment-and-obedience orientation. The
physical consequences of an action determine its goodness or
badness, regardless of the human meaning or value of these
consequences. Avoidance of punishment and unquestioning
deference to power are valued in their own right, rather than in
terms of respect for an underlying moral order supported by
punishment and authority (the latter being Stage 4).

Stage 2: The instrumental-relativist orientation. Right action consists of that which instrumentally satisfies one's own
needs and occasionally the needs of others. Human relations are
viewed in terms like those of the marketplace. Elements of
fairness, reciprocity, and equal sharing are present, but they are
always interpreted in a physical, pragmatic way. Reciprocity is
a matter of "you scratch my back and I'll scratch yours," not of
loyalty, gratitude, or justice.

II. *Conventional level*

At this level, maintaining the expectations of the individual's
family, group, or nation is perceived as valuable in its own
right, regardless of immediate and obvious consequences.
The attitude is one not only of *conformity* to personal expectations and social order, but also of loyalty to it, of actively
maintaining, supporting, and justifying the order, and of identifying with the persons or groups involved in it. At this level,
there are the following two stages:

*Stage 3: The interpersonal concordance of "good boy/nice
girl" orientation.* Good behavior is that which pleases or helps
others and is approved by them. There is much conformity to
stereotypical images of what is majority or "natural" behavior.
Behavior is frequently judged by intention—"he means well"
becomes important for the first time. One earns approval by
being "nice."

Stage 4: The "law and order" orientation. The orientation is
toward authority, fixed rules, and the maintenance of the social
order. Right behavior consists of doing one's duty, showing
respect for authority, and maintaining the given social order for
its own sake.

III.   Postconventional, autonomous, or principled level

At this level, there is a clear effort to define moral values and principles that have validity and application apart from the authority of the groups or persons holding these principles and apart from the individual's own identification with these groups. This level also has two stages:

Stage 5:   The social-contract, legalistic orientation, generally with utilitarian overtones. Right action tends to be defined in terms of general individual rights and standards that have been critically examined and agreed upon by the whole society. There is a clear awareness of the relativism of personal values and opinions and a corresponding emphasis upon procedural rules for reaching consensus. Aside from what is constitutionally and democratically agreed upon, the right is a matter of personal "values" and "opinion." The result is an emphasis upon the "legal point of view," but with an emphasis upon the possibility of changing law in terms of rational considerations and social utility (rather than freezing it in terms of Stage 4 "law and order"). Outside the legal realm, free agreement and contract is the binding element of obligation. This is the "official" morality of the U. S. government and Constitution.

Stage 6:   The universal-ethical-principle orientation. Right is defined by the decision of conscience in accord with self-chosen *ethical principles* appealing to logical comprehensiveness, universality, and consistency. These principles are abstract and ethical (the Golden Rule, the categorical imperative); they are not concrete moral rules like the Ten Commandments. At heart, these are universal principles of *justice,* of the *reciprocity* and *equality* of human *rights,* and of respect for the dignity of human beings as *individual persons.*

Adapted from "From Is to Ought: How to Commit the Naturalistic Fallacy and Get Away with It in the Study of Moral Development," by L. Kohlberg. In T. Mischel (Ed.), *Cognitive Development and Epistemology.* Copyright 1971 by Academic Press, Inc. Reprinted by permission.

Kohlberg (1967) conducted a study of a group of 75 American boys over a period of a dozen years. Initially, these youngsters were preadolescent to adolescent, aged 10 to 16. He also observed youths from other cultures—Great Britain, Canada, Taiwan, Mexico, and Turkey—and concluded from these studies that there was a universal sequence in moral development despite a wide variety of differences in social, cultural, and religious factors. These and other factors, however, affected the rate at which different individuals progressed through the sequence of moral development.

The universality of the sequence of moral development was explained by Kohlberg (1967) as the tendency of people as they strive toward moral maturity to place greater emphasis on the value of human life and lesser emphasis on the value of property. Ultimately, they reach the stage at which they may even regard the stealing of property as moral when to do so results in the saving of a life. Social-learning theory has also offered an explanation of moral development (Bandura & Walters, 1963). This theory suggests that conditioning and imitation are the primary forces affecting a youngster's moral behavior—behavior that can occur even in the absence of direct rewards and punishments. However, this approach does not seem to provide an adequate answer to the question of how moral behavior moves from a conventional orientation to a principled orientation —that is, from a level based on the expectations of one's family, peers, or society to a level based on self-chosen ethical principles. It is possible that one explanation for this change lies in the child's development of a more advanced cognitive structure.

What motivates children and adolescents to move on to the next-highest stage in the moral hierarchy? Studies (see Kohlberg, 1967) indicate that youngsters comprehend the stages in the sequence up to the point of their own moral level but not more than one stage beyond that, although they actually prefer the next-highest stage. At the same time, it should be noted that, although they go through the same sequence of moral development, not all individuals at a given age are at the same stage. Socioeconomic class and intelligence both appear to affect the maturity of moral judgment (Kohlberg, 1969); those who are brighter and of a higher social class appear to be more advanced in their moral maturity. In addition, McKinney (1975) observed that those who are motivated by internal, autonomous factors, rather than by pressure from others or from external forces, appear to be more advanced in their moral development. However, this is not inconsistent with the factor of socioeconomic class, for Rotter (1966) noted that the *locus of control* (perceived source of motivation, either inside or outside the person) is more external —that is, more subject to external forces—in lower-class than in middle-class individuals.

Not all investigators agree that social class and locus of control are important determinants in moral development. Arbuthnot (1973), in a study of 85 predominantly lower-middle-class high school juniors and seniors, to whom he administered various intelligence tests, concluded that *how* a person perceives the world is more essential to the development of moral maturity than *what* he or she perceives and that moral judgment is more closely related to such cognitive processes as reasoning and analysis than to such factors as internal/external locus of control.

Some investigators (for example, Peters, 1975) believe that Kohlberg and others have ignored the emotional components, such as guilt and remorse, in their theories of moral development. Other theorists (Maddock, 1972; Konopka, 1973) emphasize that both emotional and intellectual processes are influenced by human interaction. They believe that the formation of values is facilitated when children and adolescents are exposed to a wide variety of value systems and are encouraged to discover them and to question both themselves and others. We agree with these latter theorists and would stress the importance of the adolescent period as a crucial time for such exploration, even if it sometimes results in conflict in the thinking of adolescents or in conflict between them and their parents.

Stages of moral development in the adolescent

At what stage of moral development is the normal adolescent most likely to be? It depends on the theory to which the reader adheres. For example, Peters (1975) believes that few people are likely ever to go beyond Stage 3 (the "good boy/nice girl" orientation) or, possibly, Stage 4 (the "law and order" orientation). Therefore, he tends to stress the importance of external control and reinforcement by society in the individual's development of morality. On the other hand, Konopka (1973) believes that such punishment/reward approaches contradict basic democratic human values and are successful only in closed, authoritarian societies. Turiel (1974) notes that, among late adolescents (high school seniors and college undergraduates), many youths are in a period of transition between Stage 4 (law and order) and Stage 5 (social-contract orientation). Such young people who may appear to be regressing to Level II (the conventional level) in their moral development, are actually experiencing great conflict over the inconsistencies between conventionality and morality and between self-directed and other-controlled morality. This transition may reflect a period in adolescence when a youth has greater autonomy and exposure to a wider diversity of values, which provides the experiences that may cause him or her to begin to question the moral level of Stage 4. Apparently, as they gradually note the inconsistencies and inadequacies of that stage and as they perceive its intolerance for the views and ideas of other cultures and societies, they reject these values and gradually move to the next-higher level.

Agents contributing to moral development in the adolescent

The family

Without a doubt, education for moral development begins in the home. This is apparent from the research reported by Bengtson (1975) in which he demonstrated considerable similarity of values in three generations of the same families. These results were based on a study of 16 values of 2044 subjects ranging in age from 16 to 91: the 516 grandparents had an average age of 67, the 701 parents had an average age of 44, and the 837 grandchildren had an average age of 19. The study disclosed little evidence of a generation gap in moral values. When such gaps did exist, though, the greatest similarities in values were between grandchildren and grandparents, especially in regard to humanism; the middle generation tended to be more materialistic than either of the other two. The importance of the family in the adolescent's moral development is further substantiated by Kohlberg's research (1958), in which it was noted that the arrested moral development of juvenile delinquents could be related to family factors, such as arbitrary, inconsistent, and frustrating child-rearing practices.

How do children and adolescents obtain their initial education in moral judgment and behavior within the family structure? According to Bandura and Walters (1963), it occurs mainly through imitation. Initially, children watch their parents and siblings in certain behaviors and then later may engage in those behaviors themselves. Their decision to imitate the model, however, depends on the rewards or punishments the model received for the behavior and on the children's perception of what kind of individual the model is.

Another familial factor affecting the development of moral behavior is the type of discipline administered by the parents. When discipline is power oriented and parents use force in handling their offspring, they are serving as models of aggression for their children. The fact that lower-class parents tend to resort to more power-oriented controls then other parents do may help to explain the lag in moral development seen among many lower-class adolescents. Hoffman and Saltzstein (1967) have suggested that *induction*, one type of love-oriented discipline, wherein the parents point out to the child the serious consequences of the young person's behavior for the parents or for others, may be the most effective type of discipline in encouraging moral development. They note that an inductive approach contributes to the development of *empathy*, the capacity for experiencing the feelings or thoughts of another. This empathy, in turn, lays the foundation for emotional and cognitive development, which both seem to be necessary in the development of moral judgment. Induction appears to facilitate the development of guilt over wrongdoing and to encourage internalization of moral judgment. Hoffman and Saltzstein noted that, contrary to popular belief, a second type of love-oriented discipline, love withdrawal, is less effective than induction in the development of guilt and moral judgment.

Socioeconomic class also appears to play a role in moral development and the selection of values. Although both lower-class and middle-class parents stress the importance of honesty, consideration for others, obedience, and dependability, middle-class parents also emphasize the importance of self-direction or autonomy, whereas lower-class parents stress conformity to authority (Kohn, 1969).

Traditionally, the father has been perceived as the parent most responsible for the development of the conscience in the child, a factor essential to the formation of sound moral judgment. Recent research, however, suggests that mothers may be more important to the early development of moral behavior (Holstein, 1972). Paternal factors, such as prolonged absence or indifference, may be of greater importance in the later moral development of the male adolescent (Andry, 1957).

Unfortunately, because of the decline in family cohesiveness, the increasing incidence of broken homes, the high rate of family mobility, and the increasing number of families in which both parents work, the transfer of values from one generation of the family to the next has been considerably weakened. Hence, it is becoming more and more necessary to turn to other groups and agencies to assist in the teaching of moral and other values to young people.

Religion

Although the role of religion in the teaching of moral behavior is not so great today as it once was, its importance certainly cannot be overlooked even now. Traditionally, however, the church has tended to resort to dogma or doctrine in its moral teachings, which are presented as unquestionable wisdom or principle (such as the idea that individuals should adhere to certain values because "this is the way it has always been done"). Such rigidity is meeting with more and more youthful resistance in this last quarter of the 20th century. It is true that some church leaders are advocating the development of moral autonomy in the individual, but the means of bringing this about within the framework of the church have not as yet been devised (Purpel & Ryan, 1975). Consequently, we continue to witness a steady decline in church attendance and religious affiliation (Gallup Poll Index, 1975), and it becomes apparent that other resources are needed for the teaching of moral values.

The peer group

A third agent for the teaching of moral values is the adolescent's peer group. Douvan and Adelson (1966) have pointed out that the peer group is actually a moralizing, socializing agency in itself. It establishes standards for its members, provides limitations or external controls for their behavior, and expects its members to exercise a degree of self-control. Another investigator (Birnbaum, 1972) notes that acceptance by peers contributes to the adolescent's development of flexible moral independence from adult rule and conversely, that such moral flexibility results in greater peer acceptance. Piaget (1948) observes that the peer group is the most critical determinant in the development of a flexible, autonomous morality.

On the other hand, Bengtson (1975) believes that the family encourages young people to seek peers with similar value orientations. Thus, the peer group tends to reinforce values initially learned in the home as well as encourages further development in values. When the moral standards of a group or individual are noticeably different from those learned in the home, however, adolescents may revert back to the moral values of the family or seek out peers who have similar values.

The school

Because family, church, and peers have so often failed in the teaching of morality, our society has turned to the schools in the hope that they will be able to fill the gap in moral education. Although this may appear to be a recent innovation, educators' efforts to teach moral behavior date back to the time of the ancient Greeks. The 19th-century British philosopher Herbert Spencer asserted that "education has for its object the formation of character," and early in the 20th century John Dewey said that education should be utilized to teach students to think about moral issues and their solutions. At about the same time that Dewey was emphasizing the importance of moral education, however, rapid industrialization and widespread immigration were minimizing the school's former role as a moral teacher (Purpel & Ryan, 1975). The values of the immigrants often conflicted with those taught by the schools, and industrialization brought about such rapid changes that the values maintained by the schools frequently lagged behind those advocated by society. Thus, young people were often torn by the differences in the moral values offered by these various agents. Consequently, moral education declined to the point that, if it was taught in the schools at all, it consisted primarily of the presentation of moral standards. Students were left to make their own decisions about moral issues.

During the past few years, a new concept in the teaching of morals and other values has arisen—that of values clarification. "The process of values clarification involves knowing what one prizes, choosing those things which one cares for most, and weaving those things into the fabric of daily living" (Simon & deSherbinin, 1975, p. 679). This approach to working with people does not involve judging their values. In fact, if youths believe that a teacher or parent is judging them, they may come to reject any ideas or suggestions from that adult. According to values clarification, adolescents have to determine their own values for themselves (Raths, Harmin, & Simon, 1966); that is, they have free choice in their decision making, which involves considering (1) all the alternatives, (2) the reasons for making a particular decision, and (3) the possible consequences of that decision. The process of values clarification involves deciding what one values, publicly affirming one's values, behaving in accordance with what is valued, and repeating this behavior (thereby establishing a pattern) or revising it if necessary.

Simon and deSherbinin (1975) have noted that values clarification can enable youths to determine what is important to them by establishing a set of priorities. By listing values in descending order, beginning with those most significant to them, they can discover those values that are most meaningful for them. Such a process helps young people to become more purposeful individuals and to avoid the all-too-common practice of wasting large segments of time. Knowing their priorities also enables adolescents to become more productive and to achieve a greater sense of accomplishment.

Values clarification helps individuals sharpen their powers of critical thinking so that they are not taken in by the behavior or beliefs of others. For example, the once highly suggestible adolescent who has been well instructed in values clarification will not be so likely to be swayed by the glib peer who suggests that he or she try pot or alcohol "because everyone is doing it and it's the 'in' thing." In addition, Simon and deSherbinin (1975) have observed that values clarification facilitates better interpersonal relationships, because young people who know what they want and what they believe are better able to share and to give warmly of themselves in a relationship.

A number of high schools and colleges are using several different methods to teach values clarification (Simon & deSherbinin, 1975). One method is to teach it as one aspect of English or social studies, perhaps one day each week. Or, values clarification can be offered as an elective course that meets five days a week and that earns course credits. These approaches can use class discussion, individual study, or a combination of the two. In fact, reading can be a primary source for the formation of values, second only to that of experience (Konopka, 1973). It is unfortunate that the written word is not utilized more frequently to impart the values that society deems important to the moral development of the child and adolescent.

A novel approach to the process of values clarification has been the use of peer counseling. Adolescents who have participated in a school values-clarification curriculum are encouraged to share their experiences with their peers. Young people who do not seem to be able to talk about their problems with a regular school counselor or classroom teacher may be able to communicate with their contemporaries or possibly with students a year or two older who have been trained as peer counselors. Such counseling is often done on an informal basis through rap sessions between classes, at lunch, or after school. Generally, peer counselors offer their help only to students who seek assistance and they refrain from making value judgments. An interesting example of the success of peer counseling can be seen in the following case.

> Mark had been a typical adolescent, exploring his vast world and looking for new experiences. He began to experiment with drugs, and, during the summer before his junior year in high school, be became rather heavily involved with the drug scene. His peer-group affiliations began to change, becoming more and more "far out." Early in the fall his school grades began to drop. Mark's mother was reluctant to confront him, but she was very much aware that he was on drugs. One evening in November Mark abruptly confessed to his family that he had been using drugs for about six months but that, through rapping with a couple of his peers, he had begun to realize that his thinking was becoming cloudy and that he wasn't getting anywhere. These peers were able to help Mark clarify his values in regard to drugs and encouraged him to get involved in the peer-counseling program at their high school.
>
> As a result of their help, Mark joined the program, even admitting to the advisory teacher that he had been on drugs. This teacher,

admiring Mark's honesty and sincerity, supported his application to become a member of the peer-counseling team. For the rest of that academic year, Mark served as a peer counselor in his school. His grades began to improve noticeably, and he became a better-adjusted, more satisfied young man. At the end of the school year, Mark was awarded a citation for being the most outstanding of 12 peer counselors.

Values of importance to adolescents

Before going on to discuss the values that are important to today's adolescents, we should define the term *values*. Values are abstract psychological realities; that is, their reality lies within the human mind, not within the physical environment. Values are important because they are the source of our motivation for all our conscious, rational, purposeful behavior (Konopka, 1973).

Perhaps the most important values that have emerged in the past decade have been (1) an increasing respect for the equality of all human beings, regardless of their race, creed, or sex, and (2) a growing awareness of our social responsibilities. The numerous college students who volunteer to tutor culturally deprived children in the public schools with no more compensation than the satisfaction of helping others are excellent examples of young people who act in accordance with their values. Many of these volunteers say that they receive more from the tutoring experience than the children do. They report feeling a deep sense of satisfaction in watching disadvantaged youngsters with low self-concepts gradually begin to show improvement in their schoolwork or in watching children move, in one semester of tutoring, from utter failure to average or even better-than-average classroom performance. In instances in which a child has a parent who is ill or is recently deceased, the college student may become a surrogate parent to the youngster, providing much-needed emotional support during a period of stress.

Another value of considerable importance to the adolescent is that of honesty in interpersonal relationships (Konopka, 1973). This honesty involves an open admission of feelings to oneself and to others—a process that can sometimes prove rather painful. At the same time, there is much contempt for hyprocrisy (Bryan, 1975), which has been defined as "simulation, a feigning to be what one is not, the acting of a false part; a deception as to real character and feeling, especially in regard to morals and religion" (Whitehall, 1950, p. 849). Adolescents are keenly aware of the existence of hypocrisy among their elders, who too often verbalize moral beliefs that they do not follow.

Although adolescents value honesty in personal relationships, however, they do not always value honesty in other areas of their behavior. In a study of cheating at ten universities in the United States in the 1960s, 20% of the students admitted that they cheated regularly and estimated that more than one-third would do so if they were certain that they would not be caught (Becker, 1963). Another study of high school students, which asked "How do you feel about cheating on tests in class?" found that 72% of the students believed that cheating was wrong and never justifiable, whereas 22% stated that cheating was sometimes justifiable and 4% observed that it did no harm and was often justifiable.

In his studies of cheating, Kohlberg (1969) noted that convention-oriented youths regard cheating as bad but are likely to engage in such behavior when they are tempted, when authoritarian figures show indifference, and when others are engaged in cheating. On the other hand, a principle-oriented youth, who regards cheating as the breaking of an implicit contract with an adult, regardless of the social expectations involved, will be far less likely to take advantage of an opportunity to cheat. In a study of a college group, Kohlberg (1969) found that only 11% of the principle-oriented students cheated, whereas 42% of the convention-oriented subjects did.

Becker (1963) has also suggested that the reasons for cheating differ for college students and high school students. Becker asserts that college students cheat because of the need for social success, fear of failure, emphasis on grades instead of character, and stress on obtaining a degree rather than an education. High school students, on the other hand, are more likely to cheat when they are of average or low-average ability and are forced by parental pressure to take a college-preparatory curriculum or when they are motivated by a strong desire to gain parental approval and avoid parental punishment.

Even when students are aware that others are cheating, they are reluctant to report this behavior. They are fearful that they will be ostracized by their peers and often are not entirely convinced that classroom cheating is dishonest. Such ambivalence reflects the conflict in values with which most of us are confronted throughout life and that seems to be repeated in each new generation.

Adolescents also value active involvement in decision making (Konopka, 1973), especially in matters that will ultimately affect them. The demands made by college students for the right to participate in college administration during the late 1960s and early 1970s reflected this valuing of involvement.

The pursuit of spiritual values and the rejection of competition and materialism have also been common trends among young people (Konopka, 1973). Although they may not be so involved with the traditional church as adolescents have been in the past, the "Jesus freaks" and the followers of gurus and other spiritual leaders reflect youth's striving for meaning in life through spirituality rather than through materialism. The pursuit of spiritual values, however, is sometimes a temporary course of action; some young people return to a more formalized religion when they marry and begin to raise families of their own. Such a return emphasizes the fact that values tend to change with age and experience and that individuals and groups desire and need this right to change. However, at no other period of life are changes in values likely to be as great as they are during adolescence.

Chapter summary

One of the most important tasks of adolescence is the selection of a suitable set of values, one that is satisfying to the young person and that is acceptable to society. Over the years, a number of theories have been proposed to explain the development of moral behavior. These include the cognitive-development theories of John Dewey, Jean Piaget, and Lawrence Kohlberg, the social-learning theory of Albert Bandura and Richard Walters, and theories that emphasize emotional components, locus of control, and social class as important factors in the acquisition of values.

Social agencies that contribute to moral development in the adolescent include the family, church, peer group, and school. Recently, educators have introduced a new approach to moral education —that of values clarification. One facet of the values-clarification approach has been the trend toward peer counseling.

Values of great importance to today's adolescents include respect for equality, a desire to help others, a preference for honest and open expressions of feelings, a disdain for hypocrisy, the desirability of becoming more involved in decision making that pertains to their well-being, and the rejection of competition and materialism.

Thought provokers

1. Did you, as an adolescent, find it difficult to select moral values that were satisfying to you? When your values conflicted with those of your parents or other respected adults in your life, how did you resolve the conflict?

2. Give an example, preferably from your own experience or from that of someone you know fairly well, illustrating each of Kohlberg's six stages of moral development.
3. What stage of moral development do you think you are in now? Why do you think so?
4. Which theory of moral development do you favor? Why?
5. What psychological factors influenced your moral development? Which socializing agencies do you believe had a role in your development of morality?
6. At what stage of moral development is the normal early adolescent most likely to be? At what stage is the juvenile delinquent most likely to be?
7. What is meant by values clarification? How might you utilize this approach as a classroom teacher?
8. What values do you think are most troublesome to today's adolescents?
9. What can parents do to facilitate the development of socially acceptable and personally satisfying values in their children?

References

Andry, R. G. Faulty paternal—and maternal—child relationships, affection, and delinquency. *British Journal of Delinquency*, 1957, *8*, 34–38.

Arbuthnot, J. Relationships between maturity of moral judgment and measures of cognitive abilities. *Psychological Reports*, 1973, *33*(3), 945–946.

Bandura, A., & Walters, R. H. *Social learning and personality development*. New York: Holt, Rinehart & Winston, 1963.

Becker, L. J. The changing moral values of students. *Journal of Home Economics*, 1963, *55*, 646–648.

Bengtson, V. L. Generation and family effects in value socialization. *American Sociological Review*, 1975, *40*(3), 358–371.

Birnbaum, M. P. Anxiety and moral judgment in early adolescence. *Journal of Genetic Psychology*, 1972, *120*(1), 13–26.

Bryan, J. H. You will be well advised to watch what we do instead of what we say. In D. J. DePalma & J. M. Foley (Eds.), *Moral development: Current theory and research*. Hillsdale, N. J.: Lawrence Erlbaum, 1975. Pp. 95–111.

Dewey, J. What psychology can do for the teacher. In R. Archambault (Ed.), *John Dewey on education: Selected writings*. New York: Random House, 1964.

Douvan, E., & Adelson, J. *The adolescent experience*. New York: Wiley, 1966.

Erikson, E. *Identity: Youth and crisis*. New York: W. W. Norton, 1968.

Gallup Poll Index. *Religion in America*. Report No. 114. Princeton, N. J.: Gallup Organization, 1975. Pp. 1–5.

Hoffman, M. L., & Saltzstein, H. D. Parent discipline and the child's moral development. *Journal of Personality and Social Psychology*, 1967, *5*(1), 45–57.

Holstein, C. E. The relation of the child's moral judgment to that of the parents and to communication patterns in the family. In R. C. Smart & M. S. Smart (Eds.), *Readings in child development and relationships*. New York: Macmillan, 1972.

Kohlberg, L. *The development of modes of moral thinking and choice in the years ten to sixteen.* Unpublished doctoral dissertation, University of Chicago, 1958.

Kohlberg, L. The child as a moral philosopher. In *Readings in Psychology Today.* Del Mar, Calif.: CMR Books, 1967. Pp. 180–186.

Kohlberg, L. Stage and sequence: The cognitive-developmental approach to socialization. In D. A. Goslin (Ed.), *Handbook of socialization theory and research.* Chicago: Rand McNally, 1969. Pp. 347–480.

Kohlberg, L. The cognitive-developmental approach to moral education. *Phi Delta Kappan,* 1975, *56*(10), 670–677.

Kohn, M. L. *Class and conformity: A study in values.* Homewood, Ill.: Dorsey, 1969.

Konopka, G. Formation of values in the developing person. *American Journal of Orthopsychiatry,* 1973, *43*(1), 86–96.

Maddock, J. W. Morality and individual development: A basis for value education. *Family Coordinator,* 1972, *21*(3), 291–396.

McKinney, J. P. The development of values: A perceptual interpretation. *Journal of Personality and Social Psychology,* 1975, *31*(5), 801–807.

Peters, R. S. A reply to Kohlberg. *Phi Delta Kappan,* 1975, *56*(10), 678.

Piaget, J. *The moral judgment of the child* (2nd ed.). Glencoe, Ill.: Free Press, 1948. (Originally published, 1932.)

Purpel, D., & Ryan, K. Moral education: Where sages fear to tread. *Phi Delta Kappan,* 1975, *56*(10), 659–662.

Raths, L. E., Harmin, M., & Simon, S. B. *Values and teaching: Working with values in the classroom.* Columbus, Ohio: Merrill, 1966.

Rotter, J. Generalized expectancies for internal versus external control of reinforcement. *Psychological Monographs,* 1966, *80*(1, Whole No. 609).

Simon, S. B., & deSherbinin, P. Values clarification: It can start gently and grow deeply. *Phi Delta Kappan,* 1975, *56*(10), 679–683.

Turiel, E. Conflict and transition in adolescent moral development. *Child Development,* 1974, *45*(1), 14–29.

Whitehall, H. (Ed.). *Webster's new 20th century dictionary of the English language.* New York: World, 1950.

Delinquent behavior 8

Of all the adult male criminals in London, not two in a hundred have entered upon a course of crime who have lived an honest life up to the age of twenty . . . . Almost all who enter on a course of crime do so between the ages of eight and sixteen.

Sir Anthony Ashley Cooper Shaftesbury
(1671–1713)

Many young people find it difficult to cope with the demands of the adolescent period in an emotionally satisfying yet socially acceptable manner. Each year thousands of these youths become alienated from the adult world: they turn to delinquency, drug abuse, suicide, runaway behavior, or teenage marriages, all of which can serve as means of escape from a society that too often has failed to accord its adolescents adequate status and a sense of their individual worth. Especially since World War II, the incidence of such behaviors has been mounting, perhaps reflecting our increasing industrialization, technological advancements, and urbanization, as well as the numerous changes in family structure and function. In addition, we

191

have been made more aware of the extent of such problems through the mass media. In this chapter, we will consider the increasing problem of juvenile delinquency: its prevalence, its degrees and types, its various causes, the means of predicting and preventing it, and a few of the recent innovations in its treatment. (The topics of drug abuse, suicide, runaway behavior, and teenage marriage and divorce will be discussed in Chapter 9.)

The term *juvenile delinquent* is very broad and difficult to define. Depending on state and local laws, the dividing line between juvenile delinquents and adult criminals varies between 16 and 21 years of age, although in most jurisdictions it is 18. The term includes those committing offenses that would be considered criminal if performed by an individual legally classified as an adult, as well as those committing *status offenses*. "A status offense is a noncriminal act that subjects the child to the jurisdiction of the juvenile court not because of the act itself—it would not be considered a crime if it were committed by an adult—but because of his status: he is a juvenile" (Gilman, 1976, p. 49). These include violations of curfew regulations, school-attendance laws, and restrictions on the use of alcohol and tobacco, as well as uncontrollable, ungovernable, incorrigible, or runaway behavior and sexual misbehavior for girls (President's Commission on Law Enforcement and Administration of Justice, 1967[1]). In most jurisdictions, almost one-half of the caseload of the juvenile courts traditionally has consisted of status offenses, for which juveniles are often confined for longer periods of time than for felonies (Gilman, 1976).

Fortunately, this practice is changing. Federal legislation passed in the mid-seventies is presently requiring that states begin to pass their own laws to get status offenders out of the juvenile-justice system and to encourage the utilization of psychotherapeutic approaches instead of detention or incarceration. However, some experts on juvenile delinquency question the wisdom of these changes. They believe that many present status offenders will eventually commit criminal acts whether they receive therapeutic intervention or not (Tillie, 1977).

Juvenile delinquency is not a new phenomenon. Research indicates that the juvenile offender has existed in the United States, Canada, and other Western countries for more than half a century. The term *juvenile delinquent* was first used in the low courts in 1899, the year that the first juvenile court was established in the United States.

[1]All subsequent references to this source will be cited as "President's Commission, 1967."

Prior to that date, most behavior now categorized as a status offense was regarded as a family problem, and youths violating criminal law, regardless of their age, were treated as adult criminals (Haskell & Yablonsky, 1974). For many years, delinquency was believed to be confined mainly to the lower socioeconomic classes. For example, although almost everyone felt the impact of the depression in the 1930s, the brunt of this economic disaster was borne by the lower classes. Unemployment in the slum areas had always been high, but it became so widespread there that the majority of household heads ultimately lost their jobs—a trend that was accompanied by a mounting problem of juvenile delinquency in these areas (Tappan, 1949).

Recent investigations, however, suggest that only a very small percentage of juvenile delinquents are ever apprehended (Gold, 1970). Juveniles from more economically secure, middle-class homes are less frequently detected, and, when they are apprehended, they are less likely to be brought to the attention of any public or private agency (Haskell & Yablonsky, 1974). For example, their parents may privately settle the costs of damages wrought by vandalism or other destructive behavior. Similarly, rural offenders are less likely than urban offenders to be arrested, because there is a shortage of courts and of legal authorities in rural areas (Robinson, 1960). Because only a fraction of those engaging in delinquent behavior are ultimately taken into custody, we must be cautious in our interpretation of all statistics dealing with the prevalence, differing degrees, and various types of juvenile delinquency.

The prevalence of delinquent behavior

Juvenile delinquency has become one of the primary domestic problems in the United States and Canada today. In 1965, 697,000 delinquency cases were handled by juvenile courts in the United States (Schafer & Polk, 1967). Since that time, the increase in the incidence of delinquency has far exceeded the rise in population within this age group. In 1971, the total number of youths reaching the juvenile courts had risen to 1,125,000 (Juvenile Court Statistics, 1972). Between 1960 and 1972, according to the Uniform Crime Reports, arrests for serious offenses, such as criminal homicide, forcible rape, larceny, and auto theft, increased 101% (FBI, 1972).

Studies on file in the Office of Juvenile Delinquency and Youth Development in Washington, D. C., indicate that in inner-city slum areas "up to 70 percent or more of all youths find themselves in trouble with the law at some point in their adolescence" (Burns &

Stern, 1967, p. 362). However, this figure is somewhat misleading. It partially reflects the heavier concentration of police in such areas and the tendency of the police to apprehend lower-class youths for behavior that would be overlooked among middle-class youths. In addition, middle-class parents often exert influence to have charges dropped or to convince the authorities that what appeared to be car theft, for example, was really "joyriding" or the brief "borrowing" of a car. Nevertheless, during any given year about 2% of all individuals between the ages of 10 and 18 are likely to appear in juvenile court, and at least 17% of all 18-year-old boys have been summoned to appear before juvenile court at least one time (Wheeler, Cottrell, & Romasco, 1967).

However, the predominance of male over female delinquents appears to be changing. The number of female-delinquent cases handled by the courts in 1970 was 228,500—more than double the 104,000 cases handled in 1964. The percentage of delinquents who are girls also rose from 19% in the years from 1958 to 1964 to 24% in 1970 (*Juvenile Court Statistics,* 1971). At the same time, it should be pointed out that 70% of the female juvenile delinquents in 1971 were being detained for status offenses, whereas only 23% of the male delinquents were (Wright & James, 1974). Nevertheless, more girls are being arraigned for felonies today than ever before. For example, the total number of arrests for burglary by girls under the age of 18 rose 177.2% between 1960 and 1972 (FBI, 1972).

Although these classifications may vary slightly from state to state, the term *felony* is generally used to describe such serious crimes as murder, robbery, arson, and grand theft. The term *misdemeanor* denotes less serious offenses, such as shoplifting or the theft of money or merchandise valued at less than 50 dollars. Often the severity of the crime is determined by the presiding judge and by the circumstances under which the violation occurred.

Juveniles in the 16- to 17-year-old age group are arrested more frequently than those of any other age (Haskell & Yablonsky, 1974). The explanation for this phenomenon appears to be the fact that most school-attendance laws permit students to drop out of school at age 16—an age for which unemployment rates tend to be very high. Unable to earn money to purchase the material items that they seek and bored because of the lack of meaningful activity in their lives, many of these youths turn to crime (Fleisher, 1966).

These figures, however, may be not only disturbing but also prophetic. A study by Glueck and Glueck (1968) disclosed that, of 438 youths originally judged delinquent in the 1940s, more than 80% had subsequent criminal arrests between the ages of 17 and 25.

Categories of delinquent acts

The use of the term *juvenile delinquency* has recently been questioned, because it attempts to encompass a wide variety of behaviors in a single category. Almost all individuals break the law at some time during their lives, but there are wide variations in the frequency and seriousness of these violations (Horrocks, 1969; Gold, 1970). Only a small number of these infractions are likely to be legally recorded as delinquent acts.

One approach to the classification of juvenile misconduct has been mentioned already: delinquent acts are divided into status offenses and offenses that would be considered misdemeanors or felonies if committed by adults. Some authorities, such as the Board of Directors of the National Council on Crime and Delinquency, believe that status offenses should be removed from the jurisdiction of the juvenile courts, because court punishment is often unjust and too severe for the acts committed. Others (for example, Martin & Snyder, 1976) disagree; they believe that removal of such offenses from the juvenile-court jurisdiction would result in a reduction in services (such as referral to mental-health centers, social workers, and so on) to families of disturbed juveniles and that, on the contrary, there is a real need "for more facilities and programs to provide the court with a set of realistic alternatives at the dispositional stage" (p. 44). Martin and Snyder further note that status offenders have the highest rate of parole revocation, indicating that this group is more difficult to help than other categories of delinquents. We, on the other hand, believe that, although juvenile courts might well need to continue to intervene in some cases, referring to status offenders as juvenile delinquents often only adds one more burden to the troubled adolescent, who may simply be seeking escape from an intolerable family situation (for example, by running away). What is more often needed under such circumstances is intervention through family counseling or placement in a suitable foster home, rather than referral to a juvenile detention center.

Another method for classifying delinquents is that of Guttmacher (1958), who developed the following five categories: (1) *Normal delinquents* (75–80% of all delinquents) are antisocial adolescents who identify with asocial segments of society, such as the delinquent gang, and usually have parents who are morally and socially defective. (2) *Accidental or occasional delinquents* (a very small group) are the young people who have healthy consciences but are overwhelmed by circumstances with which they feel inadequate to cope. (3) *Organically or constitutionally predisposed delinquents* (very few in number) are a diverse group composed of a number of subgroups, such as the mentally retarded, the epileptic, and the post-encephalitic. (4) *Psychopathic or sociopathic delinquents* (10–15% of all delinquents) are not psychotic but engage in irrational antisocial behavior; they are complex individuals, difficult to handle and not likely to be responsive to therapy, punishment, or incarceration. (5) *Psychotic delinquents* are youths whose criminal behavior is symptomatic of their psychosis; they suffer from one of the major mental disorders.

Another distinction in delinquent behavior has been found in the different categories of misbehavior most frequently committed by girls and by boys. For example, girls are more likely to be apprehended for sexual offenses than for any other delinquent acts, although, as noted earlier, they are engaging in other antisocial behavior more extensively today than ever before. Nevertheless, in many instances they are initially brought to the attention of legal authorities because of venereal infection or nonmarital pregnancy. Boys, on the other hand, are seldom arrested for sexual misconduct, unless a complaint of rape is filed by a girl's family (Reiss, 1969). Actually, however, of those adolescent boys and girls arrested for stealing, most have also violated sexual-conduct norms, and, conversely, those apprehended for sexual offenses generally have a background of other law-breaking activities.

There are three types of delinquent behavior with which school administrators and teachers come in especially close contact: truancy, vandalism, and violence. We will discuss each of these in some detail.

Truancy

Generally the school's closest contact with delinquency is through the act of truancy, or unlawful absence from school. While engaged in truant behavior, a young person often participates in other illegal activities as well, such as vandalism and theft. However, it should be noted that, although truancy is a violation of school regulations and legal norms, it may also be symptomatic of certain normal behavior patterns. According to Kvaraceus (1966),

> truancy may be: a healthy rebellion of a normal adolescent who is willing to pay the price for this once-in-a-lifetime indiscretion; a representation of demand behavior of gang members who hold the school in low esteem; a brief emotional recess period from a confusing and unfriendly classroom climate; an indication of a serious conflict with parents who pressure a child to succeed and who are

attacked by this act; or a symptom of a child's inability to face and cope with the realities of his daily life [p. 59].

When truancy is symptomatic of delinquent behavior, however, the school is often a major contributing factor through (1) its provision of so many frustrating experiences and so few satisfying ones, (2) its inability to recognize and deal with learning disabilities, (3) its failure to maintain student interest, and (4) its failure to provide suitable channels for the release of adolescent energy and tension (Moore, 1964). Indeed, school policy may even encourage truancy: "When students are suspended for truancy or tardiness, the crime and the punishment are identical" (Horn, 1975, p. 83). Although some schools have turned to other forms of discipline, such as "internal suspension," (the practice of suspending a student from classes but requiring him or her to report to school each day to spend the time in the office detention area or with a school counselor) this punishment also fails to solve the problem, because it still removes the student from an academic situation that he or she wanted to escape in the first place.

The most important point to be made about truant behavior, however, is that in the history of the delinquent adolescent there is almost invariably a pattern of repeated truancy. Glueck and Glueck (1950) found in their research that 94.8% of delinquents, in contrast to only 10.8% of nondelinquents, had been involved in truancy at some time during their school careers. Of 474 delinquents who had been truant, two-thirds had been truants persistently and one-third had skipped school occasionally. This same study also noted that a high proportion of these delinquents began to be truants before age 11; the average age for the first act of truancy was 10.

Vandalism

Another category of delinquent acts that is of particular concern to educators is vandalism. School vandalism has increased tremendously in recent decades, and in 1976 it was estimated by the United States Office of Education that the cost of vandalism to public elementary schools and high schools is about 600 million dollars each year ("Terror in Schools," 1976).

Clinard and Wade (1969) defined vandalism as "the deliberate defacement, mutilation, or destruction of private or public property by a juvenile or group of juveniles not having immediate or direct ownership in the property so abused" (p. 257). Vandalism usually does not involve theft and is sometimes referred to as "malicious mischief," "destructiveness," "disorderly conduct," or even "assault." Regardless of its label, however, such destruction of property, which is especially common among adolescent boys, has proved to be more costly to the American public in recent years than the combined cost of all other offenses against property. The seriousness of an act of vandalism is determined by a number of factors, including the relationship of the property owner to the offender, the danger of punishment to the vandal, the possibilities of real injury to the owner, and the type of property involved and its value. Too often, acts of vandalism have been looked upon as youthful pranks, because at one time or another most American males, who generally have had more freedom and less parental supervision than girls, are involved in such activity (Clinard & Wade, 1969). In general, when adolescents engage in vandalism, adults consider the act deliberate and malicious. But vandalism is often the result of a sudden, impulsive, spur-of-the-moment urge that is without malice. And although society may look upon them as vandals, youths engaging in such activity are more likely to regard themselves merely as pranksters, describing their own behavior as mischievous rather than malicious.

What factors underlie the current widespread incidence of vandalism? Clinard and Wade suggested that "property destruction appears to function for the adolescent as a protest against his ill-defined role and ambiguous status in the social structure" (1969, p. 262).

In many instances, vandalism directed against the schools may reflect youths' disenchantment with their educational experiences. Among adolescents of lower socioeconomic status, such acts could also be a form of rebellion against what is regarded as symbolic of the middle-class establishment.

Violence

Closely associated with vandalism, but of a far more serious nature, is the recent upsurge of violence in the schools. This problem is approaching near-epidemic proportions in many metropolitan areas. In fact, some school systems have found it necessary to employ security guards in their schools in order to control student violence.

In investigating the extent of this problem, a United States Senate subcommittee reported that, between 1970 and 1973, school-related crimes had increased as follows: homicide, 18%; rapes and attempted rapes, 40%; assaults on students, 85%; and assaults on teachers, 77%. At the same time, the committee noted that (1) most of these offenses were committed by only about 10% of the student body, (2) this 10% included both girls and boys, and (3) children as young as 8 years old were involved in these crimes ("Terror in Schools," 1976). Although there have been attempts to indicate that a majority of these crimes are committed by males from disadvantaged homes, most such youths do not become involved in school-related violence. The problem of violence in the schools exists in both advantaged and disadvantaged neighborhoods.

In 1975 the Council for Educational Development and Research suggested a number of factors that might be contributing to this unfortunate trend toward school violence ("Terror in Schools," 1976). These included: (1) a strong relationship between early truancy and later vandalism and violence, (2) a prolonged period of adolescence, (3) students' lack of participation in the schools' decisions affecting them, and (4) a lack of parental participation in school affairs (although in some communities, it was noted, parents are not always welcomed when they do attempt to become involved in school matters). Other factors that appear to have had an impact on student violence include the tremendous increase in drug abuse and drug addiction and the prevalence of youth gangs, whether the gang members are enrolled in school or simply idly hanging around the school grounds.

To prevent or reduce the incidence of such vandalism and violence demands the concerted efforts of both educators and society as a whole. A number of suggestions have been made for counteracting these problems, including the recommendation that there be more, and much firmer, discipline in our schools. Students would be expelled for carrying weapons to school, parents would be required to pay for their children's misdeeds, and the hard-core 10% of students responsible for most of the school violence would be placed in special schools ("Terror in Schools," 1976). Also, educators and society need to encourage student and community pride in the schools by making the buildings attractive and by encouraging good, responsible citizenship. Increased use of school facilities outside of school hours could help to reduce vandalism, which occurs primarily at night and on the weekends. And since temptation often provides the motivation for delinquent behavior, school grounds should be kept free of rocks that could be hurled through windows, all rooms should be kept locked when not in use, and keys and school equipment should be carefully inventoried (Irwin, 1976).

Types of delinquents

We have been talking mainly about delinquent acts rather than delinquent youths per se. At this point we should note that the incidence of delinquent behavior varies according to socioeconomic

class and sex and that there are also differences in the types of delinquent acts in which adolescents of different social classes tend
to engage.

The lower-socioeconomic-class delinquent

There is little question that recorded delinquency is more
prevalent in the slums than elsewhere and that slum delinquency is
characterized by an extremely high number of serious offenses (Reiss
& Rhodes, 1961; President's Commission, 1967). The underlying
causes of this prevalence will be discussed shortly under the topic
"Primary Causes of Delinquent Behavior." However, it should be
stressed here that it is not the poverty and deprivation alone that
contribute to the vast number of delinquent offenses among lower-
socioeconomic-class adolescents. As noted earlier, police efforts tend
to be concentrated in slum areas, detection and apprehension of
offenders are greatest in lower-class areas, and the *self-fulfilling
prophecy* is more likely to play a role in the lives of disadvantaged
children. In addition, the school, which is one of the most important
institutions in the lives of adolescents and which provides their major
experiences during this period, too often fails to help youths, especially those from the lower class, achieve the roles they envision for
themselves (Haskell & Yablonsky, 1974). As a consequence, these
youths become frustrated and embittered and seek other means,
perhaps deviant and illegitimate, to achieve roles offering status and
recognition from their peers.

Understandably, the poor in our society frequently resent
the affluent majority. The distinctions between the "haves" and the
"have-nots" have also been magnified by our mass media, which
stimulate the desire among all socioeconomic classes for a life of
luxury (Toby, 1967). Actually, the vast majority of offenses committed
by youths from the lower classes involve crimes against property
rather than crimes against people.

> The preponderance of crimes against property sheds light on the
> tendency of crime rates to rise in the most affluent countries. People
> steal, not because they are starving, but because they are envious, and
> they are more likely to be envious of the possessions of others in
> countries with rising standards of living [Toby, 1967, p. 132].

However, other factors play a role in determining whether
lower-socioeconomic-class youths become delinquents. Living in a
middle-class neighborhood where the crime rate is low rather than in
a crime-ridden slum area and attending a primarily middle-class

school rather than a slum-area school make the lower-class youth less likely to pursue (or get caught at) illegal behavior. Apparently those from the lower class are least likely to become delinquents when they are in the minority.

> What seems more apparent is that the largest proportion of delinquents for any status group (low, middle, or upper-class) comes from the more homogeneous status areas for that group and that the delinquency-life chances for *all* status groups tend to be greatest in the lower status area and in the high delinquency rate areas [Reiss & Rhodes, 1961, p. 729].

Perhaps this tendency can be partly explained by the fact that there are generally fewer desirable models to copy in lower-status neighborhoods.

The affluent delinquent

From 1948 to 1960 the number of juvenile delinquents between the ages of 10 and 17 increased 100%, although the number of young people within this age range in the total population increased only 19% during the same period. These statistics may reflect the rising incidence of delinquency among middle-class adolescents (England, 1969), or they may reflect the fact that, in the past, middle- and upper-class parents shielded their children's delinquent behavior from unfavorable publicity, so that society was simply not aware of its prevalence (Pine, 1966). Delinquent acts of affluent adolescents are less likely to be included in official statistics than the acts of lower-class youths. This is so not only because detection is less common among the affluent but also because, if they are apprehended, their rehabilitation is likely to fall into the hands of psychiatrists, psychologists, guidance clinics, or other private facilities—all of which are beyond the framework of legal institutions.

One of the authors of this text (B. R.) recalls the incident of a middle-class boy and girl, each about 15, who ransacked a summer camp. They did considerable damage to the recreation hall and totally destroyed a piano. Apprehended by the authorities, both young people were released by the juvenile-court judge with the provision that they receive regular psychotherapy at the local mental health treatment center. In this case, as in many others, emphasis on rehabilitation is often a more effective means of combating delinquency than is commitment to a reformatory or inadequate supervision by an overworked probation officer.

A number of other suggestions have been offered to explain the rise in delinquency among the affluent (Pine, 1966). The adolescent period is extended even more for youths in the middle and upper classes than for those in the lower classes. Affluent young people are much more likely to attend college, which often necessitates their remaining economically dependent for an extended period of time and delays their acquisition of an occupational status. This prolonged transitional period may lead them to feel that they are living in an "existential vacuum," in which life lacks purpose and meaning. As a consequence, they may resort to deviant and rebellious behavior in attempts to establish their identities and develop some status.

In addition, the experiences and roles afforded by such institutions as the school sometimes reinforce youthful feelings of inadequacy (for example, by according low status to students, showing lack of trust in them, and so on). Such reinforcement of negative learning is referred to as the "structure of opportunity," a form of social organization that facilitates the learning and carrying out of unacceptable behavior (Cloward & Ohlin, 1960). Among middle-class adolescents this structure appears to revolve around the peer group and youth culture. Vaz (1967) has suggested that middle-class delinquency increases with the amount of time young people spend with their peers; deviant behavior is greatest among those who spend most of their leisure time in such activities as dating, "hanging around," or cruising around with peers in cars. However, Polk (1971) questions this differentiation of middle-class from lower-class delinquency on the basis of peer-group involvement. He points out that, for both groups, delinquent behavior tends to be concentrated among those who do poorly in school and who are thus more likely to become part of an antischool, rebellious peer culture.

Affluent delinquents may also be subject to extreme pressures to achieve by their middle- or upper-class parents. Such pressures can create much anxiety in these adolescents about the discrepancy between their aspirations and their achievements. Delinquent behavior in such cases often serves as a means of calling attention to distress over problems with which the adolescent feels unable to cope. In addition, the middle-class emphasis on the desirability of deferring immediate gratification in favor of long-range goals is losing its importance for many affluent adolescents. Taking its place are impulse buying and long-term credit, which were formerly practiced mainly by the lower socioeconomic classes. Also, lower-class dress, music, fads, and behavior are being adopted by middle-class youths. All of these trends may help to explain why affluent delinquency appears to be on the increase.

Several investigators, however, have suggested other factors as being primarily responsible for the rise in affluent delinquency. For example, Lelyveld (1964), in a *cross-sectional study* of juvenile delinquents from suburban well-to-do or middle-income families in an Ohio and a New York town, concluded that these adolescents had committed crimes because (1) they were bored and (2) they felt that their parents were not concerned about them.

Another study (Tobias, 1969) of 100 delinquents and 100 non-delinquents from middle- and upper-middle-class families in a Midwestern suburban community disclosed that both groups agreed that three factors contribute to delinquent behavior: (1) the influence of friends; (2) boredom, restlessness, and a lack of activity; and (3) a lack of parental guidance or interest. This same study revealed that non-delinquents, as compared to delinquents, tended to participate more frequently with their parents and to have closer relationships with them, were responsible for more household chores, held part-time jobs more often, and had a clearer and more concise image of whom they would emulate as adults. Affluent delinquents, on the other hand, were more preoccupied with money, financial security, and a job, but at the same time they were less certain about their future goals.

Many affluent parents believe they are demonstrating their love, affection, and concern for their children when they provide for all their material needs and desires. Fairfell (1965) observed that delinquency among upper-class suburban boys reflects a tendency of parents to give their children too much freedom and insufficient guidance and attention. Many of these youths commit their infractions against the law in a way that calls attention to their misconduct; one could hypothesize that such behavior is actually a cry for help.

The types of delinquent acts committed by affluent adolescents also differ from those committed by lower-class youths. Often, affluent delinquency revolves around the automobile, which is a status symbol, for them. In fact, Crumbaugh (1968) has stated that

> the automobile is such a constant companion in American culture that it has, in many segments of society, become part of the body-image. Children grow up in such an intimate relationship with the car that it parallels clothes, jewelry, hair style, make-up, and the like as a personal attribute that delineates the individual's status and identity [p. 349].

Consequently, it is not surprising that the car becomes the focal point for considerable adolescent misconduct, especially among the affluent. When affluent delinquents have access to an automobile, they may violate speed limits, drive while under the influence of alcohol and/or other drugs, or drag race with their friends. As a consequence, such adolescents are much more likely to be apprehended for traffic violations than are lower-class youths, who are much less apt to own a car (Reiss & Rhodes, 1961). Youths whose parents have provided them with a car but who have no funds to maintain it may turn to pilfering gasoline, tires, and other articles essential for automobile maintenance. Or, if they do not own a car at all, they may "borrow" one for joyrides, a violation of the law that can fall into the category of a felony (England, 1969; Schepses, 1969).

The female delinquent

Although formerly they engaged primarily in status and sexual offenses, female delinquents are being charged and convicted of more and more crimes similar to those of male delinquents (Kratcoski & Kratcoski, 1975). For example, the number of violent crimes committed by girls under the age of 18 increased 22% between 1970 and 1971.

Konopka (1966) and Kratcoski and Kratcoski (1975) have suggested that five factors contribute to female delinquency: (1) the unique sudden onset of puberty in girls, (2) the complex process involved in the resolution of the female identity crisis (because the female role in our society has always been slightly less rigid than the male role—"girls can be tomboys but boys can't be sissies"), (3) the changing role of the female in our society, (4) the often impersonal attitude of adult authority and the resultant loneliness for many girls, and (5) the high degree of family dissolution and the lack of familial cohesiveness. These factors indicate that the outlook for stabilizing or reducing female delinquency rates is not very bright. In fact, as girls assume more and more roles formerly denied to them, the chances are that the incidence of delinquency among females will continue to rise. A comparison of female and male delinquent behavior in the 1970s can be made from Table 8-1 on pages 206–207.

Primary causes of delinquent behavior

No case of juvenile delinquency is the result of any one factor. Although there are many variables, however, certain contributing causes appear with greater frequency than others. They fall into six general categories: (1) socioeconomic factors, (2) family factors, (3) educational factors, (4) peer-group factors, (5) mass-media factors, and (6) personality factors.

Socioeconomic factors

It is common for poverty to be transmitted from one generation to the next. In fact, among numerous lower-class U. S. families the third successive generation is now receiving welfare benefits. The regulations of the welfare program in the United States often discourage fathers from remaining in the home, and the program has not provided the necessary training, skills, or job opportunities to enable youths to escape from poverty and secure gainful employment with possibilities for advancement (President's Commission, 1967). As a consequence, a general attitude of hopelessness, defeat, and despair tends to pervade lower-class families.

In addition, poverty-stricken neighborhoods are commonly characterized by bars that sell liquor to minors, by extensive gambling, and by organized adult crime. This environment can provide the opportunity for adolescents to learn to emulate antisocial behavior, such as the use or selling of illicit drugs (Leinwand, 1968). The lower-class adolescent, lacking a more exemplary model, may seek out a criminal who is highly regarded in the neighborhood to use as a model of power and affluence (President's Commission, 1967).

Since lower-class parents frequently have only a grammar-school education, they are likely to feel inferior to their offspring who go further in school. As a result, they may be reluctant to discipline their children because they believe that the younger generation knows so much more than they do (Cervantes, 1965).

The family

The family probably has greater impact on the development of delinquency than socioeconomic class does. Although many people believe that a broken or one-parent home is the main familial factor contributing to juvenile delinquency, it is not the only one (Sheppard, 1965; Leinwand, 1968). Although a broken home can result in a disorganized family life marked by a lack of parental supervision, guidance, and control (President's Commission, 1967; Leinwand, 1968), it is perhaps more crucial that a majority of broken homes have a woman as head of the household. This situation can lead to hypermasculine behavior in the male children, especially among lower-class adolescents, for whom there is a demand (by family, culture, and peers) for strong sex-role adherence. When there is no satisfying male figure with whom to identify, boys may develop conflict over their sexual role and an obsessive concern with their masculinity. Their

Table 8-1. Profiles of delinquent behavior in the 1970s

Category			Male	Female
Home Environment	1. Socioeconomic environment:	a. below average	56%	61%
		b. average	35%	31%
		c. above average	9%	8%
	2. Source of family income:	a. all or part from public assistance	35%	44%
		b. self-supporting	65%	56%
	3. Placed in foster homes prior to Youth Authority commitment		15%	44%
Family	1. Parents not living together at time of commitment:	a. due to divorce or separation	14%	13%
			43%	53%
		b. due to death	14%	13%
	2. Parents' education:	a. completed high school (one or both)	37%	39%
		b. neither parent went beyond 8th grade	24%	20%
	3. Father (or father substitute) with no known criminal record		79%	73%
Schooling	1. Attitude toward school:	a. indifferent or negative	67%	76%
		b. positive	33%	24%
	2. Misbehavior record in school:	a. serious misbehavior on more than an occasional basis	53%	67%
		b. no serious misbehavior	13%	7%

3. Last grade in which student was enrolled prior to commitment:		
a. high school level	73%	66%
b. beyond high school	6%	7%
4. Achievement-test level:	8th grade 6th grade	8th grade 7th grade
a. reading comprehension and vocabulary	81%	88%
b. arithmetic	6%	5%

Developmental Behavior

1. IQ level as tested by nonverbal measures	91	92
2. No evidence of serious psychological disorder	76%	54%
3. Friends:		
a. tended toward delinquent orientation	81%	88%
b. mainly nondelinquent	6%	5%

Delinquent Behavior

1. Delinquent contacts prior to commitment by Youth Authority:		
a. three or more	87%	85%
b. none	3%	3%
2. Prior commitments to a juvenile institution:		
a. none	41%	63%
b. one	34%	27%
c. two or more	25%	10%
3. No use of weapons in past or present offenses	58%	83%
4. No alcohol involved in past or present offenses	68%	84%
5. Committed crime without co-offenders	52%	63%
6. Narcotic history:	15%	10%
a. none		
b. used marijuana or dangerous drugs	64%	56%
c. used opiates	21%	34%
7. Median age at time of first delinquent contact	14	14

Compiled by Joan M. Vater from statistics of the California Youth Authority for 1971.

delinquent acts may function as a means of resolving this sex-role conflict (Bacon, Child, & Barry, 1963).

Glueck and Glueck (1950) have reported a higher incidence of delinquency among boys from homes "broken by desertion, separation, divorce, or death of one or both parents, many of the breaches occurring during the early childhood of the boys" (p. 280). The fathers of male delinquents tend to be more irresponsible than the fathers of nondelinquents about both family and work. If they are unemployed, their sons may fail to identify with them (President's Commission, 1967).

In fact, most delinquents do not identify with anyone—a fact that reflects shallow emotional ties to their families and a lack of close relationships with others (Baugh & Carpenter, 1962). One study by Bandura and Walters (1958), for example, noted that antisocial boys experience a lack of paternal affection as well as parental rejection, which prevent identification with parental standards and values. A report by Allen and Sandhu (1967) of 179 institutionalized delinquents and 178 nondelinquents disclosed that low family affect (little display of affection) was characteristically reported by the delinquents.

Family psychopathology among delinquent youths is also a fairly frequent pattern. A study by Lewis, Balla, Shanok, and Snell (1976) revealed that, in many instances, delinquent behavior and parental criminality are manifestations of the entire family's underlying problem in social adaptation. They noted the prevalence of psychiatric treatment among parents of delinquents and the positive relationship between a parent's history of psychiatric care and that parent's criminal behavior. The researchers suggest that delinquent behavior reflects a failure by the parents to provide adequate socialization and supervision, because of the parents' own psychiatric problems. This failure results in the children's greater vulnerability to stress and in an inability to cope with the stress because of their unsupportive families. In many cases, then, delinquency may be symptomatic of a disturbed family, just as emotional disorders among children and adolescents frequently are.

Family structure and cultural patterns are also of extreme importance in the development of delinquent behavior. Slocum and Stone (1963) conducted a self-report study of adolescents who had engaged in delinquent behavior but had not been formally adjudged delinquents. Their results disclosed that: (1) adolescents from democratic and cooperative families are less likely to become delinquent and are more prone to conformity, (2) those who regard their parents' discipline as fair are less likely to become delinquents, and

(3) students from unaffectionate families are more likely to become delinquent and less likely to conform.

Often parents, both in the suburbs and in the slums, label their children early in their lives as "wicked," "troublemakers," or "bound to turn out bad." Such parental attitudes toward offspring contribute to the development of similar attitudes and perceptions in the children themselves. A child who has been labeled a troublemaker may begin to act accordingly (Senay, Nihira, & Yusin, 1976). This is known as the *self-fulfilling prophecy* and is especially likely to occur in the slums, where professional counseling and guidance are usually unavailable (President's Commission, 1967). At the same time, these youths who have such low self-concepts understandably perceive themselves as being unloved and misunderstood.

An interesting phenomenon that may well be a factor contributing to delinquency is the "faint smile syndrome." This is a form of nonverbal communication by parents that can betray unconscious approval of a consciously condemned act. Concerned parents who consciously attempt to prohibit certain behavior in their offspring may actually vicariously enjoy their children's misconduct. They may reveal this underlying approval in many ways, including through their facial expressions (Leland, 1961).

Delinquency and the schools

In recent years there has been increasing evidence of a high correlation between academic failure of adolescents and the prevalence of delinquency. For example, one study (Polk & Richmond, 1966) disclosed that among "blue-collar" boys, or those of the lower-middle and lower classes, the rate of delinquency was almost seven times as high for those who failed in school as for those who did not fail.

For children who have not received adequate supervision at home, the teacher represents their first encounter with authority. Having been previously left to their own devices, these youths may rebel against this new authority. The ways in which the school authorities and classroom teachers react to such rebellious behavior may well determine whether or not such children will turn to delinquency.

Teachers who adopt a firm but positive attitude based on an understanding of the factors causing the rebellion can encourage such students to learn. Other instructors, however, who choose to ignore the disruptive child because of fear and/or in an attempt to avoid open conflict, are unlikely to elicit the child's trust or intellectual curiosity. Furthermore, teachers who regard any infractions of their rules as an affront to their position, who label as misbehavior any violations of their often rigid regulations, and who quickly classify certain youths as troublemakers are likely to reinforce the tendency of these young people to rebel against the school and its authority. A vicious cycle ensues, and it becomes increasingly difficult to modify the behavior of these students. They find a way of gaining recognition through their unacceptable, disturbing behavior, and, since it is the attention and notice that they crave, they continue to engage in such behavior until ultimately they become the delinquents that the schools have claimed them to be all along (President's Commission, 1967).

In other cases, teachers and school administrators label certain students as rebellious or deviant because of their friends, appearance, or reputation, rather than because of their actual behavior. Once again the self-fulfilling prophecy takes hold, and such students begin to see themselves as deviant and to imitate the behavior of others similarly labeled (Schafer & Polk, 1967).

Nor can one overlook the impact of the conscious or unconscious negative attitudes of many classroom teachers toward their Black, Spanish-American, or other minority-group students. Although they may be unaware of it, educators often unknowingly demonstrate considerable intolerance and lack of understanding of those from non-Anglo-Saxon backgrounds. Many educators, reared in middle-class environments with middle-class values, find it difficult or almost impossible to accept youths who are reared with different values. Not surprisingly, young people from minority groups may fail to develop a healthy, positive self-concept, and rebellious behavior becomes their only means of releasing the tensions that arise from the many frustrations, conflicts, and pressures with which they are confronted each school day.

School buildings in the inner cities are often deteriorating and poorly equipped. Inadequate facilities and teaching resources, a limited number of textbooks and library books, inexperienced and incompetent teachers, overcrowded classrooms, and racial and economic segregation all contribute to the poor, and often short-lived education of so many lower-class adolescents (President's Commission, 1967).

But perhaps a more serious disadvantage in such schools is their failure to provide supervised study and recreational facilities after school hours. Many youths in the slums come from homes in which there are no books or other learning tools, no educated parents to give them assistance, and no quiet places to study, and their playgrounds are likely to be the streets of the city or the corner pool hall.

Too often, schools also fail to recognize the presence of *learning disabilities* in their students (a topic to be discussed in more detail in Chapter 10). In fact, Poremba (1967) estimated that one-half of the delinquents referred to the juvenile courts exhibit a specific learning disability. Miller and Windhauser (1971) cite four studies that disclose a significant positive relationship between reading disability and delinquency. They suggest that a high-risk student (one who has a family and socioeconomic background typical of many delinquents) who cannot attain success in reading becomes frustrated and may then become a truant, later a school dropout, and ultimately a delinquent. Dayan (1975) believes that the school, in its failure to discover and deal with youths who have learning disabilities, breaks the close attachment that most children and adolescents feel for their schools, thereby crushing their aspirations for achievement. To compound the problem, alienation from the school is likely to cause such young people to seek friends who have also been "turned off" by education and to resort to acting-out behavior to relieve the anxiety brought about by a threatening classroom situation.

In summary, the following educational factors appear to be primary contributors to delinquency: (1) the cumulative effects of academic failure combined with a thirst for success and no satisfying means of attaining it, (2) an education perceived as having no relevance to later life, (3) a lack of commitment to the accepted values of both the community and the school, and (4) teachers' and administrators' ineffective management of and lack of understanding and tolerance of students who frequently resort to misconduct in school (Schafer & Polk, 1967).

The gang and delinquency

Not all gangs are necessarily delinquent gangs. According to Haskell and Yablonsky (1974), there are actually three categories of gangs; the social gang, the delinquent gang, and the violent gang. The social gang engages in activities of a socially constructive nature. Youths join together in a relatively permanent group, whose functions mainly revolve around social activities such as athletics, dances, and other socially approved behaviors. The delinquent gang is characterized by delinquent behaviors, such as theft or assault, that are undertaken primarily for material gain. The violent gang is one that engages in extreme violent behavior, such as homicide, to gain prestige and to obtain emotional gratification. It is this third group that is most likely to become involved in purposeless, senseless gang warfare.

After a close study of 1313 gangs in Chicago in 1926, Thrasher (1963) defined a gang as a group forming spontaneously and having no special attachment to any existing segment of society. Such gangs tend to consist of boys, usually from the same neighborhood and the same ethnic group, in the age range from 11 to 25. The gang structure generally involves a core group of members that often contains the leader or leadership clique and a fringe group of followers (Cartwright, 1975). The delinquent and violent gangs are of particular concern to those working with adolescents, because an estimated 60% to 90% of all delinquent acts occur in the company of others (President's Commission, 1967). At the same time, it should be noted that gang activity does not necessarily always involve all members. Often, small cliques of two or three gang members will engage in delinquent behavior without involving the rest of the group (Cartwright, Tomson, & Schwartz, 1975).

Membership in a delinquent or violent gang appears to be "a result of ineffective family supervision, the breakdown of parental authority and the hostility of the child toward the parents; in short . . . the delinquent gang recruits members who have already achieved autonomy" (Cohen, 1955, p. 31). Such delinquent subcultures apparently fulfill two essential functions for their members: they provide a sense of belonging and they provide a certain status (Miller, 1958; Cartwright et al., 1975). Belonging may be achieved by youths who demonstrate an awareness of and a desire to adhere to the standards and values established by the gang. Status may be acquired and maintained by those who show that they possess certain traits valued by the gang, such as toughness, smartness, or the ability to dupe others. Although delinquent and violent gangs can be found among middle-class youths, they are most prevalent among lower-class youths, who are much more likely to experience status deprivation because of academic failure, poverty, and inadequate parental support.

The stealing patterns of many gangs support the hypothesis that delinquent behavior is a function of the need to belong and be respected by fellow gang members. In many instances gang members do not particularly need or want the articles they steal; they engage in theft for "kicks." In fact, in certain delinquent subcultures stealing leads to increased social status for the adolescent (Cohen, 1955). Youths shoplift in order to obtain recognition and acceptance by their peers.

An associated characteristic of delinquent-gang behavior is what Cohen (1955) describes as "short-run hedonism." Members act impulsively, doing whatever offers excitement to them at the moment. They strongly reject organized and supervised recreation and much prefer spur-of-the-moment fun, which, even among the most delinquent groups, turns into delinquent behavior only a small percentage of the time (Cartwright, 1975). In fact, delinquent-gang members spend a major portion of their time just hanging around, and it has been estimated that no more than 13% of their delinquent activity involves violence.

Group cohesiveness is important to delinquent gangs. Gang members are encouraged by their peers to resist pressures from any outsiders, including family, school, and other gangs. Often relationships with other delinquent gangs are marked by indifference or hostility (Cohen, 1955). In fact, most gang violence involves rival gangs who engage in gang fights in order to protect or obtain territory or to improve their status (President's Commission, 1967).

Perhaps the most common basis for gang cohesiveness is the gang members' deliberate and extensive repudiation of middle-class values. Because they perceive a certain amount of hypocrisy and phoniness in the older generation (as was pointed out in Chapter 7), gang members consciously pursue goals that are in opposition to adult middle-class values. They refuse to compromise with middle-class morality and want it clearly understood that they conform to no standards but their own. Consequently, they turn more and more to the gang for their values, which in turn leads to greater alienation from adults and to antisocial or delinquent behavior. It has even been suggested that the destruction of property by delinquents is deliberate behavior undertaken as a direct attack on the middle and upper classes. Since property is perceived as the main status symbol for upper socioeconomic groups, gang members attack this most vulnerable point.

However, for most delinquent adolescents, delinquent behavior would probably not be chosen as a way of life if it were not "socially legitimized"—that is, if it were not given a certain degree of respectability, at least within a limited group (Cohen, 1955). According to Reiss and Rhodes (1961), very few delinquents are consciously interested in careers as criminals; they simply conform to peer expectations. Cohen (1955) offers a similar hypothesis: ". . . there is a certain chemistry in the group situation itself, which engenders that which was not there before, . . . group interaction is a sort of catalyst which releases potentialities not otherwise visible" (p. 136).

The mass media and delinquent behavior

A number of behavioral scientists believe that the mass media, especially television, play a role in the development of delinquent behavior. A longitudinal study (Eron, Huesmann, Lefkowitz, & Walder, 1974) of youths in a semirural county in New York State investigated aggression and its causes. This study disclosed a significant positive correlation between aggressive behavior at the age of 8 and at the age of 19. It was found that, whereas TV violence often encourages and reinforces the expression of aggression in boys, such violence may serve girls, who are not trained to express aggression directly, as a positively sanctioned social activity by which they may express their aggressiveness vicariously. However, Eron et al. noted that this difference could change as girls continue to become more assertive. These researchers pointed out that the study finding that was most relevant to the prediction of aggressiveness was the fact that the television-viewing habits of 8-year-old males were the most important influence on their later aggressiveness. They suggested that the violent behavior seen on television served as a model of behavior for these youthful viewers.

Another study by Liebert, Neale, and Davidson (1973) also reported similar findings—that is, that there is a definite relationship between the violence children watch on television and the violence they exhibit in their own behavior. It has also been reported on a number of occasions that adolescents who perpetrate especially violent and unusual crimes admit that they obtained their idea for the crime from television. The fact that lower-class adolescents tend to spend more time than middle-class youths viewing television (Coleman, 1961), and thus have more exposure to this violence, might be one of several factors contributing to the high incidence of violence among youths from deprived environments. In any case, it is apparent that the mass media should not be ruled out as one of the contributing causes of delinquent behavior.

Personality factors and delinquency

The personality traits of juvenile offenders have been studied for years by numerous psychologists. In general, these researchers have concluded that true delinquents—those who repeatedly commit crimes against society—possess certain deviant personality patterns that contribute to (and/or result from) their delinquent behavior.

After administering a series of tests and correlating the results, the California Youth Authority delineated three major "interpersonal maturity levels" among delinquents (Riggs, Underwood, & Warren, 1964). At maturity level 2 (I_2), which is the first level, individuals are described as being impulsive and self-centered. They see others only as people who can serve them in some way. They believe that the world owes them a living, and they are oblivious to the needs of others and to the effects of their behavior on others. At maturity level 3 (I_3)

individuals manipulate their environment and the people in it. They use people to attain their goals, but, in contrast to those at level 2, they are aware that their behavior can have an impact on others. Generally, they conform to the wishes of those in power or maneuver those people in such a way as to obtain what they want. However, they deny experiencing any disturbed feelings over such manipulative behavior or having any strong emotional involvement in their interpersonal relationships. At maturity level 4 (I_4), individuals internalize standards and values by which they judge their own behavior and that of others. They wish to emulate the people they like and may experience guilt when they believe that they are not measuring up to their own internalized standards. In such cases they may feel inadequate and guilt ridden to the point that they develop neurotic symptoms or resort to acting-out behavior. They may identify with delinquent models and internalize delinquent values.

These three levels of interpersonal maturity are further subdivided into the following classifications (Riggs et al., 1964):

Maturity Level	Delinquent Subtypes
I_2	Unsocialized, aggressive
	Unsocialized, passive
I_3	Conformist, immature
	Conformist, cultural
	Manipulator
I_4	Neurotic, acting-out
	Neurotic, anxious
	Cultural identifier
	Situational emotional reaction

All of these levels describe people who are characterized by immature behavior, unsatisfactory interpersonal relationships, and questionable values and morals.

Baugh and Carpenter also agree that delinquents are pathologically disturbed. According to one of their studies (1962), a majority of those boys institutionalized at least twice for delinquent offenses display serious emotional disorders. These disorders apparently result from the early frustrating experiences of a childhood characterized by lack of love, emotional deprivation (due to parents' inability to express emotional warmth), maternal deprivation, and excessive punishment. These boys appeared to be engaging in delinquent behavior in order to master their antisocial, aggressive feelings and thoughts by attributing these feelings to others. This is a defense mechanism known as projection. These delinquent boys lack trust in themselves and therefore project this feeling by believing that others cannot be trusted.

Whereas it is evident that juvenile offenders act out much of their aggression, it seems that they also turn much of their hostility inward, perhaps as an indication of atonement for their guilt and of their need for punishment (Baugh & Carpenter, 1962). Thus, delinquent acts may actually be designed to call attention to one's misbehavior and may reflect an unconscious desire for punishment.

The use of the Rorschach ink-blot test has revealed certain personality traits that distinguish delinquents from nondelinquents (Glueck & Glueck, 1950). For example, delinquents are more socially assertive, defiant, and ambivalent toward authority than nondelinquents. They are also more resentful, hostile, suspicious of other people, and destructive, often to a sadistic extent. In addition, they show greater impulsivity and vivaciousness and decidedly more extroverted behavior.

At the same time, Glueck and Glueck (1950) point out, these delinquents are less concerned about failure and defeat than are nondelinquents. They are less cooperative with and dependent upon other people and display more unconventional ideas, feelings, and behavior than do normal youths. Delinquents are also less self-punitive and demonstrate less self-control than nondelinquents.

Scarpitti (1965) reported that delinquents, regardless of age, race, and school grade level, tend to reject middle-class values and to be aware of their limited access to opportunity. Because of inadequate socialization, juvenile offenders have a poor image of themselves and of others, and it is their low self-concept that appears to be the crucial factor differentiating these youths from nondelinquent middle-class and lower-class youths. Apparently, a favorable self-concept serves as a shield, protecting the adolescent from the effects of an adverse environment.

Jaffee and Polansky (1962) have noted that the inability to communicate is another personality trait of many delinquents. They suggest that, due to parental inconsistency and emotional neglect, young delinquents tend to use primitive ways of discharging their drives; that is, they act out rather than verbally express their feelings. It has also been hypothesized that the frequent adherence to pseudomasculine traits among delinquents inhibits verbal expression of emotions. Such verbal inaccessibility may even be a conscious attitude on the part of these delinquent youths, who would be unlikely to trust others enough to express their inner thoughts to them.

Apparently they are reluctant both to look inward at their feelings and to share those feelings with others.

Despite common beliefs to the contrary, the delinquent's IQ score does not differ appreciably from that of the nondelinquent (Prentice & Kelly, 1963). However, because standardized paper-and-pencil intelligence tests rely so heavily on verbal skills and reading ability, which are likely to be below average for delinquents for many reasons, IQ-test scores for such youths often do not reflect their actual mental ability.

However, one study (Pontius & Ruttiger, 1976) did disclose the existence of a subgroup of delinquents, composing about 15% to 20% of the total, who have a neurophysiological maturational lag of the frontal-lobe system of the brain. This lag is reflected in the youths' difficulty in switching in a flexible manner from ongoing behavior to new behavior. Such a behavioral pattern, which will be discussed further in Chapter 10, has also been found in some types of minimal brain dysfunction or specific learning disabilities (Pontius, 1972). At this point, it should be noted that the presence of such a neurological pattern suggests the need for extensive psychological and neurological examination of delinquents.

Prediction of delinquency

Authorities have often suggested that, if future delinquency could be accurately predicted, much of it might be prevented through early treatment. Because most juvenile delinquency is likely to begin shortly after the age of 8 (Thomas, 1967), some investigators have recently suggested that every child between the ages of 6 and 8 should be evaluated through the use of *projective techniques* in order to detect those children who are most likely to develop antisocial behavior.

Perhaps a bit less dramatic but nonetheless outstanding is the research undertaken by Glueck and Glueck (1950, 1959). These criminologists believe that early prediction is the most rational approach to the problem of delinquency. They suggest that, by assessing certain predictive factors even before a child enters school, it is possible to determine which children are most prone to delinquent behavior. If such early detection is then followed by preventive measures, the number of juvenile offenders would ultimately be reduced (Glueck & Glueck, 1959).

Maintaining that there are many traits and factors in the early life of a child that foretell the development of delinquent behavior,

Glueck and Glueck (1950) developed the Glueck Social Prediction Table. This was designed to be used by trained social workers to identify potentially antisocial behavior in boys at the time of their entrance into school. The table includes five factors, all pertaining to the family: (1) discipline of the boy by his father—whether it is firm and kindly or too strict, inconsistent, or lax; (2) supervision of the boy by his mother—whether it is unsuitable, fair, or suitable; (3) affection of the father for his son—whether the father is indifferent, hostile, warm, or overprotective; (4) affection of the mother for her son—whether she is indifferent, hostile, warm, or overprotective; and (5) the cohesiveness of the family—whether the family is uninte- grated, partly intact, or strong in its unity. Eleanor Glueck believes that it might be possible to identify a potential delinquent as early as the age of 3 (Brown, 1965), and two constitutional factors (personality traits) were later added to a revised Glueck Social Prediction Table: infant destructiveness and resistance to authority. Unfortunately this table was designed strictly for use with boys, and no comparable evaluation presently exists for girls.

According to Glueck and Glueck (1959), male delinquents are most likely to come from a family in which (1) the father's discipline is harsh, unreasonable, or inconsistent and the mother's discipline is unsuitable because of her careless supervision (for example, leaving her son to his own devices or in the hands of an incompetent substi- tute), (2) both parents are indifferent or hostile toward their male offspring, and (3) there is little family cohesiveness.

If a boy has a high likelihood of becoming a delinquent accord- ing to the Glueck Social Prediction Table but only a slight chance according to the results of the Rorschach ink-blot test and a study of the child's personality dynamics, the possibilities of preventing the onset of antisocial behavior through modification of the family envi- ronment are great. On the other hand, if the Social Prediction score is low but the Rorschach and personality-dynamics results are unsatisfactory—that is, if they indicate personality disorders— preventive action is likely to be unsuccessful. In such instances the problem would probably be too deeply rooted, and prevention of delinquency would be difficult, since it would demand a basic reor- ganization of the entire character structure (Glueck & Glueck, 1950).

Another approach to the prediction of delinquent behavior is the use of a teacher rating scale of personal/social behavior exhibited by children in kindergarten and the primary-level grades. Conger, Miller, and Walsmith (1975) reported on one such study involving 2348 urban tenth-grade boys who had been rated earlier by their teachers in kindergarten through third grade. Controlling for such variables as socioeconomic class, intelligence, and ethnic background, the researchers found that, by the third grade, teachers perceived future delinquents differently from future nondelinquents. (Delinquents were classified as those tenth-graders who had had cases presented in the juvenile court.) The teachers had noted that the future delinquents

> appeared to have less regard for the rights and feelings of their peers; less awareness of the need to accept responsibility for their obligations, both as individuals and as members of a group; and poorer attitudes toward authority, including the failure to understand the need for rules and regulations in any well-ordered social group, and to abide by them [p. 442].

In addition, these students were more readily distracted from academic work, engaged in more daydreaming, experienced a shorter attention span, and were less likely to demonstrate any special ability or unique interest. In many instances it was believed that these problems reflected underlying emotional problems emanating from a disturbed home situation.

Wright and James (1974) identified behaviors that they believe are signals that children or adolescents are experiencing problems in coping with their environment—problems that probably call for therapeutic intervention. These behaviors are listed in Table 8-2. They have also identified a large number of environmental factors, both in the home and at school, that they believe tend to elicit delinquent behaviors. These are shown in Table 8-3.

The prevention of delinquency

> The traditional institutions of America—the family, the school, the church, the law—have become decreasingly responsive to the realities of people's lives. The traditional sanctions, services, and structures which they have provided and the stability which these have represented no longer illustrate either the aspirations or the needs of a growing number of Americans [Office of Education, 1967, p. 280].

If delinquency is to be prevented or at least reduced, these traditional institutions will have to be modified. Community leaders and law-enforcement officials consider a disturbed family life to be the major cause of juvenile delinquency (Wright & James, 1974).

Table 8-2.   Behaviors by a child that indicate a need for treatment intervention

---

The behaviors listed below are signals that a child may be experiencing difficulty in coping with his environment. Behaviors listed under "A," "B," and "C," should be treated in the community. Only serious illegalities which cause observable harm should be cause for removal from the community to a restrictive environment.

A. *Childhood behavioral problems* (that persist into adolescence or adulthood)
    1. Thumbsucking
    2. Nail biting
    3. Temper tantrums
    4. Enuresis (bed wetting)

B. *Antisocial behaviors*
    1. Child makes a majority of sarcastic or negative comments to peers.
    2. Child uses physical violence (from fighting to pinching, pushing) towards peers when angered or when wanting attention.
    3. Child interacts with peers less than two to four times per day (withdrawn).
    4. Child smiles only occasionally.

C. *Undisciplined or delinquent behaviors*
    1. Child rarely finishes assigned tasks.
    2. Child is truant from school.
    3. Child runs away from home for at least one night.
    4. Child fights at least once a week.
    5. Child does not carry out parents' orders or rules.
    6. Child vandalizes school or community property.
    7. Child violates curfew.

D. *Serious illegalities*
    1. Larceny
    2. Breaking and entering
    3. Selling and/or possession of drugs
    4. Robbery
    5. Assault
    6. Rape
    7. Phoning in bomb threats
    8. Homicides

From J. Wright, Jr., & R. James, Jr., *A Behavioral Approach to Preventing Delinquency,* 1974. Courtesy of Charles C Thomas, Publisher, Springfield, Illinois.

Table 8-3.   Environmental situations that tend to elicit delinquent responses

Parental discipline is an important factor in a child's adjustment. The formula for proper child rearing is: "sensible discipline in a context of love." A child will survive poorly administered or excessive discipline if he feels secure in the love of his parents. Kids forgive their parents for stupidity more readily than they do for meanness.

Factors in the Environment That Do Not Allow a Child to Be Taught Proper, Legal Behaviors

A. *One or more parents, guardians, adult models absent from, or ineffective in, home environment*
    1. Family members who are important to child consistently use negative verbal and physical punishers, regardless of child's proper or improper behaviors.
    2. Family members consistently use positive verbal and physical reinforcers, without regard to child's proper or improper behaviors.
    3. Family members ignore majority of child's proper and improper behaviors.
    4. Family members ignore child's proper behaviors and verbally and physically punish improper behaviors.
    5. Family members ignore child's improper behaviors and punish proper behaviors.
    6. Family members are inconsistent with reinforcers and punishers.
        a. Members make threats about consequences of child's improper behaviors, then do not carry through.
        b. Members make "contracts" for proper behaviors, then do not carry through.
            1. Contracts are not balanced: too difficult a task for insufficient rewards.
            2. Contracts are set up for too long a time span.
            3. Contracts are set up under improper antecedent conditions.

B. *"Vice" in the home*
    1. One or more parents or other family members drink excessively.
    2. One or more family members consistently take drugs.
    3. Mother or other female family members are prostitutes.
    4. Father or other male family members are gigolos.
    5. One or more parents bring different sexual partners into the home on a weekly basis.

Table 8-3. Continued

      6. At least one member of the family has a court record with at least two offenses—or one very serious offense (or in prison).

C. *Economic insecurity*
1. Income of family is within $100.00 of minimum average family income set by Social Services.
2. One or more adults in the family who are responsible for furnishing income change jobs two, three, or more times per year.
3. One or more adults in the family lose job for two months or more without other full-time employment.

D. *Unsupervised recreation: "Hangs out in bars, poolrooms, etc."*
1. Child stays in presence of adult models who display improper, or illegal, problem behaviors.
2. Child is reinforced by peers or adult models for imitation of improper (or illegal) problem behavior.

E. *Negative school experiences*
1. Child's report card has a majority of D's or F's.
2. Child's score on "citizenship" grading is in the lower 50 percentile.
3. Child's teacher uses a majority of negative reinforcers in classroom (physical and verbal).
4. Child's teacher yells or loses temper at least one time a day.
5. Child has few friends—no more than two.

From J. Wright, Jr., & R. James, Jr., *A Behavioral Approach to Preventing Delinquency*, 1974. Courtesy of Charles C Thomas, Publisher, Springfield, Illinois.

Therefore, it is within the framework of the family that the most effective prevention can be undertaken. Society must seek ways of reducing the incidence of child abuse, cementing family relationships, and strengthening the role of the parents in the familial structure in order to facilitate more positive socialization of children. Parents need to be taught effective child-rearing techniques. The introduction of parenting classes into the high school curriculum is one way to prepare adolescents for future roles as parents. Such programs may stress effective means of disciplining children and adolescents and alternatives to physical punishment, which tends to have a significant correlation with delinquency. These alternatives to physical punishment are particularly important because children who see their parents resorting to physical aggression as a form of discipline are likely to resort to aggressive acting-out behavior themselves. Unfortunately, classes in effective parenting are seldom attended by those who are already parents and who need assistance in establishing or reestablishing their parental authority within the family. Many parents may also require help in learning how to become actively involved in the academic lives of their children. Schools and parents need to establish a closer relationship with each other.

Public schools today are responsible for many aspects of a child's life other than education, primarily because other agents—family, church, community services—do not have the time, money, personnel, or facilities to fulfill the child's needs. Thus, school facilities, as noted earlier, need to be used year round not only as centers for the education of children but also as places for recreation, adult education, and even counseling (Schafer & Polk, 1967). Teachers and administrators need to find new methods for effectively disciplining problem youths. For example, the suspension from school of a student who is placed on legal probation for a delinquent act may simply provide the youth with the opportunity to commit additional delinquent acts. A more positive approach to discipline within the schools might involve the use of *behavior modification,* which is a learning technique that applies conditioning procedures to the modification of behavior. For example, in some North Carolina schools a process known as "contingency contracting" is being utilized. A token-economy system is used to enable students to "buy" their free time, games, privileges, and preferred activities, with some schools even featuring a school store (Wright & James, 1974). Through such an approach, one might even acquire the opportunity to "earn" time off from school, which could well serve as one means of preventing truancy.

A similar approach was helpful in curbing the truancy of a 16-year-old girl. Her telephone and dating privileges were contingent on her attending school and bringing home a note, first on a daily basis and later on a biweekly basis, confirming that she had been attending her classes. The results were very impressive in that her absences declined from 30 out of 46 days in the first semester to no absences in the second semester (Thorn, Tharp, & Wetzel, 1973).

Educators must avoid placing the blame for misconduct on an individual student when the fault may lie with the school's handling of the situation. Teachers, for example, must be certain that they provide students with the necessary time, information, and materials to carry out their assignments. Punishing a student for not completing an impossible assignment only leads to anger and frustration for the student and may even contribute to eventual delinquent behavior.

Even though teachers are often in a position to help recognize the delinquent or delinquency-prone youth, they need to be careful to avoid labeling students as troublemakers and, thereby, burdening them with a negative reputation that is passed on from year to year and from one teacher to another. Ultimately such young people begin to live up to the name by which they have been branded. They then discover what they have in common with other misbehaving adolescents and wind up with a deviant peer group, which is bound to establish its own standards and openly flaunt the regulations of the school (Schafer & Polk, 1967).

Because dropping out of school and engaging in delinquent behavior are so closely related, special attention needs to be given to the school curriculum and to alternative approaches to education. Often, curriculum adjustments are necessary in order to include such activities as arts and crafts, radio broadcasting or repair, choir, and band, which will hopefully encourage the development of responsible behavior. Such courses can lead students to discover hobbies or even vocations that will enable them to earn a livelihood. Alternatives to the regular public school may include "store-front schools" for dropouts or special public schools that students are free to attend. One such special public school that we know of has been especially effective in appealing to expectant teenage mothers, to those who do not wish to conform to the rather rigid dress codes of the regular schools, and to those desiring to smoke at school. In such programs students proceed at their own speed, and the flexibility of the curriculum enables them to take part-time jobs. A few years ago the U. S. Post Office became involved in a similar program when it opened "store-front academies" in several cities. The purpose of these schools was to educate ghetto-area school dropouts, aged 16 to 21, through a four-month program of vocational training and part-time jobs with the Post Office ("News and Trends," 1970).

There is also a need for special youth agencies, to which other agencies can make referrals and to which parents and their children can go for help on their own. In California, Colorado, and Texas a system of nonprofit centers has been established to provide services for troubled youth and their families. The program, called Social Advocates for Youth, was started in 1970 and is geared mainly toward predelinquents aged 7 to 14 years. Referrals are made by police, probation officers, mental-health officials, schools, physicians, families, and sometimes by the children themselves. Through the use of volunteers, a one-to-one relationship is established with the goal of improving family relationships. Parent-education courses are also offered. When needed, residential treatment homes, day-care centers, crisis-intervention hotlines, juvenile-court intervention, and planned recreational activities are available (*VIP Examiner*, 1976).

Adolescents also need help in learning to make decisions, in finding meaning in life, and in learning to care what happens to them and to society as a whole. Too many delinquent and predelinquent adolescents either make unfortunate life decisions or fail to make them at all because (1) they lack specific data about themselves and their environment and (2) they lack critical decision-making skills (Rutherford, 1976). One of the functions of education should be to help adolescents learn to make decisions—a process that should teach them *how* to choose, rather than *what* to choose. To develop responsible behavior in young people, adults should encourage them to help to plan, organize, operate, and develop community programs for other youths (President's Commission, 1967). The effectiveness of such programs can be seen in the success of peer counseling, mentioned in Chapter 7.

Treatment of delinquency

Current practices in dealing with juvenile offenders usually include one or more of the following: (1) a court hearing with no final disposition of the case, which is sufficient to deter some from future delinquency; (2) assessment of a fine and restitution for any property damaged or destroyed, to be paid by the offender and not by his or her parents; (3) placement of the youth on probation, which may range from friendly counseling to serious surveillance; (4) referral of the adolescent and/or the parents to a community-based program, such as the Social Advocates for Youth; or (5) placement of an adjudged delinquent in a state institution for an indefinite period of time (Wheeler, Cottrell, & Romasco, 1967).

Although juvenile courts have existed in the United States for over three-quarters of a century, they have generally failed in the functions for which they were initially created. According to Paulson (1967), "A contact with the juvenile court not only is unlikely to assist a youngster to become a better citizen but, according to respectable theory today, the contact is likely to lead him (her) into further delinquency" (p. 70). "Recidivism (recommitment to a correctional institution) among young people who have been institutionalized is extremely high" (Burns & Stern, 1967, p. 355). Court records, although supposedly confidential, often prevent delinquents from being employed, cause them to be excluded from membership in labor unions, and prohibit them from participating in certain apprenticeship training or from being licensed in certain occupations (President's Commission, 1967). It has been suggested that status offenses be removed from the jurisdiction of the courts and that certain types of delinquency, such as truancy, be handled by the schools, rather than by the courts. Otherwise, at the present time few positive approaches to the *legal* handling of delinquency have come to the fore.

Because institutions for delinquents have too often become places to learn more delinquent behavior, a number of alternatives to commitment to a reformatory or training school have been introduced throughout the United States and Canada. Many of these, such as Social Advocates for Youth (*VIP Examiner,* 1976), operate in the community in which the juvenile offender resides. Some programs involve a treatment center where adjudged delinquents participate in daily group therapy while living at home and working or attending school. Other programs encourage delinquents to help bring about change in other law-breaking youths through such approaches as peer counseling—a philosophy somewhat similar to that of Alcoholics Anonymous.

In Jefferson Parish, Louisiana, a suburban area of New Orleans, a unique program called Project Choice has been introduced by Juvenile Court Judge Sol Gothard (1977). Juveniles apprehended for delinquent behavior are given a choice of going before the juvenile court or attending an intensive eight-week program involving three hours of concentrated study in academic basics each day and active participation in a behavior-modification program. Their families must also agree to participate in the program, which involves, among other professionals, three full-time psychologists. Some 800 youths with a background of serious academic problems and delinquent behavior are going through this program each year.

Shore and Massimo (1969) suggest that the identity crisis is more severe for lower-class boys, who realize their limited opportunities, than for those of the more affluent classes. They also note that lower-class youths often entertain unrealistic fantasies about their abilities but lack the academic skills demanded by even low-level jobs. Thus, they propose that treatment of delinquency among lower-class adolescents include a program of comprehensive vocational training. These two behavioral scientists (Massimo & Shore, 1963) reported on one such program—a ten-month, experimental, vocationally oriented psychotherapeutic program undertaken with 20 adolescent boys (10 in an experimental group and 10 in a control group), ranging in age from 15 to 17, with IQs from 85 to 110. A single practitioner served each youth in the experimental group in all therapeutic capacities, starting when the subject was expelled from or dropped out of school. Contact was initiated through offers to help the adolescent obtain a job. Preemployment counseling with emphasis on job readiness was undertaken. Because the program was not compulsory, it encouraged the adolescents to fulfill their potential and helped alleviate their fears of dependency. It was flexible and geared to the needs of each youth, and it focused on the acquisition of a sense of responsibility. A job was selected by the boy and his therapist according to the boy's interests and abilities. Following job placement, the counselor's emphasis shifted from job readiness to work problems. Remedial education was initiated according to work performance; it was introduced when the subject was ready to improve his skills on the job.

The results of this interesting study were that those in the program improved first in their self-image, second in their control of aggression, and last in their attitude toward authority. In addition, they improved academically and showed a much better employment record than the control group; seven out of ten subjects still held jobs and the other three were back in school at the end of the ten-month period. On the other hand, in the control group, three boys remained unemployed during the entire ten months and a fourth boy was unemployed at the time of the final contact; the members of this group also held more jobs for shorter periods of time than did those in the experimental group (Massimo & Shore, 1963).

The positive results of this study suggest that the experience of success reduces the need for delinquents to resort to aggressive behavior in their dealings with the world and its frustrations. Perhaps most important of all, however, this study indicates the need for intervention on an individual basis by those trained and interested in working with delinquent offenders in a wide range of activities.

Paraprofessionals and volunteers can often be taught to work with delinquents. A successful example of such an approach is the VIP program (Volunteers in Prevention, Prosecution, Probation, Prison, and Parole), which is a division of the National Council on Crime and Delinquency. It was initially started in 1960 at Royal Oak, Michigan. In 1965, under a grant from the National Institutes of Mental Health, an evaluation was undertaken to determine the effectiveness of a citizen-participation and volunteer program in rehabilitating delinquents. The Royal Oak Municipal Court sent delinquents who were on probation to the VIP program, while a reasonably comparable, unnamed court used routine probationary methods. Two testings of these youths for hostility, aggressiveness, belligerence, and other antisocial attitudes were made 18 months apart for both groups. In Royal Oak, for 94 White male-delinquent probationers aged 17 to 25, 73.8% showed definite improvement in these areas, 15.3% displayed no change, and 11.7% had regressed. In the unnamed court, with 82 youthful offenders, 17.8% improved, 34.2% showed no change, and 48% had regressed. Recidivism was only 7% at Royal Oak, whereas, in many communities, a 25% rate is considered satisfactory. The VIP volunteers are carefully screened, receive orientation and training, and are carefully supervised in their work with youths on probation. Some 500 volunteers offer their services, valued at some $300,000 a year, to this program that operates on a $17,000 a year budget. There are also half a dozen retired individuals who serve as full-time administrators and are paid the maximum permitted by Social Security (Department of Health, Education, and Welfare, 1968).

Many organizations are utilizing behavior modification in the treatment of delinquents. Token-economy systems are being used and proving successful in such places as the R. F. Kennedy Youth Center in Morgantown, West Virginia. In such programs, delinquent offenders improve dramatically in their self-concepts and experience a shift from external control to internal control as the source of their motivation. They also improve in their achievement orientation (Eitzen, 1975). Still other approaches are stressing the desirability of family therapy (Rueveni, 1976; Stumphauzer, 1976).

The Florida Ocean Science Institute in 1969 began doing research with juvenile boys referred from the local courts. This juvenile-rehabilitation project is both academic (although fairly informal) and vocational. After an introductory period of 30 days, boys meet with groups of (male) advisers and peers to consider the long-range program. If the boys decide to stay, they sign a contract that specifies the obligations and aims of both the researchers and themselves. They are then assigned an adviser, who may become personally involved with the boys. The framework of the program is not rigid; advisers may be changed and the boys may drop out if they desire (and still receive counseling). Although the results are not conclusive and the number of boys involved in the program was not mentioned, a degree of success is indicated by the fact that over a three-year period the recidivism rate was less than 10% (Khanna, 1975).

If it is necessary for delinquent youths to be sent away from the community, one approach that is certainly preferable to the usual reformatory is that of the Vermont Weeks School. Although it looks like a boarding school for upper-class youths, it is actually a training school for court-committed delinquents ranging in age from 10 to 19. The school is designed to help these youths acquire the education they have failed to get in the public schools. Small classes provide individual attention. No grades are given and no students are failed; instead, they are encouraged to like what they learn and to continue learning. When they acquire a basic foundation, they are permitted to attend the public high school in the community, with all of the obligations and most of the privileges of regular students, including extracurricular activities other than sports. Weeks School has its own athletic program, and its teams compete against other local teams. Adolescents who are old enough are encouraged to seek jobs in the community in order to earn spending money. They are also permitted to mix socially with students from town, and after a few months they are allowed to go home for weekends and vacations, provided their home is a stable one. Discipline involves the withholding of privileges, and, although there are occasional runaways and some recidivism, there is more success than failure (Levine, 1968).

In another institution, for delinquent girls, a three-month pilot project was undertaken that was based on the theory that much antisocial behavior is the result of educational failure due to a learning disability (Poremba, 1967; Dayan, 1975). Both remediation of the academic deficits and a modification of the maladaptive behavior were stressed in this program. Referred to as *educo-therapy*, the program was undertaken with ten institutionalized delinquent girls who were considered to have educational disabilities (reading difficulties due to poor educational beginning), or learning disabilities (due to organic or functional disorders), and/or behavioral disorders (possibly related to such disabilities). The philosophy underlying the treatment was fourfold: (1) each girl should experience success in school, especially in reading, (2) each one should learn socially acceptable modes of behavior, (3) each girl should achieve an enhanced self-concept, and (4) each one should learn to assume responsibility for her behavior and its consequences (Rice, 1970).

As a result of this three-month educationally oriented therapeutic project, the girls' reading levels advanced anywhere from 2 to 13 months (as measured by standardized reading-achievement tests) with a corresponding increase in their IQs. There was also improvement in the girls' personal appearance and social behavior, hostility level, incidence of aversive behavior, and group cohesiveness. "It was felt that the aversive gang or peer influence, which so often determines delinquent behavior, had changed somewhat to encouragement of socially adaptive behavior" (Rice, 1970, p. 23). As a result, three girls were released from the institution at the end of the three-month program. Another encouraging outcome of this project was the tendency of the other institutionalized girls to copy the behavior of those in the educo-therapy program.

Chapter summary

Youths who have difficulty achieving a satisfactory emotional adjustment during the adolescent period may turn to drug abuse, suicide, runaway behavior, delinquency, or a combination of these as a means of escaping from a world that they often consider to be intolerable and frustrating. The rapid increase in delinquency since World War II is the outgrowth of many factors: socioeconomic conditions, including the mass media's emphasis on affluence, the disintegration of the family, the failure of the schools to provide an education that emphasizes the basics and yet is relevant to the needs of young people, and the widespread display of violence in the media. There has also been an increase in the incidence of delinquent behavior among the affluent classes, but whether this is the result of increased parental failure or better detection and record keeping is unknown. In addition, there has been a substantial rise in serious criminal delinquency by females, who formerly had been apprehended primarily for status or sexual offenses.

To prevent or reduce the incidence of juvenile delinquency demands the concerted efforts of federal, state, and local governments, the schools, and parents. Educators need to be particularly concerned about truancy, which is often a forerunner of more serious delinquent acts, and about vandalism and violence, which are often both costly and harmful to education but frequently reflect the inadequacies and failures of our schools.

Certainly incarceration is failing as a deterrent to delinquency and may even be contributing to its higher incidence. However, new innovations—often community-based programs—in prevention and treatment are being introduced throughout the United States and Canada. These encompass various therapies, including psychological, vocational, and educational approaches, offered by professionals, paraprofessionals, and trained volunteers. Several of these programs show promise of proving to be much more effective than the traditional reformatories and training schools.

Thought provokers

1. How is the term *juvenile delinquency* defined in the state in which you live? What types of offenses does it encompass? Do you think status offenses should be considered delinquent behavior? Why?

2. What do you think the reasons are for the increase in juvenile delinquency since World War II?
3. Do you think that all juvenile delinquents should be grouped together? Why?
4. Do you agree or disagree with Guttmacher's classification of delinquents? Why?
5. Have you ever committed an act that would be regarded as delinquent behavior?
6. Why is truancy such an important aspect of juvenile delinquency?
7. What can be done to curb vandalism and violence in the schools?
8. What distinguishes the lower-socioeconomic-class delinquent from the affluent delinquent?
9. What new approaches might be utilized by society in the prevention of delinquency? Beyond those cited in your text, do you know of some unique approaches in the treatment of delinquency? Why have the traditional approaches not been very successful?
10. Do you personally know of anyone who has been apprehended and adjudged a delinquent? If so, what factors do you believe contributed to this individual's delinquent behavior?

References

Allen, D. E., & Sandhu, H. S. A comparative study of delinquents and nondelinquents: Family affect, religion, and personal income. *Social Forces*, 1967, *24*(1), 263–269.

Bacon, M. K., Child, I. L., & Barry, H. A cross-cultural study of correlates of crime. *Journal of Abnormal Psychology*, 1963, 66(4), 291–300.

Bandura, A., & Walters, R. H. Dependency conflicts in aggressive delinquency. *Journal of Social Issues*, 1958, 14(3), 52–65.

Baugh, V. S., & Carpenter, B. L. A comparison of delinquents and nondelinquents. *Journal of Social Psychology*, 1962, 56, 73–78.

Brown, V. Future delinquents can be seen at age 3. *Alexandria Daily Town Talk*, December 20, 1965, p. B-1.

Burns, V. M., & Stern, L. W. The prevention of juvenile delinquency. In The President's Commission on Law Enforcement and Administration of Justice, *Task force report: Juvenile delinquency and youth crime*. Washington, D. C.: U. S. Government Printing Office, 1967. Pp. 353–408.

Cartwright, D. S. The nature of gangs. In D. S. Cartwright, B. Tomson, & H. Schwartz (Eds.), *Gang delinquency*, Monterey, Calif.: Brooks/Cole, 1975. Pp. 1–22.

Cartwright, D. S., Tomson, B., & Schwartz, H. (Eds.), Preface. *Gang delinquency*. Monterey, Calif.: Brooks/Cole, 1975. Pp. v–vi.

Cervantes, L. F. *The dropout: Causes and cures.* Ann Arbor: University of Michigan Press, 1965.

Clinard, M. B., & Wade, A. L. Juvenile vandalism. In R. S. Cavan (Ed.), *Readings in juvenile delinquency* (2nd ed.). Philadelphia: J. B. Lippincott, 1969. Pp. 257–263.

Cloward, R. A., & Ohlin, L. E. *Delinquency and opportunity: A theory of delinquent gangs.* Glencoe, Ill.: Free Press, 1960.

Cóhen, A. K. Delinquent boys: The culture of the gang. New York: Free Press, 1955.

Coleman, J. S. The adolescent society. New York: Free Press, 1961.

Conger, J. J., Miller, W. C., & Walsmith, C. R. Antecedents of delinquency: Personality, social class and intelligence. In P. H. Mussen, J. J. Conger, & J. Kagan (Eds.), Basic and contemporary issues in developmental psychology. New York: Harper & Row, 1975. Pp. 433–450.

Crumbaugh, J. C. The automobile as part of the body-image in America. Mental Hygiene, 1968, 52(3), 349–350.

Dayan, C. Delinquency and learning disabilities. Unpublished manuscript. Adolescent Service, Central Louisiana State Hospital, Pineville, Louisiana, 1975.

Department of Health, Education, and Welfare. National Institutes of Mental Health and the Royal Oak Municipal Court preliminary research study report. Royal Oak, Mich.: VIP, a division of the National Council on Crime and Delinquency, 1968.

Eitzen, D. S. Behavior modification on the attitudes of delinquents. In Behavior research and therapy (Vol. 13). London: Pergamon Press, 1975. Pp. 295–299.

England, R. W., Jr. A theory of middle class juvenile delinquency. In R. S. Cavan (Ed.), Readings in juvenile delinquency (2nd ed.). Philadelphia: J. B. Lippincott, 1969. Pp. 106–115.

Eron, L. D., Huesmann, L. R., Lefkowitz, M. M., & Walder, L. O. Behavior-aggression. American Journal of Orthopsychiatry, 1974, 44(3), 412–423.

Fairfell, W. Delinquency in the United States. Boston: Beacon Press, 1965.

Federal Bureau of Investigation, U. S. Department of Justice. Uniform crime reports for the United States. Washington, D. C.: U. S. Government Printing Office, 1972.

Fleisher, B. M. The economics of delinquency. Chicago: Quadrangle Books, 1966.

Gilman, D. How to retain jurisdiction over status offenses. Crime and Delinquency, 1976, 22(3), 48–51.

Glueck, S., & Glueck, E. Unraveling juvenile delinquency. Cambridge, Mass.: Harvard University Press, 1950.

Glueck, S., & Glueck, E. Predicting delinquency and crime. Cambridge, Mass.: Harvard University Press, 1959.

Glueck, S., & Glueck, E. Delinquents and non-delinquents in perspective. Cambridge, Mass.: Harvard University Press, 1968.

Gold, M. Delinquent behavior in an American city. Monterey, Calif.: Brooks/Cole, 1970.

Gothard, S. Interview. Jefferson Parish, Louisiana. February 1977.

Guttmacher, M. S. The psychiatric approach to crime and correction. Law and Contemporary Problems, 1958, 23(4).

Haskell, M. R., & Yablonsky, L. Juvenile delinquency. Chicago: Rand McNally, 1974.

Horn, J. Kicked-out kids. Psychology Today, 1975, 9(7), 83–84.

Horrocks, J. The psychology of adolescence (3rd ed.). Boston: Houghton Mifflin, 1969.

Irwin, G. How to reduce school theft and vandalism. The Education Digest, 1976, 41(9), 9–11.

Jaffee, L. D., & Polansky, N. A. Verbal inaccessibility in young adolescents showing delinquent trends. Journal of Health and Human Behavior, 1962, 3(2), 105–111.

Juvenile Court Statistics. Washington, D. C.: Department of Health, Education, and Welfare, 1971.

Juvenile Court Statistics. Washington, D. C.: Department of Health, Education, and Welfare, 1972.

Khanna, J. L. New treatment approaches to juvenile delinquency. Springfield, Ill.: Charles C Thomas, 1975.

Konopka, G. The adolescent girl in conflict. Englewood Cliffs, N. J.: Prentice-Hall, 1966.

Kratcoski, P. C., & Kratcoski, J. E. Changing patterns in the delinquent activities of boys and girls: A self-reported delinquency analysis. *Adolescence*, 1975, *10*(37), 83–91.

Kvaraceus, W. C. *Anxious youth: Dynamics of delinquency.* Columbus, Ohio: Charles E. Merrill, 1966.

Leinwand, G. (Ed.). *Crime and juvenile delinquency.* New York: Washington Square Press, 1968.

Leland, T. W. The faint smile syndrome. *American Journal of Orthopsychiatry*, 1961, *31*, 420–421.

Lelyveld, J. The paradoxical case of the affluent delinquent. *The New York Times*, October 4, 1964.

Levine, R. A. The personal touch. *American Education*, 1968, *91*(4), 14–17.

Lewis, D. O., Balla, D., Shanok, S., & Snell, L. Delinquency, parental psychopathology, and parental criminality: Clinical and epidemiological findings. *Journal of the American Academy of Child Psychiatry*, 1976, *15*(4), 665–678.

Liebert, R. M., Neale, J. M., & Davidson, E. S. *The early window: Effects of television on children and youth.* New York: Pergamon Press, 1973.

Martin, L. H., & Snyder, P. R. Jurisdiction over status offenses should not be removed from juvenile court. *Crime and Delinquency*, 1976, *22*(1), 44–47.

Massimo, J. L., & Shore, M. F. The effectiveness of a comprehensive vocationally oriented psychotherapeutic program for adolescent delinquent boys. *American Journal of Orthopsychiatry*, 1963, *33*, 634–642.

Miller, W. Lower class culture as a generating milieu of gang delinquency. *Journal of Social Issues*, 1958, *14*(3), 5–19.

Miller, W., & Windhauser, E. Reading disability: Tendency toward delinquency. *The Clearing House*, 1971, *46*, 113–118.

Moore, B. M. The schools and the problems of delinquency: Research studies and findings. In R. S. Cavan (Ed.), *Readings in juvenile delinquency.* Philadelphia: J. B. Lippincott, 1964. Pp. 182–197.

News and Trends. *Today's Education*, 1970, *59*(3), 3.

Office of Education, U. S. Department of Health, Education, and Welfare. Delinquency and the schools. In The President's Commission on Law Enforcement and Administration of Justice, *Task force report: Juvenile delinquency and youth crime.* Washington, D. C.: U. S. Government Printing Office, 1967, Pp. 278–304.

Paulson, M. G. The role of juvenile courts. *Current History*, 1967, *53*(312), 70–75.

Pine, G. J. The affluent delinquent. *Phi Delta Kappan*, 1966, *48*(4), 138–143.

Polk, K. A reassessment of middle-class delinquency. *Youth and Society*, 1971, *2*(3), 333–354.

Polk, K., & Richmond, L. *Those who fail.* Unpublished paper. Lane City Youth Project, Eugene, Oregon, 1966.

Pontius, A. A. Conceptual model of minimal brain dysfunction. General Discussion, Proceedings of Minimal Brain Dysfunction Conference, 1972. *Annals of the New York Academy of Sciences*, 1972, *205*, 61–63.

Pontius, A. A., & Ruttiger, K. F. Frontal lobe system maturational lag in juvenile delinquents shown in narratives test. *Adolescence*, 1976, *11*(44), 509–518.

Poremba, C. The adolescent and young adult with learning disabilities: What are his needs: What are the needs of those who deal with him? *Academic Therapy Publications*, 1967.

Prentice, N. M., & Kelly, F. J. Intelligence and delinquency: A reconsideration. *Journal of Social Psychology*, 1963, *60*, 327–335.

President's Commission on Law Enforcement and Administration of Justice. *Task force report: Juvenile delinquency and youth crime.* Washington, D. C.: U. S. Government Printing Office, 1967.

Reiss, A. J., Jr. Sex offenses. In R. S. Cavan (Ed.), *Readings in juvenile delinquency* (2nd ed.). Philadelphia: J. B. Lippincott, 1969. Pp. 263–274.

Reiss, A. J., Jr., & Rhodes, A. L. The distribution of juvenile delinquency in the social class structure. *American Sociological Review*, 1961, *26*(5), 720–732.

Rice, R. D. Educo-therapy: A new approach to delinquent behavior. *Journal of Learning Disabilities*, 1970, *3*(1), 16–23.

Riggs, J: E., Underwood, W., & Warren, M. Q. *Interpersonal maturity level classification: Juvenile*, C. T. P. research report no. 4. Sacramento: California Department of Youth Authority, 1964. Pp. 1–2.

Robinson, S. M. *Juvenile delinquency*. New York: Holt, Rinehart & Winston, 1960.

Rueveni, U. Family network intervention: Healing families in crisis. *Intellect*, 1976, *104*(2375), 580–582.

Rutherford, R. B. Behavioral decision model for delinquent and predelinquent adolescence. *Adolescence*, 1976, *11*(41), 97–106.

Scarpitti, F. R. Delinquent and non-delinquent perceptions of self, values, and opportunity. *Mental Hygiene*, 1965, *49*(3), 399–404.

Schafer, W. E., & Polk, K. Delinquency and the schools. In The President's Commission on Law Enforcement and Administration of Justice, *Task force report: Juvenile delinquency and youth crime*. Washington, D. C.: U. S. Government Printing Office, 1967. Pp. 222–277.

Schepses, E. Boys who steal cars. In R. S. Cavan (Ed.), *Readings in juvenile delinquency* (2nd ed.). Philadelphia: J. B. Lippincott, 1969. Pp. 244–256.

Senay, R., Nihira, K., & Yusin, A. Crisis in adolescence: Parental attitudes about children's behavior. *Psychological Reports*, 1976, *38*, 423–429.

Sheppard, B. J. The orbiting teenager—a seminar: The delinquent juvenile—1963 status. *Medical Times*, 1965, *93*(2), 209–210.

Shore, M. F., & Massimo, J. L. The chronic delinquent during adolescence: A new opportunity for intervention. In G. Caplan & S. Lebovici (Eds.), *Adolescence: Psychosocial perspectives*. New York: Basic Books, 1969. Pp. 335–342.

Slocum, W. L., & Stone, C. L. Family culture patterns and delinquent type behavior. *Marriage and Family Living*, 1963, *25*(5), 202–208.

Stumphauzer, J. S. Modifying delinquent behavior: Beginnings and current practices. *Adolescence*, 1976, *11*(41), 13–24.

Tappan, P. *Juvenile delinquency*. New York: McGraw-Hill, 1949.

Terror in Schools. *U. S. News & World Report*, January 26, 1976, pp. 52–55.

Thomas, J. H. Lecture on the Louisiana Probation and Parole Program. Presented at Louisiana State University at Alexandria, April 1967.

Thorn, U. L., Tharp, R. G., & Wetzel, R. J. Behavior modification techniques: New tools for probation officers. In J. S. Stumphauzer (Ed.), *Behavior therapy with delinquents*. Springfield, Ill.: Charles C Thomas, 1973. Pp. 266–278.

Thrasher, F. M. *The gang: A study of 1,313 gangs in Chicago (1927)*. Chicago: University of Chicago Press, 1963.

Tillie, R. Interview. Alexandria, Louisiana. February 1977.

Tobias, J. J. Work activities and future goals of the affluent suburban male delinquent. *Vocational Guidance Quarterly*, June 1969, pp. 293–299.

Toby, J. Affluence and adolescent crime. In The President's Commission on Law Enforcement and Administration of Justice, *Task force report: Juvenile delinquency and youth crime*. Washington, D. C.: U. S. Government Printing Office, 1967. Pp. 132–144.

Vaz, E. W. (Ed.). *Middle-class juvenile delinquency*. New York: Harper & Row, 1967.

VIP Examiner. Flint, Mich.: National Council on Crime and Delinquency, 1976, *5*(1), 4.

Wheeler, S., Cottrell, L. S., Jr., & Romasco, A. Juvenile delinquency—its prevention and control. In The President's Commission on Law Enforcement and Administration of Justice, *Task force report: Juvenile delinquency and youth crime.* Washington, D. C.: U. S. Government Printing Office, 1967. Pp. 409–428.

Wright, J., Jr., & James, R., Jr. *A behavioral approach to preventing delinquency.* Springfield, Ill.: Charles C Thomas, 1974.

Other adolescent problems 9

When one is young and on the threshold of life's long deception, rashness is all.

Francoise Sagan
"A Certain Smile"

No text on adolescent behavior can adequately cover the topic without dwelling on some of the major problems confronting young people today. In this chapter we will discuss the more prevalent problems, including drug abuse, adolescent suicide, runaway behavior, and teenage marriage and divorce. We will take a look at some of the underlying causes and factors contributing to these difficulties and suggest possible solutions for some of these problems.

Drug use and abuse

Since the early 1960s, few problems have aroused greater concern among adults than the problem of drug use and abuse among young people. Traditionally, a "drug" was defined as a substance prescribed by a physician for the treatment or prevention of an illness or for the alleviation of pain. Such substances that were believed to be habit forming or addictive were necessarily subject to legal control. Within the framework of our discussion, however, a more precise definition of the term drug is "any substance that by its chemical nature alters structure or function in the living organism" (Modell, 1967, p. 346).

In high schools and even junior high schools (Linder, Lerner, & Burke, 1974) drug use has become so widespread that "turning on" has virtually become the puberty rite for entry into the adult world (Ungerleider & Bowen, 1969). Particularly disturbing to adults is the fact that drug use is generally illegal and is often a felony rather than a misdemeanor ("Pop Drugs," 1969), although there has been a recent trend toward decriminalization in regard to the possession of small amounts of marijuana. During the past decade, considerable research was undertaken to study the consequences of drug use and abuse, but controversy continues to rage, especially over the long-range effects of some drugs.

A brief history of drug abuse in the United States

Although the misuse of drugs has been evident throughout history, it was not until the turn of the 20th century that society began to show concern about this abuse. Kolb (1962) noted that there was an upsurge in drug usage between 1910 and 1920; in 1919 a special committee appointed by the U. S. Secretary of the Treasury reported that there were many heroin addicts under the age of 20 in this country. The use of drugs began to decline in the mid-twenties but increased again after World War II. This increase, which reached a crest during 1951 and 1952, may have reflected a favorable report on marijuana that was issued in 1944. In the early 1940s, Mayor LaGuardia of New York City appointed a committee to study the effects of marijuana. The group found that this substance was not addictive, that physical dependence and tolerance did not develop, and that its use did not lead to the use of addicting drugs, despite the fact that many addicts began as marijuana users (Mayor's Committee on Marijuana, 1944). A decline in drug use occurred again in the late 1950s. Then, during the decade of the sixties, another flareup occurred, greater than that of any previous era and characterized for the first time by widespread indulgence in drugs by White, middle-class college students, as well as by middle-class high school and even junior high school students ("Pop Drugs," 1969). Since the sixties there has been some decrease in the consumption of certain illegal drugs but a substantial increase in the use of alcohol, even at the junior high school level (Linder, Lerner, & Burke, 1974).

The phenomenon of the drug myth

Perhaps never before in history has there been a period when people turned so readily to drugs as during the years since the early 1960s (Holden, 1975). From every side, the public has been beseiged by the wonders that science can perform in relieving physical and psychological aches and pains. One parent takes *tranquilizers* to "soothe the nerves" and often administers them as well to a hyperactive child to keep him or her reasonably manageable. Another drinks liquor to relax after the stresses and strains of a hard day's work. And the young child, long before he or she learns to read, is given a rudimentary course in *physiology* and *pharmacology* by the advertisers who display their wares on television. Small wonder, in this chemical age (Forsythe, 1969), that a myth about drugs has developed—a myth that states that "drugs, with the exception of the ill-defined group referred to as 'dope,' are to be used readily to combat and correct any personal or physiologic disturbance of equanimity; they are the miracles of modern science developed essentially to cure various afflictions which are bad, and therefore the drugs themselves are good and presumably safe" (Pollard, 1967, p. 613). With such a viewpoint, it is not surprising that, in our search for instant solutions and prompt relief from our stresses, we have become possibly the most drug-oriented society on earth (Ray, 1972). Nor should it surprise us that young people, who tend to emulate adults, have turned to drugs in ever-increasing numbers and at all socioeconomic levels in the belief that such substances can give meaning to or relief from a humdrum, purposeless existence (Forsythe, 1969).

Why do adolescents turn to drugs?

The motivating factors underlying adolescent drug use are varied and numerous (Ray, 1972; Sorosiak, Thomas, & Balet, 1976). Undoubtedly, one of the primary factors is youthful rebellion, because adolescents often like to do the opposite of that which is expected of them. Thus, taking drugs can serve as a means of getting even with parents, whom the adolescent may regard as hypocritical because they depend on mood-altering substances (such as alcohol and tranquilizers) while vehemently disapproving of their children's use of similar mood-altering drugs. Using drugs also gives youths a feeling of achieving adult status, which they may mistakenly believe is symbolized by the consumption of alcohol and certain prescription drugs.

Adolescents may also take drugs for their pleasurable effects or to decrease emotional discomfort. In addition, using such substances may reflect a desire for adventure and flirtation with danger, and many young people try out drugs for the first time strictly as an experiment or to satisfy an urge for "kicks." Another, possibly crucial, explanation for drug usage is peer pressure, although one investigator (Tec, 1972) questions whether teenagers use drugs because their friends do or whether they seek out friends who are already engaged in drug use. In any case, use of these substances is often regarded as a means of improving communications with one's peers. Many adolescents report that, under the influence of drugs, their ability to participate and share in group experiences increases.

There are also other factors, possibly of less significance, that may contribute to an adolescent's decision to use drugs. One of these is the frequent, overt use of drugs by certain admired artists, writers, musicians, and would-be messiahs. For example, many rock musicians are well-known drug takers, and their compositions frequently contain references to drugs ("Pop Drugs," 1969). The mass media are probably another cause of the rising incidence of mind-altering drug use, because youths in one section of the country can instantly learn what drugs those elsewhere are using. Finally, the easy availability of drugs, especially in many large urban areas throughout the United States, makes drug use simpler today than it once was.

A distinction between drug use and drug abuse

It should be noted that the vast majority of adolescents do not *abuse* drugs; they *use* drugs for kicks and for experimentation. They may take a drug on several occasions and then quit or use it only intermittently and in moderation ("Pop Drugs," 1969; Yankelovich, 1975). It is not these youths who are of greatest concern to adults; rather, it is those who become habituated or addicted to these substances who distress us.

We must also distinguish between the terms *addiction* and *habituation*. The World Health Organization (1950) defined drug addiction as "a state of periodic or chronic intoxication detrimental to the individual and to society produced by the repeated consumption of a drug, natural or synthetic" (p. 6). Addiction is typically characterized by an overwhelming desire or need to continue using the drug and to obtain it by any means possible, by the need for ever-increasing dosages in order to maintain the same effect, and by both psychological and physiological dependence on the drug's effects. It is the third factor that is the most important in distinguishing addiction from habituation (Pollard, 1967), because habituation is characterized primarily by psychological, rather than physiological, dependence on a substance (Hinsie & Campbell, 1960).

Sociological and psychological patterns characteristic of the drug abuser

Laskowitz (1964) has suggested that drug abuse (also called "substance abuse") develops primarily in a psychological context and that physiological dependence is of less importance. He points out, as have others who treat drug abusers (Saint, 1969), that in most instances abuse occurs among those individuals who have emotional disorders. Another investigator (Schwartzman, 1975) describes the physical-dependence factor as a fallacy and a myth. He believes that it is the pleasurable effects of the drug that cause the abuser to persist in his or her drug use. It is not so much an inability to tolerate abstinence because of physiological dependence, according to Schwartzman; it is the social context or environment, especially the abuser's family, that causes the abusive behavior to persist. In such situations, both the family and the abuser believe that he or she cannot stop and should not be held responsible for his or her behavior while under the influence of the drug or be expected to refuse the drug when it is available. This reinforcement of the abuser's feeling of powerlessness is particularly typical of the mother, who often believes that her drug-abusing offspring should stay home and be taken care of by her (Schwartzman, 1975).

Without a doubt, the pattern of emotional dependency on the mother or on a mother figure is one of the most striking traits of male drug abusers (Siegler & Osmund, 1968; Schwartzman, 1975). Evidence indicates that this dependency is fostered by the mother's undue pampering and overprotective behavior. Often this protectiveness is an attempt to compensate for the absence of a stable father figure in the home or for the presence of a "cop-out" father—that is, one who is emotionally detached from his family (Lieberman, 1974). Without a strong father figure to serve as a model, a son may experience sex-role confusion. Such boys often identify with other substance abusers, who provide them with a certain sense of status and belonging that they failed to acquire within the home. Even though such identification may be negative, these boys usually find it preferable to role confusion (Lieberman, 1974). When the father is present in the home, the drug-abusing son may be confronted by a *double-bind* message, wherein he receives conflicting communications from his parents. He is torn between a father who says "To be a man you must work hard" and a mother who says "You don't have to work because you're sick" (Schwartzman, 1975, p. 156). Not surprisingly, drug abusers often perceive themselves as inadequate individuals.

Numerous other personality traits appear with considerable frequency among drug abusers and addicts. The absence of gang affiliation is one pattern noted by Laskowitz (1964), who pointed out that abusers show a preference for associating with one or two individuals with whom they can share the risks and rewards of obtaining drugs. Addicted youths tend to control social situations through their passive manipulation of those around them. They often resort to such techniques as soft-spoken "sweet talk" (Zimmering, Toolan, Safrin, & Wortis, 1951). Consistent with this behavior is the addict's preference for structured situations, which can be more readily evaluated and controlled (Laskowitz, 1964). And although they prefer authoritarian attitudes in others, reflecting their need for control and their distaste for ambiguity, they manipulate others, including those in authority, to such an extent that authority figures may lose any control they have over the addict—a fact of which teachers and others working with such young people need to become cognizant.

Substance abusers are much more likely than nonusers and moderate users to experience frequent bouts of depression and anxiety (Yankelovich, 1975). They also report feeling angry and frustrated much of the time. Because they have generally received inadequate preparation for dealing with stress, drug abusers tend to avoid overt displays of anger toward the objects of their frustrations (Laskowitz, 1964). They seek solutions to their stress through techniques that involve a minimum of conflict with others and that absolve themselves of all blame for any transgressions. Consequently, the expression of their emotions is minimized to such an extent that they fail to resolve their feelings of frustration.

Difficulty in deferring immediate gratification is also common among drug abusers (Laskowitz, 1964). Waiting is intolerable for them because future gratification is uncertain. Substance abusers do not trust authority, which reflects their belief that significant individuals in their lives will not live up to their expectations.

Of special interest to educators are the abusers' fears of failure and their attempts to resolve conflict through avoidance behavior, a pattern that is manifested in their selection of their school programs (Laskowitz, 1964). They also have difficulty in persevering and, thus, often fail to complete what they begin (Yankelovich, 1975). They avoid even diluted academic courses, preferring pleasurable, unpaced activities such as painting, physical education, woodworking, and music. Although these activities offer a refuge from more demanding academic courses, they may at the same time provide the abuser with the opportunity for peer-group recognition and may awaken latent interests and talents of which the young person was previously unaware.

Because substance abusers usually have limited vocational training and a poor academic background, however, they are often restricted to routine, unstimulating jobs. Seldom finding that such work satisfies the demand for immediate gratification that is typical of drug abusers, these youths are swiftly diverted from vocational pursuits and persist, instead, in seeking out the gratification so quickly available through drugs (Laskowitz, 1964).

There is one other area in which the drug abuser shows a pattern of behavior that distinguishes him or her from the nonuser and the moderate user. A study by Westermeyer and Walzer (1975) of a group of young psychiatric patients, aged 17 to 25, disclosed that 17 out of a total of 38 nonusers had attended church during the month prior to hospital admission, whereas only 3 out of 23 drug abusers had attended church during that time. The nonusers tended to come from families that practiced regular church attendance. The researchers suggest three possible explanations for the greater decline in church-going among the substance abusers. First, the termination of church attendance and the commencement of drug usage could both be considered forms of adolescent rebellion. Second, church attendance often serves as a major means of establishing social relationships. Without this source of social interaction, a young person might employ drugs as a substitute. Although primitive cultures and early civilizations frequently combined drug intoxication with religious ritual, drugs and religion are seldom combined today. And, third, drug usage may enable some people to achieve a psychological and emotional state similar to that attained by others through religious practice. In fact, drug abusers might even argue that they and the churchgoers have similar goals but achieve them through different pathways.

Types of drugs used by adolescents

There are numerous substances, both synthetic and natural, available to those who want to use drugs (see Table 9-1). The Maryland Psychiatric Case Register alone listed 77 mood-altering drugs that had been encountered in an eight-month period (Klee, 1969). The imagination and ingenuity displayed by adolescents in their search for substances that will produce the desired psychic effects are at times amazing, although, as marijuana and alcohol have become more

Table 9-1. The types, uses, and effects of drugs: A summary of significant factors related to drug misuse

Drug	Addicting	Habit forming	Tolerance	Withdrawal symptoms	Manner used	Physical complications	Mental complications during use	Mental complications after use	Death by overdose	Conventional therapeutic usage in U.S.A.	Source of drug	Illegal manufacture and sale	Illegal possession
heroin	yes	yes	yes	yes	sniffing, injecting	related to manner of drug use, and kind of life user is living	intoxication	unknown	respiratory failure	none	Europe, Asia, Middle East	felony	felony
barbiturates	yes	yes	yes	yes	oral, injecting	drug related	intoxication	psychosis	convulsions, respiratory failure, shock	yes	U.S.A.	felony	felony
alcohol	yes	yes	yes	yes	oral	drug related, non-drug related	intoxication	brain damage, psychosis	coma, respiratory failure	yes	U.S.A.	felony	misdemeanor
cocaine	no	yes	yes	no	oral, sniffing, injecting	drug related non-drug related	agitation, intoxication	psychosis? brain damage?	convulsions, respiratory failure	none	South America	felony	felony
amphetamines	no	yes	yes	yes	oral, sniffing, injecting	drug related non-drug related	agitation, intoxication	psychosis, brain damage?	convulsions, coma, cerebral hemorrhage	yes	U.S.A.	felony	felony
marijuana	no	yes	no	no	oral, smoking	drug related	intoxication, rare panic or paranoid state	rare psychosis?	unknown	none	grows in almost all climates	felony	felony
LSD	no	yes	yes	no	oral, injecting	drug related	panic, paranoid state	psychosis, paranoia, anxiety reactions, brain damage?	unknown	yes	U.S.A.	felony	felony
airplane glue	no	yes	yes?	yes?	sniffing	drug related?	intoxication	brain damage?	asphyxiation	none	U.S.A.	city and state laws	none, or state misdemeanor

From *The Use and Misuse of Drugs*, by Stanley Einstein. © 1970 by Wadsworth Publishing Company, Inc. Reprinted by permission of the publisher.

and more accessible over the past few years, improvisation is no longer so necessary as it once was. Some of the substances used, however, are successful mood alterers more because of wishful thinking and user expectations than because of any pharmacological effects.

Zinberg (1967) differentiated two types of drug users and pointed out that the kind of drug used depends largely on the group to which the user belongs. The first group, described as "oblivion-seekers," is composed of those mainly from the lower socioeconomic class who use drugs as a means of escape from what they regard as an intolerable environment. The second group, classified as "experience-seekers," consists of those who indulge in drugs not to escape life but to embrace it. Some investigators today, however, would object to describing all experience-seekers as drug abusers. They would be inclined to distinguish between moderate users and heavy users (Holroyd & Kahn, 1974; Yankelovich, 1975). The occasional or moderate user uses drugs for the same reasons that the adult social drinker takes a drink at a party—that is, as a relaxant and tension releaser. On the other hand, the drug abuser's whole world revolves around drugs, and he or she prefers to "turn on" alone or to socialize only with other heavy drug users.

Hamburg, Kraemer, and Jahnke (1975) suggest that there is a hierarchy of mind-altering substances: (1) coffee and tea; (2) beer, wine, and tobacco; (3) marijuana and hard liquor; (4) hallucinogens, depressants, and stimulants; and (5) narcotics. Their research indicates that, in moving up the hierarchy from one level to the next, individuals experience a time interval that allows them an opportunity for new decision making before each new level. The results of this research tend to disprove the idea that the use of one drug invariably leads to the use of others.

Let's take a look at some of the most frequently used substances in this hierarchy of drugs.

Tobacco. Although you might disagree that tobacco is a drug, the fact that it has the power to relax and to relieve tension certainly places it in the category of a mood-altering substance. Although no causal relationship seems to exist, the smoking of tobacco is highly related to the consumption of alcohol and the use of illegal drugs (Milman & Su, 1973). A recent Canadian study (Hanley & Robinson, 1976) of over 73,000 students disclosed that the prevalence of smoking is increasing, especially for girls, who are starting to smoke at progressively younger ages. This research revealed that boys are most likely to begin experimenting with tobacco between the ages of 12 and 16 and that, although girls might start a bit later, their behavior changes from experimenting to serious smoking at a more rapid rate. It also emphasized that one or two experiences with smoking did not necessarily lead to regular smoking. By age 16, however, 52% of the boys and 46% of the girls in the study were serious smokers. The major determinant of whether or not these adolescents started serious use of tobacco seemed to be the smoking behavior of the parents. When at least one parent smoked, the chances were greater that the offspring would do so, particularly for girls whose mothers smoked and for boys whose fathers did so. Hanley and Robinson believe that too many young people regard smoking as a prerequisite for social acceptance by their peers, and they suggest that the social climate be gradually modified so that smoking will no longer be considered a sign of glamour and sophistication.

Alcohol.   Because alcohol is a mind-altering substance, it can readily be classified as a drug, although it differs from most other drugs in that it can be legally purchased, by anyone who is 18 years old or older. Alcohol, which has existed since the era before Christ, is a substance that depresses central-nervous-system activity. This does not mean that excessive consumption of alcohol causes depression; rather, it means that alcohol tends to weaken one's inhibitions. This is why many individuals appear to be stimulated by alcohol. A moderate relaxation of the inhibitions may even be desirable, as in the case of an extremely shy person who becomes somewhat sociable when he or she has had a drink. Excessive amounts of alcohol, however, can weaken the inhibitions to such an extent that they virtually cease to exist. The drinker may then become extremely aggressive and abusive. Alcohol is also an addicting drug, although alcohol addiction, unlike other drug addictions, may take a number of years to develop (Einstein, 1970).

During recent years, there has been a tremendous increase not only in adolescent experimentation with liquor but also in regular use and frequent abuse of alcohol at the junior high and high school levels (Albrecht, 1973; Linder, Lerner, & Burke, 1974). What is even more alarming is the fact that alcohol is often used in conjunction with marijuana and other illicit drugs, a trend reflecting "an unusually urgent drive for oblivion" (Holden, 1975, p. 639) and one that could readily lead to untimely death.

Numerous explanations have been advanced for the increased use and abuse of alcohol. Because most mood-altering drugs are illegal, many young people turn to alcohol, which older adolescents can usually obtain legally and which younger adolescents can obtain fairly easily through older friends or acquaintances. In addition, the possession of alcohol, unlike that of other drugs, is not likely to result in legal proceedings against the young person. A third explanation for the increased use of alcohol is peer influence. One study of 26,000 high school seniors in South Carolina disclosed that 50% of them gave their reason for drinking as "going along with the group" (Kimes, Smith, & Maher, 1969). The desire to assert one's independence and to proclaim one's adult status is also a factor that contributes to the use of alcohol (Maddox, 1970), as are curiosity and the desire to experience the physical and psychological sensations produced by this substance. In addition, drinking serves as another means of "sowing one's wild oats" (Offord, 1965). And, finally, some young people undoubtedly drink in order to achieve the oblivion of drunkenness.

According to many observers, the primary factor in determining whether a young person will drink is the drinking behavior of significant adults in his or her life, particularly the parents (MacKay, Phillips, & Bryce, 1967; Maddox, 1970). In reviewing 11 studies of high school drinking behavior, Maddox (1970) concluded that young people are generally offered their first drink in the home and that their decision to drink is often influenced by the drinking habits of both family and friends. He also found that the adolescent who drinks typically reports that at least one parent drinks and that the abstaining youth has parents who are both abstainers. Maddox further noted that in the United States people learn to drink during adolescence, rather than childhood, and that most young people will have at least experimented with liquor by the time they graduate from high school, although they will not necessarily have established a regular drinking pattern.

Although the majority of adolescents are moderate in their use of alcohol, the incidence of alcoholism among teenagers is rising. According to one investigation, half of all American high school students report attending drinking parties at least once a month, and a majority of these (61%) admit to becoming intoxicated once a month (*Communication Strategies on Alcohol and Highway Safety,* 1975). As each state lowers the legal age at which alcoholic beverages can be purchased, there is an increase in the incidence of new youthful drinkers who fail to learn how to drink in a controlled manner (Ryback, 1975).

A study by Ray (1972) of adolescents who had been referred to an alcoholism clinic for treatment disclosed that all of the youths had one or both parents who were alcoholics. Although many of these young people expressed considerable anxiety about their own drinking, alcohol reduced this anxiety, and hence they continued to drink.

Ray even suggests that one motive for their drinking was to prove that they could outdo the alcoholic parent. Another pattern noted in this group was that adolescent alcoholics generally engage in group, not solitary, drinking, perhaps because they are seeking a substitute for the family ties they were unable to establish at home (Ray, 1972).

Personality traits of the alcoholic include low frustration tolerance, lack of perseverance, impulsiveness, occasional hostile behavior (which not surprisingly leads them to report feelings of isolation) and intense conflict over dependence versus independence needs (Ray, 1972).

Marijuana. Despite a decade of research, the greatest controversy over drugs revolves around the substance known as marijuana, or "grass," which is a relaxant/euphoriant that, in high doses, can become a hallucinogen. Although many oblivion-seekers start their drug consumption with marijuana, this drug's main appeal has been to experience-seekers, who come primarily from the middle- and upper-socioeconomic classes. The United States first declared marijuana an illegal narcotic in 1937, and until recently its use was considered a felony in most states. In 1973, however, the National Commission on Marijuana and Drug Abuse recommended that penalties for possession of marijuana for private use be abolished. The most common argument presented in favor of the decriminalization of marijuana is that the damage done by arresting, convicting, and, consequently, giving permanent criminal records to the many marijuana users is far greater than any harm that might ensue from the decriminalization of the drug.

Marijuana has a history of use dating back 3000 years, and, according to the World Health Organization (1950), there are more than 50 million users throughout the world, most of them using marijuana illegally. Although the LaGuardia Committee (Mayor's Committee on Marijuana, 1944) declared this drug to be harmless and pointed out that its use results only in nonproductive and apathetic behavior, the controversy continues to rage. For example, Kolansky and Moore (1971) reported that they had seen hundreds of patients with psychiatric and neurological symptoms resulting from marijuana use—symptoms that seemed to appear simultaneously with the use of the drug and disappear within 3 to 24 months following cessation of marijuana use. More recently (Kolansky & Moore, 1975) these researchers have suggested that there is a correlation between the symptoms their patients exhibited from marijuana use and the duration and frequency of their use of the drug. They have concluded that, with extensive consumption of the drug, biochemical and structural changes take place in the central nervous system. Included among the symptoms that Kolansky and Moore described were decreased self-awareness and judgment, slowed thinking, shortened attention span, decreased goal-oriented behavior, and blunted affect characterized by artificial calm, a sense of well-being, and the illusion of newly developed insight and emotional maturity.

On the other hand, Maugh (1975) has observed that adverse effects of marijuana use were found only among those who used the drug in large quantities for prolonged periods. He has seen no evidence that casual, infrequent use of marijuana produces any ill effects.

The research is obviously inconsistent and contradictory. Why? Among the problems, according to Tinklenberg (1975), are the following: (1) lack of agreement about what constitutes heavy use, (2) the wide use of retrospective studies that rely on the often inaccurate recollections of subjects, (3) difficulty in obtaining an accurate baseline of metabolic traits for subjects even if they stop smoking marijuana for a few days prior to testing, (4) difficulty in applying the results of marijuana research on animals to human beings, and (5) the short duration of most research projects, which eliminates the possibility of studying the long-range effects of marijuana use.

Why do adolescents find marijuana so appealing? Apparently, in small amounts this drug acts as a mild euphoric agent and sedative somewhat comparable to alcohol. When taken in large doses, however, its effects resemble those of the hallucinogens or *psychedelic* drugs (McGlothlin & West, 1968). Some users report that marijuana gives them feelings of pleasure, enhances their creativity, provides insight, and generally enriches their lives (Keeler, 1967). Others use the drug as a means of demonstrating their nonconformity (Cunningham, Cunningham, & English, 1974). Because people are often moved to defy laws they regard as unjust—as demonstrated by defiance of the Prohibition laws of the 1920s—many individuals believe that the decriminalization of marijuana possession would reduce its appeal for the adolescent.

It should be noted, however, that marijuana users do differ from nonusers, at least at the college level, in certain psychological and sociological traits and attitudes. A study of 547 University of Texas undergraduate students disclosed that marijuana users were characterized by greater dissatisfaction, disillusionment, and alienation than nonusers (Cunningham et al., 1974). These traits apparently reflect their greater discontent with politics, their lack of concern with status or socioeconomic class, and their indifference toward social responsibility. Marijuana users are also distrustful of society and believe that organized religion has little to offer them, because they disagree with the values of traditional religious institutions. At the same time, marijuana users tend to be flexible, unconventional, and responsive to new ideas and perspectives, whereas nonusers are likely to be conservative, dogmatic, and unworldly.

This same study by Cunningham et al. (1974) disclosed that users came from higher socioeconomic backgrounds than nonusers. Three possible explanations were offered for this phenomenon. It was suggested that more affluent students are better able to finance their use of marijuana. In addition, these young people demonstrate confidence that, if they should be apprehended, their case would in all likelihood be dismissed. And, last, because of the economic success of their parents, these students feel frustrated by the probability that they will be unable to exceed their parents' accomplishments, whereas adolescents from less affluent backgrounds can see opportunities for personal advancement within the conventional system.

Hallucinogenic or psychedelic drugs.   Psychedelic drugs are considerably more dangerous than alcohol and marijuana, and, fortunately, they are not used so extensively by young people (Pollard, 1967). Probably the best known among this group is *LSD* (lysergic acid diethylamide). These drugs are sometimes described as *psychomimetic* because they create effects in normal individuals that mimic psychosis or severe emotional disorders. "Under the guise of bringing about increased creativity and greater feelings of harmony and loving kindness, many students have been given these drugs— with tragic results in some cases" (Blaine, 1966, p. 76). The temporary pseudopsychotic experiences induced by hallucinogenic substances can produce states of panic and, in extreme cases, can even lead to suicide. Flashback episodes (fleeting recurrences of the drug experience) have been reported weeks and even months after the individual has ceased taking the drug.

The reasons given for taking hallucinogenic drugs are varied. A desire to escape from problems and frustrations, pressure from peers, and the belief that such drugs can increase creativity, insight, and self-knowledge are some of the explanations offered by users of these drugs. Consider the case of Jonathan.

> Jonathan, who was an extremely bright young man with considerable literary talent, was the son of a deceased Air Force officer. Consequently, he and his family had lived all over the United States. Because of his superior intellectual ability, Jonathan had skipped two grades in the public schools. However, because he was physically quite small, he had developed a low self-concept. The fact

that he was so much smaller than his classmates prevented him from keeping up with their social development, and ultimately he dropped out of school. He then drifted to a large city, where he began taking LSD, perhaps with the hope that it would raise his image of himself in his own eyes as well as in the eyes of others.

There has been some evidence that LSD can damage human chromosomes and that users therefore take the risk of passing on birth defects to their children (Cohen, Marinello, & Back, 1967; Ginott, 1969). However, the findings are not conclusive, because impure LSD, malnutrition, and inadequate prenatal care may also be contributing factors. Nevertheless, evidence is accumulating that women who use LSD during pregnancy do experience a higher incidence of miscarriages and give birth to more infants with *congenital* deformities (Ray, 1972). For some young people, knowledge of such possibilities has proved to be a sufficient deterrent to using LSD. Unfortunately, however, this drug is still easily made and readily available in many areas of the United States and Canada.

Stimulants and depressants.   There are many young people taking stimulants such as *amphetamines* (for example, Benzedrine) and *barbiturates* (for example, Nembutal) strictly for kicks. Unfortunately, barbiturates can be as addictive as narcotics, and an overdose of Benzedrine, which stimulates the central nervous system, can lead to extreme excitement marked by hallucinations and delusions of persecution (Ray, 1972).

One of the most dangerous of the amphetamines is Methedrine, more commonly called "speed" ("Pop Drugs," 1969). Taken in moderation for a short time, such stimulants can be safe and helpful in treating depression and in curbing the appetite. Individuals who wish to elevate their moods, however, consume many times the normal medical dosage. Such overdoses, especially of the drug Methedrine, can provoke psychoses similar to *schizophrenia* and, in some cases, can raise the blood pressure to such an extent that death results.

Heroin.   This addictive drug, a derivative of opium, is one of the most hazardous and is usually the choice of the oblivion-seekers. Heroin provides a greater kick but at the same time a greater pull toward physical dependency than any other drug that has been discussed. The potential heroin taker knows that he or she will be breaking the law and generally becoming dependent on this drug. Such dependence usually reaches the point that addicts need six injections a day at four-hour intervals (Ray, 1972).

Family patterns are rather distinctive for the potential oblivion-seeker. More than half of them come from homes broken by a parental death before the child reached age 16. Frequently, such addicts are only children or the youngest in the family. The dependency on the mother that we discussed earlier in relation to the behavioral traits of drug abusers was reconfirmed in a study by Zinberg (1967). This study reported that large numbers of addicts in their 20s and 30s live with their mothers or with other female relatives.

The dangers of using heroin are readily apparent. In 1969, in New York City alone, more than 200 adolescents died as a result of heroin use ("Why Did Walter Die?" 1969). Such tragedies are sometimes due to an overdose, but more often they are the result of unsterile conditions under which the drug is injected, causing hepatitis or tetanus, or they are the outgrowth of malnutrition and other disorders resulting from the addict's indifference to his or her physical well-being (Einstein, 1970; Ray, 1972).

There is much controversy over the incidence of narcotics addiction in this country. In 1972 the Bureau of Narcotics and Dangerous Drugs estimated that there were over a half-million narcotics addicts in the United States. That same year Ray (1972) suggested that the rate of new users appeared to be declining and that the total number of addicts seemed to have stabilized or perhaps even decreased. In 1975, however, Holden declared that, although progress had been made during the early 1970s in curtailing the use of heroin, the progress was only temporary; heroin use was again flourishing and had even increased.

Present incidence of drug use and abuse in the United States

The extent of drug use and drug abuse seems to vary according to geographical location and according to the age of the adolescents. Towns near the Mexican border, cities with large international airports, and large seaports are areas in which such substances are often smuggled into the country and, thus, provide adolescents with relatively easy access to many drugs. Because of the ready availability of drugs in such cities, drug use is much more widespread than in other localities.

A study (Blum, Aron, Tutko, Feinglass, & Fort, 1969) of a suburban high school in the San Francisco Bay Area in the spring of 1968 revealed the beginning of a trend that has persisted, with few exceptions, to the present. At that time, it was noted that the illegal use of drugs had increased two to four times over the rates disclosed by studies of other high schools in the same area 18 months earlier. The 1968 research also revealed that, once an adolescent began to use drugs, the chance of his or her continuing to do so was great, particularly when the drug was marijuana. The investigators hypothesized that the increased drug usage reflected (1) a considerable increase in exposure to such substances, (2) greater experimentation with drugs, and (3) widespread use of drugs among middle-class students in the San Francisco Bay Area (Blum et al., 1969).

Another study (Linder, Lerner, & Burke, 1974) undertaken in this same area in 1972 focused its attention on seventh- and eighth-grade students, because the consumption of drugs had continued to increase not only in high schools but also in junior high schools. These researchers reported that, of 201 seventh-grade boys, one-fourth had used marijuana and, of 160 eighth-grade boys, one-third had used this substance. Among 223 seventh-grade girls, one-fifth had at least tried marijuana and, of the 192 eighth-grade girls, almost one-third had used it. Such figures are indeed disturbing, but it should be noted that, because San Francisco is a busy seaport, drug use in that city is undoubtedly much greater than in other areas of the United States. More conservative figures can be seen in another 1972 study (Sorosiak et al., 1976) of 3348 students in grades 8–12 in a medium-sized town in the Northeastern part of the United States. Only 8% of these 8th-graders reported having used marijuana, although, by the 12th grade, the number of users had risen to 42%.

In the use of hard liquor, the San Francisco study (Linder, Lerner, & Burke, 1974) reported that 43.6% of the 7th-grade boys and 40.1% of the 7th-grade girls had consumed hard liquor and that over two-thirds of the boys and almost one-half of the girls in the 8th grade had done so. Again, these rates were much higher than those reported in the Sorosiak et al. study, which disclosed that only 29% of the 8th graders had used alcohol, although 73% of the high school seniors had. This latter study, however, did not distinguish between beer/wine and hard liquor. Since several religions use wine in their services, studies of alcohol use that do not distinguish between hard liquor and other alcoholic beverages may report slightly inflated alcohol-use statistics. In fact, with the wide discrepancy in figures reported from various parts of the United States and Canada, it is difficult to ascertain just how widespread the use and abuse of alcohol and other drugs actually is.

Also of great concern is the trend toward polydrug, or multiple drug, use. The National Commission on Marijuana and Drug Abuse (1972) reported a positive correlation between the use of tobacco (and, to a lesser extent, alcohol) and the use of marijuana and other drugs.

As noted earlier in this chapter, some combinations of drugs (for example, alcohol and barbiturates) can be fatal. At the same time, research does show that the vast majority of marijuana users do not go on to use other drugs. In fact, the majority either continue to use only marijuana or forsake marijuana in favor of alcohol.

Resources for coping with drug use and abuse

From the widespread misuse of drugs, it is apparent that parents, teachers, and legal authorities have been very ineffective in handling the drug problem. Certainly, schools that expel drug-using students and parents who report their drug-using children to law-enforcement officials have not deterred these youths from using such substances.

Apparently, few adolescents, whether users or nonusers, shy away from drugs for moral or legal reasons (Blum, 1969). Those who abstain from drug usage often report that they do so because of their concern about physical damage that might result from drug use. Some adolescents simply believe that drug use is inappropriate for them; they lack interest in drug-induced euphoria or in expanding their experiences and sensations through the use of such substances.

Unfortunately, most drug education in the secondary schools has been an utter failure (Bard, 1975). In fact, some programs have even inadvertently encouraged drug use or taught students how to use drugs more effectively. The negative effects of many of these programs are exemplified in the following case. A selected group of junior high school students in Ann Arbor, Michigan, were given a ten-week course that was established to "expose the dangers of drugs." A followup study on the effectiveness of the instruction disclosed that these young people not only had become less apprehensive about drug use but also had significantly increased their purchase and use of marijuana and LSD (Bard, 1975).

Because of the ineffectiveness of many of these programs, experts are saying that schools would do well to eliminate them. In fact, the National Commission on Marijuana and Drug Abuse (1973) even called for a nationwide moratorium on all drug-education programs being offered in the schools and requested that state legislatures repeal all laws requiring such instruction (about one-half of the states had made drug education compulsory).

Criticisms of drug-education programs have been numerous. Many teachers of these courses are poorly trained and, consequently, know less about drugs and drug abuse than their students do. Typically, drug-education courses are guilty of "overkill"; they inundate the students with lectures, brochures, and films that are often hastily and inaccurately produced. These materials are usually crisis oriented, exaggerated, inaccurate, and sermonizing. Many of the programs reflect adult bias and thereby contribute to the vicious cycle of a greater generation gap and increased drug usage (Bard, 1975).

What can the schools do to counteract the rising incidence of drug abuse? One interesting suggestion came from Ungerleider and Bowen (1969). They proposed that each school employ an ombudsman, or impartial referee, to serve the students' interests without any obligation to the school administration. This individual would be an approachable and understanding teacher with several months of special training and education in drug use and abuse. Ungerleider and Bowen define the role of this person in the following statement:

> The ombudsman may best be described as a parent surrogate who is "not square" (but who does not use "pot," "acid," or "speed"), who is not afraid of discussing drugs, and who has some training in recognizing severe degrees of emotional disorder—enough to refer the chronic drug abuser (rather than the curious experimenter) for further help [p. 1696].

The ombudsman would be available to students at almost any time. He or she would be granted the right of privileged communication —that is, the ombudsman would not be required to reveal students' confidences to parents, the police, or school authorities. Such an individual not only could counsel young people troubled about drug use but also could provide information to students requesting it that would enable the students to make more informed decisions about whether to use drugs.

A somewhat similar approach has been tried in San Jose, California, where a popular young teacher was assigned to learn about the drug culture by going on "buys" with police, attending trials of "busted" drug pushers, and working in drug-treatment centers. Upon returning to school, this teacher assumed two roles; that of teacher and that of counselor of students with drug problems. As a result of this effort, there was a sharp decline in drug abuse at that school (Bard, 1975).

Some drug-education specialists believe that it would be a mistake to scrap all drug-education programs. They believe that such programs should continue but should focus their attention on "high risk" abusers, rather than attempt to educate all students (Bard, 1975).

However, many drug abusers are also troubled adolescents who have an underlying psychopathology. In such instances, professional counseling may be needed in addition to the drug education.

Other researchers think that the best approach to working with drug abusers is an indirect one (Irwin, Hayes, & Grunden, 1975). They believe that schools should attempt to modify the low self-concept that is typical of drug abusers and that often precipitates the decision to turn to drugs. By teaching the skills needed for sound decision making and problem solving and by helping adolescents develop a capacity for self-understanding and awareness of self and others, educators could help them acquire higher self-esteem and greater self-reliance. Because many users prefer to obtain drug information from their peers (Schaps, Sanders, & Hughes, 1974), peer-counseling programs (which were discussed in Chapter 7) might be another useful means of working with drug users and abusers.

Adolescent suicide

A second major problem of adolescents is that of suicide. Although suicide is not unique to this age group, it is more prevalent in this group than in any other except that of the aged. Over 4000 of the 25,000 suicides in the United States each year are committed by those between 15 and 24 years of age. Since 1954, the suicide rate for this age group has risen 150%—from 4.2 per 100,000 in 1954 to 10.6 per 100,000 in 1973. Among males aged 15 to 24, the increase has been even greater; it has gone from 6.7 per 100,000 in 1954 to 17 per 100,000 in 1973 (Hendin, 1975a). For those aged 15 to 19 (see Table 9-2), the suicide rate increased between 1960 and 1967 from 3.6 per 100,000 to 4.7 per 100,000, and suicide now ranks as the third leading cause of death for this age group (Miller, 1975). Among college-age students, suicide is the second highest cause of death, being surpassed only by accidents (Knight, 1968). However, it should be noted that some accidents are also conscious or unconscious suicide attempts (Shneidman & Dizmang, 1967).

The ratio of male to female adolescent suicide is about 3:1. Females, however, make suicidal attempts twice as frequently as males. The discrepancies in these ratios may reflect not so much differences in attempt rates as differences in the effectiveness of the methods used (Morris, Kovacs, Beck, & Wolffe, 1974). Among college students, for every completed suicide there are some 50 unsuccessful attempts (Finch & Poznanski, 1973). Thus, it can readily be seen that suicidal behavior should be a major concern for those who deal with young people.

Table 9-2.   Breakdown of suicide rates for 15- to 19-year-olds

15-19 Years of Age	PER 100,000 POPULATION							
	1960	1961	1962	1963	1964	1965	1966	1967
Suicides	3.6	3.4	3.8	4.0	4.0	4.0	4.3	4.7
Males	5.6	5.3	5.5	6.0	6.3	6.1	6.5	7.0
Females	1.6	1.5	2.0	1.9	1.7	1.9	2.1	2.4
White	3.8	3.6	3.9	4.2	4.2	4.1	4.4	4.9
Males	5.9	5.5	5.8	6.4	6.7	6.3	6.7	7.5
Females	1.6	1.6	2.0	1.9	1.7	1.8	2.1	2.2
Nonwhite	2.4	2.5	2.8	2.9	2.9	3.8	3.6	3.7
Males	3.4	3.7	3.7	3.7	4.0	5.2	4.8	3.8
Females	1.5	1.3	1.9	2.0	1.8	2.4	2.4	3.5

From Vital Statistics of the United States, Volume 2: Mortality, United States Department of Health, Education, and Welfare Public Health Service, 1968.

There appears to be a typical sequence of events leading up to suicide. Usually there is a history of problems beginning in childhood, which we will discuss in more detail in a moment. These childhood problems escalate for a time, and often new problems arise. Ultimately, there is a cyclical reaction in which an unhappy child withdraws from others and, the more he or she withdraws, the more alienated from both parents and peers the child becomes (Jacobs & Teicher, 1967). The precipitating event (the incident that finally causes the person to attempt suicide) may seem somewhat trivial to others (for example, breaking up with a boyfriend or girlfriend), and the suicidal behavior may thus appear to be a sudden, impulsive reaction to this distressing event. However, in many instances suicidal thoughts have been present for some time before the actual attempt takes place (Draper, 1976).

Suicidal attempts can be placed into three categories: (1) half-hearted attempts that are really cries for help, (2) serious attempts that are made once but never repeated, and (3) attempts that are successfully completed (Jacobs & Teicher, 1967). When the suicidal reaction appears to be out of all proportion to the precipitating event, there is usually a history of very ineffective, superficial mechanisms for coping with stress, poor impulse control, a low self-concept, and a tendency to overreact (Hofmann, 1975).

The ways in which people in a society learn to cope with their aggression are reflected in the society's rates of suicide (aggression against self) and homicide (aggression against others). "No one kills himself who did not want to kill another, or at least, wish death to another" (Havighurst, 1969, p. 59). Because those in the lower socioeconomic classes often experience greater frustration and because parental discipline techniques in these classes usually model aggressive behavior, lower-class individuals often possess less effective controls over their aggressive impulses than those in the middle and upper socioeconomic classes. Consequently, they more frequently resort to both suicide and homicide.

What precipitates suicidal behavior? After surveying the research on this question, we believe that one of the primary factors is the family situation. The loss of one parent through death or divorce is a very common familial pattern among those who commit suicide (Barter, Swaback, & Todd, 1968; Haider, 1968; Hendin, 1975b). Many suicidal adolescents report feeling unloved by their parents, and, indeed, they may be. Sabbath (1969) has described what he calls the "expendable child." He suggests that parents of such children have a conscious or unconscious wish, which may or may not be verbalized, to be rid of the child. The adolescent perceives this wish. Teicher and Jacobs (1966) noted that 88% of the adolescent suicide attempts they studied occurred in the home and that, frequently, one or both parents were in the next room at the time of the attempts. They suggest that this reflects the extent of adolescent alienation from their parents or, perhaps, that it indicates the parents' denial of self-destructive behavior in adolescents they no longer want.

In other instances, the suicidal adolescent's family is disrupted. That is, there is much conflict between the parents, or a troubled (or troublesome) relative living in the home is receiving the parents' attention and/or emotional support at the expense of the suicidal child. Compounding these family problems that are typical of suicidal young people is the fact that all youths, as they leave their childhood behind them, experience an increased psychological distance from their parents. The parents, although concerned about their offspring, may be unaware of the growing inner stress of their adolescent children and of the communication problems that their offspring are experiencing. Even when communication has not previously been troublesome, these youths may suddenly find themselves unable to express the distress they feel about their increasing, ill-defined unhappiness (Hofmann, 1975). When an unsuccessful suicide attempt is made, the family may react with anger and rejection, because they feel disgraced by the adolescent's action. Hence, what initially may have been a gesture and a cry for help can lead to repeated attempts and to the increased risk of lethality (King, 1971).

Another factor contributing to adolescent suicidal behavior is that of family mobility. For example, in one study of immigrants to

Great Britain, it was found that, although immigrants composed only 12% of the population, suicide attempts by these newly arrived people constituted 20% of the total rate. In this study, in which most of the immigrants were from the West Indies, it was reported that children were often separated from their parents for a considerable period of time; often they were living with grandparents in the West Indies until their parents could afford to send for them (White, 1974). Similarly, Puerto Rican immigrants, who constitute 11% of the population of New York City, are responsible for 22% of that city's suicide attempts (Jacobziner, 1965).

An additional family factor is that of birth order, or ordinal rank, of the adolescent in the family structure. In an investigation of 56 children and adolescents, aged 6 to 19, who were hospitalized for suicide attempts, 20 of the 56 were the eldest children in the family (Haider, 1968). There may be a number of reasons for such statistics. One explanation might be that many young couples are unprepared for parenthood and, thus, make mistakes with their first child that they do not make with subsequent children. Eldest children are also likely to be subjected to the greatest pressure to succeed. On the other hand, suicide attempts are also frequent among the youngest members of large families—children who may have been unplanned and unwanted and, thus, do not receive enough love and attention.

Scholastically, suicidal adolescents in junior high and high school tend to lag behind their classmates anywhere from one to four years (Finch & Poznanski, 1973). However, one study (Seiden, 1966) reported that, although suicidal college students generally have a high grade-point average, they are often social isolates who try to compensate for their loneliness through increased study and absorption in their academic work (or, conversely, their loneliness could result from their devoting too much time to their studies). This research also noted that there was a pronounced drop in grades during the semester preceding the suicide (Seiden, 1966). Such findings raise the question of whether the emotional difficulties preceding the suicide interfered with the students' studies or whether depression and suicide were reactions to the lower grades. The fact that the families of suicidal college students are usually more highly educated than those of nonsuicidal students suggests that greater pressure for academic achievement may be one of the causes of such suicides (Blaine & Carmen, 1968).

A lack of strong religious affiliation is also a common factor among suicidal adolescents (Corder, Shorr, & Corder, 1974). The decline in formal religious affiliation among adolescents has removed a source of moral and emotional support and made more difficult the tasks of establishing a philosophy of life and resolving the identity crisis (Knight, 1968). Other causes of adolescent suicidal behavior include the rapidly changing values in our society (which was discussed in Chapter 7), concern over sex, fear of academic or social failure, excessive competitiveness, and stress and depression resulting from difficulties in interpersonal relationships.

Suggestibility may also be a factor in adolescent suicide. Teicher and Jacobs (1966) noted that 44% of their suicidal patients had a friend or close relative who had attempted or committed suicide. One of your authors (B. R.) recalls a time in the early 1970s when there were five attempted suicides in one dormitory in a single semester.

How can parents, teachers, and other adults recognize potentially suicidal behavior? There are three major kinds of clues that indicate that an individual may be contemplating suicide: verbal, behavioral, and situational. The most obvious verbal clue, of course, is the individual's threat to commit suicide. Such threats should never be ignored, because, contrary to popular belief, those who verbalize such thoughts are likely to attempt suicide. In fact, 90% of all individuals who attempt suicide have told at least one person of their intention to do so. Another type of verbal clue is the specific request for help. Fortunately, 80% of those who ask for help can indeed be helped; only 10% seriously intend to kill themselves when they make suicide attempts, and a mere 10% are clinically insane (Gallagher, 1976). Behavioral clues include changes in the potential suicide's normal behavior pattern. A sudden withdrawal from association with others, loss of appetite, reluctance or refusal to talk, and changes in sleeping habits can all be indications of an imminent suicide attempt. The last category, situational clues, includes an incident in the person's life that might act as the "last straw" or precipitating event for the suicide. Loss of a significant other through death, separation, or divorce, failure at a task that the individual considers important, and rejection by others are all events that might serve to precipitate a suicide attempt (Gallagher, 1976).

King (1971) notes the dangers that professionals encounter in responding only to symptoms manifested by suicide-prone youth and not to the causes of these symptoms. He suggests the importance of bringing together the suicidal adolescent and others who may be contributing to his or her problems (for example, feuding parents). He also points out the need for helping suicide-prone young people avoid the social isolation that so easily arises in our impersonal society by providing them with adequate social and therapeutic support and followup contact. Although professional assistance may be needed in most cases of suicidal behavior, additional support for troubled youths can be provided through such programs as peer counseling.

Runaway behavior

In an attempt to escape from their problems, many adolescents turn to runaway behavior, which is a status offense in most states. Basically, running away is defined as leaving the home of one's parents (or guardians) for longer than one night without parental consent (Deisher, 1975). Between 600,000 and 1 million American teenagers run away from their homes each year, most of them from white, middle-class, suburban areas. Numbers of male and female runaways are approximately equal. The average age of runaways is 15, but many are no older than 13 or 14 ("Runaway Children," 1972; Zastrow & Navarre, 1975). Since 1970 there has been a steady increase in the number of runaways in the United States each year—an increase that cannot be accounted for solely on the basis of population growth (see Table 9-3).

Table 9-3.   Number of youths arrested as runaways in the United States, 1968–1971

Age Groups	1968	1969	1970	1971
10	4,929	5,402	5,189	5,702
11–12	7,983	10,153	11,075	12,639
13–14	44,173	47,545	53,966	64,220
15	37,525	40,973	46,618	53,664
16	35,005	37,319	42,175	47,418
17	17,637	18,076	20,050	20,901
Totals	136,252	159,468	179,073	204,544

From *Uniform Crime Reports: 1968–1971*, Federal Bureau of Investigation, U. S. Department of Justice. Washington, D. C.: U. S. Government Printing Office, 1972.

There are a number of different methods of classifying runaways (Stierlin, 1973; Council of Planning Affiliates, 1973; Deisher, 1975), but generally runaways belong to one of the following five groups:

1. Runaways who are adventurous and who leave home to see the world. These are often older teenagers, and many are emotionally stable.
2. Runaways who break their connections with "the Establish-

ment," including their families, because of discontent. These, too, are often older adolescents, and they might be described as rebels. They are interested in causes and/or movements that are in conflict with their parents' beliefs.

3. Runaways who have been emotionally or psychologically damaged by their families, their schools, and/or their communities. Many of these youths come from broken or disintegrating homes, and they often have difficulty relating to others.

4. Runaways who leave home because of the intense pressures that have been placed on them by the family and the school. These young people often have no goals and, consequently, may wander aimlessly and indefinitely.

5. Runaways who do not fit into one of the other groups. These are sometimes referred to as *abortive runaways* or *floaters*. They attempt to run away but never seem to get very far, which often reflects their ambivalence about such behavior.

Regardless of the classifications used, however, these youths are more likely than not resorting to runaway behavior in order to escape from disturbed home environments. Their running away reflects their feelings of being unwanted, and, indeed, in many instances they are unwanted children. Not surprisingly, such adolescents are likely to have a low self-concept; they often feel worthless, discouraged, and afraid (Jenkins, 1971).

Runaway behavior has become an important social problem because of its very serious consequences. In fact, only drug abuse, with which running away has many connections, compares in importance as an issue in the mental health of the American adolescent (Stierlin, 1973). Although the law does not always classify runaways as delinquents, these youths are often picked up by the police and treated as delinquents because there are no other resources available for dealing with runaways. They may even be confined at a youth facility or a local jail until their parents are contacted. Often these young people run away again within a short time. When runaways are located by the police, counseling, which is often needed, is rarely provided either for the adolescents or for their parents. And if they are not picked up, runaways may wander the streets of large cities, finally taking refuge in "crash pads" where they may find themselves in the company of drug addicts, sexual perverts, or others with a negative impact on adolescents (Deisher, 1975).

As a result, a number of runaway centers have opened around the country, mainly in large cities. These centers are usually staffed by volunteers, who are often college students. One such center, called Briarpatch, was established in 1972 at Madison, Wisconsin, to serve as both a runaway center and a youth-advocate service (Zastrow & Navarre, 1975). It provides emergency shelter, care, and counseling for runaways and their parents. Because it is a licensed child-care agency, Briarpatch is able to recruit and license foster parents. Youthful runaways are placed in these foster homes, which are staffed by unpaid volunteers, for periods of up to two weeks. This center requires that the parents of the runaways be notified that their offspring are in contact with the agency, and parental consent must be obtained in order for the youths to be placed in foster homes. The center also makes referrals for legal, medical, and psychiatric services. Nearly 80% of the runaways who contact Briarpatch eventually return to their homes (Navarre & Zastrow, 1974).

Another type of runaway center is the street clinic. One such clinic, in Boston, is called Project Place. This nonprofit, multiservice agency is a "runaway house" outreach facility that was established to provide brief counseling for runaways under the age of 18 and for those commonly described as "street people" (Project Place, 1971). In 1970 this center recorded visits from 649 runaways, 60% males and 40% females. In a sample of 41 (18 females and 23 males) of these runaways, Howell, Emmons, and Frank, (1973) reported that a majority of the youths were primarily troubled by rather common problems of growing up. Almost two-thirds of these adolescents felt, in retrospect, that running away had provided them with a positive growth experience despite the difficulties involved, such as little or no money. However, this sample included only youths from "stable" two-parent families, and it is possible that many of those not covered by this particular study may have had more serious personality problems.

It is apparent that runaways are usually troubled adolescents and that runaway behavior may actually be a cry for help. Counseling for these youths and their parents should be considered as a means of determining and correcting the underlying causes of runaway behavior.

Teenage marriage and divorce

Many adolescents might not view teenage marriage as a problem. However, about one-half of all teenage girls are pregnant when they marry (Gagnon & Simon, 1968), and about one-half of all teenage marriages break up within five years (Farber & Wilson, 1967). One can only speculate about how many of these marriages are solely the consequence of nonmarital pregnancy and how many are the result of genuine, mature love. This raises the question of whether it is wise to compound one mistake (premature pregnancy) with another (premature, hasty, and immature marriage).

Suicide rates are much higher for married adolescents than for those who are unmarried. These rates persist, although progressively dropping, until age 24. Adult suicide statistics, on the other hand, are lower for marrieds than for singles (King, 1971). For all of these reasons and others, teenage marriage has become a major problem for young people, their parents, and society as a whole.

Factors contributing to the high incidence of teenage marriage

In addition to nonmarital pregnancy, there are many other explanations offered for the widespread phenomenon of teenage marriage in the United States (Broderick, 1967; Burchinal, 1960; Cadwallader, 1967; Ginzberg, 1967; Hechinger, 1967; Moss, 1965). Probably the most significant factors are the following:

1. There is a growing tendency to push youngsters into teenage behavior, especially dating, at age 10 or younger.

2. As early as junior high school there is an emphasis on going steady, which may lead to sexual experimentation. Because of the lack of sex education that stresses responsible sexual behavior, this adolescent sexual experimentation can lead to pregnancy and a marriage of necessity rather than choice.

3. By the time they reach their late teens, adolescents will have undergone so many experiences in our affluent society that marriage may remain one of the few that they have not yet tried. They may decide to "try" matrimony, often with the idea that, if it fails, the marriage can be easily dissolved.

4. Physical maturity is occurring earlier in life than it did in previous generations, and the opportunity for sexual fulfillment is being delayed.

5. The failure of many parents to place clearly defined limits on adolescent behavior has contributed to considerable insecurity among young people, who may try to find security in marriage.

6. The responsibilities demanded by marriage are often overlooked in our society, which emphasizes the pursuit of personal happiness and instant satisfaction.

7. The mass media often encourage early wedlock by focusing on the romance and glamour in marriage, rather than the commitments and responsibilities.

8. The refrain that "everybody is doing it" may push an adolescent into marriage before he or she is emotionally ready for it.

9. Marriage is often seen as a way to escape from an unpleasant

situation in the home, school, or elsewhere, and many young people think it will serve as a means of resolving personal or social problems.

10. Because of the availability of financial assistance from the government, there is less economic risk in early marriage today than there was a generation ago. Affluent parents are also often able to support these young married couples.

11. Getting married is frequently viewed as a means of obtaining the adult status that society has denied the adolescent.

12. Many adults and adolescents equate a girl's early marriage with success in life, reflecting another sex-role bind.

Predicting early marriage

Almost no research has been done on ways to predict and reduce the incidence of teenage marriage and divorce. However, several common characteristics of these married adolescents suggest that they follow certain patterns of behavior. For example, Glick (1957) noted that marital instability is more frequent in teenage marriages between school dropouts. He proposed not that one caused the other but that a lack of perseverance might be a contributing factor to both. On the other hand, Bauman (1967) suggested that both marital instability and dropping out of school are related to the age of the youths at the time of their marriage. Those marrying at an early age are more likely to drop out of school than are those who marry later. Those who marry early often feel that they have missed the freedom and fun of adolescence and may be tempted to terminate a marriage in order to belatedly enjoy those missed experiences. Some schools still have outdated policies prohibiting married students from attending classes, and many schools have regulations forbidding pregnant girls to continue in their regular schools, although they may permit them to attend special classes in special schools. In other instances, married adolescents may be forced to drop out of school because of financial pressures. Regardless of the reasons, however, dropouts do experience greater marital instability than those completing school (Bauman, 1967).

Other factors also appear with considerable frequency among married teenagers. Those who marry young are likely to come from lower- or working-class backgrounds, have limited education, earn low incomes, and need continued financial support from their parents (Burchinal, 1965). Also, rural adolescents are more likely to marry than their urban counterparts. Broderick (1968) pointed out that, among adolescents not bound for college, almost five times as many engagements occur during high school and the years immediately following as occur during this time among college-bound students. The rate of teenage marriages is also much higher among non-Whites than among Whites, and preparation and education for marriage, in both groups, are often inadequate or nonexistent. Those marrying before high school graduation generally have lower IQ scores and have histories of poorer academic achievement than unmarried high school students.

Results of teenage marriages

Probably most important of all statistics relating to teenage marriage is the stark fact that the divorce rate is 50% higher for such couples than for the general population (Burchinal, 1965; Farber & Wilson, 1967).

Two studies (Burchinal, 1959; DeLissovoy, 1973) focused attention on married teenagers' self-evaluations of their satisfaction with marriage. Burchinal's research disclosed that from one-third to over one-half of these adolescents stated that they regretted marrying when they did. DeLissovoy's investigation of 48 couples who married while in high school and who were primarily from rural areas disclosed that high risks of marital failure were associated with pre-marital pregnancy, dropping out of school, a low socioeconomic background, marriage between two partners under age 18, and inadequate income.

In addition, teenage marriage can cause problems for the offspring of such unions. Young couples, often poorly informed about parenthood, may not be ready for the responsibilities of rearing children and may neglect or abuse these children through ignorance or immaturity.

At the same time, however, not all youthful marriages are doomed to failure or unhappiness. Many such unions result in successful and satisfying relationships. Age per se is not an adequate criterion for predicting the marital success of two young people (Burchinal, 1965). Many factors relating to marriage readiness are correlated with age, but these are factors that are open to change or modification. School dropouts may ultimately complete their education; friends, family members, or community agencies may provide help or instruction in parenting, and financial assistance from parents or the government may help to ease some of the problems caused by limited financial resources. Four factors seem to be especially predictive of success in the teenage marriage: (1) lengthy acquaintanceship prior to the marriage, (2) favorable parental attitudes toward the couple before the marriage, (3) a church-sanctioned wedding ceremony, and (4) favorable parental attitudes toward the couple after the marriage (DeLissovoy, 1973).

Deterrents to teenage marriage

All high schools should offer realistic, honest programs to educate adolescents about marriage, family living, and child care. Such courses would partly answer the demands of many young people for relevance in education. The success of such a program would require well-qualified, understanding educators with suitable professional training. The emphasis of such courses should not be so much on the risks involved in early marriage as on practical knowledge and the means by which young people might develop their personalities, interests, and potentials both in and out of marriage (Burchinal, 1965).

Parents and other adults should be alerted to the dangers of the self-fulfilling prophecy as it relates to teenage marriage. Too often adults are punitive in their attitude toward youths who marry in their teens. School boards may suspend married students or require them to withdraw, because of the mistaken belief that such a policy acts as a deterrent to early marriage. Parents who warn their children that such marriages will never succeed actually contribute to the high incidence of failure in teenage marriages. At the same time, parents may also *encourage* such marriages, especially when a pregnancy is involved, by such statements as "If he were any kind of man, he'd marry you."

Chapter summary

Adolescents in our society may experience many problems— drug use and abuse, depression and suicidal behavior, runaway behavior, and teenage marriage—that some people believe are unique to our rapidly changing world. However, a study of history reveals that, although drug use and abuse are more prevalent and noticeable today than in the past, these problems have existed almost throughout recorded history. It is true that adolescent suicidal and runaway behavior are much more common now than in the past; nonetheless, they, too, are not unique to the present. The problems of teenage marriage and divorce reflect the difficulties created by the length of the adolescent period and the long period of economic dependence for adolescents in our society, as well as changing attitudes toward nonmarital adolescent sex and toward divorce.

We have suggested certain ways of alleviating these adolescent problems, with particular emphasis on practices by which the schools and society might come to grips with them. These suggestions are not offered as a final panacea; they are offered in the hope that they may provoke the reader to give serious thought and consideration to the special problems of adolescents in our society.

Thought provokers

1. Have you tried any of the drugs discussed in this chapter? What factor or factors do you think caused you to try these drugs?
2. What is the difference between addiction and habituation?
3. Do you know any drug addicts or alcoholics? What special personality traits do they exhibit?
4. Why is it difficult to determine when drug use becomes drug abuse?
5. What suggestions can you offer that might be used to combat the rising trend in drug and alcohol abuse?
6. Why is suicidal behavior considered a major adolescent problem? What causes contribute to the development of youthful suicidal behavior?
7. Do you know of anyone who committed suicide or made an attempt to do so? If so, what factors do you think were responsible?
8. What might be done to lower the incidence of adolescent suicide attempts?
9. Why do you think that the number of runaways has increased so rapidly since 1970? What measures might be undertaken to combat this problem?
10. What factors do you believe have contributed to the rising incidence of teenage marriages? What might be done to counteract this increase?
11. Do you know any couples, married at least five years, who married in their teens and seem to be relatively happy? If so, what factors do you believe have contributed to their successful marital adjustment?

References

Albrecht, G. The alcoholism process. In P. G. Bourne & R. Fox (Eds.), *Alcoholism: Progress in research and treatment.* New York: Academic Press, 1973, Pp. 11–42.

Bard, B. The failure of our school drug abuse programs. *Phi Delta Kappan,* 1975, 57(4), 251–256.

Barter, J. T., Swaback, D. O., & Todd, D. Adolescent suicide attempts: A follow-up study of hospitalized patients. *Archives of General Psychiatry,* 1968, 19(5), 523–527.

Bauman, K. E. The relationship between age at first marriage, school dropout, and marital instability: An analysis of the Glick effect. *Journal of Marriage and the Family,* 1967, *29*(4), 672–680.

Blaine, G. B., Jr. *Youth and the hazards of affluence.* New York: Harper & Row, 1966.

Blaine, G. B., Jr., & Carmen, L. R. Causal factors in suicidal attempts by male and female college students. *American Journal of Psychiatry,* 1968, *125*(6), 834–837.

Blum, R. H. Life style interviews. In R. H. Blum & Associates (Eds.), *Students and drugs.* San Francisco: Jossey-Bass, 1969. Pp. 209–231.

Blum, R. H., Aron, J., Tutko, T., Feinglass, S., & Fort, J. Drugs and high school students. In R. H. Blum & Associates (Eds.), *Students and drugs.* San Francisco: Jossey-Bass, 1969. Pp. 321–348.

Broderick, C. B. Going steady: The beginning of the end. In S. M. Farber & R. H. L. Wilson (Eds.), *Teenage marriage and divorce.* Berkeley, Calif.: Diablo Press, 1967. Pp. 21–24.

Broderick, C. B. Dating and mating among teen-agers. *Medical Aspects of Human Sexuality,* 1968, *2*(8), 16–19.

Burchinal, L. G. Comparison of factors related to adjustment in pregnancy-provoked and non-pregnancy-provoked youthful marriages. *Midwest Sociologist,* 1959, *21,* 92–96.

Burchinal, L. G. School policies and school age marriages. *Family Life Coordinator,* 1960, *8,* 45–46.

Burchinal, L. G. Trends and prospects for young marriages in the U. S. *Journal of Marriage and the Family,* 1965, *27*(2), 243–254.

Cadwallader, M. L. In search of adulthood. In S. M. Farber & R. H. L. Wilson (Eds.), *Teenage marriage and divorce.* Berkeley, Calif.: Diablo Press, 1967. Pp. 15–20.

Cohen, M. M., Marinello, M. J., & Back, N. Chromosomal damage in human leukocytes induced by lysergic acid diethylamide. *Science,* 1967, *155,* 1417–1419.

Communication strategies on alcohol and highway safety, Vol. 2: High School Youth, (Department of Transportation—H.S. 801–401) Springfield, Va.: National Technical Information Service, 1975.

Corder, B. F., Shorr, W., & Corder, R. F. A study of social and psychological characteristics of adolescent suicide attempters in an urban disadvantaged area. *Adolescence,* 1974, *9*(33), 1–6.

Council of Planning Affiliates. *Report of the committee on wandering youth.* Seattle, Wash.: Author, 1973.

Cunningham, W. H., Cunningham, I. C. M., & English, W. D. Sociopsychological characteristics of undergraduate marijuana users. *The Journal of Genetic Psychology,* 1974, *125,* 3–12.

Deisher, R. W. Runaways: A growing social and family problem. *The Journal of Family Practice,* 1975, *2*(4), 255–258.

DeLissovoy, V. High school marriages: A longitudinal study. *Journal of Marriage and the Family,* 1973, *35*(2), 245–255.

Draper, E. A developmental theory of suicide. *Comprehensive Psychiatry,* 1976, *17*(1), 63–80.

Einstein, S. *The use and misuse of drugs.* Belmont, Calif.: Wadsworth, 1970.

Farber, S. M., & Wilson, R. H. L. (Eds.). *Teenage marriage and divorce.* Berkeley, Calif.: Diablo Press, 1967.

Finch, S. M., & Poznanski, E. O. *Adolescent suicide.* Springfield, Ill.: Charles C Thomas, 1973.

Forsythe, M. J. Youth and drugs—use and abuse, educational and sociological aspects. *The Ohio State Medical Journal,* 1969, *65,* 17–23.

Gagnon, J. M., & Simon, W. Sexual deviance in contemporary America. *The Annals of the American Academy of Political and Social Science*, 1968, *376*, 106–122.

Gallagher, W. Why people kill themselves. *Today's Health*, 1976, *54*(2), 46–50.

Ginott, H. G. *Between parent and teenager*. New York: Macmillan, 1969.

Ginzberg, E. Work and life plans. In S. M. Farber & R. H. L. Wilson (Eds.), *Teenage marriage and divorce*. Berkeley, Calif.: Diablo Press, 1967, Pp. 9–14.

Glick, P. C. *American families*. New York: Wiley, 1957.

Haider, I. Suicide attempts in children and adolescents. *British Journal of Psychiatry*, 1968, *114*(514), 1133–1134.

Hamburg, B. A., Kraemer, H. C., & Jahnke, W. A hierarchy of drug use in adolescence: Behavioral and attitudinal correlates of substantial drug use. *American Journal of Psychiatry*, 1975, *132*(11), 1155–1163.

Hanley, J. A., & Robinson, J. C. Cigarette smoking and the young: A national survey. *Canadian Medical Association Journal*, 1976, *114*(6), 511–517.

Havighurst, R. J. Suicide and education. In E. S. Shneidman (Ed.), *On the nature of suicide*. San Francisco: Jossey-Bass, 1969. Pp. 53–67.

Hechinger, F. M. Tradition: Security or restriction. In S. M. Farber & R. H. L. Wilson (Eds.), *Teenage marriage and divorce*. Berkeley, Calif.: Diablo Press, 1967. Pp. 1–8.

Hendin, H. Growing up dead. *American Journal of Psychotherapy*, 1975, *29*(3), 327–338. (a)

Hendin, H. Student suicide: Death as a life style. *The Journal of Nervous and Mental Disorders*, 1975, *160*(3), 204–219. (b)

Hinsie, L. E., & Campbell, R. J. *Psychiatric dictionary* (3rd ed.). New York: Oxford Press, 1960.

Hofmann, A. D. Adolescents in distress: Suicide and out-of-control behavior. *The Medical Clinics of North America*, 1975, *59*(6), 1429–1437.

Holden, C. Drug abuse 1975: The "war" is past, the problem is as big as ever. *Science*, 1975, *190*(4215), 638–641.

Holroyd, K., & Kahn, M. Personality factors in student drug use. *Journal of Consulting and Clinical Psychology*, 1974, *42*(2), 236–243.

Howell, M. C., Emmons, E. B., & Frank, D. A. Reminiscences of runaway adolescents. *American Journal of Orthopsychiatry*, 1973, *43*(5), 840–853.

Irwin, S., Hayes, R. M., & Grunden, L. R. Education for living: Awareness and creative choice (Alternatives to drugs). *Journal of Psychedelic Drugs*, 1975, *7*(1), 49–58.

Jacobs, J., & Teicher, J. Broken homes and social isolation in attempted suicides. *International Journal of Social Psychiatry*, 1967, *13*, 139–149.

Jacobziner, H. Attempted suicides in adolescence. *Journal of the American Medical Association*, 1965, *191*, 7.

Jenkins, R. L. The runaway reaction. *American Journal of Psychiatry*, 1971, *128*(2), 60–65.

Keeler, M. H. Adverse reactions to marijuana. *American Journal of Psychiatry*, 1967, *124*(5), 674–677.

Kimes, W. T., Smith, S. C., & Maher, R. E. *Alcohol and drug abuse in S. Carolina Schools*. Columbia, S. C.: South Carolina Department of Education, 1969.

King, M. Evaluation and treatment of suicide prone youth. *Mental Hygiene*, 1971, *55*(3), 344–350.

Klee, G. D. Drugs and American youth. A psychiatrist looks at the psychedelic generation. *Medical Times*, 1969, *97*, 165–171.

Knight, J. A. Suicide among students. In H. L. P. Resnik (Ed.), *Suicidal behaviors*. Boston: Little, Brown, 1968. Pp. 228–240.

Kolansky, H., & Moore, W. T. Effects of marijuana on adolescents and young adults. *Journal of the American Medical Association*, 1971, *216*, 486–492.

Kolansky, H., & Moore, W. T. Marijuana: Can it hurt you? *Journal of the American Medical Association*, 1975, *232*(9), 923–924.

Kolb, L. *Drug Addiction*. Springfield, Ill.: Charles C Thomas, 1962.

Laskowitz, D. Psychological characteristics of the adolescent addict. In E. Harms (Ed.), *Drug Addiction in Youth*. New York: Pergamon Press, 1964. Pp. 67–83.

Lieberman, J. J. The drug addict and the "cop out" father. *Adolescence*, 1974, *9*(33), 7–14.

Linder, R. L., Lerner, S. E., & Burke, E. M. Drugs in the junior high school: Part 1. *Journal of Psychedelic Drugs*, 1974, *6*(1), 43–49.(a)

Linder, R. L., Lerner, S. E., & Burke, E. M. Drugs in the junior high school: Part 2. *Journal of Psychedelic Drugs*, 1974, *6*(1), 51–56.(b)

MacKay, J. R., Phillips, D. L., & Bryce, F. O. Drinking behavior among teenagers: A comparison of institutionalized and non-institutionalized youth. *Journal of Health and Social Behavior*, 1967, *8*(1), 46–54.

Maddox, G. L. Drinking prior to college. In G. L. Maddox (Ed.), *The domesticated drug: Drinking among college students*. New Haven, Conn.: College and University Press, 1970. Pp. 107–120.

Maugh, T. H., II. Marijuana: New support for immuno and reproductive hazards. *Science*, 1975, *190*(4217), 865–867.

Mayor's Committee on Marijuana. *The marijuana problem in the city of New York*. Lancaster, Penn.: Cattell, 1944.

McGlothlin, W. H., & West, L. J. The marijuana problem: An overview. *American Journal of Psychiatry*, 1968, *125*, 370–378.

Miller, J. P. Suicide and adolescence. *Adolescence*, 1975, *10*(37), 11–24.

Milman, D. H., & Su, Wen-Huey. Patterns of illicit drug and alcohol use among secondary-school students. *Journal of Pediatrics*, 1973, *83*, 314–320.

Modell, W. Mass drug catastrophes and the roles of science and technology. *Science*, 1967, *156*, 346.

Morris, J. B., Kovacs, M., Beck, A. T., & Wolffe, A. Notes toward an epidemiology of urban suicide. *Comprehensive Psychiatry*, 1974, *15*(6), 537–547.

Moss, J. J. Teenage marriage: Cross-national trends and sociological factors in the decision of when to marry. *Journal of Marriage and the Family*, 1965, *27*(2), 230–242.

National Commission on Marijuana and Drug Abuse. *Marijuana: A signal of misunderstanding*. Washington, D. C.: U. S. Government Printing Office, 1972.

National Commission on Marijuana and Drug Abuse. *Drug use in America: Problems in perspective*. Washington, D. C.: U. S. Government Printing Office, 1973.

Navarre, R., & Zastrow, C. *Briarpatch evaluation report*. Madison: Wisconsin Council on Criminal Justice, 1974.

Offord, D. R. The orbiting teenager—A seminar. Problems with smoking, alcohol, and drug abuse. *Medical Times*, 1965, *93*(2), 207–208.

Pollard, J. C. Teenagers and the use of drugs: Reflections on the emotional setting. *Clinical Pediatrics*, 1967, *6*(11), 613–620.

Pop drugs: The high as a way of life. *Time*, September 26, 1969, pp. 68–78.

Project Place, 1971 Report. Boston, Massachusetts.

Ray, O. S. *Drugs, society, and human behavior*. St. Louis: Mosby, 1972.

Runaway children: A problem for more and more cities. *U. S. News and World Report*, 1972, *72*(17), 38–42.

Ryback, R. S. Teen-age alcoholism, medicine, and the law. *The New England Journal of Medicine*, 1975, *293*(14), 719–721.

Sabbath, J. C. The suicidal adolescent—The expendable child. *Journal of the American Academy of Child Psychiatry*, 1969, *8*(2), 272–285.

Saint, C. L. Interview. Pineville, Louisiana. December, 1969.

Schaps, E., Sanders, C. R., & Hughes, P. H. Student preferences on the design of drug education programs: Drug users and non-users compared. *Journal of Psychedelic Drugs*, 1974, *6*(4), 425–434.

Schwartzman, J. The addict, abstinence, and the family. *American Journal of Psychiatry*, 1975, *132*(2), 154–157.

Seiden, R. H. Campus tragedy: A study of student suicide. *Journal of Abnormal Psychology*, 1966, *71*(6), 389–399.

Shneidman, E. S., & Dizmang, L. How the family physician can prevent suicide. *The Physicians Panorama*, 1967, *5*(6).

Siegler, M., & Osmund, H. Models of drug addiction. *International Journal of the Addictions*, 1968, *3*(1), 3–24.

Sorosiak, F. M., Thomas, L. E., & Balet, F. N. Adolescent drug use. *Psychological Reports*, 1976, *38*, 211–221.

Stierlin, H. A family perspective on adolescent runaways. *Archives of General Psychiatry*, 1973, *29*(1), 56–62.

Tec, N. Some aspects of high school status and differential involvement with marijuana: A study of suburban teen-agers. *Adolescence*, 1972, *6*, 1–28.

Teicher, J. D., & Jacobs, J. The physician and the adolescent suicide attempter. *Journal of School Health*, 1966, *36*(9), 406–415.

Tinklenberg, J. R. (Ed.). *Marijuana and health hazards*. New York: Academic Press, 1975.

Ungerleider, J. T., & Bowen, H. L. Drug abuse and the schools. *American Journal of Psychiatry*, 1969, *125*(12), 1691–1696.

U. S. Department of Health, Education, and Welfare Public Health Service. *Vital Statistics of the United States, Volume 2: Mortality*. Washington, D. C.: U. S. Government Printing Office, 1968.

Westermeyer, J., & Walzer, V. Drug usage: An alternative to religion. *Diseases of the Nervous System*, 1975, *36*(9), 492–495.

White, H. C. Self poisoning in adolescents. *British Journal of Psychiatry*, 1974, *124*, 24–35.

Why did Walter die? *Time*, December 26, 1969, p. 12.

World Health Organization. *Expert committee on drugs liable to produce addiction: Second report*. World Health Organization Technical Report Series No. 21. Geneva: World Health Organization, 1950.

Yankelovich, D. Drug users versus drug abusers: How students cool their drug crisis. *Psychology Today*, 1975, *9*(5), 39–42.

Zastrow, C., & Navarre, R. Help for runaways and their parents. *Social Casework*, 1975, *56*(2), 74–78.

Zimmering, P., Toolan, J., Safrin, R., & Wortis, S. B. Heroin addiction in adolescent boys. *Journal of Nervous and Mental Disorders*, 1951, *114*, 19–34.

Zinberg, N. E. Facts and fancies about drug addiction. *The Public Interest*, 1967, *6*, 75–90.

The adolescent and education

10

Adolescents who have difficulty learning in the classroom are conveying a vital message about themselves. They may be telling us that they have limited mental ability or a *sensory* or *perceptual/motor handicap*. They may be informing us that they lack readiness for the subject matter because of the inadequacy of their previous education. Or they may be demonstrating, through their poor concentration, comprehension, and recall in the classroom, an inability to cope with physical, social, or emotional problems (Hewitt, 1964).

Rarely are these messages clearly understood, however, and rarely are the explanations for learning problems simple and specific, because various physical, environmental, and psychological factors

273

often overlap. It is important that teachers learn to recognize learning difficulties, to study student behavior patterns for clues to causes of such problems and to be aware of community resources available to assist in correcting these difficulties.

Causes of learning problems

Intelligence is often closely related to academic achievement. Potential for academic achievement is determined through the use of tests that measure the intelligence quotient, or IQ—that is, the ratio of the mental age (MA) to the chronological age (CA). (The mental age is computed by comparing one's raw score on an intelligence test with the scores of others of the same chronological age.) The concept of intelligence has two distinct meanings and may be interpreted in two ways. It can be defined as the innate or inherited intellectual potential or as the average level of performance or comprehension of an individual at a given time (Wrightsman & Sanford, 1975).

Frequently in the seventh and eighth grades, teachers encounter students with IQs of 75 to 90—that is, in the *borderline-defective* or *dull-normal* range (Ames, 1968). These adolescents have often lagged behind their peers in elementary school and, in junior high, appear to reach the upper limits of their intellectual potential. Such young people are above the intellectual level that would permit them to attend special classes for the retarded but below the level that would assure them of graduating from high school with their peers. These students can benefit from some heterogeneous grouping with brighter students, but they will also require special tutoring and a special curriculum geared to their particular needs.

In many instances, however, these students possess greater intellectual potential than they demonstrate on the typical group paper-and-pencil IQ tests administered by the schools. They may be the victims of cultural deprivation and, because of a limited vocabulary and poor reading comprehension, may do poorly on such tests, which measure previous learning, rather than basic mental ability. Especially when there is an irregular profile of subtest scores—some high and others low—the teacher or guidance counselor would be wise to refer the student for individual testing. Tests such as the WISC (Wechsler Intelligence Scale for Children, 1974), for example, which is administered by a trained examiner on a one-to-one basis, minimize the effects of previous learning and cultural background. Culture-fair tests such as the Raven Progressive Matrices, which do not rely on the use of language, may also be utilized. Alzobaie, Metfessel, and Michael (1968), in using certain culture-fair tests with tenth-grade adolescents, reported that these tests provided an alternative means of predicting the school performance of disadvantaged students who have language difficulties.

IQ is not constant or unchanging. If youths are beset by emotional problems or family difficulties at the time of testing, they may demonstrate a lower level of intellectual functioning than at another time. For this reason, one IQ score should never be taken as an absolute evaluation of an individual's mental ability. Such emotional stress can also affect academic performance, as can learning disabilities and such physical problems as poor vision, impaired hearing, or endocrine disorders (these will be discussed in more detail later in this chapter).

The self-fulfilling prophecy may also be operating; that is, the teacher's expectations of a student's performance may have a strong impact both on that person's IQ level and on his or her academic achievement (Rosenthal, 1969). Students who have been categorized as "dull" and unworthy of any special time and effort may languish in the classroom. They often lose all motivation and simply kill time until they can legally drop out of school.

Recognizing students with organic disorders

When a student who has traditionally done satisfactory work begins to slip in his or her scholastic performance, one explanation may be the presence of a physical disorder. For example, the development of an endocrine imbalance is not uncommon among adolescents.

John, who had always maintained a B average in his school work, began having difficulty in the seventh grade. When his grades fell to a D average, he was referred to a center for developmental reading for help. His attention span was exceedingly short, and his grades were not reflecting his intelligence quotient, which was in the bright-normal range. Following a complete psychological workup, the center referred John to his family doctor for a physical checkup. The doctor discovered that the boy was suffering from an underactive thyroid gland—a condition that often manifests itself in adolescents through *hyperactive behavior* and an inability to concentrate. After the correction of the physical imbalance through medication and after two months of concentrated tutoring in remedial reading, John's reading level advanced 1.2 grade levels, and his school grades returned to a B level.

An excellent illustration of the impact of physiological factors on behavior and academic performance was cited by Kirk (1962). A 12-year-old boy was causing extreme difficulties in school. He behaved fairly well in the early morning but, by late morning, began creating profound disturbances within the classroom. After lunch he would behave satisfactorily for an hour or two and then begin to pant, run around the classroom, fight with the other children, and, at times, attempt to jump out the window. When the teacher referred the boy for psychiatric examination, one psychiatrist diagnosed him as a psychopathic personality. Another, more psychoanalytically oriented, ascribed the child's behavior to a traumatic experience in early childhood. A third believed that there might have been a brain injury as a result of undiagnosed encephalitis.

These diagnoses, however, did not help the teacher to deal with the child in the classroom. The boy's erratic actions continued from year to year, and he was finally sent to an institution for mental disorders when the school could no longer handle him within a classroom situation.

In the institution, the erratic behavior persisted. Teachers would accept him for a week or two and then ask that he be removed from the class, because they could not teach with him in the room. Teacher after teacher tried to control the boy's behavior, but to no avail.

Finally, it was decided that, when the boy began to misbehave in the classroom, the teacher should summon the psychiatric social worker. The social worker would then take him out of the class, walk him around the block, give him a piece of candy, discuss his problems with him, calm him down, and then return him to the classroom. This routine usually occurred once in the morning and once in the afternoon.

No one was able to determine what triggered the abnormal behavior or what diminished it. Finally, a pediatrician, in reviewing the boy's medical record, discovered that he had never had a blood-sugar tolerance test. The doctor hypothesized that the piece of candy that the boy always received from the social worker during their walk might have had some relationship to the subsequent decrease in his hyperactive behavior.

An examination revealed that the boy had hypoglycemia—a condition characterized by a severe deficiency of sugar in the blood. The treatment prescribed was to give him a glass of milk with sugar in it at ten o'clock in the morning, at two o'clock in the afternoon, and again in the evening. From that day on, the boy became a model child and a much more rapid learner. This boy's deviant behavior had apparently been an attempt on his part to reduce the tension or suffocation his body was experiencing when the blood sugar was used up.*

Recognizing students with learning disabilities

Many students who fail to learn in school are the victims of learning disabilities. The term *learning disabilities* is extremely difficult to define, but the definition most widely adopted is that of the National Advisory Committee on Handicapped Children of the U. S. Department of Health, Education, and Welfare (1968). It states:

> Children with special learning disabilities exhibit a disorder in one or more of the basic psychological processes involved in understanding or in using spoken or written languages. These may be manifested in disorders of listening, thinking, talking, reading, writing, spelling, or arithmetic. They include conditions which have been referred to as perceptual handicaps, brain injury, minimal brain dysfunction, dyslexia, developmental aphasia, etc. They do *not* include learning problems which are due primarily to visual, hearing or motor handicaps, to mental retardation, emotional disturbance, or to environmental disadvantage [p. 34].

Although research in the area of learning disabilities began at the end of the 19th century, it was not until 1960 that psychologists and educators started to pull together all of the available information and undertake research in the field as it relates to education.

Many hypotheses have been suggested to explain the *etiology*, or causes, of learning disabilities. Among the most frequently named are physiological factors, such as minimal brain injury and damage to the central nervous system (Strauss & Kaphart, 1955; Hallahan & Cruickshank, 1973). However, this kind of brain-injury explanation has actually been used more as a diagnostic category than as an etiological explanation. There is also evidence that *genetic* factors are involved in learning disabilities—that is, that learning disabilities appear more frequently in particular families (Shedd, 1969; Delker, 1971; Silver, 1971).

For example, an acquaintance of one of the authors (B. R.) recalled that she had had great difficulty meeting the academic requirements in art school because she had trouble reading. Her brother had also had academic problems and had finally flunked out of college. Two decades after art school this woman learned that three of

*Case paraphrased from *Educating Exceptional Children*, by S. A. Kirk. Copyright © 1962. Used with permission of the publisher, Houghton Mifflin Company.

her four children had been diagnosed as having learning disabilities. In all probability, she and her brother had also suffered from such difficulties.

Biochemical defects have also been suggested as possible causes of certain learning disabilities (Wallace & McLoughlin, 1975), although this idea has not yet been substantially proven. A history of traumatic and difficult prenatal, perinatal, and postnatal conditions has also been introduced as a possible contributor to learning disabilities. For example, Pasamanick and Knoblock (1960) reported that a group of children with reading difficulties had experienced more complicated prenatal development than another group with no reading problems. Nutritional deficiencies and sensory deprivation are also factors that could partially explain the presence of learning disabilities; deficits in these two areas can impede normal development of the neurological and psychological bases necessary for learning (Hallahan & Cruickshank, 1973).

Some investigators believe that a maturational lag in the development of certain elements of the central nervous system is related to the development of learning disabilities (Bender, 1968). However, such a lag can also be the outgrowth of inadequate nutrition or a complicated pregnancy or birth (Bryant, 1972).

Teachers, of course, are particularly interested in the recognition of learning disabilities, primarily for three reasons. First, it has been estimated that learning disabilities, which occur four times as frequently among boys as among girls (Wender, 1971), affect anywhere from 3% (National Advisory Committee on Handicapped Children, 1968) to 15% of the population (National Advisory Committee on Dyslexia and Related Reading Disorders, 1969; Meier, 1971). Second, this condition often goes unrecognized among disadvantaged youths, delinquents, and potential dropouts. Third, and most important, emotional disorders can develop as a result of learning disabilities (Kappelman, Kaplan, & Ganter, 1969; Tarnopol, 1970). And because students with learning disabilities are overlooked many times by their elementary-school teachers, who may have come to regard them as immature, lazy, or lacking in motivation, secondary education teachers should be alert to such disorders.

A number of tests have been devised to identify students with learning disabilities. There are also numerous symptoms characteristic of such individuals—symptoms of which classroom teachers should be aware—including the following.

1. Learning-disabled students are frequently perceptually handicapped. ("*Perception* refers to the cognitive ability of the individual to both recognize and *integrate* external stimuli"; Wallace

& McLoughlin, 1975, p. 82.) Their vision is normal, but somewhere in the central nervous system a *dysfunction* causes the visual message to be perceived erroneously by the brain. Hearing is also normal, but there is often difficulty in perceiving differences in auditory stimuli (for example, there may be difficulty discriminating between the sounds *gym* and *gem*). As Stern (1968) succinctly stated the problem, "the child is able to see, but not necessarily able to look; the child is able to hear, but not necessarily able to listen." A number of investigators regard such perceptual disorders as the primary problem of the learning disabled; some states regard the terms *perceptually handicapped* and *learning disabled* as synonymous (Cruickshank, 1975; Wallace & McLoughlin, 1975).

2. Motor coordination is poor, both gross, or large, muscle coordination (such as would be necessary to play baseball, for example) and fine, or small, muscle coordination (such as would be used in handwriting). The learning disabled often stumble and fall without apparent cause, and their locomotive gait is frequently *dysrhythmic.* Their poor muscle coordination is also evident in their speech, which tends to be slurred or mumbled. Directionality, or the ability to recognize right from left and up from down, is limited, because the learning disabled often lack *laterality,* or internal awareness of the two sides of the body and their differences (Jones, 1967; Shedd, 1968; Wallace & McLoughlin, 1975).

3. The reading ability of learning-disabled individuals is generally inadequate. As a consequence, these individuals often demonstrate a dislike for books and other reading materials. Problems in visual discrimination (for example, the inability to recognize the difference between such letters as *b* and *d* or even such whole words as *was* and *saw*) make reading difficult and frustrating for them. They fail to perceive the internal details of words; that is, words that are very similar in appearance, such as *defeat* and *defect,* are often mistaken for each other by the learning disabled. Disturbances in long-term memory are also common among these young people. For example, in spelling they often form letter combinations that are impossible in the English language. They may obtain perfect scores on spelling tests because of memorization and prompt recall, but a week later they are unable to recognize the same words when they see or hear them. Their handwriting is also likely to be difficult to decipher. The letters tend to be angular, scrawled, and poorly formed, and *t*s and *x*s are often crossed with a right-to-left motion, rather than the usual left-to-right one (Jones, 1967; Shedd, 1968; Wallace & McLoughlin, 1975).

4. Sequences are often difficult for the learning disabled, who

frequently confuse such common sequential material as the days of the week or the months of the year.

5. Those with learning disabilities tend to *perseverate*; that is, they cling to one activity and have difficulty changing to another. If they begin by multiplying problems on a page, for example, they will continue to do so even when the directions change (Jones, 1967; Shedd, 1968).

6. The learning disabled are likely to show various emotional and behavioral problems. One of the most prevalent is the presence of a low self-concept, which is not surprising in view of the fact that these students are unable to accomplish tasks that most of their class-mates master quite readily. The learning disabled are also quite dis-tractible. They have very short attention spans, and, as a consequence of their disability, many demonstrate disruptive behavior in the classroom. This behavior is usually aggressive and can be of consid-erable concern to the teacher. Others with learning disabilities re-sort to withdrawal in the form of excessive daydreaming and mini-mal contact with both peers and adults. Still others demonstrate a lack of motivation, temper tantrums, or a low level of frustration tolerance. And, as noted in Chapter 8, many engage in antisocial behavior—behavior that may ultimately lead to delinquency (Wallace & McLoughlin, 1975).

An excellent illustration of the widespread effects of learning disabilities can be seen in the following case:

> Billy, who was born prematurely and who exhibited many symp-toms of hyperactive behavior from the time of birth, entered school at 6¾ years, at which time he was taught to read phonetically. He liked reading until he reached the fourth or fifth grade. Then he showed a gradual loss of interest in it, and his grades began to slip. In the ninth grade he failed French, although he just managed to pass his other subjects. In the tenth grade, Billy developed a peptic ulcer, frequent headaches, and a chronic "sick stomach." That same year, he was finally diagnosed as having *dyslexia*, one of the most common types of learning disabilities. A case history revealed that both his father and his uncle had probably had dyslexia, although neither Billy's two older brothers nor his older sister had shown any evidence of it.
>
> After his ulcer had been treated, he spent the summer being tu-tored in *phonetics*, during which time his reading speed went from 150 to 500 words per minute. Unfortunately, at that time the community in which he lived had no instructors trained to teach dyslexics.
>
> Billy eventually attended college but dropped out for a while because of the stress involved and the insistence of the administra-

tion that he master a foreign language in order to graduate. On his return, Billy was excused from the language requirement and received weekly counseling from a university guidance counselor. Thus, he was able to meet the other academic demands without undue stress. Billy not only completed his undergraduate training but also went on to graduate school at a larger university, from which he eventually received a master's degree in social welfare.

This case exemplifies many facets of the learning-disability problem, including: (1) the close correlation between learning disabilities and psychosomatic disorders, (2) the fact that learning disabilities are not always apparent during elementary school, although the most common age of referrals for dyslexics, for example, is 9 (Clements, 1968), and (3) the fact that learning disabilities and their effects can often be treated at several different levels—that is, educationally, medically, and psychologically.

Even when the problem is not recognized until the child reaches junior high school, it is still not too late to provide training in perceptual development. In Natchez, Mississippi, where a three-year federal grant made possible the evaluation of all suspected dyslexic children and the special training in perceptual development of those so diagnosed, the results of such training at the junior high school level were most encouraging. During the first year of the program, 23 young people aged 11 to 15 were diagnosed as dyslexics. Their IQs ranged from 83 to 116 (average IQ, 96) and their reading levels varied from 2.3* to 6.8 grade level. The average improvement following eight months of specific reading remediation for the learning disability was 2.4 years, with the range of improvement running anywhere from 1 year to 4.7 years (Jones, 1968).

Not only reading ability but also IQ can improve with perceptual training, as shown in the following case from McCarthy (1968).

David's intelligence-test score indicated an IQ of 65, which is in the range of mild retardation. His test scores also indicated that he had a learning disability, but he was initially classified as too slow to attend special classes dealing with such problems. Fortunately, a professional worker in the area of perceptual development believed that David would benefit from intensive remedial study in this field, and she undertook three years of concentrated work with him. As a consequence of their efforts, David's IQ rose to 94, which is in the low-average range of intelligence-test scores.

*These figures indicate "second grade, third month," "sixth grade, eighth month," and so on.

Underachievers

In the past, an *underachiever* was quite likely to be described as "lazy." Today, a more informed approach looks to the personality and temperament of such students, as well as to the learning situations with which they are confronted, for explanations of their poor academic performance.

The term *underachiever* can describe a wide variety of students, but it usually refers to those whose academic achievements do not reflect their academic potential (Wellington & Wellington, 1965). Within this framework, however, are three distinct groups: (1) those, primarily from low-income, urban families, who underachieve because of cultural deprivation; (2) those who do average work in school but have the potential to achieve more, despite their often unstimulating working-class homes and uninspiring school programs; and (3) those, mainly middle-class underachievers, who have superior intelligence but whose academic achievements do not measure up to this ability because of an unwillingness or inability to make the commitment necessary to achieve. These latter adolescents demonstrate a considerable degree of self-doubt and are frequently disillusioned with society. Hence, they find it difficult to make any social commitment, whether academic or otherwise. Indeed, some of them resort to a kind of sit-down strike—attending classes but virtually refusing to learn—in order to resist the academic demands placed on them by their schools (Havighurst, 1966a). All three of these underachieving groups contain students with intelligence levels ranging from below-average to gifted, and they can be found at all academic levels from the first grade through college.

At this point, however, we are concerned primarily with adolescent underachievers. They may be young people with a history of poor academic success throughout their school careers, or they may be students who display a sudden drop in their grades as they reach puberty. The potentially superior, but uncommitted, adolescents are those most likely to demonstrate the sudden onset of underachieving behavior as they enter junior high or middle school. Havighurst (1966a) suggests that, at puberty, some of these bright, sensitive young people, disheartened by the world around them, become reluctant to commit themselves to a difficult, questionable future. They seem to find it especially stressful to cope with the identity crisis and, therefore, suffer from identity diffusion. In their preoccupation with this problem, they are unable to marshal their energies to tackle the demands of the academic world. Sometimes these youths go on to become "late bloomers" in college.

Underachievement can be one of the most subtle and insidious forms of adolescent rebellion (Blaine, 1966). It is subtle because it is rarely recognized as a manifestation of rebellion by either adolescents or adults. It is insidious because it often begins in a quiet, unobtrusive manner and, consequently, may go unnoticed until a promising academic career is threatened or destroyed.

Kotkov (1965) has described a number of characteristics of the underachiever. One of these is the belief that skill and knowledge are inborn in certain people and that those people do not have to struggle in order to succeed. This belief leads the student to view himself or herself as a passive receiver, rather than an active achiever. Alice's roommate in the following example is one such passive receiver.

> Alice, an honors college student, had a roommate who had the mistaken notion that Alice had only to "wave a magic wand" in order to achieve her outstanding scholastic record. On the contrary, Alice admitted studying diligently during many long hours both day and night. She was unable to convince her roommate, however, of the efforts she expended in order to achieve her grades. Maintaining her belief that academic skill is inborn, the roommate, who had the potential but lacked the necessary motivation to do average college work, remained on scholastic probation and was finally forced to drop out of school.

Such young people are frequently the victims of maternal overprotection. As a result, they are poorly prepared for independent achievement and are likely to overreact to minute frustrations (Kotkov, 1965). They tend to display apathy, a lack of motivation, and a certain sense of helplessness.

Another behavior pattern frequently observed in underachievers, according to Kotkov, is that of youths who possess a high level of aspiration and a high degree of perfectionism but face each new learning task with a fear of failure. They have internalized the pressures to succeed that are placed on them by their demanding parents and have become acutely aware of their own shortcomings. To circumvent what they believe will surely prove to be imperfect performances, they withdraw from scholastic competition. Guilt then arises and is transformed into feelings of inadequacy or inferiority, which in turn lead to fears of further failure.

Such persistent feelings of inferiority may be present despite superior test results and an occasional superior performance to the contrary. As long as they don't put forth wholehearted effort, these adolescents can regard their academic record as less than a true reflection of their actual capacity. Their halfhearted efforts also provide them with the opportunity to rationalize their failures. According to Blaine (1966), this pattern is particularly noticeable among children who have a low ordinal rank in the family. These young people develop expectations of defeat, which prevent them from attempting to compete even when the odds are in their favor. And too, often, teachers add to this problem by comparing later-arriving students with their brothers and sisters who preceded them.

Many individuals have an unconscious fear of success, a fear that is especially prevalent among females. Horner (1969) notes that bright women are caught in a double-bind situation. When they are confronted with achievement-oriented situations, they become apprehensive not only about failure but also about success, because achievement has traditionally been regarded as incompatible with the female role. For example, Horner reports that, when females compete with males, they manifest higher test-anxiety scores than do the males. She suggests that bright women, if they fail in their striving to succeed, will not have lived up to their own standards for success. On the other hand, if they do succeed, they will have exceeded the limits of what society has traditionally considered suitable behavior for females. Hence, they experience much anxiety in such situations—anxiety that contributes to the "motive to avoid success" (Horner, 1969). In addition, Horner reports that male college students regard female achievers with some suspicion and distrust and that the motive to avoid success becomes more pronounced as females move from one grade level to the next. As Gornick (1975) has succinctly stated,

> Girls get dumber and dumber as they get older and older. We all know that. We have all *always* known that. The girl child matures early, levels off fast, and then slowly retrogresses. Thousands of females, who are positively brilliant in grade school, become merely bright in high school, simply very good in college, and finally, almost mediocre in graduate school [p. 212].

With the existence of such a behavior pattern, it is not surprising that there are a large number of females who never fulfill their potential.

Some adolescents fear success because they don't want to attract attention by being above average. Such students are often shy and reticent. For adolescents who seek high acceptance from their peers, success can be a very uncomfortable position—one to be avoided at all costs. They fear being teased, disliked, or rejected by their classmates as a result of the praise and academic recognition they might receive (Blaine, 1966).

Roth and Meyersburg (1963, p. 538) describe the existence of a nonachievement syndrome in terms of the following behavior patterns:

1. Poor academic achievement
2. General self-deprecation; lack of recognition of pleasure at "being"
3. No clear system of personal goals or values
4. Vulnerability to disparagement by others
5. Immature relations with parents
6. Frequent depressions
7. Lack of insight about self and others
8. Free-floating anxiety

Anxiety, if sufficiently severe, will cripple or interfere with intellectual functioning. According to the expectancy-value theory of motivation, anxiety is aroused when individuals expect the consequences of behavior to be negative. The anxiety acts as an inhibiting factor and, thereby, produces what behavioral scientists refer to as an *"avoidance* motive," which describes what someone will *not* do rather than what he or she *will* do. Anxiety, of course, may occur because of conflicts outside as well as inside the classroom. Inner conflicts and emotional stress can be so energy consuming that they interfere with the student's ability to concentrate. For example, a young boy's concern about his delayed sexual development can seriously affect his academic performance.

When learning is impeded by emotional stress, the pattern of scholastic behavior is often mystifying. Typically the student suffering from emotional stress will miss easy problems but solve more difficult ones or solve a given problem one day but be unable even to understand the same problem the next day. Frequently, such young people experience test panic, in which their minds go blank at the sight of an exam, even when they are well prepared for the test. This anxiety may even carry over to their performance on intelligence tests, so that an IQ score may not be an accurate evaluation of their academic potential (Wattenberg, 1963). A vicious cycle can result: anxiety leads to scholastic failure, which leads to further emotional stress, which leads to continued academic failure (Bakwin & Bakwin, 1960).

The etiology of the nonachievement syndrome described by Roth and Meyersburg (1963) has its roots in a common pattern in the parent/child relationship. In this pattern either the parents ignore the accomplishments and failures of their offspring, or they pay attention to the failures (by punishing the child) but ignore the successes, which are taken for granted.

These early experiences in the parent/child relationship can lead to serious *pathological* disorders in children (Roth & Meyersburg, 1963). One of these disorders is the development of a characteristic pattern of self-deprecation. In their attempts to maintain a relationship with their parents, the children learn to perceive themselves as failures. They restrain their productive impulses and blame themselves for their weaknesses and failures. They direct their hostility only against themselves, thereby reinforcing their low self-concept. The opinions of others acquire far greater significance than their own opinions, consequently interfering with the development of autonomy and self-direction, which, in turn, reinforces their self-deprecating attitudes. They usually acquire poor academic skills, and for this reason their perception of themselves as failures is reinforced, the growth of their *phenomenal* world, or environment as they perceive it, is curtailed or limited, and their intellectual development is arrested or impeded. Their unsatisfied longing for approval makes them especially susceptible to the peer-group acceptance awarded the unscholarly. These students are unable to delineate definite boundaries between themselves and others. Whatever they see or hear, they *introject,* or accept as their own without modification, thereby acquiring no individual value system. In other words, they are easily led by others and rarely question the ideas or standards of those whom they follow.

Tests as a factor in underachievement

Many students are "labeled" by the results of intelligence tests that are administered to them periodically throughout their education. Those who earn low scores are promptly described as having limited intelligence; the self-fulfilling prophecy comes into play (Rosenthal, 1969), and a number of those so labeled immediately become underachievers who never are encouraged to display their innate ability. Some educators and psychologists believe that present-day IQ tests only legitimize the existing social order, reinforcing the class structure (White, 1975). Some states, such as California and Massachusetts, have banned intelligence testing in public-school classrooms (Sheils, 1976).

Other psychologists and educators believe that plural tests of human ability—that is, tests that include items of verbal ability, spatial ability, mechanical ability, and so on—should be adopted in place of the traditional intelligence tests (White, 1975). Cattell (1974) has suggested that there are two kinds of intelligence: fluid and crystallized. Crystallized intelligence is reflected in judgmental skills evolving primarily from cultural experience and environmental influences: verbal facility, mathematical skills, mechanical knowledge, a good, well-stocked memory, and, possibly, habits of logical reasoning. Such skills are measured by traditional tests of intelligence. On the other hand, fluid intelligence can be assessed by culture-fair perceptual and performance tests; such tests measure forms of judgment and reasoning that are considered to be relatively free of cultural influences. These tests require the individual to complete classification problems, analogies, matrices, and so on—tasks that do not require much of an educational background. Cattell believes that a dual IQ score is needed that would contain both a fluid culture-fair test score and a crystallized test score. Although existing IQ tests contain both fluid and crystallized elements, the scores cannot be broken down and separated according to type of intelligence measured.

Like many other psychologists, Cattell (1974) also notes that IQ scores and intellectual functioning vary from day to day and that scores for both crystallized and fluid abilities can increase as a result of test sophistication and familiarity with test instructions. As a consequence, Cattell suggests discarding the results of tests administered when the child first enters school, especially for those who are unaccustomed to paper-and-pencil tests.

There are other types of standardized tests that are commonly used to measure achievement or to predict aptitude for future learning. Many of these appear to be utilized excessively—that is, they are administered too often and the schools rely too heavily on the test results—or they do not actually measure learning at all. The results of these tests, too, can be used to label students. For example, a student may be held back in a grade on the basis of an achievement-test score even though other factors indicate that the student is ready for the next grade. In fact, no single test has yet been developed that "can measure the potential ability and capacities of children with different backgrounds, languages, and life experiences" (Intellect, 1976, p. 349). However, some tests, called "criterion-referenced" tests, are being developed. It is hoped that these tests will be able to evaluate where the individual student is academically and whether he or she needs specific help with the school program.

The teacher as a factor in underachievement

A common factor in the inadequate performance of underachieving adolescents is teacher expectations, which may often outweigh all other factors in affecting behavior (Chess, 1968; Rosenthal, 1969). Young people are likely to make a positive adaptation to the requirements of school when teacher demands are consistent with the capacities of the students. Learning will be impaired, however, when these demands do not allow for the individual differences among students and become a source of stress. For example, hyperactive adolescents often have difficulty attending to what their teachers are saying and may, therefore, need to have directions repeated more than once. When this need is not met, or when it is met in an unpleasant, impatient manner, the teacher becomes a source of stress for the student.

Sometimes teachers evaluate their students as underachievers when they are, in fact, achieving at their full potential. Such educators may believe that, because a youth is from a middle-class background and has an adequate command of English, he or she should be performing at a specific level. And it is not only teachers who make such false assumptions; well-educated parents can also harbor such misconceptions about the abilities of their children.

Educators should not overlook student temperament and its impact on learning (Chess, 1968). One individual may welcome new experiences and deal with them confidently. Another may initially withdraw from new experiences and be able to deal with them only after several exposures. And still another individual may be selective in his or her approach to new stimuli, approaching new people, perhaps, but withdrawing from new surroundings and new academic demands. Teachers may inaccurately assume that those students who do not readily accept new learning experiences simply lack academic readiness for them.

> Sue, a superior student with above-average intelligence, looked forward to her entry into senior high school, where she quickly made many new friends. However, accustomed to a relatively small junior high school, where all of her teachers knew her and where she was regarded as a class leader, she found herself overwhelmed by the size of her new school. She was bewildered by the lack of personal attention accorded her by the teachers and by the amount of responsibility she was expected to assume in her class assignments. As a result, her academic average slipped, and she soon joined the ranks of the underachievers.

Often, repeatedly exposing such students to a new learning task without making them feel stupid or uncooperative can help them gradually develop a sense of security. These students discover that they respond slowly to new materials and learn to allow themselves more time to adjust (Chess, 1968). Some individuals are naturally more adaptable than others; those who both adapt slowly and have a negative reaction toward new demands will be confronted by a double problem. Instructors need to keep these students from becoming disheartened, because discouragement can trigger a cycle whereby students who avoid a particular subject because they lack confidence in their ability to learn it are assumed by others to lack motivation. In reality, their low motivation is only a secondary reaction to their lack of confidence.

There are wide individual differences in distractibility (Chess, 1968). A student who is easily distracted by incidental activities in the classroom may simply be more alert to what is going on than other students are. The teacher must be able to recognize that the highly distractible adolescent isn't necessarily deliberately failing to listen. In fact, high distractibility can be a kind of responsiveness to a learning situation, reflecting a high degree of mental alertness to one's surroundings. From the viewpoint of social adjustment, the distractible student, possibly because of his or her alertness, may actually have a capacity for empathy and constructive behavior that less distractible pupils lack.

Traditionally, educators have regarded a long attention span and marked perseverance as classroom assets (Chess, 1968). A long attention span, however, can prove to be a liability; if such students become annoyed at having their attention diverted, either by the teacher or by other students, they may respond negatively (for example, by sulking or dawdling). On the other hand, it is probably desirable to reduce distractibility whenever feasible. Distractibility can be caused by hyperactivity, which has a number of possible causes (Walker, 1974). In such instances, the teacher might suggest to the parents that the child receive a physical checkup to ascertain whether the hyperactivity has a physical basis. If physical causes are eliminated, the parents can be encouraged to investigate the possibility of psychological factors that might be contributing to the hyperactivity. But in some cases the term *hyperactive behavior* is merely a label that a rigid educator has misapplied to a normal, active, curious student.

Sometimes highly distractible students respond favorably to a well-structured academic environment that has a high stimulus intensity and a minimum of outside distractions. Small enrollments and individualized instruction, perhaps with the assistance of teacher aides or tutors, can also be helpful to these easily distracted young people.

The culturally deprived adolescent

A major problem in our society is education of culturally deprived, or disadvantaged, young people. "In an educational context, 'disadvantaged' refers to children with a particular set of educationally associated problems arising from and residing extensively within the culture of the poor" (Frost & Hawkes, 1966, p. 1). Frequently, only Blacks are considered culturally deprived; but Whites in urban slums, the rural poor, migrant workers, Mexican Americans, Puerto Ricans, and Native Americans also are often culturally deprived.

A number of unfortunate consequences result from the impoverished living conditions of these groups. They include (1) a vast number of school dropouts, (2) a high delinquency rate, (3) mental retardation that is more often the result of a deprived, unstimulating environment than of organic problems, and (4) educational retardation (Frost & Hawkes, 1966; Ulibarri, 1972). Because of these problems, most culturally deprived youths possess a very low self-concept—one that is too often reinforced by their classroom teachers (Chang, 1976).

From the sociological point of view, the disadvantaged can be delineated in three ways: according to family traits relating directly to the child, according to the personal traits and behavior of the young person, and according to the social-group traits of the family (Havighurst, 1966). The family environment of the culturally deprived adolescent is characterized by parents who frequently fail to answer their children's questions or even discourage the asking of questions. It is no wonder that these young people are reluctant to ask questions of their teachers when they don't understand what is going on in the classroom. In their personal behavior, these disadvantaged adolescents often display inferior auditory and visual discrimination and poor understanding of time, numbers, and other basic concepts. Often these youths have not learned how to pay attention or to concentrate. Because disadvantaged adolescents frequently come from large families who live in a few crowded rooms, they often learn to "tune out" the noise around them. Such behavior is readily carried over into the classroom, where it interferes with learning. The social-group traits of these disadvantaged families usually include low income, a rural background, and considerable experience with social and economic discrimination (Havighurst, 1966b).

Teachers must be alert to the traits that characterize the classroom behavior of culturally deprived young people. Riessman (1962) identified the following traits as being more or less typical of these students: (1) They are slow at cognitive tasks, often because of the lack of intellectual stimulation at home. (2) They learn more readily through physical, concrete approaches than through reading, at which they are often quite deficient. (3) They are frequently anti-intellectual, appreciating knowledge for its pragmatic uses rather than for its own sake. (4) They are often superstitious, traditionally oriented (adhering to the customs of their family and ethnic group), somewhat religious, often rigid and inflexible about their beliefs and practices, reluctant to change their ideas and traditions, and hesitant about accepting innovations. (5) They generally come from male-centered cultures, except for a large number of Blacks, who come from families headed by females. The deprived from both the male-centered and the female-centered cultures, however, place a high premium on so-called masculinity. The males tend to pursue behavior that they consider appropriate to the male role, and they regard intellectual activities as "sissified." (6) They often feel alienated from society and have a sense of hopelessness and frustration about both the present and the future. (7) They frequently place the blame for their misfortunes on others. (8) They desire a higher standard of living but are reluctant to adopt the middle-class way of life. (9) They show deficits in communication skills, which may be the outgrowth of their coming from homes in which little or no English is spoken or in which the primary language is substandard English. (10) They demonstrate deficient auditory attention, possibly resulting from the necessity of "tuning out" much of what goes on around them in their homes.

At the same time, these disadvantaged learners exhibit many positive traits on which the effective classroom teacher can build (McCreary, 1966). Some of the most provoking behavior of these young people is actually reasonable, useful, and rewarding when viewed within the framework of the lives they lead. These adolescents often possess special skills and practical knowledge that take the place of much of the "book learning" that middle-class youths receive. For instance, disadvantaged youths can often be entrusted with major responsibility in caring for younger siblings, because the mother is frequently required to work, either in addition to the father or in place of an absent father. Through such experiences, deprived adolescents can learn something about parenting as well as about the realities of economics and social institutions. Teachers can capitalize on these experiences by teaching subject matter in a more relevant, realistic, and authentic manner. The practical experiences of the disadvantaged can be made to work in the classroom in an affirmative way (for example, by teaching math in terms of family budgeting).

These adolescents also demonstrate strong loyalty to their peer group through mutual aid, a feeling of kinship, and reciprocity (McCreary, 1966). This peer-group cooperation can be explained partly by the fact that disadvantaged young people are not nearly so competitive and are not under so much pressure to establish themselves as individuals as are middle-class youths (Riessman, 1962).

Youths from deprived homes develop early self-reliance, autonomy, and independence—behavior that is sometimes in conflict with the school's attempts to control, supervise, and direct student activities (McCreary, 1966).

> John, a high school sophomore of 15, is accustomed to fending for himself. With his mother deceased, his father employed as a taxi driver from 3 to 11 P.M., and no other siblings or relatives at home, John has learned to depend on himself. He comes and goes as he pleases, prepares his own meals, and plans his own entertainment. It is not surprising that he often defies the school, whose rigid directives demand that he eat in the school cafeteria, not leave the school during the day, and not smoke anywhere in the school building or on the school grounds.

And, last, the culturally deprived appreciate the value of an education, if not the value of the school (McCreary, 1966). These young people frequently dislike school. They feel alienated from it as a consequence of the cumulative effects of a too-demanding curriculum, inadequate training in the basic skills, especially reading, and teachers whom they often view as the source of their frustrations. Their parents often feel (rightly) that the school regards their children as second-class citizens. But many of the disadvantaged do recognize that education represents the one opportunity for improving their lives by preparing them for better jobs than were available to their parents.

The education of disadvantaged and bilingual adolescents

One of the problems now facing educators is that of deciding the role of the school in the education of the disadvantaged and the bilingual. One group rejects the idea that there should be special school curricula for these minorities. This group favors providing math and reading readiness for these students in preschool programs but teaching all students the standard curriculum once they reach primary school (Havighurst, 1966b). Another group of educators, however, believes that the socialization of these minority-group members is more important than their formal education (Bettelheim, 1966). Their assumption is that, if these young people have not been adequately socialized before coming to school, this task must be accomplished in the classroom. They believe that teaching these children such things as moral standards, the unacceptability of antisocial behaviors, self-discipline, and so on is far more important, both to the young people and to society, than teaching them math and reading. Still other educators believe that the school should provide disadvantaged and bilingual students with a practical preparation for life—that is, with an education that will prepare them for a trade, teach them how to obtain and hold a job, and teach them how to get along with supervisors and fellow employees. Undoubtedly, additional research is needed to determine which goals will most effectively meet the needs of these special groups and of society as a whole.

Regardless of the ultimate aims of the curriculum, however, there are certain classroom practices that can enhance the teacher's effectivenss in working with minority students. Goldberg (1966) has vividly described a hypothetical model of successful teachers of the disadvantaged and bilingual. Before all else, such teachers respect their students. They do not judge the subcultures in which these students live; instead, they learn as much as possible about these subcultures through both study and personal contact. They recognize and understand the unwillingness of these youths to strive toward goals that provide little or no visible, immediate rewards for their efforts. These teachers are aware of the deficiencies such youths possess as the result of inadequate stimulation in their environment and are familiar with the varied family structures from which their students spring. They know the impact of ethnic-group cultures on these adolescents' self-images and concepts of the world and recognize the functional qualities of the languages these students speak at home and on the streets. These teachers use test scores only as measures of achievement and not as measures of potential.

With their knowledge of the special problems of these minorities, such teachers accept certain youthful behaviors without necessarily condoning them. They attempt to modify behavior only when it seems both necessary and important to do so. In establishing clearly defined limits on behavior with a minimum of discussion, they remain impersonal, consistent, and strict but not punitive. They decide which behavior is unimportant and can be ignored and which should be rigidly restricted. For example, they may decide to ignore gum chewing in the classroom but place very firm, consistent limitations on the use of obscene language.

Successful teachers of the culturally deprived, recognizing the dangers in the self-fulfilling prophecy, inform their students of their expectations for them, always expecting just a bit more than the adolescent believes that he or she can achieve. At the same time, these teachers do not set their standards so high that their students regard them as too remote to strive toward.

Perhaps most important of all, these hypothetical effective

teachers of disadvantaged and bilingual students have a certain idealism. They are dedicated teachers who sincerely desire to render help and service to their students.

Hopefully possessed of the traits just described, the successful teacher is also aware of the importance of effective motivation among these students. Ausubel (1966) has pointed out that the kindling of a cognitive drive, or *intrinsic motivation* for learning—that is, learning for the sake of knowledge, in order to satisfy one's curiosity and one's need to explore and manipulate the environment—is probably the most promising technique for teaching cultural minorities. For a student with intrinsic motivation, learning is much more potent, relevant, and lasting than it is for one with *extrinsic motivation*, who desires an education solely as a means to a job. The lower socioeconomic classes often manifest a pragmatic attitude toward education; that is, they are extrinsically motivated. But, often, intrinsic motivation can be combined with extrinsic motivation, including visible rewards, which are important in improving the self-concept and in encouraging the development of responsibility through reinforcement of the desired behavior.

> An "effective" ninth-grade biology teacher in an urban school decided to try to foster both extrinsic and intrinsic motivation in her students. Dividing the class of 30 into pairs, she gave each pair a small piece of land on the school grounds and provided each with the necessary means for planting and raising a miniature vegetable garden. The students were encouraged to prepare the ground, fertilize it, water it, and plant the seeds they had been given. They were expected to keep their gardens weeded and watered, and weekly written reports of the garden's progress were required. Although it is unlikely that any of these urban-reared adolescents would ever become truck farmers, the presence of both extrinsic and intrinsic motivation in this project was quite evident. The students' curiosity about the growth and development of plants provided their intrinsic motivation, whereas their ability to grow something enhanced their feelings of achievement, which satisfied their external motivation. In addition, the enthusiasm generated by this project later resulted in several students' undertaking gardening as a hobby.

A number of special programs have been developed during the past decade to encourage and assist talented students who have economic, cultural, or educational handicaps. Such programs, which are sponsored by the U. S. Office of Education, enable these youths to complete high school and/or continue with postsecondary study. These programs are offered throughout the United States and its possessions and include Talent Bank, Upward Bound, Special Services for Disadvantaged Students, and others. Their goal is "to give students from deprived backgrounds the same chance for a secondary and post-secondary education that youngsters in more auspicious circumstances now enjoy" (American Education, 1976, p. 27).

Of special concern to many teachers are the cultural minority-group members who speak little or no English. According to Masarato-Horowitz (1976), non-English-speaking students should not be considered culturally deprived, because they have a culture of their own, although it may not be a White, middle-class "American" culture. We can call members of cultural minorities "disadvantaged" only if they are required by the schools to do all of their work, learn concepts, and display their abilities in the English language, which is not their native tongue. These students are not necessarily slow—their intelligence may range from retarded to superior; for most of them, the only barrier to learning is a language barrier.

Masarato-Horowitz (1976) reported on a 1974 case brought before the courts in New York City by the Puerto Rican community. The Puerto Ricans claimed that their children were not receiving equal educational opportunities because of the language barrier in the schools. The court ruled that New York City be required to educate these children in their native tongue.

There are two basic types of bilingual programs: (1) the truly bilingual program is one in which all students are permitted to learn at all levels and in all subjects in their native language until such time as they become sufficiently proficient in English to be able to learn in English-speaking classes. Unfortunately, there are very few truly bilingual programs on the secondary level, which makes school especially difficult for individuals immigrating to the United States in their mid-teens. The federal government has provided funding for such bilingual programs on the secondary level but has not spelled out the means for implementing the programs. (2) The second type of bilingual program simply provides for the teaching of English as a second language (called ESL). This program is the most common type offered at the secondary level. Under this plan, students have one class in which they are taught English as a second language, and all their remaining classes are conducted in English. Not surprisingly, young people in these programs do become or remain "disadvantaged," because it can take two years or more for a non-English-speaking student to become truly English speaking and English thinking (Masarato-Horowitz, 1976).

Masarato-Horowitz (1976) conducts two truly bilingual classes for Puerto Rican children—one in social studies and the other in English—using Spanish as the common language until the students attain a degree of proficiency in English. From the very beginning, students are given the option of doing their work in English or in Spanish, and gradually they begin to choose to do more of their work in English.

In California, school districts are being encouraged to permit non-English-speaking students to attend classes conducted in their native tongue until they can compete with their peers in English. One alternative to this approach is the use of one language in the mornings and the other language in the afternoons (Hamilton, 1975). Unfortunately, one of the main deterrents to such programs is the difficulty of finding bilingual teachers who are certified to teach subjects other than languages.

It is also important that programs for cultural-minority groups be not only bilingual but also bicultural. These students should be given a good background in their own culture and encouraged to take pride in their cultural heritage. In fact, a booklet of curriculum guidelines for multiethnic education (*Social Education*, 1976) stresses the following: (1) Ethnic diversity should be recognized and respected at individual, group, and societal levels. (2) Ethnic diversity provides a basis for maintaining societal cohesiveness and survival. (3) Equality of opportunity should be afforded to members of all ethnic groups. (4) Identification with one's ethnic group should be optional.

The school dropout

Frequently, failure to recognize the existence of learning problems or to undertake their modification results in adolescents' ultimately dropping out of school. Actually, many dropouts have the ability to do passing or even superior academic work. Elliott, Voss, and Wendling (1966) have estimated that as high as three-fourths of all dropouts have sufficient native intelligence to complete high school.

According to estimates of the U. S. Census Bureau, at any given time there are at least 2.4 million American youths between the ages of 7 and 19 who belong to a group described as "nonenrollers." These are young people who drop out because of scholastic failure or because parents or educators have discouraged them from further school attendance ("2.4 Million Children," 1976). These figures should be of considerable concern to our society for a number of reasons: (1) The United States is becoming increasingly more urbanized and less agricultural; thus, there are greater demands for educated, skilled workers and fewer demands for physical, unskilled labor. (2) Automation is becoming more common, and millions of unskilled and semiskilled jobs have become, or will shortly become, obsolete. (3) Vast numbers of young people, many of them highly educated, are experiencing great difficulty in finding employment. This problem, which was already serious because of the great numbers of young people in the United States, has been aggravated by the recession and inflation of the 1970s. (4) As the civil-rights movement of the 1960s pointed out to us, the low socioeconomic groups have a high incidence of school dropouts (Tannenbaum, 1966).

According to Greene (1966), "The dropout is defined . . . as any student who leaves school without graduating" (p. 3). However, Greene goes on to point out that this definition includes both those who leave school voluntarily and those who are expelled from classes by school officials. Many students are suspended or expelled as disciplinary measures for anything from smoking to fighting, and such expulsions often involve minority-group students. For example, a nationwide study in 1974 disclosed that three times as many Blacks as Whites were suspended from school ("2.4 Million Children," 1976). Greene further noted that his definition overlooks the fact that some dropouts continue their education in private trade schools, adult-education classes, correspondence courses, and programs offered by the armed services.

How can a teacher learn to identify the potential dropout in order to take preventive action? Unfortunately, the high school teacher is often at a considerable disadvantage, because many potential dropouts who can and should be recognized by the third grade or sooner (Fitzsimmons, Cheever, Leonard, & Macunovich, 1969) are overlooked at that stage. By the time they reach secondary school, these adolescents have usually passed the point at which they can be most effectively helped.

The major factors in determining whether adolescents drop out of school or remain to graduate are as follows (Cervantes, 1965; Greene, 1966):

1. Potential dropouts are frequently older than their classmates, usually because they have been retained in a grade at least once. Because of this age difference, these students often have difficulty relating to their classmates and, consequently, have few friends among them. This lack of peer acceptance, especially at the high school level, becomes more important to these adolescents than academic achievement, or the lack of it. The friends they do have usually have similar social and scholastic problems and either intend to drop out of school or have already done so.

2. Dropouts are generally failing in their school work when

they decide to leave school, and their academic history is one of consistent failure to achieve in the regular school program. Their poor scholastic performance leads to a cycle in which the pattern of academic failure results in a low self-concept, limited role expectations, and a low level of aspiration. These, in turn, reinforce the expectation of continued failure.

3. During high school, potential dropouts average many more absences than they did in elementary school. Almost all research points to a marked attendance regression as potential dropouts move from elementary to secondary school.

4. Most dropouts are markedly retarded in their reading ability. In fact, studies indicate that they are usually at least two years behind in reading, and many of them are as much as five to six years behind. A high percentage of these youths have undiagnosed learning disabilities. And because reading is necessary for approximately 90% of all subjects taught in school, their reading retardation is a severe handicap.

5. Dropouts characteristically have limited mental ability, although this is not necessarily responsible for their dropping out.

6. Dropouts usually lack interest in school and are dissatisfied with the curriculum, the faculty, and the school activities. In fact, Greene (1966) reported that dropouts cited disinterest and dissatisfaction as the most important factors in their decision to leave school. At the same time, these dropouts report that their teachers have exerted little influence on them while they were in school and have not encouraged them to complete their high school education. Cervantes (1965) emphasized this lack of teacher influence when he reported that two-thirds of the dropouts in his study had testified that they had never really been friends with any teacher and that one-third had maintained that the teachers were unfriendly. These are rather startling observations when one considers that the teacher has been referred to as the "key to the dropout problem." Apparently, potential dropouts do not identify with their teachers, who appear to regard them only as names in the roll book and not as individuals.

7. Potential dropouts do not become involved in school activities. One study (Bell, 1967) of 212 dropouts in Kansas disclosed that 144 (68%) of the dropouts had not participated in a single extracurricular activity, whereas nondropouts showed an average of four activities per student in large high schools and six activities per student in small high schools.

Eighteen-year-old Sam was a high school senior of limited intelligence who had a poor academic record. Under the rules of most public schools, he probably would have been prohibited from participating in varsity athletics because of his low academic average. However, because his school was somewhat progressive, Sam was permitted to play fullback on the varsity football team, a role at which he excelled. As a result of his performance with the team, he received much acclamation and recognition from his peers, which enhanced Sam's self-esteem. In another school, where he probably would have been denied the right to play football, Sam would, in all likelihood, have ended up as another dropout. Because of his success in the school's athletic program, however, and because of the understanding and acceptance of his teachers, Sam managed to stay in school and ultimately graduate.

8. Regardless of what other factors are present, the family inevitably plays a critical role in determining whether a youth becomes a dropout or remains in school. Because dropouts come primarily from the lower socioeconomic classes (Tesseneer & Tesseneer, 1958, estimated the rate at from 72% to 84%), the educational level of the parents is frequently quite low. Often such parents see little value in education and provide almost no support or encouragement for their children's academic efforts. Rarely is there much interaction between the parents and the school. These factors together form a "dropout syndrome" for which teachers should be alert.

> The dropout feels that he (or she) does not belong. He does not belong because he is retarded in school and thus separated from his age mates; he does not belong because his communication attitudes—verbal and social—seem truncated [or inadequate]. He does not belong because he is not participating in any of the activities of the school [Cervantes, 1965, p. 102].

In addition to the previously cited factors, there are other conditions, often not cited by dropouts, that can cause an adolescent to leave school. Among girls, one of the most common of these is pregnancy. Nearly half of all dropouts are girls, who are usually capable of doing better school work than many boys. Girls generally read better, fail less frequently, repeat grades less often, and even have slightly higher intelligence-test scores than boys (Pollack, 1966). Dropping out initially appears to be less catastrophic for girls than for boys, primarily because girls, unlike boys, usually are not forced to find a job when they drop out of school. In later years, however, these girls have a higher separation and divorce rate, larger families, and a greater likelihood of belonging to the lower socioeconomic classes than do nondropout girls (Hathaway, Reynolds, & Monachesi, 1969b).

On the other hand, in a study of dropout boys later in life, Hathaway, Reynolds, and Monachesi (1969a) found that these boys are characterized by a low socioeconomic level, with a tendency toward downward social mobility, a higher incidence of criminal behavior, and larger families than nondropout boys.

Alternatives to dropping out

A number of innovative programs have been introduced in recent years in attempts to counteract the problem of the dropout. For example, Boston High School now offers, as an alternative to the regular curriculum, a work-study program that provides vocational testing, occupational training, and jobs each year to some 600 students who were formerly dropouts, troublemakers, grade repeaters, and so on (Hoyt, 1976). This program, which has been in operation since the mid-sixties, has the cooperation of local banks, insurance companies, hospitals, and industries. Students are screened for their jobs in these community businesses and are supervised weekly by their teachers. When given this opportunity to earn while they learn, many of these adolescents go on to graduate from high school, and 10% even go on to college. All who graduate from the program have a job waiting for them.

In Tuskeegee, Alabama, a four-year experimental project ("2.4 Million Children," 1976) was designed to encourage school attendance, discourage dropping out, and increase parental involvement in the schools. This project employed the parents of potential dropouts at $100 per week to make certain that their own children and other children in their neighborhoods were in school. These parents were required to attend PTA meetings and to bring a minimum of five other parents with them to each meeting. Any of the parents employed by the project who did not have a ninth-grade education were required to enroll in night school.

Another small project (Csapo, 1976) involved six high school dropouts who had been placed on probation by juvenile courts. These adolescents were hired to tutor elementary-school children in reading for ten weeks during the summer. The program used the contract approach, in which requirements and goals are specified in a written contract. These contracts required, for example, that the tutors be on time for the tutoring sessions and that they use positive reinforcement with the children. The tutors were paid in accordance with their compliance with these conditions. The results of the summer's work disclosed that not only the children being tutored but also the tutors themselves showed improvement in their reading ability. In addition, the tutors improved in their personal appearance and behavior.

Until recently, school authorities discouraged pregnant girls and teenage mothers from returning to school. However, the present policy of the U. S. Department of Health, Education, and Welfare and recent court decisions have changed this practice, and a number of innovative programs have been introduced. For example, in Minneapolis a nursery has been established on the premises of one school, and teenage mothers can leave their babies there while they attend classes (Markham & Jacobson, 1976). In Atlanta an experimental program was conducted by the Department of Gynecology and Obstetrics of the Emory University School of Medicine (Ewer & Gibbs, 1976). Students in one high school served as the experimental group and those in two other high schools as controls. Girls in the experimental group were encouraged to stay in school during pregnancy and to return following childbirth. Extensive medical and counseling services were provided for them, and 51% subsequently returned to their regular high school and another 24% enrolled in other educational programs. Girls in the control groups, on the other hand, were permitted, but not encouraged, to remain in school, and only regular counseling services were provided. Of these girls, 25% returned to their regular high school and 37% went on to other educational programs. Apparently, the removal of the barriers by the schools was the most important factor in the girls' decision to remain in school.

School discipline

Many students find it difficult to adjust to the structure and discipline that are necessary in a school setting. And educators find that determining the appropriate kind and degree of structure and discipline is one of their most taxing problems.

Unfortunately, many schools use little foresight or imagination in selecting their methods of discipline. For example, during the 1972–1973 school year more than 1 million students were suspended in only nine states and Washington, D. C. (Horn, 1975), and this figure doesn't include those students who decided to drop out because they were going to be suspended or because they had been suspended a number of times. Nearly two-thirds of these 1 million suspensions involved nonviolent, nondangerous offenses, such as truancy, tardiness, smoking in school, or arguing with a teacher. Fewer than 1 out of 30 students was suspended for destroying property or engaging in other criminal behavior or for using drugs or alcohol (Horn, 1975). When the practice of suspension is widely utilized, it is likely to involve mostly minority youths. In Dallas, for example, where 50% of the students are Blacks and Mexican Americans, 70% of all suspensions involve these minorities (Cottle, 1975).

Most schools will not reinstate a suspended student until at least one of the parents comes to the school for a conference. Thus, suspension is sometimes used as a means of forcing parents to become involved in their child's problems at school. What is more likely to happen, however, is that repeated suspensions will ultimately lead the adolescent to drop out of school. When these dropouts discover that no jobs are available to them, they often turn to delinquent behavior, usually within a year or so of quitting school (Cottle, 1975).

According to Thompson (1976), there are two categories of misbehavior in school: real and perceived. Real misbehavior is that which disrupts the learning process, hindering teaching by the instructor and learning by the students. In other words, such misbehavior infringes on the freedom and rights of others to learn. Perceived misbehavior is more difficult to delineate, because it consists of those behaviors that are disturbing to some teachers but not to others. Whispering, paper crumpling, and gum chewing are forms of perceived misbehavior, and the perception of such behavior depends on the tolerance threshold of a given teacher.

Thompson (1976) also points out that, the more rules that exist in a classroom, the greater the temptation and the possibility will be for students to violate these rules. He goes on to suggest that students function best in a free, but not chaotic, environment, a free environment being one that is characterized by certain parameters of behavior and certain procedures to be followed but not by a long list of rigid rules.

Discipline, too, can be classified in two categories: remedial and preventive (Thompson, 1976). Remedial discipline, which unfortunately is the most frequently used, is action taken after misbehavior has occurred. Preventive discipline includes "all the positive steps the teacher takes to insure a productive learning environment as free as possible from the kinds of unnecessary challenges which potentially give rise to discipline problems" (Thompson, 1976, p. 410).

Most adolescents try new experiences and take risks as a normal part of their striving toward independence. The "nonsuccess" of risk taking, however, is considered to be misbehavior, and young people must learn to cope with the consequences of these nonsuccesses. Thompson (1976) observes that, in such instances, remedial discipline is most effective when it evolves from the particular risk taken. For example, if note passing is intolerable to an instructor, then a student takes a risk in passing a note. Should the note be intercepted by the teacher, it should be destroyed and thrown away without being read. This consequence, which evolves directly from the risk taken, informs the offender that such behavior will not be tolerated but does not unnecessarily embarrass or humiliate the student.

Preventive discipline "enhances the learning environment, examines the relevance of the curriculum, and challenges the traditional methodologies" (Thompson, 1976, p. 412). This kind of discipline involves giving pupils as much freedom as possible without allowing them to infringe on the rights of others. It requires that teachers recognize their roles and limitations—that is, that they resist the temptation to be not only teachers but also analysts, pals, and long-term counselors to their students. The ultimate goal of all discipline, however, should be the development in young people of the ability to discipline themselves.

A number of innovative techniques have been introduced in an effort to cope with the increasing discipline problems in our schools. One approach, behavior modification, is a group of techniques based on the principles of learning theory. In brief, this approach is based on the principle that behavior that is rewarded or that proves satisfying will be repeated, whereas behavior that is ignored or punished or that proves dissatisfying will decline. Distinguishing between rewards and punishments, however, is not always easy. For example, a teacher who scolds a student for disruptive behavior may in fact be rewarding that behavior if the student's aim was to get attention. Often, ignoring misbehavior and praising desired behavior can serve as more effective means of achieving classroom control.

On the other hand, some inappropriate behavior, such as hitting others or destroying property, cannot be ignored. One alternative to the traditional suspension is the use of a "time-out room." One of the authors (B. R.) visited a school that uses such a facility and observed its program in action. This particular time-out room was staffed by one adult, a member of the school staff who had some training in values clarification, and one student from the peer-counseling program. The function of the time-out program was to provide a place for students to ventilate their anger and frustration and to help them, through discussing the problem with the time-out-room aides, to find more effective means of coping with their problems in the classroom. In the first six months of this program's existence, 60 students out of a total school enrollment of about 1500 were referred to the time-out room, usually for one class period a day for three or four days (Pressley, 1977). There was little recidivism among these students. Table 10-1 shows the kinds of problems handled by the time-out-room program.

The function of the time-out-room aides was to help the student determine what was causing his or her problems in the classroom. In some cases, discussion revealed that communication lines had broken down between teachers and students. The student, unable to understand the teacher's assignment or requirements and reluctant

Table 10-1. Time-out record sheet

1st Assignment	2nd Assignment	3rd Assignment	4th Assignment	5th Assignment	Total	TIME OUT Month _____
						Truant behavior
						a. Skipping
						b. Fear of teacher by the student
						Disruptive behavior
						a. Goofing off
						b. Not understanding classroom material
						Disrespectful behavior
						a. Lack of communication between teacher and student
						b. Disrespect by teacher for the student
						Lying
						Stealing
						Ignorance of school discipline policy
						Refusing to give one's name to the teacher
						Not completing assignments
						Walked out of class
						a. Deliberate disrespect
						b. To prevent fighting with another student
						c. Student teasing—not corrected by the teacher
						Skipped detention
						a. Lack of fairness in being detained
						Fighting
						Personal problems (just needs to talk)

Adapted from Bolton High School time-out record sheet. Courtesy of Pat Pressley, time-out-room aide.

to ask questions for fear of appearing stupid, responded by pestering other students, being disrespectful toward the teacher, or skipping class. In such cases, the time-out-room aide would talk to the teacher to discover whether more effective means of communicating could be undertaken.

A school in Sacramento, California, has devised an alternative to the practice of suspending students for smoking, which is one of the most frequent causes of suspension (Jorgenson, 1976). In this school, students who are caught smoking are given a choice between suspension and participation in a community program called Five-Day Clinic to Stop Smoking (provided that their parents will accompany them to the clinic). In the 1969–1970 school year smoking had caused 45% of all suspensions in this school. With the availability of the clinic, which was first introduced during the 1972–1973 school year, suspensions for smoking dropped to 26% of the total, the following year they declined to 20%, and by 1974–1975 they had fallen to 13%. Although there were no data available to indicate whether the smoking incidence at the school had decreased, the community medical society reported that 70% to 80% of the adolescents and adults who attended the five-evening clinic stopped smoking—some immediately and others up to two years later.

The role of the schools

Many people erroneously believe that all students are expected to attain the same degree of mastery and skill in the various subjects they study. Actually, good teachers and a curriculum developed to meet the needs of each individual will *increase* the differences between students. It is unrealistic to expect every student to fit neatly into one of only three or four tracks, or programs of study. What is needed are programs tailored to the needs of each student. And because it is also unrealistic to expect eighth- and ninth-graders to adhere to a planned curriculum regardless of changes in their interests, aptitudes, and experiences, these individualized programs of study must be open to periodic revision. (Greene, 1966).

Schools must also recognize that each student has his or her own unique learning style. One of the problems confronting young people is the fact that they are often unaware of what that style is and how to modify it so that they can learn more effectively. Educators can help such pupils to become aware of the methods by which they learn most effectively. Riessman (1976) suggests that an informal questionnaire could be used to identify learning styles by ascertaining the time of day when the student is most alert, the easiest way for him or her to learn (that is, visually, auditorily, or expressively by active recitation), and the kind of learning situation that is most effective for that individual (studying alone or studying with others). Once a pattern is delineated and the student becomes cognizant of the setting and methods that are most effective for him or her, the learning experience may prove to be more rewarding.

The typical school curriculum has evolved from middle-class needs and values and has come to depend upon the ability of students to postpone immediate gratification in order to achieve long-range goals. However, these long-range goals are often unappealing to potential dropouts and to many minority students, whose lives have been characterized primarily by failure and frustration. Therefore, a suitable curriculum for such students would offer specific, concrete subjects that place more emphasis on practical experience, such as writing letters of application for jobs, and less emphasis on theory. Those students going on to college, on the other hand, would have special courses that stress theory. For example, all students would take a general English course that stresses the skills necessary for effective communication. In addition, however, the college-bound would have a course in formal language structure, and the potential dropouts with reading deficits would receive special training in visual and auditory perception.

Often dropouts, potential dropouts, and some minority-group students with problems in communication might prefer and respond more favorably to the flexibility of certain innovative programs or to adult-education courses, which are usually individualized and thus enable students to proceed at their own rate of speed. For example, in recent years, some unique schools have been established that cater strictly to the needs of potential dropouts. One such school was opened in the fall of 1974 in Pineville, Louisiana (Johnson, 1975). Operating in two shifts of 45 students each, this school provides individualized instruction by its four teachers, who use much programmed learning material and other up-to-date methods. During the first year of its operation, 12 students, who probably would have become dropouts at a regular school, succeeded in graduating and were granted diplomas from their original high schools.

Schools should also recognize that the composition of a class can have an impact on the emotional and social well-being of the students (Drews, 1964). One study of 600 ninth-graders who were described as slow learners disclosed that these adolescents did better emotionally and socially in homogeneous remedial sections than did a matched group left in regular heterogeneous classes. The slow learners were divided into classes of only 15 to 20 students each in order to ensure that each student would receive individual help. They were given reading material on a level that they could understand and were encouraged to work on topics of interest to them. This program resulted in increased teacher acceptance, peer acceptance, and self-acceptance. Among other dividends was the development of leadership in those who, for the first time in their lives, had an opportunity to assume such roles both socially and scholastically.

Chapter summary

Learning problems among adolescents are not restricted to those students enrolled in special-education classes. Many adolescents in regular junior high and high school classrooms also suffer from such problems. Some of these students have never had their learning difficulties recognized and, therefore, are in urgent need of help. In other instances, the learning problem was identified early but continues to require modification.

Learning difficulties have a variety of causes, including physical disorders, limited mental ability, learning disabilities (such as dyslexia), emotional disturbances, and cultural deprivation. Certain learning problems cannot be identified without the assistance of a physician, but others require only the alertness and sensitivity of a concerned teacher. The nature of the difficulty and the point in the student's development at which treatment is begun are factors that determine whether remediation of the problem is carried out in the regular classroom or in special classes.

A number of innovative measures have been introduced during the past decade in attempts to combat learning problems. These include bilingual programs for cultural-minority groups, individualized instruction, perceptual training, and special schools for potential dropouts. The problem of school discipline also has led to the use of new techniques, including behavior modification and time-out rooms.

Adolescents with untreated learning disorders frequently exhibit a low self-concept, a generalized expectation of failure, and frustration that often manifests itself in disruptive or destructive behavior. Thus, failure to identify and remedy learning problems can have widespread repercussions for the student, the school, and society as a whole.

Thought provokers

1. What are some of the factors that teachers, parents, and tutors might consider as possible causes when a student develops a serious learning problem?

2. What seems to be the primary cause of learning disabilities?
3. What are some of the traits that teachers, parents, and tutors might look for in identifying students with learning disabilities?
4. When a child has a serious learning problem, why should the teacher first suggest that that student be given a physical examination?
5. Are you an underachiever or do you know of anyone who could be classified in this manner? If so, what are some of the traits that you have observed to be characteristic of such an individual? What familial factors are present in the background of this underachiever that might have contributed to the problem?
6. In what ways can teachers and tutors help underachieving adolescents?
7. What is meant by "the motive to avoid success"? Do you know of any students or are you a student who tends to fear success? If so, what factors do you think contributed to the presence of this behavior?
8. How would you, as a teacher, cope with the culturally deprived students in your classroom so that they do not become so frustrated that they ultimately become dropouts?
9. In your own experiences as a student, do you think that intrinsic motivation, extrinsic motivation, or a combination of the two has proved most effective in motivating you to learn? Why?
10. What factors have you observed to be most characteristic of those you have known who dropped out of school?
11. What can classroom teachers do to reduce the number of school dropouts?
12. Do you know of any innovative methods that have been introduced in your community to cope with the rising incidence of disciplinary problems in the schools?

References

Alzobaie, A. J., Metfessel, N. S., & Michael, W. B. Alternative approaches to assessing intellectual abilities of youth from a culture of poverty. *Educational and Psychological Measurement*, 1968, *28*, 449–455.

American Education. Special programs for disadvantaged students, 1976, *12*(2), 27.

Ames, L. B. A low intelligence quotient often not recognized as the chief cause of many learning difficulties. *Journal of Learning Disabilities*, 1968, *1*, 735–739.

Ausubel, D. P. A teaching strategy for culturally deprived pupils: Cognitive and motivational considerations. In J. L. Frost & G. R. Hawkes (Eds.), *The disadvantaged child.* Boston: Houghton Mifflin, 1966. Pp. 237–243.

Bakwin, H., & Bakwin, R. M. *Clinical management of behavior disorders in children* (2nd ed.). Philadelphia: Saunders, 1960.

Bell, J. W. A comparison of dropouts and nondropouts on participation in school activities. *Journal of Educational Research*, 1967, *60*, 248–251.

Bender, L. Neuropsychiatric disturbances. In A. H. Keeney & V. T. Keeney (Eds.), *Dyslexia*. St. Louis: Mosby, 1968. Pp. 84–89.

Bettelheim, B. Teaching the disadvantaged. In S. W. Webster (Ed.), *The disadvantaged learner: Knowing, understanding, learning*. San Francisco: Chandler, 1966. Pp. 423–429.

Blaine, G. B., Jr. *Youth and the hazards of affluence*. New York: Harper & Row, 1966.

Bryant, N. D. Subject variables: Definition, incidence, characteristics and correlates. In N. D. Bryant & C. Kass (Eds.), *Final report: LTI in learning disabilities*, Vol. 1. Tucson: University of Arizona, 1972. Pp. 5–158.

Cattell, R. B. Are IQ tests intelligent? *Readings in Psychology Today* (3rd ed.). Del Mar, Calif.: CRM Books, 1974. Pp. 226–231.

Cervantes, L. F. *The dropout*. Ann Arbor: University of Michigan Press, 1965.

Chang, T. S. Self-concepts, academic achievement, and teachers' ratings. *Psychology in the Schools*, 1976, *13*(1), 111–115.

Chess, S. Temperament and learning ability of school children. *American Journal of Public Health*, 1968, *58*, 2231–2239.

Clements, S. *A note of caution on learning disabilities*. Paper presented at the third annual state convention of the Louisiana Association for Children with Learning Disabilities, October 1968.

Cottle, T. J. A case of suspension. *The National Elementary Principal*, 1975, *55*, 4–9.

Cruickshank, W. M. Perceptual and learning disability: A definition and projection. *Educational Digest*, 1975, *41*, 31–33.

Csapo, M. If you don't know it, teach it. *The Clearing House*, 1976, *49*(8), 365–367.

Delker, L. L. *The role of heredity in reading disability*. Glassboro, N. J.: Graduate division of Glassboro State College, 1971.

Drews, E. M. The schools: Climate affects fallout. In D. Schreiber (Ed.), *Guidance and the school dropout*. Washington, D. C.: Personnel and Guidance Association, 1964. Pp. 24–39.

Elliott, D. S., Voss, H. L., & Wendling, A. Capable dropouts and the social milieu of the high school. *Journal of Educational Research*, 1966, *60*, 180–186.

Ewer, P. A., & Gibbs, J. O. School return among pregnant adolescents. *Journal of Youth and Adolescence*, 1976, *5*(2), 221–229.

Fitzsimmons, S. J., Cheever, J., Leonard, E., & Macunovich, D. School failures: Now and tomorrow. *Developmental Psychology*, 1969, *1*, 134–146.

Frost, J. L., & Hawkes, G. R. *The disadvantaged child*. Boston: Houghton Mifflin, 1966.

Goldberg, M. L. Adapting teacher style to pupil differences: Teachers for disadvantaged children. In J. L. Frost & G. R. Hawkes (Eds.), *The disadvantaged child*. Boston: Houghton Mifflin, 1966. Pp. 345–362.

Gornick, Y. Why women fear success. *Annual editions: Readings in psychology 75/76*. Guilford, Conn.: Dushkin, 1975. Pp. 212–216.

Greene, B. I. *Preventing school dropouts*. Englewood Cliffs, N. J.: Prentice-Hall, 1966.

Hallahan, D., & Cruickshank, W. M. *Psychoeducational foundations of learning disabilities*. Englewood Cliffs, N. J.: Prentice-Hall, 1973.

Hamilton, A. The old equalizer. *American Education*, 1975, *11*(2), 748.

Hathaway, S. R., Reynolds, P. C., & Monachesi, E. D. Follow-up of the later careers and lives of 1000 boys who dropped out of high school. *Journal of Consulting and Clinical Psychology*, 1969, *33*(4), 370–380. (a)

Hathaway, S. R., Reynolds, P. C., & Monachesi, E. D. Follow-up of 812 girls ten years after high school dropout. *Journal of Consulting and Clinical Psychology*, 1969, *33*(4), 383–390. (b)

Havighurst, R. J. Unrealized potentials of adolescents. *National Association of Secondary School Principals Bulletin*, 1966, *50*, 75–96. (a)

Havighurst, R. J. Who are the socially disadvantaged? In J. L. Frost & G. R. Hawkes (Eds.), *The disadvantaged child*. Boston: Houghton Mifflin, 1966. Pp. 15–23. (b)

Hewitt, F. M. A hierarchy of educational tasks for children with learning disorders. *Exceptional Children*, 1964, *31*, 209–214.

Horn, J. Kicked-out kids. *Psychology Today*, 1975, *9*(7), 83–84.

Horner, M. S. Fail: Bright women. *Psychology Today*, 1969, *3*(6), 36–38.

Hoyt, J. H. The story of hardnosed Boston high. *American Education*, 1976, *12*(4), 10–14.

Intellect. What's wrong with standardized testing? 1976, *104*(2372), 348–349.

Johnson, N. *The halfway-plus school: 1974-1975*. Alexandria, Louisiana: Rapides Parish School Board, 1975.

Jones, H. L. *Information packet*. Perceptual development center for dyslexic children, Natchez, Mississippi, 1967.

Jones, H. L. *Project Evaluation*, Title 3 ESEA Grant No. 67-04991-0, September 1967-July 1968. Natchez, Mississippi, 1968.

Jorgenson, J. An alternative to suspension for smoking. *Phi Delta Kappan*, 1976, *57*(8), 549.

Kappelman, M. M., Kaplan, E., & Ganter, R. L. A study of learning disorders among disadvantaged children. *Journal of Learning Disabilities*, 1969, *2*(5), 262–268.

Kirk, S. *Educating exceptional children*. Boston: Houghton Mifflin, 1962.

Kotkov, B. Emotional syndromes associated with learning failures. *Diseases of the Nervous System*, 1965, *26*, 48–55.

Markham, M., & Jacobson, H. Unwed teenage mothers. *Parents Magazine*, 1976, *51*(6), 36–38.

Masarato-Horowitz, B. Interview. Central Islip School District, New York. November 1976.

McCarthy, J. *Direction of learning disability program*. Paper presented at the third annual state convention of the Louisiana Association for Children with Learning Disabilities, October 1968.

McCreary, E. Some positive characteristics of disadvantaged learners and their implications for education. In S. W. Webster (Ed.), *The disadvantaged learner: Knowing, understanding, educating*. San Francisco: Chandler, 1966. Pp. 47–52.

Meier, J. H. Prevalence and characteristics of learning disabilities found in second grade children. *Journal of Learning Disabilities*, 1971, *4*, 6–21.

National Advisory Committee on Dyslexia and Related Reading Disorders. *Reading disorders in the United States*. Washington, D. C.: U. S. Department of Health, Education, & Welfare, 1969.

National Advisory Committee on Handicapped Children. *Special education for handicapped children*. First annual report. Washington, D. C.: U. S. Department of Health, Education, & Welfare, January 31, 1968.

Pasamanick, B., & Knoblock, H. Brain damage and reproductive causality. *American Journal of Orthopsychiatry*, 1960, *30*, 229–305.

Pollack, J. H. The astonishing truth about girl dropouts. *Educational Digest*, 1966, *32*(3), 14–16.

Pressley, P. Interview. Bolton High School, Alexandria, Louisiana. March 1977.

Riessman, F. *The culturally deprived child*. New York: Harper & Row, 1962.

Riessman, F. Students' learning styles: How to determine, strengthen, and capitalize on them. *Today's Education*, 1976, *65*(3), 94–98.

Rosenthal, R. Self-fulfilling prophecy. In *Readings in Psychology Today*. Del Mar, Calif.: CRM Books, 1969. Pp. 464–471.

Roth, R. M., & Meyersburg, H. The non-achievement syndrome. *Personnel and Guidance Journal*, 1963, *41*, 535–540.

Shedd, C. L. Ptolemy rides again or dyslexia doesn't exist? *Alabama Journal of Medical Science,* 1968, 5, 481–503.

Shedd, C. L. Address at workshop for teachers sponsored by the Perceptual Development Center for Dyslexic Children, Natchez, Mississippi, January 1969.

Sheils, M., with Monroe, S. A ban on I.Q. tests? *Newsweek,* 1976, 80(12), 49.

Silver, L. Familial patterns in children with neurologically based learning disabilities. *Journal of Learning Disabilities,* 1971, 4, 349–358.

Social Education. Curriculum guidelines for multiethnic education, 1976, 40(6).

Stern, A. *Learning disabilities.* Keynote address presented at the third annual state convention of the Louisiana Association for Children with Learning Disabilities, October 1968.

Strauss, A. A., & Kaphart, N. C. *Psychopathology and education of the brain injured child: Vol. 2, Progress in theory and clinic.* New York: Grune and Stratton, 1955.

Tannenbaum, A. J. *Dropout or diploma.* New York: Teachers College, Columbia University, 1966.

Tarnopol, L. Delinquency and minimal brain dysfunction. *Journal of Learning Disabilities,* 1970, 3(4), 200–207.

Tesseneer, R. A., & Tesseneer, L. M. Review of the literature on school dropouts. *Bulletin of the National Association of Secondary School Principals,* 1958, 42, 141–153.

Thompson, G. Discipline and the high school teacher. *The Clearing House,* 1976, 49(9), 408–413.

2.4 million children who aren't in school. *U. S. News and World Report,* March 22, 1976, pp. 43–44.

Ulibarri, H. The bicultural myth and the education of the Mexican American. *Journal of Comparative Cultures,* 1972, 1, 83–95.

Walker, S. W., III. Drugging the American child: We're too cavalier about hyperactivity. *Psychology Today,* 1974, 8(7), 43–48.

Wallace, G., & McLoughlin, J. A. *Learning disabilities: Concepts and characteristics.* Columbus, Ohio: Charles E. Merrill, 1975.

Wattenberg, W. W. In A. Deutsch & H. Fishman (Eds.), *The encyclopedia of mental health* (Vol. 5). New York: Encyclopedia of Mental Health, 1963. Pp. 1803ff.

Wechsler, D. *Wechsler Intelligence Scale for Children* (Rev. ed.). New York: Psychological Corporation, 1974.

Wellington, C. B., & Wellington, J. *The underachiever: Challenges and guidelines.* Chicago: Rand McNally, 1965.

Wender, P. H. *Minimal brain dysfunction in children.* New York: Wiley Interscience, 1971.

White, S. H. Social implications of I.Q. *National Elementary Principal,* 1975, 41(1), 6–10.

Wrightsman, L. S., & Sanford, F. H. *Psychology: A scientific study of human behavior* (4th ed.). Monterey, Calif.: Brooks/Cole, 1975.

Career selection 11

Work is the basis for getting acquainted with one's self and one's creativity.

Paul Brodsky
"Problems of Adolescence"

One of the most important developmental tasks of the adolescent period, and perhaps the most difficult to fulfill in our society, is the acquisition of self-esteem and status in the community. All individuals, regardless of age, need to feel some measure of importance to themselves and to others. In Chapter 1 we said that, as adolescents make the transition from childhood to maturity, they must mature in four ways—physically, intellectually, socially, and emotionally. One aspect of social maturation is the individual's achievement of responsibility in the world of work.

When the United States and Canada were basically rural, agricultural societies, everyone in the family helped to maintain the home and the farm. Young people, who shared in these responsibilities, could feel important and needed, and they developed a sense of personal worth and status (Fredenburgh, 1968). Now that the family farm has virtually disappeared, however, many adolescents have little opportunity to contribute to the family's well-being. Although adolescents (especially girls) from the lower socioeconomic classes and from certain ethnic groups, such as the Chinese Americans, still perform numerous chores around the home and help care for younger siblings, many others, from the urban middle and upper classes, have no such opportunity. In addition, many young people are denied the opportunity to find employment because of the minimum-age requirements for working in industry and business and because of the refusal of some parents to permit their children to become gainfully employed during the early adolescent years.

A century ago very few Americans finished high school; however, by the year 1973 over 75% were doing so, and this additional education has reduced and postponed occupational work experience for the typical adolescent (Mincer, 1973).

Even summer employment for young people has become extremely limited. For example, during one recent summer the U. S. Department of Labor, the U. S. Civil Service Commission, the U. S. Department of the Interior, and the National Alliance of Businessmen expected to have 1.5 million, 54,000, 26,000, and 221,900 summer job openings, respectively, but these job figures were exceeded by the number of youths seeking summer employment ("Chances of Finding Work," 1976). Of all those programs, none was open to adolescents from middle- or upper-income families, although they could apply to the state employment agencies, which were also available to the other youths. During this same summer, in New York City, 65,000 young people had jobs and 435,000 did not; in New Orleans, 25,000 applications were expected for the 5602 summer jobs that had been created with federal funds. The prospect of obtaining a job in private industry was even more bleak ("Chances of Finding Work," 1976).

It is difficult to reduce teenage unemployment because of: (1) the vast numbers of teenagers seeking jobs each year, (2) the minimum-age restrictions that bar youths from employment, (3) licensing restrictions in many fields that set age requirements, (4) minimum-wage laws that discourage some employers from hiring inexperienced teenagers, (5) the union membership required of workers in certain jobs, and (6) the many teenagers who receive insufficient career counseling in school and therefore find their skills ill suited to the job market ("Why It's Hard to Cut Teen-Age Unemployment," 1976).

Adolescent employment since 1930

The early 1930s witnessed a gradual decline in the exploitation of child labor with its long hours and low pay (up to 80 hours per week at five to ten cents an hour). At the same time, however, the

Children's Bureau of the U. S. Department of Labor ("Child Labor Comes Back," 1933) noted that there were 250,000 homeless and jobless boys living in the streets and scrounging for an existence. The explanation for this inconsistency lies in the fact that numerous states had begun to raise the age at which children could be employed in many industries and factories ("Child Labor," 1932). By 1937, eight state legislatures had established 16 as the minimum age for gainful employment ("Brearley Bulletin," 1937).

During the thirties approximately 86% of the young people between the ages of 10 and 13 who were classified as employed were engaged in agriculture, in most instances on the farms of parents or other relatives ("United States Summary," 1932). But with the coming of widespread droughts and depressed prices for farm products, some of those in middle adolescence moved into manufacturing, mechanical, and mercantile occupations; others became messenger and delivery boys; and still others—in fact, quite a large number—entered domestic service ("Brearley Bulletin," 1937). Although legislation against child labor was gradually becoming more stringent, a larger percentage of adolescents were gainfully employed in the thirties than today.

By 1940, more than 60% of those between the ages of 14 and 19 were working, whereas only 40% of those between the ages of 20 and 25 were ("Youth in the Labor Market," 1941). Apparently, not all states were yet enacting or enforcing minimum-age legislation, although in many areas such laws were becoming quite common. During the early forties about 2 million youths left school each year, either as graduates or as dropouts. Many were dropping out of school when they reached age 16, which was rapidly becoming the minimum legal age for leaving ("Post-War Planning," 1945).

In the 1950s, jobs for young people started to disappear. One survey did reveal, however, that 32% of the adolescents of that decade were gainfully employed in widely diverse occupations, ranging from office work to modeling ("Getting and Spending the Teenage Allowance," 1957). Other youths found summer employment on farms, where they could drive tractors, work milking machines, and care for poultry, or in offices, where they were employed as temporary typists, file clerks, and switchboard operators ("About That Summer Job," 1957). Nevertheless, it was becoming more and more difficult for the young person between the ages of 14 and 16 to find afternoon and summer jobs, which are so essential to provide adolescents with initial work experience and the opportunity to acquire the status associated with gainful employment ("New Look," 1958).

Many of the job openings requiring little or no training, such as certain factory and farm occupations, had largely disappeared by the

1960s. Hamel (1964) noted that many youths seeking employment simply did not have the necessary skills for the jobs that were available. And Krauss (1964) observed that additional education was being demanded for the more desirable jobs in our rapidly expanding technological society.

According to Rosenfeld (1963), unemployment is usually most widespread among youths who have been in the job market for a relatively short time, especially among those with the least education, training, and experience. Thus, job applicants without a high school diploma began to find it more and more difficult to secure work during the 1960s. Despite the national average of 4% unemployment, teenagers were experiencing a 12% unemployment rate (U. S. Department of Labor, 1966). Some of these young people were seeking only summer or part-time jobs, and their failure to find such employment usually meant that they remained financially dependent on their parents. Such extended dependence not only denies adolescents the opportunities and experiences that accompany employment but also delays their achievement of self-reliance.

Duncan (1965) stated that "widespread unemployment of young people could lead to feelings of frustration or worthlessness. It could also contribute to the development of antisocial attitudes, to crime, or even in some circumstances, to the growth of totalitarian political movements" (p. 123). Perhaps this trend of declining employment was one of the factors that contributed to the unrest and militancy of the late 1960s.

Almost a decade later, in 1974, only 4% of the labor force was composed of American workers of Spanish background. The 16- to 19-year-olds among these workers had a median of only 11.2 years of education, whereas the national average for this age group was 12.5 years. In fact, in 1974, 69% of the total labor force (16 years old and older) had completed 12 years of school as compared to 56% who had done so in 1964, with workers of both Spanish and non-Spanish background attaining a gain in educational level over the decade (McEaddy, 1975).

The majority of workers in the United States by 1974 were employed in occupations that were service-related, such as finance, trade, government, public utilities, and business and personal services. The adolescents of the late 1970s and early 1980s will have the opportunity to work in many of these service areas, because it is predicted that by 1985 about 60 million workers will be employed in such jobs (Calhoun & Finch, 1976). Yet, as Rogers (1973) has stated, "There is no orderly or effective system of vocational training and supportive services for youth in America and none allowing for continuing interchange and movement between school and work" (p. 472). Despite legislation designed to improve job opportunities for young people (for example, the Equal Pay Act of 1963, the Age Discrimination in Employment Act of 1967, and Title IX of the Vocational Education Amendments of 1972), adolescents entering the job market today still face a variety of problems (Calhoun & Finch, 1976).

It is apparent that the past 50 or 60 years have seen numerous changes in the types and number of jobs available to the adolescent. Nevertheless, the reasons for young people's desire to work have remained basically the same. Adolescents need to experience some degree of independence, which they can achieve only by earning at least some of their own spending money. In addition, work provides young people with the opportunity to acquire status within the community, enhance their feelings of adequacy and self-esteem, and engage in the role testing that is necessary in order for them to resolve the identity crisis. Besides working to satisfy their needs for status and independence, however, adolescents often seek employment to obtain money for secondary and higher education. Many students from disadvantaged homes must purchase their own school supplies, clothing, and even food while still in junior high and high school. And, finally, married adolescents must work in order to support themselves and their families.

Career education

Based on the premise that a career should provide an identity as well as a sense of accomplishment, a model for "career education" was developed by the U. S. Office of Education (1973) that requires the cooperative efforts of school, family, business, and community. The thesis for the model is that, from kindergarten through high school, students should be made aware of the wide variety of careers available, the types of tasks they involve, the requirements for entering them, and opportunities they offer.

The career-education model developed by the Office of Education is similar to the one developed by the State of Ohio (Tolbert, 1974, p. 15), which includes the following career concepts:

1. Awareness, grades K–6: introduction to the work world through the study of occupational clusters
2. Exploration, grades 7–9: selection and in-depth investigation of those clusters of particular interest
3. Job skills at entry-level, grade 10: participation by all students in actual work experience

4. Preparation for post-high-school work, grade 12: preparation of students for entering the work world or furthering their education or training at the end of grade 12.

The U. S. Office of Education guidelines for career education (1973) state that academic subjects should: (1) be structured around career development, (2) include extensive counseling for decision making, and (3) prepare students for a career of their choice or for advanced education.

There were over 100 career-education pilot projects with almost 750,000 students enrolled during 1973, and by 1974 about 5000 of the 17,000 school districts in the United States had instituted career-education programs. Some of the pilot projects were Upward Bound, Talent Search, and Career Opportunities Program.

> Career education provides a core for the total educational program, using the job as the unifying force for all school disciplines. In this sense, career education represents a total system wherein all general education offerings take on new meanings relating to career and work. Career education emphasizes student awareness and orientation to work, appreciation for the dignity of work, exploration of career opportunities and requirements, and specialized vocational preparation [Calhoun & Finch, 1976, p. 4].

The adolescent whose education has emphasized career options and decision making and who has been exposed to many areas of the work world is better able to make responsible, informed decisions at all career stages, from the educational preparation for the first job to reeducation for reentry into the job market (Shafer, 1975).

Educational selection

During the past two decades, the growing number of technological occupations, the need for increased education for the more desirable jobs, and the greater availability of education have encouraged most parents, and society in general, to emphasize to young people the importance of education and the necessity of obtaining a high school diploma. However, about 32% of all young people are still not completing high school (Tolbert, 1974), and another 30% are completing high school in a way that is dissatisfying both to them and to their parents (Stripling, 1967).

What are some of the factors contributing to this dissatisfaction? Perhaps one of the most important factors is selection of an improper curriculum. By the ninth grade, most schools begin pressuring students to decide whether they will pursue an academic or a vocational curriculum. Unfortunately, those who elect a vocational- or commercial-training program sometimes decide two or three years later that they want to enter college, only to discover that they have not had certain academic courses required for college admission. Conversely, students enrolled in college-preparatory curricula are often restricted to studying only those subjects demanded for college entrance; they are given little opportunity to explore their interests in subjects outside their chosen curriculum.

Another factor contributing to unsuitable curriculum selection is the lack of sufficient numbers of qualified counselors at the junior high level to help students identify and investigate subjects and occupations of interest to them before their entrance into high school. Ideally, there should be one counselor for every 250 students (Tolbert, 1974). However, in most school systems a ratio of one counselor for every 500–750 students is more common. As a result, counselors are usually engaged in routine group testing and clerical work and have little time to help individual students explore the educational possibilities available to them.

Society's emphasis on the need for a college education also contributes to unsatisfactory curriculum selection. Since World War II, a college degree has been a symbol of prestige, and it is regarded by many as the only means to achieve upward socioeconomic mobility. Therefore, many individuals enroll in a college-preparatory curriculum, and eventually in college, not because they desire a higher education but because their families believe that college is the only door of opportunity open to young people. Fredenburgh (1968) suggests that some of the radical activist behavior on college campuses in the 1960s may have been a reflection of these young people's frustration at the pressures their parents placed on them to attend college and to compete for high-prestige occupations. Such goals often reflect not the students' choices but rather the unfilled aspirations of the parents. In many instances, these students are also frustrated by the discovery that their college degree doesn't bring them instant success.

Vocational-high-school enrollments, which reached 4 million in 1969, are expected to decline to less than 3.4 million by 1980, whereas enrollments in postsecondary technical-education programs, especially community colleges, are expected to increase (Feldman, 1971). This is due partly to the fact that many community colleges are now offering vocational/technical training. Many of the young people entering colleges today, of whom one-half do not graduate (Tolbert, 1974), might be happier and better suited to a two-year technical-training curriculum, a vocational or trade-school program, or an apprenticeship or on-the-job training program.

The selection of appropriate training and a satisfying occupation should be made by the youths themselves, of course, but assistance from parents and other interested adults is often needed. Such assistance can take many forms. Discussions with adults employed in various fields, school-sponsored seminars and lectures on career opportunities, and the many available pamphlets and brochures describing different training programs can all be quite informative.* School counselors should acquaint students with the results of their group achievement tests and discuss the ways in which their particular talents, as indicated by the test scores, can be utilized in the world of work. When young people are not fully aware of their abilities and interests, individual vocational testing may be indicated. This testing can often be done by the school counselor or through the guidance programs of nearby colleges. The type of education desired and the financial resources available to the student must also be considered.

One factor that is often of considerable importance in the selection of an educational facility is its proximity to the student's home. Many high school graduates attend colleges and universities within a 50- to 75-mile radius of their homes. Those students who commute to their schools receive the same educational benefits as those who live on campus, but they do not always have the opportunity to participate in the extracurricular activities and cultural events that may be offered by the school. In addition, these commuters do not experience the independence gained in living away from home. Nevertheless, for the young person who must economize by residing at home and might not otherwise be able to obtain a higher education, commuting is frequently the only option. In addition, such an arrangement often enables less mature adolescents to attain a degree of maturity before leaving home. It is estimated that eventually 75% of all college-bound youths will begin their higher education at a junior college or technical school, to which most of them will commute (Stripling, 1967).

According to Calhoun and Finch (1976), since 1970 only two out of every ten jobs has required a college education, and, consequently, a greater emphasis has been placed on the importance of vocational/technical education. Therefore, it is essential that adolescents be made aware of the numerous avenues through which they

*Counselors and school libraries should make such books as the following available for students' use: The College Blue Book, A Handbook for Counselors of College Bound Students, The College Finder, Lovejoy's College Guide, Student Financial Aid Manual for Colleges and Universities, An Introduction to Junior Colleges, Vocational and Technical Institute Courses, Vocational Training Directory of the United States, Lovejoy's Vocational School Guide, and Directory of Vocational Training Sources, Career World–The Continuing Guide to Careers.

can achieve occupational and vocational competence outside college. For example, federal, state, and local governments offer vocational and technical training in many areas, including homemaking, commercial occupations, auto mechanics, practical nursing, electronics, and agriculture. There are also private schools that offer courses in business and in technical and trade areas. Sometimes students can even start their vocational training in high school and continue it after graduation. Many medical schools throughout the United States are now providing training for such careers as nursing, laboratory technician, medical technician, medical-records librarian, and dental technician.

In numerous skilled-labor occupations, on-the-job training and apprenticeship training are available. Certainly, the adolescent who selects an occupation with such a training program is exposed more quickly to the world of work than is the one who continues in formal education. No matter how extensive his or her formal education may be, however, every student will eventually need to acquire some type of preliminary experience in the job or profession he or she chooses to follow. In recent years, more and more professions have been emphasizing practical experience and demanding internships.

The selection of a vocation

Theories of vocational choice

> Having a vocational objective is important in a society in which earning a living is important, in which occupational roles are of major significance, and in which education is, in effect, if not avowedly, occupationally oriented; having a vocational preference, in this context, gives a purpose to behavior and makes possible education and vocational decisions [Super, 1961, p. 35].

As an authority in the area of vocational selection whose ideas have had a profound effect on current theories of occupational choice, Super has come to regard vocational selection as a part of the developmental process that reflects the individual's feelings about himself or herself.

Korman (1969), elaborating on Super's theories, pointed out that "Basically, the high self-esteem person seems to look at himself and say, 'I like what I see and I am going to give it its desires and needs,' whereas the low self-esteem person seems to say when looking at himself 'I do not like what I see and I am not going to give it its desires and needs' " (p. 191). Even when the individuals with a low self-concept have their desires fulfilled, they do not necessarily experience emotional satisfaction, although continued fulfillment could conceivably lead to a self-reassessment that could change the determinants of their satisfaction.

There have been numerous theories advanced to explain how one goes about selecting a vocation. In 1951, Ginsberg, Ginsberg, Axelrod, and Herma suggested that an occupational choice is a compromise between fantasy and reality. They saw the individual as moving through three definite stages in the process of making a vocational choice: the "fantasy period," the "tentative period," and the "realistic period." During the fantasy period, which encompasses the first decade of life, a child's thoughts about a future vocation are not related to ability, training, or the availability of job opportunities. This stage of development is marked by frequent changes; one day the child expresses a desire to be an astronaut and the next day, a doctor and in neither case does he or she consider the qualifications necessary for or the future offered by the vocation being considered. During the tentative period, which covers part of adolescence, the individual begins to be concerned with the working conditions and requirements of the various vocations open to him or her. Consideration is given to the young person's particular interests and, toward the end of the period, to the aptitudes and education demanded by various occupations and to the individual's personal values and goals. In the period of reality, which begins around the age of 17, the adolescent starts to resolve the problem of vocational choice, recognizing the need to compromise between fantasy and reality. Hollander (1967) studied 4616 students in grades 6 through 12 and found that vocational choices do become more realistic with advancing age.

In 1956, Roe introduced the idea that vocational selection reflects the adolescent's personality type, which develops in large measure as a result of the early parent/child relationship. She pointed out that each personality type demands the satisfaction of certain psychological needs, such as the need for power and prestige, which the individual seeks to fulfill through various life roles. In adolescents these needs are partially expressed through the selection of a vocation. For example, an individual who demonstrates a need for power and prestige might select a career in politics.

Lambert (1967), using a revision of the Roe-Siegelman Parent-Child Relationship Questionnaire, did a study of vocational motivation among eighth-grade girls attending an urban junior high school in the Oklahoma City metropolitan area and among both boys and girls in the seventh and ninth grades attending a junior high school located on the outskirts of the city (with a half rural and half urban enrollment). The results disclosed that adolescent girls tended to select occupations that do not involve working directly with people (for example, computer programming) if the relationship with the dominant parent was a loving and rewarding one and that they were more likely to select occupations that involve many personal contacts (for example, teaching) when the parental attitudes toward the child's activities were casual.

Holland (1962) listed six vocational areas, each of which represents a unique vocational environment with its own life-style. He believed that the individual's personality determines which of these areas he or she will ultimately enter. Each person must learn to adjust to one of these patterns and must acquire the skills demanded by the selected area. The six vocational fields are as follows:

1. The *realistic* area stresses physical skills, with little emphasis on interpersonal relationships or verbal ability (construction workers).
2. The *intellectual* area involves working with ideas rather than with people (scientific researchers).
3. The *social* area places its emphasis on interpersonal relationships (teachers).
4. The *conventional* area is structured and characterized by rules and regulations that give it a certain inflexibility (the military).
5. The *enterprising* area involves the pursuit of status through domination and manipulation of others (politicians).
6. The *artistic* area stresses the emotional and esthetic expression of the inner self (composers).

According to Caplow (1954), many vocational choices occur by accident. He notes that certain preliminary choices leading to a vocation must be made as early as the eighth grade, such as the decision of whether to enroll in a college-preparatory curriculum or a vocational-training program. Because students are frequently badly informed about occupations at this stage in their development and because their training is often irreversible, they tend to stumble into their life's work. He also observes that some careers attract people because of the prestige attached to them. Tyler (1969) suggested that choosing an identity is synonymous with choosing an occupation, and Calhoun and Finch (1976, p. 6) state that "an occupation is an important source of social identity. A person's occupation has direct significance for self-fulfillment and social prestige."

In any case, however, it is apparent that occupational development should be a subject of concern to educators and counselors of young people. Tolbert (1974) has suggested that the principal premises of vocational development include the following: (1) Vocational development should be considered an essential part of the total educational program of grades K through 16. (2) Such development is shaped both by the home and by the school. (3) The personality traits that contribute to career selection are identifiable. (4) There are several different approaches (such as work/study programs, volunteer work, and vocational testing and counseling) that can be utilized in career development. (5) Young people must make their own career choices and must accept responsibility for them. (6) Vocational development is a lifelong experience. (7) Making a career choice requires one to grow and to synthesize an understanding of the self with an understanding of the environment. (8) Vocational selection evolves from the interaction of psychological, physiological, sociological and economic factors. Whether you believe in one, several, or none of these premises, they do offer a framework for interpreting vocational selection as a developmental process and suggest that choosing an occupation is a much more complex process than is commonly assumed.

Sociological factors in vocational selection

Numerous sociological factors affect vocational choice, and probably none has greater impact than the family. For example, Super (1957) noted that the family *inculcates* in young people certain habits and expectations of success that form the foundation for later success. The adolescent growing up in a home in which success is recognized and rewarded usually develops a pattern of successful achievement that carries over into all phases of life: school, social life, and, ultimately, career. Conversely, those in whom success is ignored and failure condemned tend to develop patterns of failure that become self-perpetuating.

Some individuals pursue the careers of their parents or grandparents because of interest, economic feasibility, lack of motivation to follow another career, or family pressure. However, this phenomenon of family occupations is gradually disappearing. Duncan and Hodge (1963), in a study of 1000 Chicago males, noted that only 10% entered their fathers' vocations; it is probable that some of these were examples of "forced inheritance," wherein they found themselves in their fathers' jobs because of restricted opportunity and cultural deprivation that made it difficult to escape from the parents' low-status occupation. Werts (1968), comparing fathers' occupations to the career choices of over 76,000 boys at the other end of the socioeconomic scale, found that the sons of physical scientists, social scientists, and medical people more frequently selected the careers of their fathers than might ordinarily be expected. And a study by Goyder and Curtis (1975) disclosed that, for middle-class males and females, the congruence between the subject's and the father's occupational status was similar to that between the father's and the paternal grandfather's. This finding tends to indicate the existence of a relatively stable pattern of occupational-status inheritance.

A second sociological factor, the school, also contributes substantially to vocational selection. Through their experiences at school, adolescents gradually acquire an awareness of their vocational assets, liabilities, and interests, which largely provide the basis for their educational and vocational aspirations.

One's socioeconomic class and one's sex also appear to have an impact on the selection of an occupation. For example, Osipow (1968) noted that "social class membership is an important situational determinant and affects attitudes towards education and work, the amount and kind of education and training acquired, and the economic resources one has to implement his career plans" (p. 216). Omvig and Thomas (1974) reported that vocational-interest data for affluent junior high school students, compared to like data for inner-city, disadvantaged students, disclosed that: (1) the disadvantaged showed greater consistency than the affluent between their verbally expressed interests and their tested interests; (2) disadvantaged males displayed greater consistency between these two factors than disadvantaged females; (3) high-socioeconomic-class females demonstrated greater congruence between these factors than high-socioeconomic-class males; (4) disadvantaged females showed high tested interest in service occupations (for example, nursing); (5) females of high socioeconomic levels also showed tested and expressed interest in service occupations but in addition displayed a preference for the performing arts; (6) disadvantaged males manifested high tested interests for training in music, applied technology, entertainment/performing arts; (7) high-socioeconomic-class males also demonstrated a strong tested interest for applied technology but in addition an attraction to computational fields; (8) disadvantaged males verbally expressed high interest in music, management, supervision, and machine work; and (9) high-socioeconomic-class youths (both male and female) verbalized strong interest in crafts, precision operations (computer science, for example), promotion/community (such as public relations), agriculture, and medical occupations. Other research (Thomas, 1976) has indicated that the vocational expectations and choices for low-socioeconomic-class youths—both Black and White—are usually realistic, although the lower class shows a greater proportion of unrealistic preferences and plans than does the middle class.

In recent years, numerous studies have concentrated on the vocational interests and goals of adolescent girls, which for too long were ignored or minimized. One investigator (Burlin, 1976) noted that many adolescent females are influenced in their occupational aspirations by external (environmental) cues and that they aspire to sexually nonstereotyped occupations in their ideal choices but not in their real choices. She points out that "our culture's sex role ideology has limited and continues to limit the occupational aspirations of many female adolescents" (p. 129). Now that traditional barriers to various forms of professional or vocational-technical education have come down and . . . barriers to many forms of employment have been removed" (Shafer, 1975, p. 124), girls are just as much in need of occupational information, role models, and career education as are boys.

The issue of vocational selection by girls, however, continues to be complicated by the question of whether to plan for a career, marriage, a career during marriage, or simply a vocation to fall back on in case of marital failure or economic necessity. One study (Epstein & Bronzaft, 1972) of 1063 females from predominantly lower-middle-class and working-class backgrounds who were first-year students at a tuition-free public university disclosed that a plurality perceived their role 15 years hence as that of "a married career woman with children" (p. 671).

Another survey of 1200 first-year college women done by Harmon (1971) showed that the most popular career fields were those of medicine, social service, communication, and housewife, while the areas of business and clerical/secretarial were the least popular.

Regardless of ultimate vocational choice, however, it is apparent that there is a need to end career-choice sex typing, which both girls and boys have traditionally learned in childhood. Harris (1974) suggests that this stereotyping can be counteracted through group career counseling of students beginning at about the sixth-grade level.

Another factor, the mass media (magazines, newspapers, books, movies, radio, and television), also influences some adolescents' thoughts about entering certain occupations. Some industries and the armed forces advertise the adventure, education, and intellectual stimulation afforded by their organizations in efforts to recruit personnel. Such environmental forces do not always provide a realistic picture of job situations and may inadvertently deceive young people, who are quite suggestible. However, as youths mature, they tend to become more realistic about their abilities and therefore become less susceptible to the vocational ideas presented by the media.

Occasionally, community facilities play a positive role in assisting young people in their selection of a suitable career. In 1969, the University of Texas Medical Branch in Galveston began helping youths in that city to explore opportunities in vocations related to medicine (*Galveston Daily News,* 1969) through a project called the Health Occupation Cooperative Training Program. This program introduced high school juniors and seniors to certain medical occupations and helped them decide, through an on-the-job training plan, whether they were qualified for and interested in any of these areas.

And, last, the peer group can also play a role in vocational selection. For example, upper-middle-class youths who prefer to work with their hands in skilled laborers' jobs may be dissuaded from doing so for fear that they will be ostracized by their college-bound friends.

Other factors influencing vocational choice

In addition to the numerous sociological influences just cited, there are still other factors influencing vocational selection. For example, Powell and Bloom (1962) reported that, when senior high school students were asked to name the occupational factors they considered to be the most important in vocational choice, they most frequently stated that "interest in their work" was the primary consideration, with a desire for security being another strong motivating factor.

According to Tseng and Carter (1970), achievement motivation is critical to an individual's choice of a career, as is the perceived prestige of different occupations. On the other hand, Slocum and Bowles (1968) found no correlation between the prestige rankings of an occupation and the expressed attractiveness of that job to high school seniors.

Another factor that would be expected to have much impact on vocational selection is intellectual ability. Although this element cannot be ruled out, the average adolescent bases his or her ultimate occupational decision on factors other than the intelligence demanded by a given career (Horrocks, 1976). Certainly, limited mental ability would limit entrance to higher-level occupations, but being highly intelligent does not necessarily indicate that a young person will enter or succeed in a high-level career.

It is interesting to note that there is a certain degree of stability in occupational choices. Despite many changes in ambitions that individuals undergo in childhood and adolescence, once a career decision is made during high school, there appears to be a greater stability of choice than one might expect. Followup studies on a high school class initially investigated in 1966 were done in 1968 and again in 1974 (Lambert, 1975) to discover whether the students had pursued the academic and/or work experiences that each had chosen during the senior year and whether their IQs, as measured by the Navy Classification Test, were related to the stability of their long-term occupational or educational choices. The 1968 survey reported that IQ was not a factor in either choice, but the 1974 survey did disclose a small relationship between IQ and the stability of the vocational selection. Although many of the young men in the group had been required to serve in the armed forces, thus interrupting their career plans, 75% of the subjects in the 1968 survey disclosed the same career choice that they had expressed in 1966, and 70% of the group in the 1974 survey still retained the same vocational goals they had had in the 1966 survey (Lambert, 1975).

Regardless of the motives, conscious or unconscious, underlying the selection of a vocation, however, the more occupational information to which adolescents have access and the more knowledge they have about themselves, the greater the opportunities are for them to arrive at a wise choice. Certainly it is preferable for young people to select a career that will utilize their talents and enhance their self-esteem. At the same time, it is essential for both the adolescents and the adults counseling them to recognize that, in addition to the professions, there are many equally important jobs that demand responsible, qualified workers. Young people should be made aware of the disparity that often exists between the availability of certain jobs, especially within the professions, and the numbers of individuals desiring to enter such fields.

The adolescent's selection of a vocation is an important step in role testing and in striving toward maturity, but that selection should not be regarded as irreversible. Because it is estimated that within a decade many jobs will be obsolescent and will ultimately disappear, and that many others, presently nonexistent, will emerge, it is important that youths, whether technically or academically educated, recognize that changing jobs can sometimes be a sign of vocational growth.

Adolescent participation in volunteer work

Selecting an occupation and finding employment are two major goals that many young people hope to accomplish during their teens. Both are necessary for fulfilling their psychological needs and their need for status. Often, volunteer work can serve as one means of achieving these aims. Such work can provide interesting learning experiences, especially in service jobs, which have outstripped over-all employment with an increase of 49% during the decade between 1960 and 1970 (Havighurst, Graham, & Eberly, 1972).

With the decline in gainful employment available to the ado-lescent, there has been a corresponding increase in the prevalence of volunteer job openings. In addition to satisfying the need to acquire both status and feelings of adequacy, volunteer work can reveal to some adolescents career possibilities that they might otherwise never have known of.

Volunteer work is often first introduced to the adolescent through the Boy Scouts, Girl Scouts, and similar organizations. These groups engage in useful community projects, such as sponsoring antipollution clean-up drives, making gifts and decorations for nursing-home and hospital patients, visiting the ill, and accompany-ing senior citizens to church. Such volunteer service develops a sense of responsibility in these young people and satisfies some of their demands for feeling needed by their community.

Many adolescents also do volunteer work through participa-tion in extracurricular activities at school. Those who assist with the school newspaper or yearbook are working and learning simultane-ously, and these activities can lead to interest in careers such as journalism and advertising. Students who serve as office helpers, counselors' aides, library assistants, and teachers' aides help their schools by lightening the loads of overworked faculty and staff mem-bers and, at the same time, learn something about the world of work. During the past several years, numerous students have assisted with the Head Start programs conducted by the public schools or have tutored disadvantaged youngsters in inner-city tutorial programs. Thus, it is apparent that the schools offer many opportunities for youths to volunteer their services.

Candy Stripers, who assist hospital staffs throughout the coun-try, perform one type of volunteer work that is often appealing to young people. These adolescents aid the staff by delivering mail and flowers, pushing wheelchairs, and doing other unskilled but neces-sary work around the hospital. Through such services, youths are exposed to the vast field of medicine, and many ultimately become interested in some type of medical career.

Some adolescents volunteer to do work in such places as research laboratories, darkrooms, and science museums, frequently because they already have an interest in some aspect of the work done there. Other young people do volunteer work at municipal zoos and parks, where they help to supervise young children visiting these facilities by serving as guides and organizing games for them. Still others discover that there is pleasure and excitement in volunteering as ushers and stagehands for local little-theater and opera groups. Such young people have an opportunity not only to do useful work and learn about interesting occupations but also to see, without charge, the performances of the groups with which they are working.

And some adolescents find enjoyment, and sometimes profit, in using their musical talents. These youths may form musical groups and play at dances and other gatherings or volunteer their performances at benefits or at meetings of fraternal organizations. Others play the guitar or the organ for church services or sing in the church or community choir group. Musical entertainment in all its forms has long been a means by which adolescents have volunteered their talents, as well as financed their educational and recreational needs.

Older adolescents, especially college students and young working people, often volunteer to help with disadvantaged and troubled young people in their communities. In many cities Big Brother and Big Sister programs have been introduced. Under these programs, each volunteer "adopts" a disadvantaged child, whom he or she sees regularly, taking the child on excursions and to sporting events and tutoring the child in school work when necessary. One of the authors (B. R.) has had over 500 college students who have done such tutoring since 1970. Many sociology, psychology, and education majors, particularly, have participated in these volunteer services, as well as in programs dealing with mental health and mental retardation. For example, young people are serving as telephone answerers, staffing hotlines for adolescents who seek help or advice with their problems, (a topic to be discussed in more detail in Chapter 12). In several Kentucky high schools and communities a number of mental-health and mental-retardation clubs have been formed. The more than 300 club members in this one state alone have published a mental-health paper, operated county-fair information booths on mental health and retardation, conducted drives for toys and equipment to be distributed to mental-health and mental-retardation services, and engaged in other related activities (Staton, Tiller, & Weyler, 1969).

In 1972 Havighurst, Graham, and Eberly recommended what they described as "action learning," a term for volunteer public service that would supplement formal academic education for young people between the ages of 15 and 20. This work would be part-time and would be related to subjects the adolescent studies in school. Academic credit would be awarded for what was learned through the work, rather than simply for having participated in the work experience. This action learning could be incorporated into school curricula in the same manner in which vocational programs have been.

From the current trends in the volunteer services in which adolescents participate, it is evident that these activities are not just "busy work" and that they actually serve several important functions in the lives of numerous young people. First, those who have elected to volunteer their energies are helping their community and its members. Second, volunteers are helping themselves to become more adequate individuals through testing various roles, acquiring a greater sense of responsibility, and developing greater self-esteem. And, third, by continuing to engage in such volunteer services, adolescents can convince society of the need to recognize their worth and value and to accord them the status they so desperately seek, frequently by less positive means.

Remunerative employment

Part-time work for the adolescent

Some adults have come to view part-time jobs for adolescents as the way to encourage positive attitudes toward work, create a sense of responsibility, and even prevent delinquency (Freedman, 1963). Whether such jobs achieve all these ends is debatable, but they certainly can prove beneficial to many high school and college students by encouraging better work habits, improving self-esteem, and creating an awareness of the importance of and need for education.

Unfortunately, many of the part-time jobs available to young people are vocationally irrelevant, rarely introducing the adolescent to skills or training that can be used in a career (Freedman, 1963). Exceptions can be found, however, in the Distributive Education, Diversified Occupations, and Cooperative Education programs offered by many schools throughout the United States. Under such plans, students attend school half a day and work under close supervision in business or industry the other half-day.

Richard was enrolled in the Distributive Education program during his junior and senior years of high school. In the mornings he studied English, history, and the Distributive Education course, which dealt with merchandising, sales techniques, and advertising display. In the afternoons he worked in a local supermarket, where he was paid while learning about various aspects of the grocery business. He worked under the close supervision of the store's manager and of his Distributive Education coordinator, who visited him on the job at least once a week. Upon graduation from high school, Richard continued to work full time at the same store. After acquiring several years of experience, he opened his own neighborhood store, where he has handled a successful business for a number of years.

Another exception to the irrelevance of part-time job experience can be found in the Junior Achievement Clubs, which introduce many students each year to the workings of free enterprise. This organization finds sponsors for youths who are interested in forming temporary corporations, issuing stock in their companies, and making or assembling articles to be sold to members of the community. In this manner, the young people learn about corporations, stocks, and dividends as well as about the various aspects of production. At the end of one fiscal year, the companies are liquidated and the stockholders are paid for their shares, depending on the profit or loss of the corporation.

> Becky was a member of her local Junior Achievement Club. She and a group of friends formed a corporation for the purpose of manufacturing cutting boards, which they sold during the Christmas season. In addition to covering all of their expenses, the sale of the articles grossed sufficient returns to pay a 7% dividend to the stockholders on each $1.00 share that had been sold. As a member of this organization, Becky learned something about the financing of private enterprise and about how to produce and merchandise goods.

The printing and publishing industry, which employs many individuals in copywork, proofreading, and classified-ad sales, for example, offers part-time jobs that provide relevant training in vocational skills. On-the-job training can also be found in many occupations calling for manual dexterity, such as watch repair and electronics. And the student attending a trade school in auto mechanics, for example, will often find a part-time market for his or her skills in various repair shops and garages in the community.

Irving (1975) reports that some adolescents are being paid as mental-health workers to act as big brothers and big sisters for children who show various degrees of emotional difficulty. These adolescents, trained and supervised by professionals, have proved effective in developing relationships with young people ranging in age from 9 to 12. They work with the permission of their parents and put in a minimum of three hours per week.

During the summers, many cities operate youth opportunity programs similar to "Call-a-Teen" (*Oklahoma City Times*, 1969), which is sponsored by the Mayor's Action for Youth Opportunity in

Oklahoma City. Call-a-Teen, which began in 1969, locates household chores for 14- and 15-year-old young people, who, as noted earlier in this chapter, are at the most difficult age for finding gainful employment. According to Schulte (1976), there was still plenty of work available for those adolescents who wanted to work. Cities like Atlanta, Georgia, had "Rent-a-Kid" programs, which matched young people with part-time work. In the summer of 1975, the Regional Youth Employment Program helped over 5000 teenagers find jobs, and the Youth Conservation Corps aided 8500 adolescents in obtaining employment in the National Park System, the National Forest System, and other public water and land areas.

Under the supervision of public schools and colleges, many jobs financed by federal programs are open to lower-class youths. However, studies (see Miller & Corwin, 1973) have found that the federal Manpower training programs of the 1960s (Neighborhood Youth Corps, Work Study Program, and Youth Opportunity Program, all operating from the Office of Economic Opportunity), although useful and effective in many ways, were successful only in some locations, because of an overemphasis on the number of young people placed and the insufficiency of jobs available.

Before we leave this topic of part-time employment, it is important to note that such employment can produce certain negative effects (Freedman, 1963). First, it may increase the adolescent's impatience with the rigid demands of high school. Second, it may alienate some adolescents from their peers, with whom some of them may already have only a tenuous relationship at best. Third, it may increase a preexisting desire to leave school. And, last, the rewards of such employment may be insufficient to convince an alienated youth with few prospects for the future of the desirability of adhering to the path of honest hard work.

Full-time employment for the adolescent dropout

Young people who drop out of school have an even greater need to work than their peers who continue their education. Dropouts particularly need to achieve, because their academic history has frequently been one of failure. Success at work will enable them to gain the self-satisfaction and feelings of accomplishment that they have failed to attain in school. In addition, work will provide them with the means to support themselves, thereby facilitating their emancipation from their parents and achievement of independence.

Many dropouts, however, have not developed the basic skills of communication and computation that are needed for employment.

Some are even incapable of adequately completing a job-application form. Others have not acquired the specialized skills or knowledge necessary for specific occupations and jobs, and this lack contributes to an unstable employment record for dropouts (Super & Bohn, 1970). Their vocational career typically consists of a series of unrelated jobs, usually semiskilled or unskilled, with little security and few prospects for growth or advancement. Super (1964) has also noted that "at a time when the bulk of opportunities for [adolescents] seem to be in technological fields and when technology is advancing at a rapid rate, the tendency is for dropouts to move down, rather than up the occupational ladder after they have acquired a few years of experience" (p. 82).

Although the dropout rate in our schools is decreasing with each passing decade, job opportunities for dropouts are shrinking even more rapidly (Bienstock, 1964). Formerly, an individual who dropped out of school and wanted to work could usually find an unskilled job. Such jobs are becoming increasingly scarce, however, and unemployment in the United States is rapidly becoming a problem of the young, with unemployment rates among teenagers running at five times the rate for those over 25 years of age. Of course, the dropout is hit hardest of all (Hedges, 1976).

Chapter summary

The United States and Canada now have industrial societies that virtually no longer require marginal (uneducated, inexperienced, unskilled) workers, who were once drawn primarily from the adolescent population (Freedman, 1963). The disappearance of the need for such workers has resulted in both opportunities and problems for adolescents. There is more time for education, because young people have little opportunity today to begin their careers during adolescence, but there is a scarcity of employment available to those youths who want to work part time or who need to work to help support their families. This scarcity of job opportunities has also increased adolescent difficulties in making the transition from school to work.

Young people, as well as the adults working with them, need to realize the importance of appropriate educational and vocational selection. Although several theories have been advanced to explain how individuals reach their ultimate occupational choice, it remains the responsibility primarily of the school to supply students with the information necessary to enable them to make wise, informed, and suitable educational and vocational decisions. A recent innovation has been the introduction of career education, which is being included in the curriculum from kindergarten through high school.

A compensatory increase in the prevalence of volunteer work has helped somewhat to bridge the increasing gap between the academic world and the world of work. Voluntary service, ranging from scouting groups to crisis-hotline workers, has encouraged youths to acquire a sense of responsibility and has enabled them to achieve status in the community and, to some extent, satisfy their need to belong.

Nevertheless, numerous young people must work part time to earn some income in order to remain in school, whereas others need to work in order to develop the habits of conscientiousness, responsibility, and so on that are necessary to hold a job and to increase their awareness of the importance of further education. Unfortunately, however, many part-time jobs are irrelevant as vocational preparation and may even have some negative effects on adolescents.

For the high school dropout, remunerative employment assumes even greater importance than for the adolescent remaining in school. Too often, however, because of a limited education and insufficient work skills, the dropout remains the last one to be hired and the first one to be fired.

Thought provokers

1. Can you see any benefits for adolescents in the changing job market? If so, what are they? What are the negative aspects of the adolescent job market?
2. Did you have any career education during your first 12 years of school? If so, during what grades in school was this offered? What topics were covered? Did you find it worthwhile and helpful in your selection of a vocation?
3. Did you find it difficult to select your educational curriculum for high school? What factors made it difficult? Are you still finding curriculum selection a perplexing decision to make? If so, what are you doing to get help with this problem?
4. Which explanations of the way vocational selection is made do you find most plausible?
5. Have you selected your vocation? What factors influenced or are influencing your choice?
6. Have you done any volunteer work? What kind? What benefits did you derive from your volunteer work? Were there any disadvantages?
7. Have you ever worked part time during your education? If so, what were the benefits and the difficulties in such work?
8. Do you know any high school dropouts? What employment problems, if any, have they faced since dropping out of school?

References

About that summer job. *National Education Association Journal*, 1957, *46*, 256–257.

Bienstock, H. Realities of the job market. In D. Schreiber (Ed.), *Guidance and the school dropout*. Washington, D.·C.: American Personnel and Guidance Association, 1964. Pp. 84–108.

Brearley Bulletin. *Review of Reviews*, 1937, *95*, 44–45.

Brodsky, P. Problems of adolescence: An Adlerian view. *Adolescence*, 1968, 3(9), 9–22.

Burlin, F. D. Locus of control and female occupational aspiration. *Journal of Counseling Psychology*, 1976, *23*(2), 126–128.

Calhoun, C. C., & Finch, A. V. *Vocational and career education: Concepts and operations*. Belmont, Calif.: Wadsworth, 1976.

Caplow, T. *The sociology of work*. Minneapolis: University of Minnesota Press, 1954.

Chances of finding work this summer—Jobs and the young. *U. S. News and World Report*, 1976, *80*(20), 72.

Child labor and school attendance. *Elementary School Journal*, 1932, *33*, 245–247.

Child labor comes back. *New Republic*, 1933, *73*, 257.

Duncan, B. Dropouts and the unemployed. *Journal of Political Economy*, April 1965, p. 123.

Duncan, O. D., & Hodge, R. W. Education and occupational mobility: A regression analysis. *American Journal of Sociology*, 1963, *68*, 629–644.

Epstein, G. F., & Bronzaft, A. L. Female freshmen view their role as women. *Journal of Marriage and the Family*, 1972, *34*(4), 671–672.

Feldman, M. J. Opting for career education: Emergency of the community college. In R. C. Pucenski & S. P. Hersch (Eds.), *The courage to change*. Englewood Cliffs, N. J.: Prentice-Hall, 1971.

Fredenburgh, F. A. An apologia for the hippie generation. *Mental Hygiene*, 1968, *52*(3), 341–348.

Freedman, M. K. Part-time work and potential early school leavers. *American Journal of Orthopsychiatry*, 1963, *33*, 509–514.

Galveston Daily News, Galveston, Texas, June 26, 1969, p. C-3.

Getting and spending the teenage allowance. *Life*, 1957, *42*, 147–152.

Ginsberg, E., Ginsberg, S. W., Axelrod, S., & Herma, J. L. *Occupational choice: An approach to a general theory*. New York: Columbia University Press, 1951.

Goyder, J. C., & Curtis, J. E. A three-generational approach to trends in occupational mobility. *American Journal of Sociology*, 1975, *81*(1), 129–138.

Hamel, H. R. Employment of school age youth. October, 1963. *Monthly Labor Review*, 1964, *87*, 767.

Harmon, L. W. The childhood and adolescent career plans of college women. *Journal of Vocational Behavior*, 1971, *1*, 45–56.

Harris, S. R. Sex typing in girls' career choices: A challenge to counselors. *The Vocational Guidance Quarterly*, 1974, *23*(2), 128–133.

Havighurst, R. J., Graham, R. A., & Eberly, D. American youth in the mid-seventies. *The Bulletin of the National Association of Secondary Principals*, 1972, *56*, 1–13.

Hedges, J. N. Youth unemployment in the 1974–75 recession. *Monthly Labor Review*, 1976, *99*(1), 49–56.

Holland, J. L. Some explorations of a theory of vocational choice: One- and two-year longitudinal studies. *Psychological Monographs*, 1962, *76*(2, Whole No. 545).

Hollander, J. W. Development of realistic vocational choice. *Journal of Counseling Psychology*, 1967, *14*, 314–318.

Horrocks, J. E. *The psychology of adolescence* (4th ed.). Boston: Houghton Mifflin, 1976.

Irving, J. E. Friends unlimited: Adolescents as helping resources. *Children Today,* 1975, 4(4), 14–17.

Korman, A. K. Self-esteem as a moderator in vocational choice: Replications and extensions. *Journal of Applied Psychology,* 1969, 53(3), 188–192.

Krauss, I. Sources of educational aspirations among working class youth. *American Sociological Review,* 1964, 29, 867–879.

Lambert, B. G. A revision of the Parent-Child Relations Questionnaire to investigate Roe's occupational choice theory with adolescent girls. *Studies in the Assessment of Parent-Child Relationships.* Monograph Series Number One. Oklahoma City: University of Oklahoma Medical Center, 1967. Pp. 34–47.

Lambert, B. G. *Career choice: An eight year follow-up study.* Paper presented at the meeting of the National Association of School Psychologists, April 1975.

Little, J. K. The occupations of non-college youth. *American Educational Research Journal,* 1967, 4, 147–153.

McEaddy, B. J. Educational attainment of workers. March, 1974. *Monthly Labor Review,* 1975, 98(2), 64–69.

Miller, S. M., & Corwin, R. D. U. S. employment from the 1960s to the 70's. *New Generations,* 1973, 2, 13.

Mincer, J. Youth, education, and work. *Teachers College Record,* 1973, 73, 309–316.

New look: Jobs for children. *Social Service,* March 1958, pp. 32–64. *Oklahoma City Times,* July 3, 1969.

Omvig, P., & Thomas, E. G. Vocational interests of affluent suburban students. *The Vocational Guidance Quarterly,* 1974, 23(1), 10–16.

Osipow, S. H. *Theories of career development.* New York: Appleton-Century-Crofts, 1968.

Post-war planning for young job seekers. *Occupations,* 1945, 24, 111–114.

Powell, M., & Bloom, V. Development of and reasons for vocational choices of adolescents through the high school years. *Journal of Educational Research,* 1962, 56, 126–133.

Roe, A. *The psychology of occupations.* New York: Wiley, 1956.

Rogers, D. Vocational and career education: A critique and some new directions. *Teachers College Record,* 1973, 73, 471–511.

Rosenfeld, C. Employment of school-age youth, October, 1962. *Monthly Labor Review,* 1963, 86, 909.

Schulte, E. L. Help wanted: Teenagers and pre-teenagers too! *Parents Magazine,* 1976, 51, 16.

Shafer, S. M. Adolescent girls and future career mobility. In R. E. Grinder (Ed.), *Studies in adolescence: A book of readings in adolescent development* (3rd ed.), New York: Macmillan, 1975. Pp. 114–125.

Slocum, W. L., & Bowles, R. T. Attractiveness of occupation to high school students. *Personnel and Guidance Journal,* 1968, 46, 754–761.

Staton, E. E., Tiller, C. B., & Weyler, E. H. Teens who care: Potential mental health manpower. *Mental Hygiene,* 1969, 53(2), 200–204.

Stripling, R. *The role of the counselor in educational programs.* Address presented at the fourth annual guidance seminar for counselors and educators at Louisiana State University. Alexandria, January 1967.

Super, D. E. *The psychology of careers.* New York: Harper & Row, 1957.

Super, D. E. Consistency and wisdom of vocational preference as indices of vocational maturity in the ninth grade. *Journal of Educational Psychology,* 1961, 52, 35–43.

Super, D. E. Vocational development of high school dropouts. In D. Schreiber (Ed.), *Guidance and the school dropout*. Washington, D. C.: American Personnel and Guidance Association, 1964. Pp. 66–83.

Super, D. E., & Bohn, M. J. *Occupational psychology*, Monterey, Calif.: Brooks/Cole, 1970.

Thomas, M. Realism and socio-economic status (SES) of occupational plans of low SES Black and White male adolescents. *Journal of Counseling Psychology*, 1976, *23*(1), 46–49.

Tolbert, E. L. *Counseling for career development*. Boston: Houghton Mifflin, 1974.

Tseng, M. S., & Carter, A. P. Achievement motivation and fear of failure as determinants of vocational choice, vocational aspiration, and perception of vocational prestige. *Journal of Counseling Psychology*, 1970, *17*, 150–156.

Tyler, L. E. *The work of the counselor* (3rd ed.). New York: Meredith, 1969. United States summary of departmental statistics, 15th census of the United States, 1930. *Monthly Labor Review*, 1932, *35*, 1334–1336.

U. S. Department of Health, Education, and Welfare. *Career education*. Washington, D. C.: U. S. Government Printing Office, 1971. P. 5.

U. S. Department of Health, Education, and Welfare. *Education in a changing world*. Washington, D. C.: U. S. Government Printing Office, 1961.

U. S. Department of Labor. *Manpower report of the President*. Washington, D. C.: U. S. Government Printing Office, 1966.

U. S. Office of Education. *Guidelines and work statement*, RFP-731-21. Washington, D. C.: U. S. Department of Health, Education, and Welfare, 1973.

Werts, C. E. Parental influence on career choice. *Journal of Counseling Psychology*, 1968, *15*, 48–52.

Why it's hard to cut teen-age unemployment. *U. S. News and World Report*, 1976, *80*(20), 74.

Youth in the labor market. *Current History*, 1941, *53*, 41.

The adult/adolescent communication gap 12

> Without trust, there can be no serious communication nor listening, only doubt and suspicion. Without communication we move in the direction of separation, alienation, rejection, paranoia, and finally self-gratification of abusive behavior.
>
> Irwin, Hayes, and Grunden
> "Education for Living: Awareness
> and Creative Choice," 1975

During the past quarter of a century there have been several books and a flood of articles in popular periodicals and professional journals dealing with the generation gap. Young and old alike have been mulling over such questions as whether this problem is unique to our rapidly changing society or whether it is one that has been with us throughout history—and even whether such a gap actually exists at all.

"Our youth now love luxury. They have bad manners, contempt for authority, disrespect for older people. Children nowadays are tyrants. They contradict their parents, chatter before company,

339

gobble their food, and tyrannize their teachers." So said Socrates in about 500 B.C.

At the root of the generation gap, whether it is new today or whether it goes back 2500 years, is the difficulty experienced by the generations in communicating with one another. To communicate means "to share or impart, to signal or tell somebody about some feelings or knowledge" (Dubbé, 1965, p. 57). But this act of communication involves both a sender and a receiver, with something of common interest flowing between the two, and until the receiver has gotten and acknowledged the message of the sender, the act of communication is not complete. Communication, however, is not always accomplished through speech; it may also involve such things as physical position, signs, facial expressions, drawings, and writings.

Communication is especially important within the family. "It is vital to basic human relationships in the one social living unit which does most to shape individual character. If wholesome, practical, affectionate, and secure relationships are worthy to be generated and sustained, then easy flow of thoughts and feelings is imperative" (Dubbé, 1965, p. 57). Unfortunately, family members sometimes have rigid, preconceived ideas about each other, which cause restrictions in the flow of communication. Such ideas are often hard to change and may cause such distortion in the sending or receiving of messages that the transmission of accurate, precise information becomes completely blocked. Thus, communication breaks down and, in doing so, may impede sound decision making on the part of the young (Boyd, Clark, Kempler, Johannet, Leonard, & McPherson, 1974). For example, parents may set a curfew for their children because they know that, if they do not do so, they will stay out until dawn. Although the decision to establish a curfew is based on the parents' worry that some harm may come to their children if they aren't home at a "reasonable" hour, the children may well interpret the decision as a manifestation of a lack of trust in their judgment. A better approach might be for the parents to discuss their concern with their children and mutually agree on an appropriate curfew.

Some investigators believe that the generation gap revolves around the differences in attitudes and values between the generations. The existence of a great values gap between adolescents and their parents is supported by Mead (1970), Bengtson (1970), Friedenberg (1969), and others, but researchers such as Douvan and Adelson (1966) suggest that such a gap is an illusion, most likely created by the mass media. These latter researchers believe that a central core of values is shared by parents and their children and that only on minor, peripheral issues do they differ. Yankelovich (1970) found significant generational differences on only three issues: the importance of organized religion and two issues dealing with sexual behavior.

Extent of the communication gap

Some problems in communication are probably inevitable between most young people and their parents. According to a study by Dubbé (1965), 95% of all youths occasionally experience some degree of difficulty when trying to communicate with their parents on certain subjects. Dubbé's findings were based on extensive research on intergenerational communication, which probably has received less attention than any other area affecting adolescent behavior.

Dubbé (1965) devised a questionnaire that included 22 reasons for difficulty in communicating with parents on 36 different topics. When subjects indicated that they were experiencing difficulty in any of these areas, they were asked to assign a score to the difficulty to indicate the intensity of the problem. Dubbé first undertook a pilot study in 1956 in western Oregon of 50 men and 50 women selected at random from 2184 first-year college students. Later, he made a second study of 100 boys and 100 girls who were first-year high school students, also selected at random from eight high schools in western Oregon with a total of 1930 ninth-grade students. In the first study (Dubbé, 1956), all but 1 of the 100 subjects admitted to some degree of difficulty when talking to their parents about some of the 36 topics; the problems encountered varied according to the sex of both the student and the parent. Boys said that difficulty in communication arose because of fear and conservatism on the part of their parents, whereas girls stated that their parents' lack of time to talk with them was an important factor in the communication breakdown. For the subjects of both the 1956 and the 1965 studies, the topics most difficult to discuss with either parent were sex, petting, and courtship. There were a few issues, such as care of property and use of the family car, that also proved more troublesome for boys than for girls in their relationships with their parents, especially their mothers.

Another study, by Johnson (1961), disclosed that, when parents were asked to cite the most difficult situation they had encountered with their adolescent children, the communication gap led all of the rest of the problems. He also noted that this gap was felt not only by the parents but also by the children. In a study of nearly 400 young people in grades 7 through 11, 40% said that it was "difficult at times" to communicate with their parents, and 11% stated that it was "always difficult."

However, this communication gap is neither inevitable nor

characteristic of all young people in our society. A survey of 1219 high school students (Rothschild, 1969)* disclosed that, although 6.5% indicated that their communication with their parents was very unsatisfactory and another 11.5% stated that their communication with parents was poor, 44% said that they had established fair or average communication with their parents, 24% said that their communication was good, and 14% described it as excellent. Typical of the statements made by students in this study were the following.

> I think parents should realize that this is a new generation and that they can't expect us to conform to all the old standards. Things that were not acceptable years ago are now considered everyday things.

> I think the generation gap is as it should be—maybe a little to the extreme, though. Many things adults say are right and many things the kids say are right, but neither would ever admit to being wrong. I think that is the whole problem.

> If you could get adults to talk to us like we're old enough to know something and not treat us like little kids . . . . They act like they're afraid to let down their defenses.

> I think the trouble occurs when teenagers don't think of their mother and father as friends as well as parents—friends who want to help them and know more about them.

> To me, there isn't much of a communication gap between parents and their children. I get along fine with my folks (most of the time).

> I just think that the gap is part of growing up.

Causes of communication problems

Johnson (1961) hypothesized that, although there has always been some communication gap, this problem has probably become a more frequent complaint since the 1920s. It is perhaps inevitable that, with social changes occurring so swiftly, the generations grow apart more rapidly. For example, McLuhan (1964) believes that today's adolescents are different from those of the past because the medium of television is such a large part of their environment. Television instantaneously envelopes the individual with visual and auditory stimuli, whereas the mass medium of previous generations, that of print, presents one stimulus at a time in an orderly sequence. McLuhan thinks that, as a consequence, today's young people have developed

*We are indebted to the late W. E. Pate, former Principal of Bolton High School, Alexandria, Louisiana, for his cooperation in making this study possible.

different ways of perceiving stimuli than those of previous generations. Another investigator, B. Pacella (1967), observes "that television has tended to induce an alienation of family members from each other, since intrafamily communication has been replaced by the one-way communication with television" (p. 1977).

Communication problems can also be caused by parents who believe that their values and beliefs are the only right ones. Research has indicated that parents who experience severe problems in their relationships with their adolescent children are usually individuals who adhere to strong and very inflexible concepts of what is right and wrong—attitudes that they strive to impose on their children. At the same time, such parents are unacceptant of any behaviors or ideas that deviate from their own (Gordon, 1970). Such deviations seem to focus particularly on the subjects of sex (Bell, 1966), allegiance to one's country, and obedience to authority. Other parents are more democratic, allowing their children to express their own points of view much more freely. However, such democracies may sometimes create problems, because young people's attitudes can seem quite alien and unacceptable even to the liberal thinkers among parents.

There are also many more young people today than there were even 25 years ago; this large population growth accounts, in part, for an increasingly impersonal society and thus for some of the adult/adolescent communication problems. In addition, adolescence, which was formerly regarded as a 5-year behavioral phenomenon, can now extend up to 15 years, because of society's increasing demands for more education and the resultant lengthening of adolescent economic dependence. This extended period of dependence often not only delays resolution of the identity crisis but also creates resentment, which can contribute to communication problems.

Whatever its specific causes, the generation gap is basically typical of human nature. If there were no differences between a 15-year-old and a 35-year-old, it would be a sad commentary on the lack of individual growth and healthy ferment and idealism in our society. However, this natural conflict between generations may be more intense today than in the past as a result of the increased pace of change; according to Neisser (1967), the amount of social, scientific, and technological innovation that once occurred over an interval of two or three decades now takes place in one.

Mead (1970) suggests that, in a *postfigurative culture* (a term that she uses to describe a stable, simple society), youths can realistically seek guidance and advice from their parents and other adults, because the older generations have the most experience in the social and occupational roles that the young people will ultimately assume.

In the recent past, Western civilization changed at a moderate rate, which made it a *cofigurative culture*, according to Mead. Under such change, young people look more often to their peers and less often to adults for advice and guidance. But in our society today, which she describes as a *prefigurative culture*, it is the younger generations and not the older ones that reflect what is to come. In such a culture, therefore, adolescents must rely on themselves, rather than on the older generations, to map the way through life.

It is only natural, then, that, as the children in the family emerge into adolescence, there will be some difficulty in communication between the two generations. As they reach adolescence, young people tend to withhold information about their personal activities, to be resentful of parents and other adults who try to pry this information loose from them, and to become much more critical of adults in general. As a result of this often abrupt withdrawal, parents may respond by prying more or by withdrawing themselves—both of which are likely to precipitate a widening of the gap between adults and youths (Bienvenu, 1967).

Sometimes, adults' attempts to reach the unresponsive adolescent and the endeavors of young people to reach the unresponsive or indifferent parent and establish some degree of emotional rapport between the two generations can be terribly frustrating undertakings for both young and old (M. Pacella, 1963). Parents of young people often misinterpret their offspring's need for privacy as standoffishness and may respond inappropriately, perhaps out of feelings of rejection. They may even experience a sense of guilt, believing that they have failed their children in some way. Youths with unresponsive parents may believe that they are unconcerned about their children's problems and well-being, and these young people may then turn to acting-out behavior in their efforts to communicate. *Acting out* is resorting to punitive behavior in problem solving, for example, by engaging in illegal drag racing, drug abuse, or vandalism.

Regrettably, few parents, teachers, and other adults perceive the adolescent's frequent detachment from parents as a right and even a necessity. This retreat from the adult world may be especially necessary for those who are trying to cope with the rapid physiological and emotional changes occurring during early adolescence.

In addition, parents who were previously placed on a pedestal by their preadolescent children may suddenly discover that they no longer serve as the ideal when their children reach adolescence. Such a discovery can be quite traumatic for the parents, who must now learn to accept the rejection of some of the values that they have worked to instill in their children. When adolescent messages are correctly decoded, they may reflect the fact that youths believe that they have the right to adhere to their own values as long as these values do not affect their parents in any tangible way. Too often adults take over certain adolescent problems and come to feel that they "own" the problems. For example, parents may feel that their son's shoulder-length hair is an adverse reflection on them, rather than an expression of the son's preference in hair styles. Such behavior by parents tends to contribute to conflict between the generations. Interestingly, adults, too, will resist the efforts of those who try to change their behavior, when they feel that such behavior is not interfering with the rights of others (Gordon, 1970).

Acting-out behavior as a form of communication

According to Levitt and Rubenstein (1959), a considerable amount of acting-out behavior among adolescents is an attempt at communication. It is important to realize, in interpreting such behavior, that adolescents often do not understand their behavior any more than their parents do, although their words and actions may often communicate a great deal to a trained, perceptive observer. Adults should take into account the fact that certain factors in the personality structure of the young person are in the process of undergoing change, which may be reflected through acting out.

Frequently, adolescent slang can convey to the perceptive adult meanings that adolescents themselves may be unaware of. Such phrases as "play it cool" stress the young person's need to remain calm at a time in life that is likely to be filled with turbulence. It is almost as if the young person were saying to himself or herself "I'm all shook up inside, but I'll play it cool and no one will know" (Levitt & Rubenstein, 1959, p. 624). Thus, it is the latent content, rather than the manifest content, through which the adolescent sometimes attempts to communicate. An adult, in order to understand such communication, "must learn to disregard the apparent logical word arrangement and to translate the language expression from the secondary elaboration to its real meaning" (Levitt & Rubenstein, 1959, p. 624).

The adolescent, through acting out as well as through verbalization, may communicate many messages to the alert observer. As we mentioned in the chapters on delinquency and suicide, acting-out behavior often represents a plea for help or for discipline. At other times, it demonstrates a need for independence and autonomy, perhaps reflecting a protest against a symbiotic relationship with the parents (Ekstein & Friedman, 1956). And in still other instances, young people may simply be expressing their genuine political beliefs or moral values.

Many social scientists believe that much of the misunderstanding and disharmony between parents and adolescents has its inception in the early parent/child relationship (M. Pacella, 1963). Parents who regard their children as a constant source of annoyance and trouble during the early periods of childhood development may sometimes verbalize their wish that the child "stop acting like a child." Often such young people are pushed into acting-out behavior because all outlets for their normal impulses and their need for communication have been denied. Thus, the frustrations and resentments that pile up during childhood persist into the adolescent period, meantime becoming far more corrosive and unmanageable. At the same time, parental frustrations also accumulate over the years, thereby creating in some families mutual rejection and recrimination between the two generations.

Communication problems contributing to psychopathology

The question arises of whether an adolescent's inability to communicate may be indicative of psychopathology. A study (Marcus et al., 1966) of all adolescents admitted to the Psychosomatic and Psychiatric Institute at Michael Reese Hospital in Chicago between 1958 and 1961 revealed that many of the young people there complained about their parents' failure to understand them and about their own inability to understand their parents. Marcus et al. studied 20 families in which both parents were present in the home and in which there were two adolescent children of the same sex in the age range of 13 to 19. In 10 of the families, one of the adolescents was a patient at the Institute. All 40 of the adolescents were given an 80-item questionnaire that asked them to describe themselves and to describe what their mothers expected of them. These questionnaires, intensive interviews with the patients, their siblings, and their mothers, and historical data from patient records were used to evaluate the effectiveness of the patients' communication. The results disclosed that family members were in better communication with each other in those families without a disturbed adolescent than in those with such an adolescent. Normal siblings of disturbed adolescents had some degree of impaired communication but the impairment was not so extensive as that in the disturbed adolescents. The patients understood that they did not meet the expectations of their mothers, thereby indicating that they had some degree of perception, but the normal adolescents recognized their mothers' expectations more clearly. The mothers, in turn, were better able to understand their normal children than their disturbed children.

Bridging the communication gap

How can adults and adolescents bridge the communication gap between them? The older generations may be held more responsible than the younger for making this effort, because adults supposedly possess greater wisdom and experience and should have moved beyond the egocentrism typical of adolescence. Adults and adolescents must be willing to give their undivided attention to each other before effective communication can begin. Especially important is the parents' willingness to listen to their children at the moment that they want to talk, as illustrated in the following example.

> One evening, Jerry, a high school senior, went into the family den to discuss with his father the question of whether he should give his girlfriend his class ring. His father, engrossed in reading the newspaper, looked up from his reading and asked impatiently "Well, what do you want?" Jerry muttered "Nothing, Dad" and stumbled out of the room, realizing that, at that moment, his father was more interested in the news than in his son's problem.

It is quite likely that a precious moment of communication was lost forever. The father, in failing to put aside his own interests for a very few minutes, inadvertently widened the gap between himself and his son. Jerry, in turn, probably felt a certain sense of bewilderment and anger and wondered whether there was anyone to whom he could turn besides his peers.

In other cases, parents and other adults are often guilty of practicing one-way communication; that is, they send numerous messages to young people without making any attempt to ascertain whether their messages have been accepted, understood, or even received. Many youths are confronted with such a flood of incoming messages that they lack the opportunity to reply to them. Such one-way communication not only can increase the possibility of misunderstandings but also can lead adolescents to finally abandon all attempts to communicate with adults (Boyd et al., 1974). They gradually "tune out" everything that adults say to them.

Adults need to ask themselves what they as individuals can do to keep the communication line open. Too often, they play the role of helper when what the adolescent needs is simply a good listener.

Such a listener does not moralize, judge, or advise, because in many instances young people possess the solutions to their problems within themselves. Instead, the good listener acts as a sounding board for the adolescent, accurately repeating back the thoughts and feelings that the young person has expressed so that the adolescent can look at his or her difficulties more objectively and ultimately arrive at a sound solution (Gordon, 1970).

It is important for parents to begin as early as possible to talk openly with their children, answering their questions fully and honestly and admitting that they do not know all the answers. Such communication involves listening with genuine interest to what even small children have to say. Failure to establish adequate communication patterns during childhood has been found by one investigator (Matteson, 1974) to contribute to the development of a low self-concept, resulting in alienation of the child and increasing inability to communicate as the young person reaches adolescence.

Communication can also be severely limited by the tendency of many adults to prejudge adolescents, particularly on the basis of appearance. Many adults are not willing to listen to young people because they believe "they're too young to know anything" or "they're all a bunch of radicals." Adults would do well, however, to listen to adolescents, who often have fresh, new ideas. Young people are often more aware of and concerned about the social issues that are important to them than adults are. And because their concern is frequently reflected in their active efforts to bring about change, rather than in mere talk, their credibility is often higher than that of many adults (Robinson, 1973). Adolescents have demonstrated this thoughtful concern in their efforts to help lower the voting age, in their demands for more active participation in the formation of educational curricula, in their insistence on their right to select their own values, and in their work with such programs as volunteer tutoring of disadvantaged children and volunteer services to the emotionally disturbed and the mentally retarded.

Parents and other adults who are constantly prying into their children's activities are quite likely to stir up resentment and create problems in communication. Young people need confidence and trust from adults. Unfortunately, many adults have overgeneralized about today's adolescents and have come to regard them as a generation of troublemakers who will inevitably become delinquents or drug abusers unless adults get tough with them (Irwin, Hayes, & Grunden, 1975). When adolescents are trusted by their parents, however, they are likely to develop self-confidence and self-trust, thereby moving toward independence and maturity.

Parents, in turn, must acquire the trust and confidence of their children. Often, parents make the mistake of failing to keep the secrets of their children or of telling tales about them that they regard as cute or funny. These actions can be regarded by young people as a betrayal of trust, because their privacy, which is particularly important during adolescence, has not been respected.

Constantly comparing a young person with his or her siblings or peers can also lead to communication problems. Teachers who assume that a student has the same interests and aptitudes as an older sibling and those parents who attempt to make one child perform or behave the way another child does can eventually convince adolescents that adults are not interested in them as individuals. Such a conviction could lead them to give up all attempts to communicate with adults. Perceptive, understanding adults do not attempt to mold young people into what they think they should be. Instead, they assume the role of observant bystanders who are ready to come forward when help is needed. They demonstrate an interest in adolescents and their problems, but they are sparing with advice and, more important, are able to withdraw a certain distance when youths indicate that they want to be on their own.

Family councils or meetings can often facilitate communication. When given such opportunities to verbalize their feelings, ideas, and opinions, adolescents may discover that, through effective communication, they are able to influence the feelings and beliefs of others in the family. Such a discovery can lead not only to increased communication but also to the development in the adolescent of feelings of competence and self worth. At the same time, such family discussions expose young people to their parents' knowledge and experience and, consequently, can give them a better perspective on adulthood and its responsibilities and potentials.

If parents, educators, and other adults were willing to change some of their own inflexible values and attitudes about young people's assertion of independence and individuality, communication between the generations might improve. As long as adults, however, continue to insist that their standards and values are the only right ones, the adult/adolescent communication gap will persist (Cross, 1967).

Recent trends in community resources for adolescent communication

It is apparent that some parents cannot bridge the communication gap, and teachers and guidance counselors, as figures of authority, are ruled out by many young people as sources of help. In the

Bolton High School study (Rothschild, 1969) of 1219 high school students, only four stated that they most often confided in their guidance counselors, and none said that they commonly discussed their personal problems with their teachers. Another study (West & Zingle, 1969) of 50 ninth-grade pupils disclosed that these young people confide in others in the following order of preference: friends of the same sex, parents, friends of the other sex, school counselors, and teachers. It appears then that adolescents often seek help and guidance from their friends, who may be as painfully ignorant as they or even from newspaper columnists, whose answers may be inadequate for the individual's particular problem.

Many young people need someone totally objective to talk to, someone unswayed by love or hate and unconcerned about punishment or reward. In the Rothschild (1969) study, over 50% of the students believed that there was a need for a center where adolescents could get help over the phone with their problems. More than one-third of these young people said that they would be likely to use such a service, and 45% stated that they knew of friends or acquaintances who they believed would avail themselves of such a service.

To meet this need for objective counseling, a number of hot-lines and telephone crisis centers were started in the early 1960s. By 1966, 13 such services had been established, and by 1971 there were 253 in operation throughout the United States. Although these centers began on the East and West Coasts, they have since spread to the inner regions of the United States. In fact, by 1973 these centers could be found in all 50 states, although mainly in urban areas (McCord & Packwood, 1973).

The range of services offered by these centers varies from place to place, but typically they supply information and counseling by telephone on such matters as family difficulties, drugs, alcohol, sex, pregnancy, and suicidal behavior. In addition, working in these centers often serves as a source of training for future professionals in such fields as psychology and social work (Mohr, 1971).

The pioneer in telephone counseling services at the university level was probably the University of Texas, which in July 1967 initiated a continuous telephone counseling and referral service designed to bring immediate aid to university students for a wide range of problems. The service is staffed 24 hours a day, 7 days a week, by trained counselors. Students can phone for personal counseling, academic counseling, consultation concerning the problems of another person, referral to other agencies or other professionals, and information about university life and events. During its first year of operation, 12,827 calls were received, of which 1361 were requests for counseling (882 calls from women and 479 calls from men). Most of the counseling calls were made late in the evening, from 9 P.M. to midnight (University of Texas, 1968). For the year 1975 a total of 17,343 calls were received. These fell into eight major categories, as can be seen from Table 12-1. In addition, the University of Texas center now provides self-help counseling tapes dealing with a variety of mental and physical problems. These tapes, which are five to ten minutes long, offer information and suggestions about how to cope

Table 12-1.   Categories of telephone calls received by the University of Texas Telephone Counseling and Referral Service in 1975

Odd Calls (Center business, inquiries about the Counseling and Psychological Services Center, crank calls, and so on)   6831

Internal Problems (Anger, fights, depression, anxiety, loneliness, social adjustment, suicidal thoughts and attempts, and so on)   1613

Family and Social Problems (Dating, marital, parent/child as reported by parent, parent/child as reported by child, and so on)   747

Sex Problems (Sex information, venereal disease, birth-control information, pregnancy, homosexuality, and so on)   534

Medical Problems (General health, illness, injury, poisons, medicines, medical facilities, alcoholism, effects of drugs, drug addiction, dependence, and so on)   303

Hassles (Vocational, housing, legal, financial, university jobs, scholarships, loans, employment, and so on)   912

Social Information (Athletic events information, entertainment, voting, information about university and committee services and meetings, and so on)   1283

Academic (Admission requirements, advising and course information, conflicts with course/instructor, homework, lecture notes, tutors, registration, withdrawal, tuition and fees, and so on)   5120

Total Number of Calls   17,343

From the *University of Texas Twenty-Four Hour Telephone Counseling and Referral Service Annual Report for 1975.* Reprinted with the permission of Dr. Ira Iscoe, Director, Counseling-Psychological Services Center, University of Texas.

with a wide range of day-to-day difficulties. By dialing a phone number, which differs from that of the Telephone Counseling and Referral Service, students can ask to listen to the tape or tapes of their choice. Suggestions for new tapes are also sought (University of Texas, 1976).

In 1967, 67 colleges and universities with enrollments of over 5000 were asked whether similar telephone crisis services were available on their campuses. None of the 47 institutions that replied had a comparable 24-hour service (University of Texas, 1968). Today such services are available on many campuses. Louisiana State University offers a 24-hour crisis-counseling and information, referral service, which is available not only to students but also to the residents of Baton Rouge. This service, which is called The Phone, was begun in April of 1970 and is staffed by student and community volunteers. Tulane University, in New Orleans, also introduced a similar service at about the same time (Mohr, 1971).

What leads young people, in particular, to use such services? There are numerous explanations. Because many telephone crisis services operate 24 hours a day, they are available to the individual at the very moment that help is needed, whereas conventional services, operating five days a week from 8 A.M. to 5 P.M., often force the troubled individual to wait hours or even days for an appointment with a counselor. Another factor is the services' protection of the anonymity of their callers—a situation that helps to reduce the natural tendency of adolescents to feel inhibited about discussing their personal problems. The telephone also provides dissatisfied callers with an easy, nonthreatening means of terminating counseling; they simply hang up (McCord & Packwood, 1973).

Many of these centers are staffed by student and community volunteers, who are closely screened and then receive 15 to 20 hours or more of training to help them develop their ability to relate to others (Bauer, 1975; Mohr, 1971). Although such telephone services are often criticized because of their utilization of young volunteers with limited training, many centers do have backup professionals —psychiatrists, psychologists, psychiatric social workers, medical doctors, and attorneys—who can be called on for help. In addition, the experience of working on a telephone crisis line sometimes leads these semiprofessional, unpaid workers to choose a related vocation, such as social work or psychology.

It is also evident that young people are more at ease when talking to their peers, with whom they can more closely identify than when talking with adults. They often believe that their contemporaries are more aware of adolescent problems and less likely to pass judgment than their elders. These young listeners are sometimes able to pick up cues in their peers' speech or voice patterns that adult listeners miss (Bauer, 1975). Regardless of the age of the volunteer, however, the primary function of such centers is not to offer "cheap advice" but to encourage young people to grapple with their problems and to come up with their own solutions (Wright, 1969).

Teachers and others working with adolescents should be aware of such community facilities and learn how referrals can be made to them. Regrettably, many educators are ignorant of the availability of these services, and, consequently, many youths in need of counseling and guidance continue to struggle with their problems alone.

Chapter summary

Although the communication gap has probably existed since the beginning of civilization, it is quite possible that this gap is wider today than ever before. Explanations of this widening breach between the generations can be found in our rapidly changing society with its tremendous technological advances, its shifting customs and values, and its extended period of adolescent economic dependence.

There are a number of ways in which the communication gap can be bridged, but all of them demand that adults and adolescents learn to listen to each other and that they refrain from imposing their own values and judgments on each other.

When personal efforts fail, adults should encourage young people to consult community-mental-health facilities, hotlines, or telephone crisis centers. Only through effective communication can the incidence of such problems as delinquency, drug abuse, and emotional disorders be reduced.

Thought provokers

1. Do you think that most adolescents experience the communication gap?
2. Did a communication gap exist between you and your parents when you were in early or middle adolescence? Does it now?
3. What particular problems in communication did you have with your parents when you were in high school?
4. Is there a telephone crisis center in your community? Have you ever used it or known anyone who used it? What kind of problem was involved? Was the center helpful?
5. In early adolescence, did you confide primarily in your parents, your friends, school counselors, or teachers? Why?

6. As a high school teacher or as a parent of adolescent children, what would you try to do to minimize the communication gap?

References

Bauer, J. The hot line and its training problems for adolescent listeners. *Adolescence,* 1975, *10*(37), 63–74.

Bell, R. R. Parent-child conflict in sexual values. *Journal of Social Issues,* 1966, *22,* 34–44.

Bengtson, V. L. The generation gap: A review and typology of social-psychological perspectives. *Youth and Society,* 1970, *2,* 7–31.

Bienvenu, M., Sr. Talking it over at home: Problems in family communication. *Public Affairs Pamphlet,* No. 410. New York: Public Affairs Committee, 1967.

Boyd, E., Clark, J., Kempler, H., Johannet, P., Leonard, B., & McPherson, P. Teaching interpersonal communication to troubled families. *Family Process,* 1974, *13*(3), 317–336.

Cross, H. J. Conceptual systems theory-application to some problems of adolescence. *Adolescence,* 1967, *2*(6), 153–165.

Douvan, E., & Adelson, J. *The adolescent experience.* New York: Wiley, 1966.

Dubbé, M. C. *Subjects which one hundred selected college students found difficult to discuss with their parents and reasons for their difficulties.* Unpublished doctoral dissertation, Oregon State College, 1956.

Dubbé, M. C. What parents are not told may hurt: A study of communication between teenagers and parents. *Family Life Coordinator,* 1965, *14*(2), 51–118.

Ekstein, R., & Friedman, S. *A function of acting out, play activity, and play acting in the therapeutic process.* Paper presented at the spring meeting of the American Psychoanalytic Association, Chicago, 1956.

Friedenberg, E. The generation gap. *Annals of the American Academy of Political and Social Science,* 1969, *382,* 32–42.

Gordon, T. *Parental effectiveness training.* New York: Wyden, 1970.

Irwin, S., Hayes, R. M., & Grunden, L. R. Education for living: Awareness and creative choice (alternatives to drugs), *Journal of Psychedelic Drugs,* 1975, *7*(1), 49–58.

Johnson, E. W. Ten pointers on talking to teen-agers. *Parents Magazine,* July 1961. Pp. 38–39*ff.*

Levitt, M., & Rubenstein, B. O. Acting out in adolescence: A study in communication. *American Journal of Orthopsychiatry,* 1959, *29,* 622–632.

Marcus, D., et al. A clinical approach to the understanding of normal and pathological adolescence: A study of communication patterns in the families of disturbed and nondisturbed adolescents. *Archives of General Psychiatry,* 1966, *15,* 569–576.

Matteson, R. Adolescent self-esteem, family communication, and marital satisfaction. *The Journal of Psychology,* 1974, *86,* 35–47.

McCord, J. B., & Packwood, W. T. Crisis centers and hotlines: A survey. *Personnel and Guidance Journal,* 1973, *51*(10), 723–728.

McLuhan, M. *Understanding media: The extension of man.* New York: McGraw-Hill, 1964.

Mead, M. *Culture and commitment: A study of the generation gap.* New York: Basic Books, 1970.

Mohr, M. G. *The Phone.* Baton Rouge: Louisiana State University, February 1971.

Neisser, E. G. *Mothers and daughters: A lifelong relationship.* New York: Harper & Row, 1967.

Pacella, B. L. The adolescent crisis today: Morals, ethics, and religion. *New York State Journal of Medicine,* 1967, *67,* 1975–1978.

Pacella, M. J. Understanding your teen-ager. *Mental Hygiene,* 1963, *47,* 273–278.

Robinson, R. Healthy criticism: Crossing the age barrier and communicating with your children. *Today's Health,* 1973, *51*(8), 12–13*ff.*

Rothschild, B. F. Unpublished study. Louisiana State University at Alexandria, 1969.

Sackett, W. W., Jr. Family problems involving the adolescent. *Southern Medical Journal,* 1965, *58*(12), 1558–1561.

University of Texas at Austin. *Annual report of the twenty-four hour telephone counseling and referral service.* Author, 1968.

University of Texas at Austin. Unpublished statistics for 1975 for the twenty-four hour telephone counseling and referral service. Personal communication, 1976.

West, L. W., & Zingle, H. W. A self-disclosure inventory for adolescents. *Psychological Reports,* 1969, *24,* 439–445.

Wright, F. Medicine today. *Ladies Home Journal,* July 1969. P. 42.

Yankelovich, D. *The generation gap: A misleading half truth.* Paper presented at the meeting of the Eastern Sociological Society, 1970.

Glossary

acting out: transferring to a new experience a learned pattern of behavior that is symbolically representative of thoughts or feelings

activism: practice or doctrine that emphasizes vigorous action to attain one's ends

adolescence: behavioral phenomenon that occurs between childhood and maturity and involves numerous physical, psychological, and emotional changes

affect: emotion or feeling

alienation: in this book, a young person's feeling that he or she cannot find a meaningful role in today's society, which leads the individual to adopt nonconforming behaviors

altruism: concern for the welfare of others, as opposed to egoism; idealism

ambivalence: coexistence of opposite feelings toward an individual or situation (such as love and hate, acceptance and denial)

amphetamine: drug used to stimulate the central nervous system, increase blood pressure, reduce appetite, and reduce nasal congestion; used by young people as an "upper"

androgen: male hormone that regulates sexual development and influences development of male secondary sex characteristics

apathy: lack of feeling or emotion; indifference

aptitude: innate potential to learn or to acquire skill

attitude: an enduring, learned, predisposition to behave in a consistent way toward a given class of objects

authoritarian: demanding unquestioning obedience and subordination from others

autoeroticism: self-arousal or gratification of erotic feelings

autonomy: independence; self-regulation

avoidance: acting so as to protect oneself from pain or conflict by not confronting the source of that discomfort

barbiturate: any of various derivatives of barbituric acid used especially as sedatives and hypnotics; used by young people as a "downer"

behavior modification: the application of operant-learning and other experimental laboratory procedures to human behavior in order to effect change

biochemical: having to do with the chemistry of living organisms and vital processes

biogenetic: referring to the development of life from preexisting life

357

bisexuality: having both male and female secondary sex characteristics; also, having sexual feeling for both sexes

borderline defective: an individual whose IQ (70–79) is below normal but who is usually considered legally competent

chemotherapy: treatment of a disease by administering chemicals that affect the causative organisms unfavorably but do not injure the patient

clique: a small, exclusive group of from two to nine persons with common interests and activities

clitoris: a small organ of erectile tissue that is part of the external female genitals; its stimulation is an important source of sexual pleasure

cofigurative culture: a culture characterized by a moderate rate of social change

cognition: process by which one learns about an object; includes perception, recognition, and reasoning

cognitive development: the process of growth in reasoning, thinking, memory, and problem solving that takes place from birth through old age

cognitive dissonance: a state of tension generated when a person holds two cognitions (beliefs) that are inconsistent with each other

cognitive structure: an individual's way of perceiving the world, both physical and social, including his or her concepts, beliefs, and expectations

coitus: the act of conveying semen to the female reproductive tract, involving insertion of the penis into the vaginal orifice, followed by ejaculation

congenital: referring to a condition, not determined by heredity, that exists at or before birth

cross-sectional study: a study of the relationship between factors in two or more groups investigated at the same time

defense mechanism: behavior used as a defense against anxiety

denial: a primitive, unconscious, or preconscious defense mechanism in which the mind refuses to admit to some threatening external reality

dependence: reliance on others in making decisions or carrying out actions

depersonalization: a state in which a person loses the feeling of his or her own reality

depression: psychological state characterized by emotional dejection, absence of cheerfulness or hope, and decreased functional activity

developmental age: age as determined by the degree of development of secondary sex characteristics and by skeletal age; may be younger or older than the chronological age

developmental tasks: accomplishments or skills that should be mastered at a particular age stage; these are critical to further achievement and happiness

displacement: a defense mechanism by which one transfers a thought, feeling, or emotion from one person or stimulation to another, less threatening one

double bind: an approach/avoidance or double approach/avoidance situation (the person is attracted and repelled at the same time)

dull normal: describing an individual whose IQ (80–89) is slightly below normal but who is not considered mentally retarded

dysfunction: impaired or abnormal functioning

dyslexia: a reading disability due to distortion in the development of perceptual motor skills that is independent of any speech defect

dysrhythmic: uncoordinated or poorly coordinated

educo-therapy: remediation of academic deficits and modification of maladaptive behavior

ego: generally, concept of self; the part of the personality that is conscious and most in touch with reality; in psychoanalytic terms, the problem-solving portion of the personality

egocentric: concerned primarily with one's self to the exclusion of concern for others

ejaculation: the sudden discharge from the penis of seminal fluid, with or without sperm

empathy: ability to experience the emotions and thoughts of another

erotic: pertaining to the sensations of sex or the emotions aroused by sex

estrogen: female hormone that regulates sexual development and influences the development of female secondary sex characteristics

etiology: having to do with causes, origins, or reasons; the part of medicine that deals with the causation of disease

euphoria: an emotional attitude that all is well and nothing can possibly go wrong; in psychiatry, an exaggerated sense of well-being involving sympathetic delusions

expressive role: a role characterized by love and affective responses

extrinsic motivation: desire to do something as a means to an end; for example, a desire to get a good education in order to get a good job, or learning in order to obtain good grades

fixation: situation in which an individual remains at one stage of development and is unable to progress to the next stage

genetic: pertaining to the genes; inherited

genital: pertaining to the reproductive organs

gonadotropin: hormone that stimulates growth and development in the gonads, or sex glands

hallucinogen: a drug that produces hallucination and false perception

heterosexuality: sexual attraction to persons of the other sex

hormone: a chemical substance produced by the endocrine glands that triggers many kinds of bodily activities and behavior

hyperactive behavior: abnormally increased activity; overstimulation

hypothalamus: a portion of the forebrain that helps control visceral functions such as sleep, hunger, thirst, sex drive, and emotion

ideal self: an individual's concept of what he or she would like to be in terms of living by his or her values; a structure of values an individual is striving to attain

identification: accepting as one's own the goals and values of another individual

identity crisis: a period during which an individual seeks to define who he or she is in relationship to society and the environment

ideology: an accepted system of ideas, beliefs, and attitudes

image: a conscious representation of sensory experience in the absence of the relevant sensory stimulation

impunitive: characterizing a reaction to frustration in which one does not blame either self or others but is more concerned with condemning what has occurred; an impunitive person may display embarrassment and shame but not anger

inculcate: to teach or impress by forceful urging or frequent repetition

individuation: in a social group, the process whereby a person emerges as a distinct unit in the group, with a distinct, even unique, role or status

induction: one type of love-oriented discipline wherein parents point out to their child the possible consequences of the child's behavior and reasons for modifying that behavior

instrumental role: a role in the family held by an individual who imparts values and goals relating to the world outside the family.

intellectualization: analysis of a problem strictly in intellectual terms to the exclusion of any emotional or practical considerations

internalization: adopting as one's own the ideas, practices, standards, or values of another person

interpersonal: referring to a relationship between two or more persons

intrapersonal: referring to an individual's relationship with his or her environment

intrinsic motivation: desire to do something for its own sake, rather than as the means to an end (for example, to learn for the sake of knowledge, rather than in order to get a better job)

introjection: internalization of the external world; in psychoanalytic terms, a defense mechanism for warding off threat by symbolic incorporation of an external object as part of one's self

kinesthesis: sense of movement, of knowing where body and limb are and what their movements are

kinesthetic method: process of treating reading disability by having students trace outlines of letters and words

laissez-faire: abstention from direction or interference with the behavior of another

latency: the period of development, from about age 4 to about age 13, during which sexual desires are relatively dormant; in general, emphasis at this time is on recognizing and coping with reality

laterality: of or relating to one side; preferential use of one side (of the body)

learning disability: inability to learn certain skills, such as reading, because of organic or functional disorder

locus of control: perceived source of motivation, either inside or outside the individual

longitudinal study: study of the same person or persons over a considerable period of time

LSD (lysergic acid diethylamide): a chemical substance derived from lysergic acid that, when taken, produces symptoms similar in some respects to those of a schizophrenic reaction

manifest content: any idea, feeling, or impulse considered to be conscious expression of an unreportable or repressed motive (the latent content); the part of a dream one can recall

marijuana: drug derived from *cannabis sativa* that induces feelings of well-being and decreases self-criticism and inhibition

masturbation: genital self-stimulation (usually by manipulation)

matriarchy: a social unit ruled by a female

menarche: the first menstruation

menstruation: the monthly discharge of blood from the uterus of a sexually mature female

microsocial: referring to the nuclear family

minority: a part of a population differing from the majority in some characteristics (often subjected to different treatment)

mixed dominance: referring to the theory that speech disorders and some other maladjustments may be due wholly or partly to the fact that one cerebral hemisphere does not consistently lead the other in control of bodily movement (for example, a right-handed person may be left-eyed)

modal values: values shared by a majority of a selected or sample population

mores: the generally accepted customs of a social group

narcotic: a drug (as opium) that, in moderate doses, dulls the senses, relieves pain, and induces profound sleep but, in excessive doses, causes stupor, coma, or convulsions; also, a drug (as LSD) subject to legal restriction similar to that of addictive narcotics whether in fact addictive and narcotic or not

nocturnal emissions: loss of semen during sleep

norm: a single value or range of values constituting the usual behavior of a given group

nuclear family: family unit consisting of parents and children living at home

nurturance: the tendency that leads one to provide nurture (food, shelter, other care, and affection) to the young or to the weak and incapable; also, the provision of such nurture

oligarche: onset of seminal emission

ordinal position: indicating place in a succession; usually the number series; first, second, third . . .

ovary: one of a pair of glandular organs producing the ovum, or egg cell; the primary female organ of reproduction

overcompensation: defense mechanism that overemphasizes one type of behavior in order to cover up felt deficiencies in other areas

ovulation: the production of eggs or the discharge of them from the ovary

ovulatory menstrual cycle: menstrual cycle marked by regular ovulation and uterine bleeding

paranoid psychopathic: tendency to grandiose ideas and/or sensitivity to real or apparent criticisms

pathological: referring to a diseased, disordered, or abnormal condition of an organism or its parts

patriarchy: a social unit ruled by a male

peer: a person deemed an equal for the purpose at hand; in this book, another of one's own age or status

penis: male external genital and urinary organ

perception: a process whereby an organism selects, organizes, and interprets the sensory data available to it

perceptual/motor handicap: a disability in the combined functioning of sensory and motor nerves in response to stimuli

perseveration: a tendency to continue in a particular activity to the extent that there is difficulty in beginning a new activity

pharmacology: the science of drugs

phenomenal: referring to the environment that is known through the senses and through experience, rather than through thought

phonetics: method of teaching reading that relates the vocal sounds to the written language

physiology: a branch of biology dealing with the processes, activities, and phenomena incidental to and characteristic of life or living matter

pituitary: an endocrine gland that secretes hormones, including the gonadotropic hormones; important for growth and development

postfigurative culture: a culture that is relatively stable and unchanging

pragmatic: describing an emphasis on practical results as determining the value of a thing; disinclination toward dogmatism or elaborate theorizing

prefigurative culture: a culture in which the younger generations, and not the older ones, represent what is to come

prepuberty: the period of transition at the end of childhood and prior to adolescence that is characterized by hormone-level changes

primogeniture: principle of inheritance by the firstborn, especially the eldest son

projection: the defense mechanism of attributing one's own beliefs and thoughts to others; method one uses to alleviate conflict by seeing in others the motives or attributes about which one is anxious

projective techniques: psychological tests (such as the Rorschach Inkblot Test) in which the individual is presented with a set of ambiguous stimuli and asked to describe what he or she sees in them (in doing so, the individual projects his or her own thoughts and feelings onto these stimuli)

promiscuity: nonselective social or (predominantly) sexual intercourse *psychedelic:* pertaining to or generating hallucinations, distortions of perception, and, occasionally, psychotic-like states

psychogenic: pertaining to the origin of psychic or psychological processes or attributes; in this book, describing illnesses with no organic basis

psychological moratorium: cessation of activity (such as dropping out of school) for the purpose of establishing one's identity or self-concept

psychomimetic: having the tendency to mimic psychosis

psychoneurosis: disorder of behavior, without gross disorganization of thought processes or perceptions, in which functional or psychogenic factors predominate

psychopath: an individual who is unable to visualize the consequences of his or her actions or to care about them and who appears to be incapable of deep emotional feelings; *sociopath* is often used synonymously

psychosexual: describing the development of a masculine or feminine role as the outgrowth of psychobiological drives, awareness, and interests

psychosis: a severe mental disorder, with or without organic damage, involving drastic personality changes, deterioration of intellectual and social functioning, and, often, partial or complete withdrawal from reality

puberty: a period of development during which reproductive organs become capable of functioning and secondary sex characteristics are completely developed

pubescence: early stage of sexual development, beginning with the menarche in girls and oligarche in boys

raison d'être: reason, or justification, for existence

rationalization: a defense mechanism whereby false, but seemingly logical, reasons are devised to justify (to self and others) one's actions in order to protect one's self-concept or self-esteem

reaction formation: defense mechanism of inhibiting, masking, or overcoming threatening impulses by emphasizing opposite ones

reality testing: testing an action to see whether it brings the intended results (to see whether it will work)

reciprocal role: referring to the explanation for sex-role learning in which children are said to identify with or model certain sex-typed behavior they observe in their parents

reference set: a group of persons, especially peers, who supply individuals with ideas regarding actions and so on

regression: psychologically, a return to less mature or earlier forms of behavior as a defense against stress and frustration

repression: a defense mechanism that automatically inhibits threatening stimuli (such as unpleasant thoughts or memories) that produce anxiety

role: behavior associated with a particular position in a group

role needs: the desire that an individual has to engage in certain stereotyped behavior patterns

schizoid: an enduring and maladjustive pattern of behavior manifesting avoidance of close relations with others and inability to express hostility and aggressive feelings directly

schizophrenia: a psychosis characterized by markedly deviant patterns of feeling, thinking, and acting; a "split-off" from reality, frequently involving hallucinations, delusions, withdrawal, and serious disturbances of emotional life

secondary sex characteristics: genetically transmitted traits, typical for either sex but not for both and not necessary for reproduction (for example, heavy growth of facial hair in males)

secular trend: a directional change in a given variable over a period of time; in this book, the trend for the onset of puberty to occur at increasingly younger ages

sedative: a drug that calms or tranquilizes nervousness or excitement

self-actualization: the fulfillment of one's potentialities

self-concept: the way an individual views, perceives, and feels about himself or herself

self-fulfilling prophecy: principle that one's expectation is a factor in determining outcome (for example, if a particular student is expected to fail, he or she may do so)

self-image: an individual's perception of himself or herself, reflecting the subjective experience of his or her uniqueness

sensory handicap: a dysfunction in the areas of sound, sight, or other senses

sex role: the pattern of attitudes and behavior that in any society is deemed appropriate to one's sex

sex-role identification: the process of gradually taking on the behavior and attitudes characteristic of members of one sex

sibling: one of two or more offspring from the same mother or same father

skeletal age: level of bone development, based on hand/wrist or knee X rays showing the relative completeness of ossification, or calcium deposit on the bones

social isolate: a person who separates himself or herself from relationships with others in society

socialization: learning to behave in a manner prescribed by one's society

socialized delinquent: an individual whose entire mode of behavior is characterized by delinquent acts, generally committed in a gang or with others

socioeconomic status: an individual's position in a given society, as determined by wealth, occupation, and social class

sociometric: a type of measuring instrument in which peer-group members rate or rank the attitudes, values, or characteristics of all fellow members in a given organization

somatic: pertaining to the body rather than to the mind

spatial orientation: relation of the external world to the physical self

spermatogenesis: formation of spermatozoa

spermatozoa: mature sperm cells capable of fertilizing an egg

status offenses: infractions of the law by persons below legal age (such as being truant, running away, buying liquor); these actions would not be considered illegal if committed by an adult

stimulus intensity: strength of a given stimulus

stress: strong, uncomfortable emotional tension

Sturm und Drang: (German) storm and stress; in this book, referring to the conflict theory of adolescence

subculture: an ethnic, regional, economic, or social group exhibiting characteristic patterns of behavior different from those of the embracing culture

superego: in psychoanalytic terms, the part of the personality structure that is concerned with moral standards; the conscience

surrogate: a person who functions in another's life as a substitute for some third person

symbiotic relationship: a close relationship between two people such that one needs the other to exist; usually, neurotic interdependency

synthesis: a combining of elements or forces to create an integrated whole

temperament: one's susceptibility to emotive situations and one's tendency to experience mood changes

testicle: the male genital gland and its enclosing structures

tranquilizer: drug used to reduce anxiety and tension

trauma: a physical or psychological injury or experience causing serious damage to the individual

underachiever: a person who performs below his or her ability

unisexual: pertaining to one sex (such as a group of boys or a group of girls)

unsocialized delinquent: an individual who has difficulty relating to others and who acts overtly hostile toward those whom he or she regards as hostile or threatening

vagina: the canal from the uterus to the exterior of the female body

validity: the degree to which a test, rating, or measurement correctly measures the variable it is supposed to measure

visual/motor integration: coordination of visual and motor systems, including eye/hand relations, eye/foot relations, movement of eyes across a page while reading, and so on

Author index

365

Subject index